Golf Tourism

Simon and Louise Hudson

Golf Tourism

Simon and Louise Hudson

 Goodfellow Publishing

(G) Published by Goodfellow Publishers Limited,
Woodeaton, Oxford, OX3 9TJ
http://www.goodfellowpublishers.com

British Library Cataloguing in Publication Data: a catalogue record
for this title is available from the British Library.

Library of Congress Catalog Card Number: on file.

ISBN: 978-1-906884-01-7

Design and typesetting by P.K. McBride, Southampton UK

Printed by Lightning Source, www.lightningsource.com

Contents

Preface

Golf tourism has been valued at US$20 billion with over 50 million golf tourists travelling the world to play on some of the estimated 32,000 courses. The industry has huge growth potential with 1000 new golf courses being built every year. There are 25 million golfers in North America, over 5 million in Europe, and participation in Asia is growing at an astronomical rate. Well-established golf tourism regions like Florida, California, Scotland, Ireland and Spain, are being challenged by emerging golf destinations such as Mexico, Egypt, Thailand, Malaysia and even China, where the number of golfers is growing by 30 percent a year. All of these golf destinations are competing for the affluent, high-value-adding tourists who generate significantly above-average per capita revenues for the destinations they frequent.

Surprisingly, there is no textbook that deals specifically with the golf tourism phenomenon. Given that golf represents the largest sports-related travel market, this is even more astonishing. We have books on the ski industry, marine tourism, sporting events, spa and health tourism, and adventure tourism, but no book, despite the availability of an increasing amount of research, dedicated to golf tourism. So this text will be a first, and we hope it will be of great value to both students and practitioners of golf tourism. With 40 up-to-date case studies from all over the world, covering all sectors of the golf industry, the book colourfully illustrates the key issues, opportunities and future challenges that lie ahead for those in the golf industry. The majority of these cases have been developed based on personal visits and in-depth interviews conducted by the authors. As well as offering numerous industry examples, the book provides comprehensive coverage of essential tourism management principles, such as understanding consumer behavior, planning issues, developing a marketing plan, and implementing the marketing mix. The text also includes sections on contemporary tourism issues such as integrated marketing communications, Internet marketing, and the environmental impacts of golf tourism.

Chapter 1 lays the foundation for the book and provides an initial insight into this growing area of tourism. It defines golf tourism, and discusses its evolution, describing the size and value of the market. The key players are introduced – the destinations, the golfers, golf hotels and resorts, golf real estate, golf attractions, golf retailers, golf tour operators, golf schools and golf tournaments. Three cases profile golf tourism in Wales, Malaysia and China, and another focuses on a US-based golf tour operator, The Wide World of Golf.

Chapter 2, *The Golf Tourist*, focuses on the tourists, who are predominately male, middle-aged or in their early retirement years, although this profile is changing with more females entering the sport. However, there are some variations worldwide, as there are differences in the way golf tourism is consumed, and so some of these variations are explained. Chapter 2 synthesizes the research that has attempted to segment the golf tourist market – one that is often segmented by golfographics or pyschographics. It ends by looking at ten key trends in consumer behaviour that are influencing golf tourism today. Cases here spotlight Legend Golf and Safari Resort in South Africa, the golf experience in Japan, Sandals Resorts Golf School in Jamaica, and golfer typologies in Scotland.

Chapter 3 looks at the *Golf Tourism Product*, which primarily consists of golf tours and packages, the courses themselves, and the hotels and resorts serving the golf tourists. An increasing number of golf tourists are also booking into golf schools and visiting golfing attractions, so these are also discussed here. There are also a number of golfing museums around the word, and the chapter highlights some of these attractions. The chapter is supported by cases on Disney's Celebration golf course, PGA Tour Golf Experiences, the Ho Chi Minh Golf Trail in Vietnam, and golf tourism at Fairmont Hotels & Resorts.

Chapter 4, *Planning for Golf Tourism*, discusses the critical importance of planning for the sustainability of golf course developments. It focuses on the initiatives and solutions most frequently applied in planning. A section on the planning process is followed by an analysis of golf course types and layout options. There are a number of design considerations in the planning and development of courses and these are discussed in turn, followed by a final section on the costs and development problems that might arise during the planning process. Cases here focus on golf tourism planning in Australia, Mexico and Canada.

Chapter 5, *The Management of Golf Tourism*, explores the various management structures in golf clubs and resorts, as well highlighting the important operational considerations for golf club managers, such as staffing, pro shops, golf cart fleets, maintenance and course management, customer service, and risk management. Supporting cases here look at Trump National Los Angeles, supposedly the most expensive course ever built; how Troon Golf manages ailing golf clubs; and key management issues for two different golf clubs in Canada and New Zealand.

The Marketing of Golf Tourism is the topic for Chapters 6 and 7. Chapter 6 investigates the marketing planning process, the key factors determining pricing decisions, key product decisions, and the distribution strategies available to the industry. Cases here look at the successful Homecoming Scotland Campaign, how the Sahara is repositioning for golf tourism, the New Mexico Golf Tourism Alliance, and the emergence of golf tourism in Kashmir. Chapter 7 focuses on integrated marketing communications and the implementation of the marketing mix. It outlines the key principles of advertising, promotions, public relations, selling and marketing, and delves into uses of the Internet for golf tourism industry marketers. Cases highlight how Kiawah Island Golf Resort has embraced social media, how the Kiwi Challenge has put New Zealand's North Coast on the international golf map, why North Carolina developed an interactive golf travel website, and how Stoke Park Club has leveraged its association with James Bond.

Chapter 8 on *Golf Events* examines the contribution that golf events – and their high-profile competitors – can make to the overall golf industry economy. It begins by looking at the different types of golf events around the world, then at the spectators that attend them. The hosting of golf events is the subject of the next part, which considers issues related to planning, marketing and operations. It concludes with a section on the impact of golf events. Cases here include a look at the draw of Tiger Woods, how Abu Dhabi uses golf events to boost tourism, the experience of Korea hosting an international PGA Tour event, and Mallorca's experience in hosting the European Senior Open in 2009.

The increasing emphasis on sustainability has important implications for the golf industry, and Chapter 9, *The Impacts of Golf Tourism*, centres on the three pillars of sustainability – the economy, the environment and society. In the past, golf tourism was encouraged for its economic benefits with little consideration for the effects on the environment and host societies. But this is beginning to change. For golf tourism to be sustainable, it is vital that its impacts are understood, so that they can be incorporated into planning and management. To highlight these issues, Chapter 9 includes cases on Justin Timberlake's new 'green' golf course, how golf resorts in Las Vegas are selling grass back to the desert to reduce their footprint, and environmental sustainability in Portugal's Algarve area. Another case looks at the economic impact of the industry in South Carolina.

The Future is discussed in Chapter 10, particularly three important themes impacting the outlook for golf tourism: the internationalization of golf and its economy, social access to participation, and environmental issues. Cases in this chapter take a look at Heli Golf in the Canadian Rockies, golf tourism in New Europe, how Alberta's Stewart Creek is juggling the needs of people and wildlife, and how junior golf is the key to the future of the golf industry.

Acknowledgements

We are grateful to the many individuals and organizations that helped to make *Golf Tourism* a reality. In particular, we would like to thank Sally North from Goodfellow for her professional support throughout the writing process, and Joyce Twizell for her expert assistance with the tables and diagrams. The book has also benefited tremendously from the people in the golf tourism industry who took the time to talk to us and provide us with valuable material. These people include Nick Faldo, Brian Curley of Schmidt-Curley Golf Design, Ashley Tait of Revelstoke Mountain Resort, Andreas Pamer of Son Gual, David Conforti of Trump National Los Angeles, Mike Vegis of Kiawha Island Golf Resort, Joan Phillips of Black Mountain, Sean Kjemhus and John Munro of Stewart Creek, Lindsey Thuell and Justin Wood of Fairmont, Graham Moore of the FPGA, Bill Hogan of Wide World of Golf, Pete Richardson of Legend Golf and Safari Resort, Philip Riddle of VisitScotland, Patti Covert of Disney's Celebration, Travis Velichko of the PGA Tour Experiences, Mark Siegel of Golfasian, Alexandra D'Cunha of Mystic Ridge, Brett Brooks of Troon Golf, Chad Thomlinson of Panorama, Leo Barber of Paraparauma Beach, Sayeed Sanadi of Tiger Sports Marketing, Julia Buxton of Stoke Park, Julie Flowers of South Carolina Department of Parks, Recreation and Tourism, António Rosa Santos of San Lorenzo Golf Course, Luke Haberman of Western Canadian Golf Tours, Brock Balog of Resorts of the Canadian Rockies and Christa Bodensteiner of Litchfield Country Club.

About the authors

Simon Hudson is the Center of Economic Excellence (CoEE) Endowed Chair in Tourism and Economic Development, College of Hospitality, Retail and Sport Management, University of South Carolina. He has held previous academic positions at universities in England and Canada and has worked as a visiting professor in Austria, Switzerland, Spain, Fiji, New Zealand and Australia. He is often engaged to speak at conferences around the world. Prior to working in academia, Dr. Hudson spent several years in the tourism industry in Europe. He plays golf to a handicap of 12.

Louise Hudson is a freelance journalist specializing in sport and travel writing. Originally trained in journalism in England, she now writes for a variety of international publications including Canada's Sun Media group, Calgary Herald, Ottawa Citizen, Globe and Mail, Canada's MORE magazine, Opulence, Alberta Parent, Calgary's Child, Travel Alberta, Fresh Tracks, and Alberta Hospitality magazine. Having been a golf widow for 25 years, Louise has recently taken up the sport in an attempt to understand its attraction from a hands-on perspective.

Visit their website at www.tourismgurus.com.

1 An Introduction to Golf Tourism

Spotlight: Wales challenging the giants of golf tourism

Celtic Manor Resort, home of the 2010 Ryder Cup, courtesy of © Crown copyright (2009) Visit Wales

The Welsh Assembly Government is counting on the Ryder Cup scheduled for October 2010 at the Celtic Manor Resort to put Wales firmly on the golf tourism map, rivalling Scotland, Ireland and England in the international arena. It is the biggest event ever to come to Wales and one of the biggest sporting attractions in the world. Scotland has always been considered the birthplace of golf with the rudimentary beginnings of the sport back in the 15th century. The first golf club was established near Glasgow in 1744. St Andrews, built in 1754, was given the royal seal in 1834 and has been hailed ever since as the bedrock of British golf. But, more recently, Wales has been identified by golf tour operators as a cheaper but good quality alternative for golfing holidays.

The Ryder Cup is slated to be a landmark for the country's tourism. The Welsh Assembly Government has recognized the importance of the Ryder Cup as a means to challenge the 'giants' of golf tourism, stressing the alliance of business and golf to attract corporate events and, as a spinoff, foreign investment. Currently, there are 500 international companies based in Wales, employing 80,000 people, and responsible for $21 billion in investments since 1983. The government is using this globally-televised event to highlight tourism in rural and urban Wales as well as business opportunities. With the national recession hitting hard throughout the UK, it's a heaven-sent chance to revitalize the economy.

Ryder Cup Wales invited Ian Woosnam to be the official ambassador for Team Wales. Captain of the victorious European team at the Irish Ryder Cup in September 2006, Woosnam wanted to raise the Welsh profile as a separate entity from England. 'Winning the bid to host the 2010 Ryder Cup gave Wales the opportunity to tell the world what it has to offer,' he said. Newport – chosen as the Ryder Cup city – has 45 golf courses within a forty-minute radius, including four championship courses. The 160 miles long by 60 miles wide country actually has more than 200 courses with a golfing tradition stretching back centuries. The Welsh Golfing Union was established in 1895, the second oldest union in the world (second to Ireland). Alongside a rich sporting history in golf and rugby, Wales also boasts 641 castles and 687 miles of coastline, adding to the broader tourism appeal.

The Ryder Cup dates back to the 1920s when it started as a contest between US and British golfers. Samuel Ryder – a successful entrepreneur – donated the trophy and the inaugural Ryder Cup matches were played at the Worcester Country Club, Massachusetts, in 1927. Since 1979 the biennial competition evolved into a USA versus Europe match, securing international TV coverage in 150 countries and territories for 2010. In the run up to the 2010 event, Wales reinforced its increased profile with curtain raisers staged during the Ryder Cup Wales 2009 summer of golf. The Bull Bay Golf Club held the Welsh Open Young PGA Professional Championship in both 2008 and 2009, sponsored by Ryder Cup Wales 2010. The Welsh Open at Chepstow in July 2009 and the Welsh National at Llanelli in September 2009 were also similarly sponsored.

The Welsh Assembly Government is also using this opportunity to regenerate golfing facilities, providing financial support to the tune of $3 million for golfing projects throughout the country via the Ryder Cup Wales Legacy Fund. In a report by Roger Pride, Director of Marketing for the Assembly, there were eight factors identified to differentiate Welsh golf from traditional, 'stuffy' images. These were:

* Easy access to tee-off times
* The unique Welsh welcome means you won't be made to feel small
* You can go at your own pace
* No unnaturally scorching sun
* The outstanding beauty of the natural environment
* You don't have to take out a loan to pay for a round of golf
* Relatively easy access
* The antidote to the English, Irish and Scottish golf scenes

Pride, who is also a Director of Ryder Cup Wales 2010 Ltd, has led the development of Wales' golf tourism strategy. He has identified their target demographic to be the 29 to 49 age group for whom time is currency. Their needs encompassed the Internet, closer destinations and shorter breaks. He also noted an increasing proportion of female golfers, linking that with Welsh Hollywood icon, Catherine Zeta Jones. The alliance between golf apparel and fashion was also underlined as well as the crossover between younger celebs from music/TV/film/soccer to playing and endorsing golf.

Sources

www.rydercupwales2010.com

Melanie Hauser, 37th Ryder Cup Official Journal, for pgatour.com.2007, www.rydercup.com/2008/rydercup/2008/usa/09/14/ryder_tv_091408/index.html,

'Challenging the giants of golf tourism', by Roger Pride, www.nationaalgolfcongres.nl/afbeeldingen/Presentatie_Roger_Pride.pdf.

Introduction

Ever since Tiger Woods first won the Masters' in 1997, golf has got sexier. No longer largely the preserve of the privileged, it's become a trendy sport with an appeal across generations, genders and cultures. The Ryder Cup is now watched on television by around a billion people worldwide. Compare that to the mere 260 million who watched the 2006 Soccer World Cup. TV has helped create golf icons across the globe with increasing tournament coverage and advertising endorsement. Golf pros promote everything from alcohol to automobiles and from beverages to bling. Two of the top three earners in all sports in 2007 were golfers. But professional golfers are not just aloof celebs. Any decent handicapped golfer can play alongside their favourite heroes at corporate pro-am competitions. Many businesses invest huge amounts in this unique opportunity for sponsorship and executive perks. Living on golf courses has become a trend over the past two decades. Golf course real estate has been spawning courses across Europe, North America and Asia.

Fashion has also entered the arena, infusing golf attire with funky fabrics, shapes, colours and detailing, pushing the limits of clubhouse etiquette. And golf gear is no longer just for the golf course. Argyle-style diamond print sweaters became city chic in 2008, reinforcing golf's street cred. Golf retail has expanded, too, moving on from small golf club collections to gigantic big box chain stores, featuring multiple designer brands and computerized, virtual fairways as well as extensive putting green practice areas to try out equipment.

Golf is becoming less corporate and more sport for all. Families world over are looking to golf as a generational-spanning game and specialized family courses are multiplying with affordable fees and lessons. Schools in Canada are even introducing golf as part of the Phys Ed curriculum. Women are increasingly attracted to the sport, with clubs developing female-only instruction and tournaments and pro shops luring them with pink and purple pretty clothing and equipment.

It is clear from the opening Spotlight that golf is big business. Whether as a primary motivator or as a secondary activity, golf attracts millions of holidaymakers worldwide, contributing over $20 billion annually. Despite this phenomenal figure, no-one has yet defined who the golf tourist really is and documented the scale of the industry. This book will examine international golf tourism spotlighting countries, clubs, courses, consumers, competition and commercial concepts.

Defining golf tourism

Golf tourism falls under the umbrella of sport tourism, one of the fastest growth areas in the tourism industry. Although sport tourism is a relatively new concept in contemporary vernacular, its scope of activity is far from a recent phenomenon.

Note: all currencies in US$. Exchange rates: 1 euro = $1.276; 1 UK pound = $1.5; 6.8 Chinese yuan = $1.

The notion of people travelling to participate in and watch sport dates back to the ancient Olympic Games, and the practice of stimulating tourism through sport has existed for over a century. Within the last few decades however, destinations have begun to recognize the significant potential of sport tourism, and they are now aggressively pursuing this attractive market niche.

The subject has also gained strong academic and public interest in recent years. This is evident in the publication of numerous textbooks related to sport tourism (e.g. Standeven and De Knopp, 1999; Hudson, 2003; Weed and Bull, 2004; Higham, 2005; Gibson, 2006), the development of the *Journal of Sport Tourism*, and a number of special journal issues devoted to sport tourism. Much of this work focuses on describing and defining the concept of sport travel, but broadly defined, sport tourism includes travel away from a person's primary residence to participate in a sporting activity for recreation or competition; travel to observe sport at the grass roots or elite level; and travel to visit a sport attraction such as a sports' hall of fame or a water park, for example.

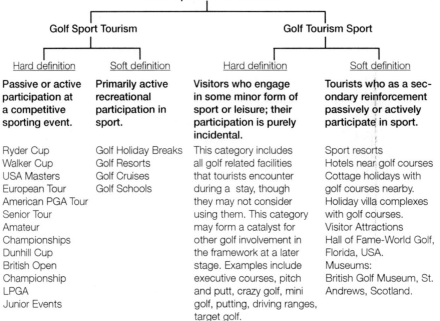

Golf Sport and Tourism			
Golf Sport Tourism		**Golf Tourism Sport**	
Hard definition	Soft definition	Hard definition	Soft definition
Passive or active participation at a competitive sporting event.	**Primarily active recreational participation in sport.**	**Visitors who engage in some minor form of sport or leisure; their participation is purely incidental.**	**Tourists who as a secondary reinforcement passively or actively participate in sport.**
Ryder Cup Walker Cup USA Masters European Tour American PGA Tour Senior Tour Amateur Championships Dunhill Cup British Open Championship LPGA Junior Events	Golf Holiday Breaks Golf Resorts Golf Cruises Golf Schools	This category includes all golf related facilities that tourists encounter during a stay, though they may not consider using them. This category may form a catalyst for other golf involvement in the framework at a later stage. Examples include executive courses, pitch and putt, crazy golf, mini golf, putting, driving ranges, target golf.	Sport resorts Hotels near golf courses Cottage holidays with golf courses nearby. Holiday villa complexes with golf courses. Visitor Attractions Hall of Fame-World Golf, Florida, USA. Museums: British Golf Museum, St. Andrews, Scotland.

Figure 1.1: Application of the sport tourism and tourism sport framework to golf (Source: Adapted from Robinson and Gammon, p. 229)

Robinson and Gammon (2004) differentiate between 'sport tourism' and 'tourism sport' and suggest that that there can be a hard and a soft definition for each. Sport tourists actively participate in competitive or recreational sport, whilst travelling to and/or staying in places outside their usual environment. The difference between the hard and the soft sport tourist is that the hard sport tourist actively or passively participates at a competitive sporting event. Tourism sport on the other hand comprises persons travelling to and/or staying in places outside their usually environment and participating in, actively or passively, a competitive or recreational sport as a secondary activity. The holiday or visit is their primary motivational reason for travel. The hard definition of tourism sport includes holidaymakers who use sport as a secondary enrichment to their holiday whilst a soft definition of tourism sport involves visitors who as a minor part of their trip engage in some form of sport on a purely incidental basis. Robinson and Gammon have applied this framework to golf (see Figure 1.1).

Golf tourism itself has also been defined in a number of ways, but for the purposes of this book, golf tourism is simply defined as travel away from home to participate in or observe the sport of golf, or to visit attractions associated with golf. Figure 1.2 is a representation of the business of golf tourism.

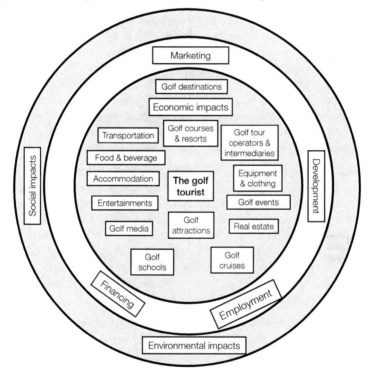

Figure 1.2: The business of golf tourism.

The figure shows the golf tourists in the middle and they can be divided into three basic categories:

♦ tourists who go on holiday principally to play golf;

♦ tourists who play golf as a secondary activity whilst on holiday or on a business trip;

♦ those who attend tournaments as spectators, or visit golf attractions.

Chapter 2 expands on the segmentation of golf tourists. They in turn are served by a number of different sectors. These include the golf tour operators (see Chapter 3), accommodation and transportation services (Chapter 3), the courses and resorts themselves (see Chapters 4, 5 and 6). In turn, these suppliers have to make important decisions regarding planning and development, marketing, financing and human resource development (Chapters 5, 6 and 7). Finally, the business of golf tourism has a number of economic, social and environmental impacts (see Chapter 9). Throughout this book, the players and elements in this model will be discussed and analysed.

The evolution of golf tourism

The origins of the game of golf have been the subject of numerous debates, but it was the Scots who created the concept that the game of golf starts with the ball situated at a point just above ground and ends with it disappearing below ground (Campbell, 1994). The first reference to the game in Scotland dates back to 1457 when the Scottish Parliament declared that golf was interfering with the defence of the realm practice of archery, declaring golf to be 'utterly cryit doun and nocht usit' (Brasch, 1972). Despite this proclamation, golf was popular with both the Scottish and English royalty (Mary, Queen of Scots was the first woman golfer) and soon spread to the common people, resulting in golf courses springing up all over the UK. The most famous of these was St Andrews which was established around 1552. The Royal and Ancient (R&A), based at St Andrews, assumed responsibility for formulating the Rules of Golf in 1897.

As the British Empire spread in the 19th century, so too did the game of golf (Readman, 2003). The first golf clubs outside Britain were in India with the establishment of the Bangalore Club in 1820 and the Royal Calcutta Club in 1829. Asia followed as courses were built between 1888 and 1890 at Taiping in Malaya, Bangkok in Thailand and a first Japanese course in 1901 on the slopes of Mount Rokko near Kobe. Courses opened in Australia and New Zealand from 1871, the most famous being Royal Melbourne. In South Africa, Royal Cape Town was founded in 1885 and a course which later became known as Royal Montreal (Canada) opened in 1873.

Golf was well established around the world by 1885 although not in the USA, the country that was to refine and define it during the 20th century. John Reid is acknowledged to be the founding father of golf in the USA. Reid, a Scottish ex-patriate businessman, imported a few clubs and balls from Scotland and in 1888 set up a rudimentary three-hole golf course near to his house in Yonkers, New York. The players of this first course formed themselves into a club called St Andrew's (its name copied from its famous Scottish predecessor – complete with an apostrophe to differentiate it). Very soon this club was forced to move on and expand, doing so by building a course on land studded by apple trees close to the Hudson River. These early club pioneers henceforth became known as the 'Apple Tree Gang'. Very quickly golf caught on. In 1890, Reid's cow pasture was the country's only golf course. By 1896, the number of courses had risen to over 80. Four years later, there were 892 courses meaning that by 1900 there were more American courses than British ones. This huge growth was spurred by the arrival of hundreds of Scotsmen in the form of architects, greenkeepers and teaching professionals (Readman, 2003).

The United States Golf Association (USGA) was formed in 1894 and, boosted by economic booms in the 1890s and the 1920s, golf continued to blossom. By the end of this period there were over 5600 golf facilities in the USA. For the next 30 years this situation remained relatively unchanged, until the 1960s when golf in the USA experienced a second growth period. This was due to two factors. First, the US government provided financing for the development of public golf facilities, changing a sport largely organized on a private club basis into one that allowed mass participation for the first time. Second, media exposure of the developing professional tours prompted a renewed interest in the sport.

Golf continued to grow in the USA and at one point in the early 1990s, golf courses were being opened at a rate of one per day. This growth was largely due to an increase in available funding (owing to deregulation of the banking industry and the new banking institutions aggressively funding new development). In addition, golf courses became a major part of real estate and new resort developments and for the first time began to attract real estate buyers to particular locations. Today, the US golf market is moving in a sideways direction. The total number of rounds played has been virtually flat at about 500 million rounds per annum for the six years up to 2008. Although there has been little change in the total number of golf facilities in the USA over the last couple of years, the net growth in supply has been falling since 2001 (see Figure 1.3). According to industry research firm IBISWorld, there were around 15,888 golfing establishments in the USA in 2008 (IBISWorld, 2008).

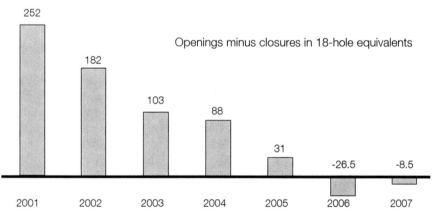

Figure 1.3: Net growth in golf facility supply in the USA 2001–07. Source: National Golf Foundation, 2008

Worldwide, during the 20th century, golf experienced similar patterns of growth to North America. In Japan the number of golf courses increased from approximately 30 prior to the Second World War to 116 in 1957 and then 1700 in 1992. In France, the number of golfers doubled between 1981 and 1985, and Spain experienced similar growth. In the 1980s the number of golfers increased by 60 per cent in the German Federal republic, 57 per cent in Italy, 42 per cent in Sweden and 41 per cent in Switzerland (Priestly and Ashworth, 1995). In Britain the Royal and Ancient Golf Club of St Andrews predicted in 1990 a need to increase the numbers of golf courses by 691 by the year 2000.

The combination of the expansion of the game of golf worldwide and the growth of international travel after the Second World War led to an increase in the desire to travel for the purpose of playing the sport. An increasing number of destinations started to develop and diversify their golf tourism products in an effort to lure strong foreign currency, and thus spur economic growth. The attraction of the golf tourist became a key tourism development strategy for many regions around the world. By allowing the building of infrastructure and the import of quality resort builders and operators, countries have been able to achieve economic growth by attracting foreign tourists. Good examples of this type of practice exist in East Asia where countries such as Malaysia (see the Snapshot on page 9), Thailand, the Philippines and Indonesia have all built golf infrastructures to attract international guests.

Reducing the seasonality impacts of tourism was another incentive for many destinations to pursue golf tourists. Destinations that traditionally attracted tourists for the reasons of hot climate and sandy beaches began to extend their holiday season by adding products that do not necessarily require these attributes. For example, in Spain, the Costa del Sol is now marketed off-season as the 'Costa del Golf' with over 30 golf developments lined up along the 50-kilometre strip of sand. There are also many examples of winter sport destinations building golf courses in order to attract tourists to the mountains in the summer (Hudson and Cross, 2005). Panorama in British Columbia, Canada, for example, spent $16 million building a golf course that is only open four months of the year, but is part of owner Intrawest's strategy to develop four-season resorts (Hudson and Cross, 2005).

Just like the tourism industry in general, the golf industry is subject to increasing globalization levels. For example, ownership and management of golf courses in the USA is not restricted to domestic firms. Similarly, some major US golf course management companies have increased their ownership of foreign courses and clubs in recent years. For example, ClubCorp Inc also operates courses in Australia, China and Mexico; American Golf Corporation has courses in New Zealand and the UK; and Troon Golf has courses in 20 other countries outside the USA including Mexico, the UK, Italy, Japan, Fiji, Australia, Kuwait, South America and the Caribbean. This trend is likely to continue as firms look to increase market share and attempt to achieve economies of scale by minimizing average administration and maintenance costs per golf course.

The design of golf courses by well-known past and present golfing professionals also contributes to the level of globalization within the industry. It is common for international golfers, such as Greg Norman (Australia) and Bernhard Langer (Germany), to design and influence US golf courses, facilities and land estates. Many US players also work on golf course designs in foreign countries. As promotion of golf courses becomes more common, the trend of using golf professionals in course design is likely to increase as this can add to the prestige and reputation of a golf course. Chapter 2 profiles the Legend Golf and Safari Resort in South Africa, where each of the 18 holes has been designed by a different pro golfer.

Snapshot: Malaysia, open for golf tourism

Penang Golf Resort Malaysia, courtesy of Tourism Malaysia

Awarded '2008 Asia and Australasia Golf Destination of the Year' by the International Association of Golfing Tour Operators (IAGTO), Malaysia is an up and coming destination for golf travellers. In 2007 around 503,348 tourists engaged in golf out of a total of 20,972,822 tourist arrivals – about 2.4 per cent. Most of these golf tourists came from the ASEAN nations (475,057) with Australia, South Korea, UK, Hong Kong, Japan and India making up the numbers. This was an increase of 150,000 over 2006, generating more than $242 million in 2007.

Malaysia's strengths as a golf destination are in its locations and year-round tropical climate but, primarily, cost. The array of over 200 courses is located by the sea, in the islands, on the highlands, in the city and in the jungle. Cheap green fees are a major advantage over regional competitors such as Thailand; they can be as low as $10. Most courses are in the vicinity of main tourism areas around the capital Kuala Lumpur, the Malay Peninsula and in Borneo, and the Ministry of Tourism has produced a booklet on 50 of the best courses in the region.

The IAGTO award was testament to the government's push to cash in on Asia's golf mania. Recognizing golfers as premium, high-spending tourists, Tourism Malaysia has been targeting golf visitors via international competitions and golf fairs.

Malaysian golf's crowning glory is the Maybank Malaysia Open which is sanctioned by the European and Asian Tours, telecast worldwide by CNBC and other major sports channels and watched by between 300 and 500 million viewers. In 1999 it became the first ever co-sanctioned tournament in Asia and has been hosted seven times by Saujana Golf and Country Club, named 'The Best Championship Course in Asia' in 2005.

Malaysia also hosts the World Amateur Inter Team Golf Championship (WAITGC). Tourism Malaysia attends the Orlando Merchandise Golf Show, PGA Golf Show in Australia, Japan Golf Fair, and the Asia Golf Show in Shanghai and participates in IAGTO's International Golf Travel Mart. The government is actively encouraging media fam (familiarization) trips to facilitate international travel press exposure. Until the 2000s, golf was not promoted separately in Malaysia, it was just one part of the tourism offering. Now the emphasis is on more specialized golf tourism promotion. There are plans to coordinate with the Malaysian Golf Association and other industry players to categorize local golf clubs with star ratings. The region boasts championship and signature courses designed by the likes of Jack Nicklaus, Robert Trent Jones Jr and Graham Marsh.

Malaysia's regional competitors are Thailand and Indonesia but Malaysia has a cost advantage as well as already having more golf facilities than current visitation numbers require. However, Tourism Malaysia is keen to work with neighbouring ASEAN countries to promote golf and tourism jointly. It is also attempting to surmount an internal obstacle of lack of coordination between club operators and government, by providing more specific golf travel packages.

With corporate golf growing in Malaysia, the government's focus on business travellers could also strengthen golf visitation numbers. Tourism Minister YB Dato' Sri Azalina Othman Said announced a new 'one-stop centre for business events' in December 2008. A budget of US$1.4 million was allocated for the establishment of MyCEB – the Malaysia Convention and Exhibition Bureau.

Sources

http://www.worldgolf.com/newswire/browse/56480-Maybank-Malaysian-Open, accessed 1 December 2008.

Tourism Malaysia, website http://www.menteripenlancongan.com, accessed 12 January 2009.

Olszewski, P.(2008), 'Cambodia sees green in bid to lure golf tourists', *Phnom Penh Post*, http://www.phnompenhpost.ocm/index.php/20080306188/Tourism-20 accessed 17 June 2008.

'Tee times: selling the country through golf', *New Straits Times*, 4 April 2008, p.15.

'Going places', Ottawa Citizen, 23 June 2007, L.6, *Style Weekly: Travel & Leisure*.

'Golf tourism, anyone?', Malaysian Business, 1 July 2006, p. 42.

The size and impact of the market

It is difficult to isolate the full extent and impact of golf tourism, since trips which include golfing or watching tournaments may very well encompass other activities, such as conventions, corporate meetings, incentives, or other leisure activities, such as cruising or skiing. However, there have been attempts to analyse economic value of the golf industry as a whole, and golf tourism in particular, for various geographic regions. According to the International Association of Golfing Tour Operators the global golf tourism market is worth over US$20 billion, and this would explain golf's global spread to places as incongruous as Kazakhstan, Nicaragua, Myanmar (Burma) and Afghanistan. Developing countries are recognizing that golf tourists spend considerably more than the average tourist, and golf tourism can therefore have a significant impact on their economies.

The golf economy can be divided into a number of interrelated subsectors of which golf tourism is just one (see Figure 1.4). The golf industry cluster begins with the golf facilities themselves and with the other core industries that produce goods and services used to operate these facilities and to play the game – golf equipment and golf apparel manufacturers, golf course architects, and club management services. Golf further enables a number of other industries, the key ones being golf-related tourism and real estate development, both of which are closely intertwined.

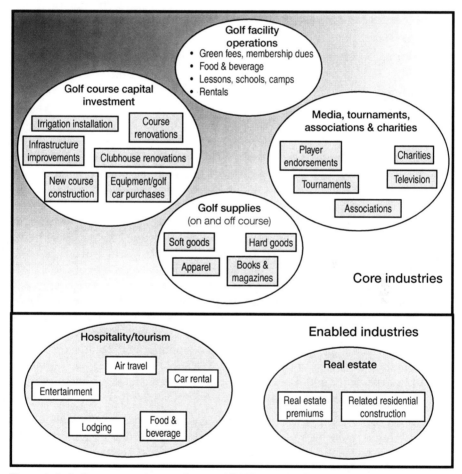

Figure 1.4: Golf economy clusters. Source: KPMG 2008a, SRI International 2008

The economic value of these sectors can be measured by adding together the direct, indirect and induced effects of golf's activities on each cluster. Direct effects relate to the spending that occurs 'on site', for example at golf courses, golf equipment retailers and the hotels in which golf tourists stay. The indirect effects relate to the economic impact on golf's supply chain, via the industry's purchases of goods and services. Induced effects are those brought about by consumer spending by employees in the golf industry and its supply chain – the proportion of their wages they spend on goods and services in the wider economy. Table 1.1 summarizes the value of the golf economy, cluster by cluster, for both the USA and Europe, the Middle East and Africa (EMA).

Table 1.1: Value of the golf economy in the USA and Europe, the Middle East and Africa by region and industry cluster. Source: KPMG, 2008a

Size of the golf economy by industry segment	EMA (2006)	US (2005)
	$ million	$ million
Golf facility operations	9,347	28,052
Golf course capital investments	3,117	3,578
Golfer supplies	2,487	6,151
Endorsements, tournaments & associations	460	1,682
Real estate	8,792	14,973
Hospitality/tourism	3,492	18,001
Charities		3,501
Total golf economy	27,695	75,938

A *Golf Economy Report* produced by SRI International in 2005, determined that the golf industry as a whole in the USA generated $76 billion in direct economic impact (SRI, 2005). It indicated that the sport generated a total economic impact of $195 billion in 2005, creating approximately two million jobs with wage income of $61 billion. The report also showed a five-year growth from 2000 of approximately $14 billion representing an average annual growth rate of 4.1 per cent, well ahead of the average annual inflation rate of 2.5 per cent during the years 2000-05. The increase primarily reflected growth in golf facility revenues, real estate and golf-related tourism. However, the industry observes a very poor level of profitability on a year-to-year basis, and IBISWorld believes that the golf courses and country clubs sector has experienced a loss over the nine years, 2000-08 (IBISWorld, 2008). The SRI report identified the financial contributions from the game's key clusters, including golf facility operations ($28 billion); golf course capital investment ($3.6 billion); golfer supplies ($6.1 billion); tournaments, golf associations, and endorsements ($1.7 billion); charities ($3.5 billion); hospitality/tourism ($18 billion) and real estate ($15 billion).

In the EMA region, golf generated a direct economic effect of $27.7 billion, golf tourism being responsible for $3.5 billion of this. Of this, 82 per cent was spent in Europe, 17 per cent on the African continent and the remaining 1 per cent in the Middle East. Most (55%) of the impact on GDP from the core golf industry occurs in Great Britain and Ireland, whereas 79 per cent of GDP derived from the enabled industries of tourism and real estate within the EMA region occurs in Western Europe. Most of the impact of the golf industry in Portugal, Spain, France and Italy reflects golf enthusiasts travelling there for golf holidays and their purchase of holiday homes built as part of golf communities and golf resorts. Overall, golf tourism supports the employment of approximately 60,000 people throughout the EMA region.

The key players

Destinations

There are 32,000 golf courses in 140 countries worldwide, and currently the top locations for golf tourism are North America, Spain and Portugal. Just over half (17,000) of the world's courses are in the USA, and golfers there spend $24.3 billion on green fees and equipment, according to the US National Golf Foundation. A further $26.1 billion goes on golfing travel, hotels, food and drink. There are approximately 6000 European golf courses, and although it is often considered a mature market, Europe still offers significant growth potential as the rate of participation in the sport remains very low – at less than 1 per cent of the population.

Of the 30 million golfers in the USA, approximately 11 million golfers travel within their country to play golf – about 42 per cent of the total golfing market (National Golf Foundation, 2003). Around 35 per cent of these trips include air travel. The most popular states are Florida, South and North Carolina, California and Arizona. Golfers in the Mid Atlantic and Northwest tend to travel outside their regions, typically venturing into an adjacent one. Golfers in the Northeast are most likely to travel to Central/South Florida, whereas Southeastern golfers are more likely to stay within their region. In Canada, about 14 per cent of adults (3.4 million) play golf while they are away from home, 31 per cent of them reporting that golf is the main reason they travel (Lang Research, 2007). British Columbia has the highest appeal for golf tourists who stay in the country, while Florida, California, Hawaii and Arizona are the most popular international destinations for Canadians.

Table 1.2 is a list of popular destinations for the four largest golfing markets in Europe. This shows the percentage of visits from regular golfers in France, Germany, UK and Sweden. The figures indicate that French golfers tend to stay in France to play golf or favour countries like Morocco or Tunisia which are French-speaking. German golfers typically travel to Spain or stay in Germany, but some make the quick journey to Austria. Golfers from Sweden like to play in Spain and Portugal and at home in Sweden. They also make the short trip to Denmark. If British golfers travel to play outside their country, they tend to go to Spain, Portugal, and the USA.

The Asian market is estimated to contribute 17–18 million golfers to the world total. Japan is the most mature golfing market in Asia, with a golfing population second only to that of the USA. More than 13 million Japanese, or around 10 per cent of the population, play golf. In 2008, there were about 2300 courses in Japan. The golf markets in Australia and New Zealand are also mature, with a fall in the number of core golfers. New developments however continue in Australia, where in 2009 there are about 1500 courses serving just over 1 million golfers. New Zealand has about 140,000 registered golf club members.

Table 1.2: Popular destinations for the four largest golfing markets in Europe. Source: SMS Golf Holidays, 2005

Country where they golf	2005 Percentage			
	France	Germany	UK	Sweden
Australia	-	0.5	0.6	0.3
Austria	0.3	10.5	-	-
Canada	-	1.0	0.5	-
Caribbean	2.3	2.6	0.3	0.3
Denmark	1.3	0.2	-	5.3
Dubai	0.7	1.9	0.5	-
Egypt	1.7	3.3	-	1.9
England	-	0.2	26.5	0.5
France	47.7	2.6	5.2	1.1
Germany	-	19.0	0.5	0.5
Italy	0.3	4.0	0.6	3.5
Malaysia	-	0.2	-	0.5
Mauritius	-	0.5	-	-
Morocco	19.3	1.7	-	-
Portugal	3.0	4.5	13.1	6.9
Rep. Ireland	1.3	1.7	5.1	1.6
Scotland	1.7	2.4	11.7	2.9
South Africa	1.3	1.7	0.8	1.1
Spain	4.7	21.9	21.2	15.7
Sweden	0.7	0.5	0.3	41.3
Switzerland	0.7	1.0	-	0.3
Thailand	-	3.1	0.9	2.7
Tunisia	7.3	4.3	0.2	7.2
Turkey	1.7	3.3	0.8	1.1
USA	1.3	5.0	5.1	1.6
Wales	-	-	3.2	0.3
Other short haul	0.7	1.2	0.3	3.5
Other long haul	2.0	1.2	2.6	-
Total	**100**	**100**	**100**	**100**

The traditional golf markets mentioned above can expect increasing competition from the emerging golf destinations that offer high quality golfing experiences at affordable prices. These include Mexico, Egypt, Thailand, Malaysia and China, where the number of golfers is growing by 30 per cent a year. KPMG Golf Advisory surveyed over 120 golf course architects in 2008 and found that Turkey, Dubai and South Africa are also expected to be among the most popular destinations for golfers in the future. Dubai is the only city in the UAE that hosts major tournaments and also has a number of courses for golf tourists, such as The Montgomerie, Al Badia Golf Course, The Dunes and Nakheel Golf's six courses. At the end of 2008 the first course in the world designed by Tiger Woods opened. Tiger Woods Dubai is a residential community and resort, as is the new Jumeriah Golf Estates.

In China, by the end of 2008, there were over 300 courses open across the country, nearly half of them located in the southern Guangdong Province (responsible for over a third of tourism arrivals to China), and the country's two major cities of Shanghai and Beijing (KPMG, 2008b). The development of the leisure and tourism industry has led to an increase in golf tourism in the country, and media exposure from hosting world-class golf tournaments (including the World Cup of Golf) has fuelled interest from overseas markets. China's most successful golf resorts include Shenzhen's Mission Hills (see the Snapshot below), Shanghai's Sheshan International, Beijing's Pine Valley and Kunming's Spring City. These are comparable to some of the best golf resorts in the world, and the trend for high quality golfing complexes is likely to continue as developers respond to the demand from the growing middle and upper classes for top quality housing and living environments.

Another emerging destination for golf tourists is India. Although golf tourism is only just beginning to be promoted there, a modest number of golf tourists are arriving from Japan and Korea. According to the Indian Golf Union there are 186 golf courses and approximately 100,000 golf club members in the country (KPMG, 2008c). Courses in India are not usually part of a residential community or an integrated component of a tourist resort, but this is changing. Residential dwellings built around a golf course are the latest trend in the Indian realty sector. For example, in 2007, Royal Indian Raj International Corporation, a foreign investment company in the India real estate sector based in Vancouver, announced a partnership with Jack Nicklaus to build as many as eight 18-hole courses as multimillion-dollar centrepieces to the firm's new resort and residential communities across India (Kumar, 2007). The growing number of international golf events hosted in India and the increasing success of professional Indian golfers on international circuits, will, like in China, lead to more positive exposure for the sport, and a continued growth in golf tourism in the country.

Snapshot: Mission Hills, China – the world's largest golf resort

Amid a Chinese golf boom, the Chu family has created the world's largest golf resort near the Hong Kong border. Boasting 12 courses, Mission Hills supplanted Pinehurst Golf Resort in North Carolina in the Guinness Book of Records in 2007 when the final two courses were added to the gigantic, three-phase development.

The courses – covering a 15-square-kilometre site – were designed by pro golfers, the first five representing five continents with Jack Nicklaus for North America, Vijay Singh for Oceania, Nick Faldo for Europe, Jumbo Ozaki for Asia and Ernie Els for Africa. Eleven of the 12 are championship courses, with the 12th designed by China's most famous golfer, Zhang Lian Wei as an 18-hole, par three layout. The 216 holes were all constructed by Brian Curley of Schmidt-Curley Design from Scottsdale, Arizona.

Dongguan Clubhouse, Mission Hills, courtesy of Mission Hills

China's first international golf event was held at Mission Hills in 1995. After the success of this World Cup of Golf final on the original Jack Nicklaus course, the International Federation of Golf Tours assigned a series of 12 World Cup finals up to 2018, which will be held on the newer, 7320-yard José Maria Olazabal course. The 18th hole abuts the gargantuan Dongguan Clubhouse.

With around 87 per cent of Chinese golfers male, Mission Hills is trying to promote women's golf with regular Ladies' Days as well as the Mission Hills Golf Academy by Cindy Reid. The Chu family also contracted Sweden's Annika Sorenstam to design her first golf course there.

Lavish hotel accommodation is at a five-star resort surrounded by impressive residential properties, some as big as 9300 square feet, designed by US and Italian architects. There are 219 rooms at Mission Hills Resort and 90 in the adjoining Savannah Wing, plus 35 meeting rooms throughout the $400 million resort. There are four spas, pools and diverse fitness facilities. The largest of the clubhouses is the Dongguan which comprises 63,000 square metres of dining, conference and retail venues, including Asia's largest golf shop and China's only golf club maintenance centre.

There is also a second golf academy, spearheaded by David Leadbetter, where local kids can take free junior programmes. One of the six driving ranges is, at 250 metres, the longest in China. The club also boasts Asia's largest tennis centre with 51 courts, including a 3000-seater stadium court.

Chinese golf courses traditionally have a higher number of staff than elsewhere in the world. Mission Hills leads the way with around 7000 employees, including 3000 mostly female caddies. Part of their job is to hand-pick weeds from the fairways and greens, to keep Mission Hills' environmental promise to avoid pesticides.

Out of China's 1.4 billion population, a substantial 230 million people live in a four-hour driving radius of Mission Hills. The Hong Kong border is just 35 minutes away and Macao's glitzy casino district, an hour's drive. A recent survey conducted by the China Golf Association suggested that 2000 new golf courses would be needed in China this decade to keep pace with the interest in the sport and the burgeoning population.

Golf course profits are heavily dependent upon real estate sales. Mission Hills is targeting China's growing middle and upper classes with promo phrases such as 'personalized environs for the elites' to describe its luxurious lifestyle. However, with an economic downturn starting to affect Chinese spending power, Mission Hills will have to look further afield to fill its beds. So far, more than 1000 properties have been sold, half to Hong Kong buyers with the remainder from Taiwan and other Asian countries.

Membership fees are notoriously high in China, averaging around US$67,000 in Guangdong Province and even more nearer Shanghai. Green fees are also the highest in the world ranging from US$50 to $200 for 18 holes. Mission Hills advertises weekend green fees of US$132 including caddie.

With China slated to become the top inbound destination in the world by 2020, timing could be good for an increase in destination visitors, attracted in part by the media exposure of over 50 tournaments which were held at Mission Hills between 1995 and 2008. The club hosted Tiger Woods' first visit to China, in order to publicize the venue in the USA. Dr David Chu, a strong advocate for golf being included in the 2016 Olympics – which would raise its profile even further – is head of the family operation. Sons Tenniel and Ken and daughter Carol all came to work within the company after graduating from universities in Canada. It was living in Toronto that first introduced Chu to golf, giving him the inspiration to bring the golf and country club model back to China on a massive scale.

Sources

Quinn, H. (2008) 'Over the wall', *West*, August/September, p. W14.

Carey, R. (2008) 'Around the world in 18 holes', *Successful Meetings*, April, p . 89.

Macintosh, R. Scott (2005) 'China's golf empire is a family affair', *International Herald Tribune*, 29 September, http://www.iht.com/articles/2005/09/29/properties/web.rechu.php accessed 18 Feb 2009.

www.golfbenchmark.com, Andrea Sartori, KPMG Golf Advisory Practice in EMA, Budapest, info@golfbenchmark.com

Golfers

There are an estimated 59 million golfers worldwide (Rees, 2008). Between 5 and 10 per cent of these golfers travel overseas each year for the main purpose of playing golf, making the international scale of the golf tourism market between 2.9 and 5.9 million. The principal market for dedicated golf tours has been golfers who regularly participate in the sport, but over the last few years there has been a noticeable stagnation and even decline in the number of 'core' golfers, particularly in the mature markets of the Anglo-Saxon countries (Mintel, 2006). However, the number of occasional golfers is growing worldwide, providing the opportunity for tour operators and resorts to offer golf as an add-on feature to holidays. Golf is also becoming an important part of meetings and conventions.

Figure 1.5 shows the percentage of golfers by region of the world. Despite the popularity of golf, there is great growth potential with only 1 per cent of the world's population playing golf at present. This compares to the USA where 10 per cent of the population plays golf. It is estimated there are about 30 million golfers in the USA, 8–9 million in Europe and about 17–18 million in other parts of the world, in places like Japan, Australia and South Africa. The main source markets for golf tourism are the USA, UK, Japan, Canada and Australia, although the number of golf tourists coming from Taiwan, Malaysia, China and Thailand is expected to rise. Chapter 2 discusses the golf tourist in more detail.

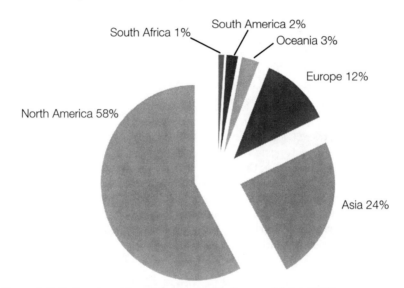

Figure 1.5: Golfers by region of the world (%). Source: Mintel, 2006.

Golf hotels and resorts

A resort typically consists of a luxury hotel with amenities – golf, beach, skiing and/or spa – that make it a destination in itself. A resort generally does not rely on a city or attractions outside its property to attract guests. Most resorts have conference centres or meeting rooms to accommodate business functions, but the majority (60 per cent) of resort guests are leisure travellers. Chapter 3 looks at golf resorts in more detail, but a significant trend in resort development is smaller golf-oriented properties: inns, lodges, and boutique hotels with fewer than 125 rooms – some with as few as 15 – and access to championship courses designed by big-name architects.

Golf course design is a lucrative business. The Middle East is a massive growth area with a company called Dubai World at the heart of it. It has set up a residential division called Leisurecorp, which makes its money from developing properties around the golf courses. It pays well-known players huge sums to be involved. David Spencer, Leisurecorp's CEO said 'for a Greg Norman golf course, to have him intimately involved, (is) in the vicinity of $2.5 million... Vijay Singh is $1.5m. And the new star in the design business is Tiger Woods who has a design fee but couples that with a guaranteed return on the real estate so his figure is quite a bit higher, in the region of $40 million' (Carter, 2008). Chapter 3 provides more information on golf hotels and resorts.

Golf real estate

Golf courses are increasingly being used to support quality residential developments. The golf real estate business is now almost five times bigger than the investment in golf courses themselves. In the USA an estimated 63,840 golf course homes were constructed in 2005 at a total cost of $11.6 billion. Additionally, SRI estimates that new golf courses in 2005 generated $3.3 billion in increased real estate value or premium (SRI, 2005). The premium is the additional amount a buyer is willing to pay for a home or property located on a golf course or in a golf community. Other studies have shown that golf courses come only second to water features as the most desirable 'amenities' for a housing community, and buyers are prepared to pay up to 30 per cent more for this premium (KPMG, 2008a).

In Europe, the Middle East and Africa, more than 150 golf-related real estate projects came to fruition in the region in 2006, providing 17,000 new villas, houses and apartments and generating a total of $24 billion. Nearly three-quarters of these properties were built in the South of France, Portugal and Spain, countries with favourable climates and strong existing images as golf tourist destinations.

Golf attractions

The definition of golf tourism presented earlier in the chapter included tourists who travel to visit golf-related attractions, and there are a growing number of such attractions. An example is the World Golf Hall of Fame, situated in the World Golf Village in Florida. With a blend of conventional museum-style exhibits and cutting-edge video presentations, the 2973-square-metre exhibition space offers hundreds of artefacts and displays from the sport's early days through to the modern game. Another example is the USGA Museum in Far Hills, New Jersey, America's oldest institution dedicated to the sport of golf. The museum celebrates the history of golf in America, with a particular focus on USGA championships. The museum dedicates extensive resources to its educational responsibilities and has developed a variety of programmes to disseminate information, scholarship, and educational programming to a broad and diverse audience. The museum has recently undergone a $20 million makeover, and there are now more than two thousand artefacts on display, as well as six new galleries, each spotlighting an iconic moment in USGA history, including Tiger Wood's record-breaking 2000 Open victory at Pebble Beach.

Golf tournaments as attractions

Golf tournaments can attract thousands of spectators and can give a significant boost to the golf economy. The British Open, for example, can pull in up to

200,000 and an average PGA championship in the USA draws crowds of up to 60,000. In 2006, the Ryder Cup was staged at the K-Club in Ireland, and according to a study by Deloitte for the European Tour, the event generated $182.5 million in direct revenues, while its total economic impact was valued at $306 million.

In 2007, there were 120 international professional golf tournaments in the EMA region, of which 84 were staged in Europe. Major tournaments in the USA directed by the PGA of America, the PGA Tour, the United States Golf Association and the Ladies Professional Golf Association generated approximately $954 million in 2005. Tournament revenues include fees generated by selling broadcast rights, corporate sponsorship of events, and spectator ticket sales and merchandise purchases.

In other parts of the world, the Japanese PGA Tour is domestically a hugely popular and rich tour covering over 39 events. Other tours include the Australasian Tour held in countries such as Hong Kong, Malaysia, India, China, the Philippines, Thailand, Australia and New Zealand. The Sunshine Tour meanders through southern Africa during the winter months, November to March. These two tours have showcased the likes of Greg Norman (Australia) and Ernie Els (South Africa) and raised the profile of golf destinations in various countries especially in the winter months. Add to these the Ladies Professional Golfers Association tours of Europe and the United States, the hugely popular Seniors Tour and a myriad of smaller tours and the result is a continually dynamic worldwide golf tournament. This travelling entourage attracts a large media circus fuelling interest and development of golf in all corners of the globe. Chapter 8 covers these golf events in more detail.

Golf retailers

In the USA the five largest golf retailers are Dick's Sporting Goods, The Sports Authority, Golfsmith, Edwin Watts and Golf Galaxy. Unit sales of golf clubs grew between 2002 and 2005, but have since levelled off as have the sales of soft goods – balls, bags, gloves and shoes (National Golf Foundation, 2008). The retail sales market for golf equipment and apparel in Europe, the Middle East and Africa is $2.4 billion (KPMG, 2008a). Europe accounts for most (96 per cent) of this market. Golf equipment is about 60 per cent of sales while the remaining 40 per cent represent the sales of golf apparel. The four largest markets in Europe are Great Britain and Ireland, Germany, France and Sweden, which also have the highest number of players. The decade since 2000 has seen a new crossover of golfing designs to fashion and, conversely, the fashion world influencing golf apparel. Equipment has also evolved recently, and self-improvement marketing has persuaded even the savviest golfer to indulge in the latest 'technology'.

Tour operators

A large number of tour operators cater to the golf tourism market, from the small specialists like Jenahura, to larger tour operators like Wide World of Golf. The travel giants like Thomas Cook tend to leave selling golf packages to these dedicated tour operators because of the need for intimate knowledge of the courses and resorts. In recognition of golf tourism as a growing niche of the travel industry, IAGTO was set up in 1997 as a representative body for a number of the world's leading golf tour operators and resorts. At the end of 2008, IAGTO's membership comprised 1136 accredited golf tour operators, golf resorts, hotels, golf courses, receptive operators, airlines and tourist boards in 75 countries worldwide with specifically 328 golf tour operators in 47 countries.

Some tour operators have been targeting golf tourists for many years. Wide World of Golf, for example, was founded in 1957 in San Francisco by Michael C. Roseto who owned a successful travel agency and began planning golf tours to Hawaii for fellow members of The Olympic Club. WWG claims to be the oldest and most experienced golf tour company in the world, operating in over 25 countries. More information about Wide World of Golf can be found in the case study at the end of this chapter.

One trend in the golf tourism industry is the packaging of golf with cruises. Golf cruises will be covered in more detail in Chapter 3, but all of the major cruise lines now offer golfers the chance to play golf ashore as part of an organized excursion. Golfers on a cruise can play on almost every continent, and golf cruises are standard in the Caribbean, Mexico, the British Isles, Hawaii, the Bahamas, and Bermuda. Itineraries for New Zealand, Australia, and the South Seas also sometimes include a golf package. Silversea Cruises even offers the opportunity to play courses in Africa as part of its Silver Links Golf Cruise programme. Caribbean Cruise Lines Ltd has set up a company called GolfAhoy.com to distribute golf cruises, and the company customizes golf packages on most Princess, Royal Caribbean, Celebrity, Carnival, Seabourn or Silversea worldwide cruise itineraries.

Golf schools

In the last decade or so, golfing instruction has been increasingly offered as a central or an add-on feature of golfing packages. Instruction packages are a good way to tap into the market of novice golfers, who are less likely to book a golfing holiday than experienced golfers with handicaps (Mintel, 2006). The largest chain of American golf schools is that of former English golfer John Jacobs. The John Jacobs Golf Schools are at 32 resort hotels in 15 states. John Jacobs also has an in-house travel department that offers complete golf tourism packages including air fare and accommodation. A Snapshot in Chapter 2 profiles the Sandals Resorts Golf School in Ochos Rios Jamaica. The school offers lessons that focus on the golfers full swing, pitch, chip, sand play specialty shots, golf psychology, and club fitting.

Case study: the Wide World of Golf

World Golf Hall of Fame, Florida, courtesy of Visit Florida

Founded in 1957, Wide World of Golf was an early pioneer of organized golf tours. Michael C. Roseto started the company in San Francisco originally as a travel agency, planning golf tours to Hawaii, then moving on to the famous courses of Scotland and Ireland as the company morphed into the first North American golf tour operator. It now conducts tours in more than 25 countries from five international offices.

Roseto instigated the first American visits to Japan to attend Friendship Cups as well as South African events. Among many other firsts, he originated golf cruises back in the 1960s and Wide World of Golf is today the official golf operator of Seabourn/Cunard Cruises. Roseto also initiated 'Around the World Golf Tours' for small groups of private clients. They fly to around ten different locations, combining golf and sightseeing over a 30-day itinerary.

As trends changed in the 1990s with golf tourists opting for more independent travel, Wide World of Golf altered its focus from larger groups to customizing tailor-made tours. Around 80 per cent of its clients now select custom tours but Wide World of Golf still produces a number of luxury group tours, corporate golf outings, golf incentive programmes, and retail package tours to events such as the British Open, US Open and The Masters.

Since the 1950s, Wide World of Golf has taken tens of thousands of golfers to more than 30 countries all over the world. Today, partners Bill Hogan and Mike Lardner head up the company, directing proceedings via the international offices as well as the licensed seasonal representatives over four continents. They organize trips ranging from three days at Pebble Beach to a 30-day round the world tour. The average package, though, is nine days at a cost of around $5,000. 'Our typical customer is a country club member, over 50, semi-retired or retired, from an affluent demographic who has both the money and time to travel internationally,' says Hogan, who has been President of the company for the past 20 years.

Traditional destinations focus on the UK where golfers can choose one-week escorted tours to the British Open, Scotland or Ireland and two-week escorted tours combining two countries. Ground travel is by luxury coach with the package price including accommodation in first class hotels, breakfast, some dinners, sightseeing trips, four rounds of championship golf at top rated courses every week plus tickets to events. With Wide World of Golf, golfers can play the prestigious courses they have seen only on television before. In Ireland there's Ballybunion or Killarney, for example; in Scotland, Royal Dornoch or one of the St Andrews courses; in California, Pebble Beach or Carmel; in Wales, Royal Porthcawl; in England, Royal Birkdale.

Alternatively golfers can opt for a Valderrama Spain golf package, visiting the 'Costa del Golf' or go on a San Lorenzo Portugal tour. The Thailand package includes Blue Canyon CC and South Africa's itinerary encompasses a Fancourt, Sun City and Cape Town golf safari. Trips to New Zealand include top lodges and courses at Cape Kidnappers and Kauri Cliffs. Australian itineraries include visits to Royal Melbourne, Kingston Heath, the Mornington Peninsula or New South Wales.

Celebrity endorsement by Hollywood film star, Russell Crowe is a slick addition to Wide World of Golf's website street cred. The link came about when Crowe's cousin, Jeff Crowe (himself a famous cricketer) worked for Wide World of Golf in New Zealand. Russell Crowe jokes about his dubious golf abilities online whilst supporting the company's customized tour options.

Golf cruises have been intrinsic to the company's offering since the 1960s and they now utilize small 30–100 passenger charter ships in the Mediterranean. In 2008 they introduced new golf cruises to the Greek Islands, Turkey, Spain and Morocco.

The company targets couples by appealing to non-golfing partners via an array of combined activities. 'We have sightseeing tours set up with a stable of step-on guides available for the day', says Hogan. 'They are all experts, so perhaps a university history professor in Edinburgh will come on board and show the clients the sights with a historical perspective.' In Scotland sightseeing may encompass whisky distilleries, woollen mills, witch tours, shopping or high tea at grandiose manor houses. 'We set up trips depending on what each country is famous for so it might be anything from battlefield tours in continental Europe to D Day landing beaches', he adds.

Combination holidays are increasingly popular for golf tourists who want a different focus off the course as well as satisfying the needs of non-golfers in the party. Wide World of Golf combines golf with fishing, wine tasting in New Zealand, photography seminars in Scotland and cookery classes safaris in South Africa at Shamwari Game Reserve where Tiger Woods got engaged. 'When you add the safari element it makes it more of a couples' destination as there is a certain level of romance that goes along with going on safari,' says Hogan. 'Golf and wine make a great pairing in New Zealand, France, Italy and Argentina and our cooking packages for Italy are quite popular. I would like to expand that side of it to attract more couples and groups of couples in areas such as France, Spain and other Mediterranean areas'.

Over the decades marketing methods have changed for the company. 'We used to play up more of the golf courses. Back in the early 80s the key selling point was the golf course line-up', remembers Hogan. Nowadays the type of accommodation and range of extra-curricular activities are equally as important in attracting customers, particularly with the addition of more women to both the golfing and non-golfing clientele. Hogan has noticed a rise in female participation in the sport and in his tours over the past ten years, not only in couples but also as women-only groups. Wide World of Golf has arranged Hong Kong golf and Christmas shopping itineraries; summer trips to London for theatre and golf; spa and golf; and Fashion Week in Paris where the ladies play golf as well as taking in the catwalk shows and associated activities.

With recession hitting the USA, Hogan is marketing good value destinations to his customers. Wales, Thailand and Argentina offer cheaper alternatives than some of the more traditional golf destinations. 'Wales has suddenly become a popular destination for us. It's somewhat undiscovered but the golf is just about as good as Ireland and Scotland for about half the price. In this marketplace, price is definitely a consideration but fortunately we've got enough recession proof customers. We do need more economical product in the marketplace, though, to attract new customers', says Hogan.

With new golf courses and resorts being currently developed in New Europe, Russia is on Hogan's radar for future expansion. 'The average North American has great curiosity about that country and destination,' he explains. He is also looking at Egypt, having first taken golfers there in the 1980s when it was a relatively popular long-haul destination. He has identified golf course developments along the Nile as a growth destination for the company. 'What we've found over the years is that a lot of our clientele have already been to lots of more mainstream places and they are looking for new, more exotic destinations to visit,' says Hogan. He has reinstated Dubai on their schedule for the first time since the 9/11 fall-out made Middle East golf less viable.

Source

Telephone interview with Bill Hogan, 12 December 2008

http://www.wideworldofgolf.com

References

Brasch, R. (1972) *How did Sports Begin*, Harlow: Longman.

Campbell, M. (1994) *The Encyclopaedia of Golf*, London: Dorling Kindersley.

Carter, I. (2008) 'Golf's growth still in credit', *Golf Monthly*, September, 55.

Gigson, H. (2006) *Sport Tourism: Concepts and Theories*, New York: Routledge.

Higham, J. (ed.) (2005) *Sport Tourism Destinations*, London: Elsevier Butterworth-Heinemann.

Hudson, S. (ed.) (2003) *Sport and Adventure Tourism*, Oxford: Haworth.

Hudson, S. and Cross, P. (2005) 'Winter sports destinations: dealing with seasonality', in J. Higham and T. Hinch (eds), *Sports Tourism Destinations: Issues, Opportunities and Analysis*, Oxford: Butterworth-Heinemann, pp. 188–204.

IBISWorld (2008) *Golf Courses and Country Clubs in the US*, Los Angeles: IBISWorld.

KPMG (2008a) *The Value of Golf to Europe, Middle East and Africa*, KPMG Advisory, download from http://www.golfbenchmark.com.

KPMG (2008b) *Benchmark Survey in China 2008*, KPMG Advisory, download from http://www.golfbenchmark.com.

KPMG (2008c) *Golf Benchmark Survey 2007: Regional Report: Benchmark Indicators and Performance of Golf Courses in India*, KPMG Advisory, download from http://www.golfbenchmark.com.

Kumar, S. (2007) 'Indian "golf cities" fuel real estate boom, attract non-residential Indians', *Noida Scoop*, 7 May.

Lang Research (2007) *Golfing While on Trips of One or More Nights: A Travel Activities and Motivations Survey*, download from www.tourism.gov.on.ca.

Mintel (2006) 'Golf tourism', *Travel and Tourism Analyst*, 5, London: Mintel Group.

National Golf Foundation (2003) *The U.S. Golf Travel Market 2003*, Jupiter, FL: NGF.

National Golf Foundation (2008) *Gold Industry Overview*, Jupiter, FL: NGF.

Priestley, G.K. and Ashworth, G.J. (1995) *Sports Tourism: The Case of Golf. Tourism and Spatial Transformations*, Wallingford, Oxfordshire: CAB Publishing.

Readman, M. (2003) 'Golf tourism', in S. Hudson (ed.), *Sport and Adventure Tourism*, Oxford: Haworth, pp. 165–201.

Rees, E. (2008) 'Taking a swing', *The Ecologist*, 38 (6), 42–45.

Robinson, T. and Gammon, S. (2004) Sports Tourism: An Introduction, London: Thompson Learning.

SRI International (2005) *The 2005 Golf Economy Report*, www.sri.com.

Standeven, J. and De Knopp, p. (1999) *Sport Tourism*, Windsor, Ontario: Human Kinetics.

Weed, M. and Bull, C. (2004) *Sport Tourism: Participants, Policy and Providers*, Oxford: Elsevier Butterworth-Heinemann.

2 The Golf Tourist

Spotlight: Legend Golf and Safari Resort

Miss Worlds promoting Legend Golf and Safari Resort in South Africa, courtesy of Legend Golf and Safari Resort

Legend Golf and Safari Resort is raising the bar in providing five-star accommodation, luxury real estate opportunities, celebrity connections and topnotch activities for golfers and their spouses. While other clubs employ one pro golfer to design and endorse their course, Legend was able to attract 18 golf celebrities to design a hole each, representing the main golfing nations of the world.

The Legend Golf and Safari Resort is in the Waterberg Region of the Limpopo Province of South Africa, encompassing the Entabeni Safari Conservancy within its 22,000 hectares. It opened for golf in March 2009, with a grand opening scheduled for later in the year. The Resort combines the culture and wildlife of the African bushveld lifestyle with championship golf, a golf academy, a driving range, hotel, recreational and conference facilities and a wellness centre. Tourists no longer have to choose between a golfing holiday or a safari – they can do both here in a rarefied enclave designed to minimize the impact on the natural environment.

The Limpopo area was formerly home to the ancient kingdom of Monomatapa at Mapungubwe followed by a second city now known as the Great Zimbabwean Ruins. This heritage is emphasized in Legend's promotional literature as well as the architecture of the resort. The Eugene Marais Museum and Pedi Cultural Village within the grounds pay homage to the myths, legends, history and archaeology of the area's people. The resort's architecture – a modern take on local stone and brick, rounded towers - blends into the environment and the golf course has breathtaking views with the Waterberg Mountains as a backdrop.

As well as the Big Five – lion, leopard, rhinoceros, buffalo and elephant – the area boasts 55 mammal species, 300 plant species, 380 bird species, countless insects, reptiles and amphibians over five diverse eco-systems – grassland, bushveld, forest, mountain and riverbed.

The golf course is an 18-hole championship course, the longest in South Africa at 7748 metres for tournament play and 6534 metres for daily play. Each hole features five different tees to allow for both professionals and amateurs. The designs of the 18 world famous golfers have been brought to reality by David Riddle. Each designer's wishes were moulded from the landscape by Riddle who has now also taken on the mantle of Director of Golf.

The first hole has been designed by local hero, Trevor Immelman. Hole three was designed by Jim Furyk (USA) and the fourth by Germany's Bernhard Langer. Colin Montgomerie (Scotland) planned the par 4 sixth hole and Canada's Mike Weir provided the variety of length and angle for the tee positions at the seventh. In a clever representation of all the chief golfing nations of the world, other notable names include Camilo Villejas, Justin Rose, Vijay Singh, Padraig Harrington, Ian Woosnam and Sergio Garcia.

But the unique 19th hole is Legend's piece de resistance. Conceived by Graham Cooke of the UK and designed by Riddle, the Extreme 19th is the longest, most dramatic par 3 in the world, set high up on the Hanglip Mountain with the tee reached only by helicopter. Measuring 400 metres, it is played from a vertical height of also 400 metres after a short flight up to the escarpment. There are three tee boxes and plans for four separate cameras with tracking equipment to enable players to follow the flight of their ball which takes an incredible 27 seconds to reach the ground. The fairway is contoured to funnel the ball to the green below which is shaped like the map of Africa. Golfers can opt to add this hole onto their 18 or play it as a one-off experience for $350 with the lure of $1 million for a hole-in-one. The price tag includes the heli ride, a special certificate plus a range of unique products and of course the six balls you get to launch into infinity!

Legend Golf & Safari Resort also houses a Golf Academy and Family Golf Centre, including a full 400 metre driving range, pitching facility and chipping and putting greens. PGA professionals direct the training programmes with tuition available for all levels and ages. A 10-hole, par 3 Tribute Course is another exceptional feature of this amazing golf facility and has been modelled on the best par 3 holes in the world. No self-respecting golf resort is without a spa these days and the Fountain of Youth Wellness Centre typically offers treatments, relaxation, fitness, yoga, meditation and aromatherapy, with customized programmes for diet, fitness and lifestyle.

Just two hours' drive from Pretoria, accessibility is one of Legend's advantages. The Legend air strip accommodates small fixed wing aircraft and of course there is a helicopter onsite. Johannesburg is just a three-hour drive away.

In addition to Big 5 game drives, guests can visit the Botanical Gardens, the Legend Ranger Training School and the traditional Pedi Village. The Field of Legends is a sports training facility focusing on soccer, rugby, netball, gymnastics, hockey, tennis and cricket. Legend is approaching tennis and swimming stars to endorse these products, too.

Well-heeled guests can even buy their own piece of the legend, with plots from 3500 square feet to 3.5 hectares. Before official golf opening, almost half of the plots had been sold mainly to South African investors. Starting from around

$300,000 per plot, buyers need another $300,000 to build the house within an 18-month period, choosing from four blueprints. Each home will also have four separate guest villas in its domain, all of which can be entered into the rental pool. The low-rise architecture is being blended into the natural surroundings. Legend Golf & Safari resort communications director, Pete Richardson is optimistic that the world recession will not unduly impact the project. 'It'll probably have a very small effect on us because, I think, it'll be mainly the middle marketplace that gets squeezed. This is an exceptionally special place so when people realize what we have on offer there is little doubt we can make the few sales remaining. After all – in the global scheme of things we only have another 230 sales to make, and I'm absolutely certain there are 230 people in the world who will be delighted to buy here. We're at the top end of the marketplace and we're unique,' he said.

With its promise to be culturally and environmentally friendly, The Legend Foundation was founded as a non-profitable entity. Its objectives include creating a sustainable financial model focusing on the development of the disadvantaged communities in the area through sport and skill development as well as assisting with the social uplifting of neighbouring populations. The Entabeni Nature Guide Training School, Legend Hospitality School and Legend Wildlife Centre have already been established, with sports academies, arts and crafts centres, nurseries and clinics planned for the future. The well-being of the community is at the very heart of the Legend project and enshrined in the ethos of the development.

The Legend Group (part of the IFA Hotels & Resorts portfolio) has been involved with game and safari lodges, coastal hotels, country lodges, city hotels and cultural villages in four of South Africa's nine provinces since 2000. No stranger to guerrilla marketing tactics and celebrity endorsement, Legend invited 112 Miss World participants to add some female cachet to the Golf and Safari Resort in December 2008. Their six-day programme involved ranger skills, wildlife lessons, cooking seminars, survival training, tree-planting and eco-awareness as well as golf instruction. This was great promotion for the new venture since 112 Miss Worlds gave Legend access to unrivalled media publicity in 112 countries. 'In addition we were able to specifically target the 18 core golfing countries,' said Richardson. 'For example, we photographed Miss Scotland on Colin Montgomerie's hole, right by the plaque with his name and were able to send that out in national press releases.'

Sources

Telephone interview with Legend's Communications Director, Pete Richardson, 20 January, 2009.

'Legend Golf Resort', *Golf Course Architecture*, March 2008, p. 63.

www.legend-resort.com; www.legendlodges.co.za; www.ifahotelsresorts.com.

Profile of golf tourists worldwide

Golfers worldwide are predominately male, middle-aged or in their early retirement years, although this profile is changing slightly with more females entering the sport. Golf tourists also earn well above average incomes and are typically business owners, managers or independent professionals. Golf tourists also tend to be even older and wealthier than the average golfer. However, there are some variations worldwide, so the next section will take a closer look at golf tourists from different countries.

America

From recent research in the USA, the average age for a golf participant is around 37 years (see Table 2.1). Around 75 per cent of US participants are males and 25 per cent females, and participation is directly related to income levels. Participation rates at incomes between $25,000 and $60,000 are around 8 per cent and 20 per cent respectively, but when income levels rise to $150,000, the participation rate increases to around 30 per cent. Table 2.2 outlines golfing participation by category of workers. Participation numbers in the USA have been around the 30 million mark for the last decade. However, regular or avid golfers, playing at least 25 rounds annually, comprise a small segment of participants, but account for 75 per cent of golf-related spending. As a result, regular golfers, rather than occasional golfers, tend to have a greater influence on the industry, as do exogenous factors, such as weather conditions and wealth levels. It is estimated that there are about 13 million of these core golfers in the USA, and half of them regularly take a golfing holiday.

Table 2.1: Golf segmentation by age in the USA (Source: IBISWorld, 2008)

Age category	Golf participants (%age)
5-11	8
12-17	9
18-29	18
30-39	21
40-49	19
50-59	12
60-64	4
65+	9
Total	100

Table 2.2: Golf segmentation by working category in the USA (Source: IBISWorld, 2008)

Category	Golf participants (%age)
Professional/management/administration	39
Clerical/sales	15
Blue collar	24
Other	6
Retired	16
Total	100

As golfers grow older, they tend to play more often, with those over 65 averaging more than one round per week. Older core golfers spend more on golf and are more likely to take golf holidays than those under 35 years of age. On average,

American golfers who take golf-related trips are older, earn more, spend more on golf-related items, and play almost three times as often as the non-travelling segment. They are also more likely to be retired and to be members of private clubs. Of those working, almost half work in management jobs, where golf is likely to be a programmed activity for corporate outings and meeting clients and business partners.

Canada

A study of Canadian golf tourists in 2007 found that about 14 per cent of Canadians had played golf on a vacation during the previous two years. Of those that golfed, 31 per cent reported that golf was the main reason for travelling. Golfers in Canada are more likely to be male (65%), married and have dependent children under 18 living at home. They are a relatively affluent segment with an above-average level of education and prefer luxury accommodation when they travel. They are also more likely than other travellers to attend sporting events while on trips and are less likely to seek intellectual and cultural stimulation than entertainment activities such as visits to casinos, spas, comedy festivals and clubs and wineries. Canadian golf tourists can be targeted most effectively through sports-related media, travel-related media and business, finance and investing magazines (Lang Research, 2007). In terms of their preferred golf destination outside Canada, golf tourists usually consider Florida, California, Hawaii and Arizona.

Europe

With the exception of the UK and Ireland, golf is a relatively young sport in Europe. The number of registered golfers has grown faster than the number of courses in Europe since 1990, more than doubling over the period to reach almost 4 million. One way of making a comparison between the USA and Europe is to compare the number of core American golfers with registered golfers in Europe (Mintel, 2006). The population of the USA is around 300 million, whereas the 35 European countries collectively boast more than 500 million inhabitants. So, on a comparable basis, the penetration of committed golfers in the USA is 4.3 per cent compared to only 0.8 per cent in Europe. However, this comparison is based on the assumption that there are no core European golfers who are not registered to a club.

The number of registered players is concentrated heavily in Northern European countries. In the UK, for example, one out of every 150 citizens is a golfer. Here, golfers are predominantly male (78%), 62 per cent are aged between 35–60, and 42 per cent are likely to be in professional, managerial, or administrative occupations. Mintel estimates that golf accounts for up to 1 million holiday trips annually in the UK – including both domestic and inbound tourists – which generate more than $1 billion (Mintel, 2006). Scotland in particular has seen a tremendous growth in golf tourism revenue, and the case study at the end of this chapter focuses on golf tourists in Scotland. As mentioned in Chapter 1, the growth of golf tourism in Portugal, Spain, and Italy is due not just to golf holidays, but the desire to purchase holiday homes built as part of golf communities and golf resorts. Golf properties are also gaining momentum in Turkey, attracting not just golfers but also people seeking an alternative lifestyle, community and environment.

Elsewhere, France is a growing destination for golf tourism – both for domestic and international golfers. Golf passes are issued for three to six courses in a region, and some, like the Biarritz Golf Pass for six courses, can be purchased on the website of Maison de France, the national tourist office. France is particularly popular for British golfers and was cited in a poll of German golfers as the third most attractive foreign country. The fastest growing age segment in France is the over 55-year-old, and, in absolute terms, the number of golfers in the 56–69 age group is around double that of the 34–37 and 38–41 segments. Germany has also seen a spurt in the growth of golfing, although adult males make up only half of participants, with women over a third and the remainder juniors. Socio-economic status seems to be a relatively more important determinant of participation than age or gender. For German golf tourists, Spain is the most popular foreign choice.

With a relatively small population of about 9 million people, golf in Sweden is very popular and around 6 per cent of Swedes play golf. Many Swedish golf courses were built in the 1980s, coinciding with a worldwide surge in popularity, and there are now around 450 courses. In the 1990s, the emergence of home grown talent such as Jesper Parnevik, Carl Pettersson and Annika Sörenstam helped raise the profile of the game. In Sweden, as in other countries, golf has undergone a transformation from an elitist 'country club' game to something for everyone, and, of the almost 500,000 Swedes who play golf, about a third are female.

Finally, golf tourism in New Europe is experiencing something of a boom. Croatia is attracting the attention of big-name developers, and Montenegro is generating some interest. At the centre of Croatia's boom is Istria, a Mediterranean peninsula that was spared the fighting in the 1990s Balkan War. The local government anticipates 22 courses by 2012, and the region has attracted many names in design including Jack Nicklaus and Robert Trent Jones Jr. But growing golf tourism will not be easy in a country with such a complicated past. Developers have struggled to obtain contiguous plots of land, and regional offices have been slow to grant building permits because of concerns over unscrupulous practices and environmental impact. While Serbia and Bosnia are unlikely to attract foreign golfers – as neither share Croatia's tradition of tourism – both are witnessing a burgeoning domestic market. However, similar challenges face developers in Bosnia and Serbia, where all that remains of the Belgrade course opened by Prince Karadjordjevic in 1936 – and bombed a few years later – is a restaurant named Golf. A new golf course in Belgrade opened in 2003 and has since seen its membership quadruple. The game is part of a new experience for Serbians, and some are beginning to cross the border into Croatia in search of a tee time.

Asia

Japan is the most mature golfing market in Asia, with a golfing population second only to that of the USA. More than 11 million Japanese, or around 10 per cent of the population, play golf on the country's 2300 or so golf courses. After many years of decline, the number of golf players in Japan reportedly rose in 2007 by 3.9 per cent, according to government data. The key to improving golf numbers is to attract the increasingly numerous retired population. While running a golf business in Japan may not be hugely different from anywhere else, there are idiosyncrasies that need to be accounted for. For example, Japanese golfers tend to play in two halves, stopping for lunch after the ninth hole. Another ritual is the post-golf soothing of strained muscles in hot baths or an *onsen*. All clubs have an *onsen*, and visitors are welcome to use them at no extra charge. The Snapshot on page 33 gives more of an insight into the golf experience in Japan.

Golf is still a strongly male-dominated sport in China, with men comprising 87 per cent of golf club members. At the moment, because there are few public courses in China, the sport is largely restricted to a narrow elite group who can afford to pay the high cost of membership, which can be as steep as $150,000. However, the number of Chinese golfers is growing 30 per cent a year, and a report published by the China Golf Association suggested that 2000 new courses need to be built by 2014 if demand continues to grow.

Elsewhere in Asia, golf has become one of the most popular sports in Thailand where there are approximately 200 golf courses and around 15 golf resorts (Mintel, 2006). The game arrived in the country a century ago and was quickly taken up by the elite and the fashionable. Among the first sponsors of the game were the armed forces and government institutions, which built and continue to own some of the finest courses in the country. The Thailand Tourist Authority has been quite proactive in attempting to attract golf tourists from all over the world, and receives upwards of 400,000 golf tourists per year. Like other Asian countries, the standard of golf played in Thailand by local golfers has rocketed over the past few years, and has led to increase in domestic golf tourism. Thongchai Jaidee is the country's most successful golfer, winning a handful of major international tournaments. Other Thais who have had international success include Prayad Marksaeng and Boonchu Ruangjit.

Malaysia too has about 200 golf courses and has been aggressively promoting its golf tourism to potential visitors (see the Snapshot in Chapter 1). According to Tourism Malaysia, golf tourism only accounted for 2.4 per cent of tourist arrivals in 2007, but this translated into half a million golf tourists. Most of them are from the ASEAN countries, and represent an attractive market for tourism officials, as golf tourists in Malaysia spend three times as much as regular tourists. Tourism Malaysia organizes the World Amateur Inter-Team Golf Championship, an annual tournament that brings together amateur golfers from all over the world to play on some of the best courses in Malaysia. Tourism Malaysia sees a huge potential in golf tourism, as golf courses in the country are currently only half utilized.

Malaysia attracts an increasing number of Indian golfers. In 2006, 35,000-38,000 outbound golf packages were sold to Indian golfers, largely to corporate travellers. At the same time, around 10,000 spa packages were sold, and golf and spa packages have become an integral part of high-end Indian travellers' itineraries. Around 80 per cent of the golf and spa holiday destinations for Indian holiday makers are still restricted to South-East Asia. Thailand, Malaysia and Singapore are the most popular golfing destinations for Indians, but Mauritius and South Africa are gaining popularity among Indian golf tourists.

Snapshot: the golf experience in Japan

Ocean Palace Nagasaki, courtesy of ©Nagasaki International Tourism and Convention Association/©JNTO

Golf has traditionally been a day-long affair for Japanese golfers who routinely play nine holes and then break for a 45-minute lunch in the clubhouse restaurant. They then return to the game to finish off the back nine, stopping on course for cups of hot green tea and snacks. The sport is followed by a visit to the *onsen* where golfers wash (at stools with pails of water) and then bathe in the mineralized waters to relax their strained muscles. Caddies are de rigueur at all courses and they tend to be women – although not necessarily the youthful women which characterize Chinese and Thai golf.

With courses designed by famous international golf course architects, many of them reflect a natural theme, and all are immaculately maintained. They can be tougher to play than western courses, as they are often narrower than European or US counterparts.

A hole-in-one comes very expensive at traditional clubs with the 'lucky' golfer having to buy presents for hundreds of club members. Insurance companies offer coverage against this. If a golfer has a good game, he is honour-bound to buy drinks and give gifts in the clubhouse afterwards. Fortunately, this only applies to members and casual players or tourists are less bound by such customs.

These cultural differences have not yet been obliterated by mass global tourism but some clubs have been trying to woo golfers with western-style innovations at their courses. Pacific Golf Group International Holdings – an affiliate of Dallas-based Lone Star – has 118 courses in Japan where it has been trying to revive participation since a decline over the past decade.

The company tried introducing earlybird and twilight games with discounted green fees to bolster weekday use which was only running at 58.5 per cent capacity. It also encouraged the practice of playing 18 holes straight without stopping for lunch. However, this strategy failed when numbers were seen to have dropped and restaurant profits halved. It just didn't tie in with the Japanese tradition of playing in two separate nines with a leisurely lunch in between. Pacific hired agronomists for its Clear View Golf Club to plant wear-resistant grass which would enable carts to drive on the fairways and thus speed up play. Pacific is also targeting seniors as baby boomers reach retirement age. It is also appealing to women and targeting youth via school golf programmes. Loyalty schemes which give points redeemable for free golf during weekdays are helping to fill tee times.

With over 2300 courses, Japan has more golf courses than it currently needs despite a golfing population of around 11 million. Since Japan is generally perceived as an expensive destination, there are challenges in attracting golf tourists. From golf's beginnings in the country around 1910, golf was an extravagant corporate entertainment, with expensive membership and green fees. In the 1980s memberships were traded like stocks and shares, raising the prices even higher. In the 1990s asset prices dropped and companies scaled back on expense accounts resulting in a 10 per cent drop in golf participation in 1998. Golf course memberships and green fees had to come down in price in an attempt to attract lower-income golfers, who hitherto had only been able to afford indoor putting facilities or high-rise driving ranges in the city. Some courses are dispensing with memberships entirely to attract more casual players. La Vista Country Club in Chiba has also cut down on caddies to keep prices down.

Japan Golf Tours organizes unique itineraries to Japan's top ranked private courses. The company's founder, John Thornton maintains that Japanese golf is no longer any more expensive than that of the UK or USA. He targets English-speaking golfers to give them a privileged insight into Japan's elite courses.

The international profile of Japanese golf is being raised by an increasing number of annual pro tournaments. One is held at the vast Phoenix Seagaia Resort on the southern island of Kyushu, which encompasses 99 holes, including a Tom Watson-designed public course. The Japan PGA Championship has been held at various courses since 1926. And, recently, a golf star has emerged in the form of a 16-year-old high school student, Ryo Ishikawa. He is the biggest sports star in Japan right now and has signed on for around $20 million in product endorsements.

Sources

Jenkins, A. 'Links of the rising sun', *Travel + Leisure Golf*, pp. 101–105.

Whipp, L. (Mar 19, 2008) 'Hopes for revival are pinned on older golfer', *Financial Times*, p. 2.

http://www.japan-golf-tours.com/japan-golf-tour-information.html.

Understanding golf tourists

A number of researchers have attempted to segment the golf tourist market in different ways. Table 2.3 summarizes these studies, and the next section explains each one in more detail.

Table 2.3: Segmenting the golf tourist market

Study	Segments identified	Key findings
Hennessey *et al* (2008) (Canada)	Infrequent Moderate Dedicated	Dedicated golfers are much more likely to be older, wealthier, from outside the region, first time, be visiting to play golf, golf in couples, be less price sensitive, and more likely to have made golf bookings prior to coming. They also spend considerably more than the other two groups.
Wilson and Thilmany (2006) (U.S.)	Enthusiasts Affluent-Resorters Networkers	Enthusiasts were most likely to bring income to the region. The Affluent-Resorters would be the easiest to attract to the mountain resorts because of aesthetics, but Enthusiasts bring more revenue into the surrounding economy. Enthusiasts are most likely to extend their stay for other mountain diversions.
Petrick (2002) (U.S.)	Infrequents Loyal-infrequents Collectors Locals Visitors Veterans	Infrequents were more satisfied than visitors, and visitors were least likely to have repurchase intentions. Collectors also had statistically lower repurchase intentions than veterans and locals. It was suggested that the segments of infrequents and loyal-infrequents are the most important for golf course management.
Correia and Pintassilgo (2006) (Portugal)	Golf tourist Householder tourist Sun-beach tourist	The concerns of the golf tourist are centred on the golf courses and game conditions whereas the householder tourist particularly values accommodation, gastronomy, landscape, weather, price and accessibility. The sun-beach tourist is mainly concerned with tourist opportunities.
Scott Parker Research (Scotland)	Golf buddies Golfing escapees Luxury golfers Golf purists Golfing tourists	For golf buddies and golf escapees, the social elements of the break are as integral as the golf, whereas golfing tourists seek a range of leisure activities and less challenging courses. Luxury golfers seek an exceptional experience which is golf centred, and golf purists are highly competitive with low handicaps.

Hennessey *et al.* (2008) have developed a framework for understanding the golf traveller (see Figure 2.3) which includes three sets of variables: influence sets, decision sets, and outcomes. The influence set is the demographic, behavioural and environmental variables that exist for the golf tourist before he or she plans to take the trip. The decision set is the motivations and 'golfographic' variables that require actions or decisions either prior to or during a trip. Golfographics is a term that is used to describe variables associated with playing golf such as rounds of golf played per year, golf vacations taken, number of years played, handicap etc.). Lastly, there are the outcomes – the value and satisfaction variables that can predict future travel plans.

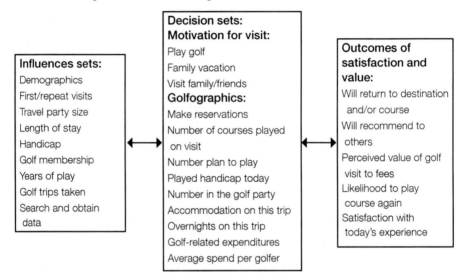

Figure 2.3: A framework of golf travellers' profiles (Source: adapted from Hennessey *et al.*, 2008, p. 10)

The authors applied the framework to golf tourists in Prince Edward Island, Canada, and found significant differences in these variables based on golfing frequency. They categorized golf tourists into three groups – infrequent, moderate and dedicated golfers. Dedicated golfers are very different from infrequent and moderate golfers on three of the four variables. They are much more likely to be older, wealthier, from outside the Maritime Provinces, first-time visitors to PEI, be visiting to play golf, golf in couples, be less price sensitive, and more likely to have made golf bookings prior to coming to the island. They also spend considerably more than the other two groups. Their expenditure on golf-related items alone was $483 per golfer. The researchers concluded that dedicated golfers can provide a tremendous boost to a region's tourist industry.

Researchers in Colorado have segmented the Colorado golf tourist population, finding three key segments or clusters (Wilson and Thilmany, 2006). The first group, named Enthusiasts, was named after the frequency with which they play golf. The second group Affluent-Resorters was named after their desire to stay in resort areas and experience 'some of the finer things in life'. Lastly, the Networkers were most likely to be Colorado residents and were presumed to be playing with business acquaintances. Of the three clusters, the Enthusiasts were most likely to bring income to Colorado as only 25 per cent were Colorado residents while 39 per cent and 82 per cent of the Affluent-Resorters and Networkers, respectively, were residents. All three groups were found to be significantly older than the Colorado golfing population in general, and all three were dominantly male. The researchers found that skill level was not particularly high amongst golf tourists as they appear to be playing golf for the leisure and enjoyment of the sport and not to improve their final score. Not surprisingly, golf tourists spend more on green fees and other travel activities than the average golfer in Colorado, and therefore have economic benefits for 'enabled' industries including lodging, entertainment, shopping and food. The study found that the Affluent-Resorters would be the easiest to attract to the mountain resorts because of aesthetics, but Enthusiasts bring more revenue into the surrounding economy. Moreover, Enthusiasts are most likely to extend their stay for other mountain diversions, especially if travel packages strategically bundle biking, rafting, hiking or boating with some golf.

One researcher in the USA utilized 'experience use history' (EUH) to create distinct, identifiable segments of golf tourists by examining their past behaviour and experience levels (Petrick, 2002). These segments were labelled as follows: infrequents (golf travellers with low experience at few resorts); loyal-infrequents (golf travellers with low experience, mainly at the study resort); collectors (golf travellers who have visited many resorts, but little experience at any one); locals (golf travellers with high experience at the study resort only); visitors (golf travellers with high experience in general, but little experience at the study resort); and veterans (golf travellers with high experience at many resorts). It was found that infrequents were more satisfied than visitors, and visitors were least likely to have repurchase intentions. Collectors also had statistically lower repurchase intentions than veterans and locals. It was suggested that the segments of infrequents and loyal-infrequents are the most important for golf course management. Since their intentions are moderate and their experiences are low, it is believed that these segments could be a viable market for the future.

A research study in Portugal identified three market segments based on the attributes that led to the choice of Algarve's golf courses (Correia and Pintassilgo, 2006). These segments were: the golf tourist, whose concerns are centred on the golf courses and game conditions; the householder tourist who particularly values accommodation, gastronomy, landscape, weather, price and accessibility; and the sun-beach tourist who is mainly concerned with tourist opportunities. The researchers found that the sun-beach tourists were mainly from the UK and Scandinavia, whereas the Portuguese players belonged to the golf tourist segment. The study emphasized the strategic importance of golf for the Algarve, given that it operates on a counter-cycle to sun-beach tourism and does not depend exclusively on the same factors.

Finally, a qualitative study in Scotland in 2006, identified five different golf tourist segments; golf buddies, golf escapees, luxury golfers, golf purists, and golfing tourists. These segments are described in more detail in the end-of-chapter case study. Other research commissioned by VisitScotland has found that those visitors who travelled the furthest also stayed the longest – and play the most courses (VisitScotland, 2007). However, it is the Swedish golfers who play most rounds per course visited (2.0), and domestic Scottish golfers who play the most rounds per day – day-trippers average 1.27 and overnight Scottish visitors 0.93. There is a significant variation in the average expenditure per day – from $120 by domestic Scottish golfers, to around $450 by visitors from the USA.

Women golfers

Although women's participation in golf has increased in the last decade, it has been suggested that the golf industry is missing a huge potential market, given the increase in female participation in other sports such as softball and volley-ball, sports that are more physically-demanding than golf (McGinnis and Gentry, 2006). However, female participation in the sport of golf is increasing, and this has not gone unnoticed in the golf tourism world. Wide World of Golf, the tour operator featured in Chapter 1, has noticed a rise in female participation in tours over the past ten years, not only in couples but also as women-only groups. To cater for this market, the company has packaged golf with spa visits, shopping, theatre and fashion shows. Wide World of Golf has also seen examples of women golfers bringing non-golfing spouses on trips.

There are also an increasing number of organizations dedicated to promoting women's golf. One example is the Executive Women's Golf Association (EWGA). The EWGA is a Florida not-for-profit corporation serving an international membership. The EWGA exists to provide opportunities for women to learn, play and enjoy the game of golf for business and for life. The association currently has nearly 20,000 members in over 120 chapters throughout the United States, along with international chapters in Canada and France, offering a wide range of organized golf activities, player development and education programmes, volunteer, social and networking opportunities for both novice and experienced golfers.

EWGA Chapter activities typically include: an annual 'kick off' event; two to three major tournaments; weekly 'after work' 9-hole league play; business networking and social functions; weekend golf outings; golf rules and etiquette seminars; education programmes; a Chapter Championship (the qualifying event in the EWGA Championship); charity fundraising events; and volunteer installation and recognition events. The EWGA Championship is the largest women's amateur golf tournament in the USA and is designed for players of all skill levels. The EWGA Championship is held annually in the fall.

Golf courses, too, are beginning to target women specifically. An example is Dragon's Fire Golf Club in Ontario, Canada. According to owner Bryan DeCunha, too many courses were long, difficult and designed to impress the game's long-hitting, low-handicap participants and earn 'Best New Course' accolades. He surveyed potential customers about what kind of golf course they wanted. Around 35 per cent of those surveyed were female, and the overwhelming consensus among respondents was that they wanted a fun, playable course, particularly for those of middling ability. So, in 2008 he opened Dragon's Fire. 'We needed a course that was very playable for the average player,' he said. 'I didn't want to design a golf course that was ideal for tour play, or that they would want to host the Canadian Open there, which makes it tough' (McCarten, 2008). The course features five massive tee decks that allow the course to stretch from about 5200 yards to nearly 7300.

However, some researchers have warned against a traditional segmentation approach by specifically targeting women. A study of women golfers and potential golfers in the USA found that overt attempts to cater to female golfers and to make them 'feel at home' may alienate men to some extent, while at the same time alienating women as well (McGinnis and Gentry, 2006). The same study found that intrapersonal constraints were important inhibitors to women's involvement in the game of golf. Such factors as knowledge of the game, self-confidence, and anxiety influence whether women stick with the game. For current female golfers, interpersonal constraints such as difficulty finding playing partners and non-verbal communication when interacting with males on the golf course can be more influential than intrapersonal constraints. Moreover, structural constraints, such as family obligations and time, were heavily cited among the female golfers as reasons for limiting their golf participation.

In terms of behaviour, women golf tourists spend slightly less than men on golf travel (National Golf Foundation, 2003). But that hasn't stopped golfing hotels and resorts packaging golfing holidays specifically for women's tastes. For example, Daytona Oceanfront Hotels in Florida were offering a Girls and Golf package in 2008 that included two nights' accommodation, a 30-minute hydralift facial and a 30-minute Swedish massage, a round of golf for two, and a gift basket filled with snacks, a make-your-own cosmo kit and a picture frame – all for $269 per person.

Influences on the demand for golf tourism

In terms of golf participation generally, research in North America (IBISWorld, 2008, p. 15) suggests that the demand determinants of services offered by golf courses and resort are influenced by many factors, including:

♦ The golf participation rate
♦ The number of golf courses and clubs available for participants
♦ The condition of golf courses
♦ The status associated with being a member of a club
♦ The price to participate in a round of golf
♦ The popularity of other sports
♦ The average level of leisure time
♦ Weather patterns
♦ The desire to increase sport participation and fitness levels
♦ The success of US golfers on the professional golf circuit.

Another study in North America, found that price sensitivity and the promise of good weather are by far the top considerations when choosing a golf destination (National Golf Foundation, 2003). Golfers were given a list of characteristics and asked to rate their importance in planning a trip that includes golf. Table 2.4 shows the percentage of golfers who responded 8, 9 or 10 on a scale of 1 to 10 where '1' was 'Not all important' and '10' was 'Very Important'.

Table 2.4: The importance of characteristics when choosing a golf destination (Source: National Golf Foundation, 2003, p. 15)

Characteristic	All golfers (%)	Best customers (%)
Overall price	72	74
Weather/climate	76	85
Location	60	65
Past experience	55	62
Resort/hotel reputation	49	57
Other amenities (pool, dining, etc.)	46	46
Quality of courses in area	46	65
Other area attractions	42	40
Golf packages available	41	55
Natural surroundings/scenery	40	40
Destination within one-day drive	36	38
Family/friend recommendation	36	41
Family activities	35	30
Number of courses in area	33	50
Shopping in area	20	22
Courses highly rated by golf media	16	25
Spa	13	13
Courses close to interstate	12	15
Courses close to major airports	10	12
Golf schools	4	6

According to research by KPMG, the typical golf tourist spends 4–7 days on a short-haul golf holiday, and 7–14 days on a long-haul one (KPMG, 2008). These golf tourists generally play 4–6 rounds of golf on 3–5 different courses during a one-week golf holiday. Figure 2.2 shows how golf tourists in Europe choose their golf destination according to tour operators that serve them. Golf tourists care more about the climate of a location and quality of the golf course, although they are still price sensitive. Golf tourists care less about entertainment and sightseeing opportunities.

A research study in Portugal found that the driving motivations behind the demand for golf courses in the Algarve were typically the social environment associated with golf; the leisure opportunities provided by the region; the golf course and the game conditions; and the price and proximity/accessibility (Correia and Pintassilgo, 2006). This tends to support the comments of Bill Hogan from Wide World of Golf (see the case study in Chapter 1) who says that the key selling point in the 1980s was the golf course itself, whereas now the type of accommodation and range of extra-curricular activities are equally as important in attracting customers, particularly with the addition of more women to both the golfing and non-golfing clientele. 'Typically if a group of men went to Scotland, all they needed was good golf and the local pub. Ladies want a more well-rounded itinerary,' says Hogan.

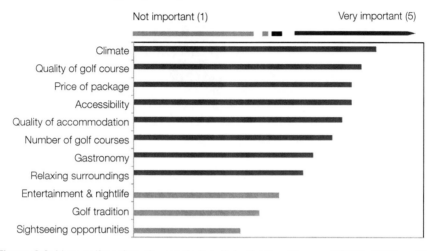

Figure 2.2: How golf tourists choose their golf destination (Source: KPMG, 2008, p. 8)

Researchers in the USA have looked at how well golfographic variables can predict golf travellers' perceived value (Petrick and Backman, 2002a). They found that the variables of frequency of play, average score, years of play, and golf trips taken are poor indicators of golf travellers' perceived value. Instead, they found that the attributes of resort facilities, resort service, and golf information were the best predictors of overall satisfaction. Therefore, in order to differentiate itself most effectively in the market, resort management would be better off providing superior resort facilities and service than its competition. However, the researchers found that golf resorts may have a more difficult time pleasing older golf tourists with more experience. Thus, to retain customers that are older, golf resort management may need to use more resources.

Spending habits of golf tourists

Compared to other leisure tourists, golf tourists spend significantly more on their vacations. In addition to the golf course facilities, they support a wide range of businesses such as hotels, restaurants, retailers, and car rental agencies. According to research by KPMG, golf tourists in Europe spend on average $190–230 per day on a short trip, and approximately $320 per day while on a long-haul golf trip (KPMG, 2008). Figure 2.3 presents the estimated breakdown of golf tourist spending during a long-haul trip of 7–9 days.

In terms of clothing and equipment, Figure 2.4 shows that sales of golf clubs between 2002 and 2005 in the USA were impressive, but have tailed off since then. Sales of soft goods – balls, bags, gloves and shoes – generally keep track with rounds played which have also levelled off (see Figure 2.5).

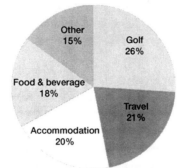

Figure 2.3: Spending by golf tourists during a long haul trip (Source: KPMG, 2008, p. 6)

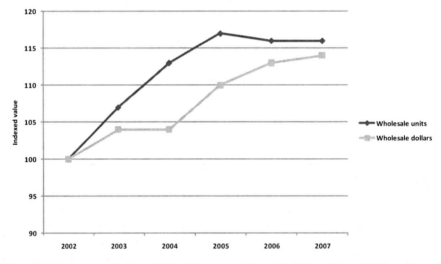

Figure 2.4: Sales of golf clubs 2002–7 (Source: National Golf Foundation 2008, p. 1)

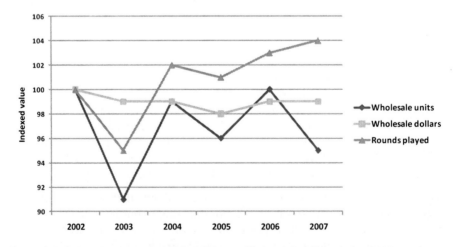

Figure 2.5: Sales of soft goods 2002–7 (Source: National Golf Foundation 2008, p. 1)

The early 2000s have seen a new cross-over of golfing designs to fashion and, conversely, the fashion world influencing golf apparel. As Roger Pride, Director of Marketing for Welsh Assembly Government, says 'Lyle & Scott and Pringle are putting golf fashion on the street and Burberry is putting fashion on the golf course.'

Golf for Women – a Golf Digest publication – brought out a 'Style Issue' in July/ Aug 2008 full of attractive and innovative golf ensembles, modelled by trendy golf pros and available as prizes in a Win a Golf Wardrobe online contest. Styles included pants outfits, skirts and sleeveless tops, funky dresses and preppy cardigans in variegated colours, metallics and wild prints in a fusion of fashion and utility. Golf shoes are undergoing a metamorphosis, too, with a wide variety of colours and non-traditional styles. No longer do you have just one pair of golf shoes – you need a pair to match each outfit.

Titania Golf, a design company from Australia, brings pastels and printed Capri pants to the tee. These are the kind of clothes that can be worn out to lunch, shopping or the beach after a round of golf. Designers like Liz Claiborne and Ralph Lauren in the USA have come to the 'fore' also, producing signature golf apparel collections. And it's not just for the women – with England's Ian Poulter's cutting-edge outfits monopolizing TV golf coverage, golf fashion is no longer an oxymoron. Poulter sells his brightly-coloured line via the Internet specializing in pants made from traditional plaids in updated colours and styles. Frumpy polyester pants are no longer acceptable nor are stereotypical cotton shirts. Fabrics are now technological triumphs with lightweight, heat and sweat wicking properties borrowed from running, tennis and ski-wear.

Equipment has also evolved recently. It's come a long way from the original wooden clubs and stones characterizing 15th century golf. Nowadays, self-improvement marketing has persuaded even the savviest golfer to indulge in the latest 'technology' despite the well-known adage 'a bad workman blames his tools'. An increasing number of golf clubs and resorts are offering high quality club rentals to cater for golf tourists.

Trends in consumer behaviour influencing golf tourism

The final section of Chapter 2 focuses on ten key trends or demands in consumer behaviour that are influencing golf tourism today.

1. Learning and enrichment

One of the major trends in tourism today is the desire of the tourist to have a learning experience as a part of the vacation. A recent survey found that half of North American travellers want to visit art, architectural, or historic sites on vacations, while one-third would like to learn a new skill or activity. Today's travellers are seeking experiences that provide them with a greater insight, increased understanding, and a personal connection to the people and places they visit. Rather than choose their vacation by the destination, many are first determining the experiences they want, and then choosing the destination where these experiences are located. Learning and enrichment travel refers to vacations that provide opportunities for authentic, hands-on, or interactive learning experiences, featuring themes such as adventure, agriculture, anthropology, archaeology, arts, culture, cuisine, education, forestry, gardening, language, maritime culture, mining, nature, science, spirituality, sports, wine, and wildlife – to name only a few!

The case study in Chapter 1 showed how Wide World of Golf is packaging golf alongside historical tours, photography seminars, and cooking packages. PerryGolf also books trips to Scotland and Ireland that combine golf with explorations of centuries-old castles. As mentioned in Chapter 1, golfing instruction has been increasingly offered as a central or an add-on feature of golfing packages, tapping in to this desire to learn on vacation. Even all-inclusive resorts are promoting golf instruction. Sandals, for example, has introduced its first Sandals Resorts Golf School at Sandals Golf & Country Club, Ochos Rios, Jamaica. The Snapshot below gives more details.

Snapshot: Sandals Resorts Golf School, Jamaica

Sandals Resorts Golf School, Jamaica, courtesy of Sandals

A current tourism trend is for vacations that teach. Whether it is educational, environmental, skills, crafts or sports, the baby boomers are clamouring for a significant purpose to their valuable free time. Sandals – renowned for its all-inclusive, adult-only lazy beach holidays – is catering to this trend by establishing its first Golf School at the Sandals Golf & Country Club, at Ocho Rios in Jamaica. To facilitate publicity for this new offering, Sandals Resorts International teamed up with trade magazine *Travelweek*, with a survey for travel agents and the chance to win a golf-instruction trip. The survey – sent out by eblast in November 2008 just one month after the launch of the world-class golf training facility – involved four questions designed to accumulate information on best practices for selling golf holidays.

Open to resort guests and the public, the new Sandals Golf School focuses on private instruction as well as multi-day lessons and corporate golf retreats, utilizing technology to enhance the procedure. The School is supported by Nike Golf for clothing and equipment, with club fitting facilitated by the Nike 360 degree system. The teaching area covers 1000 square feet, featuring up-to-date JC Video Motion Analysis software to analyze and improve performance. There's also a 10,000 square yard short-game teaching area for performance enhancement up to 100 yards.

Private lessons don't come cheaply – $125 for a one-hour, one-on-one session. But there are more affordable packages for one– to five–day group courses with a maximum ratio of four students to one coach. Renowned for its cozy couple environment, Sandals is also offering couples' golf lessons. Programmes are tiered to benefit all ability levels. To ensnare the next generation, Beaches Resorts (the sister brand of family resorts) offers a Junior Golf Camp which runs weekdays for ages eight to 16, including 20 hours of supervised instruction, competitions and on-course play for $299 per person. Sandals is sufficiently sure of its instruction programmes to offer a money-back guarantee.

Included in the prices are rentals, golf towels and transportation. All students take home a DVD evaluation of their swing along with coach's comments plus an instruction manual with individually customized tips. For those unsure about going back to school, there's a taster golf clinic two days a week which is free. And the children of staff members are given free lessons every weekend.

Opened in 1992 as a par 72, 18-hole championship course, Sandals Golf & Country Club was positioned as the most elite golf course in Jamaica. Dubbed 'the land of wood and water' by Jamaica's first inhabitants, the Arawaks, the course is very scenic. It also boasts a plantation-style clubhouse, perched 700 ft atop the Ocho Rios hills. For mid-round snacks, there's an authentic Jamaican Jerk Shack on the course. There's a driving range, too, and all Sandals guests get unlimited, complimentary green fees. The School was the brainchild of CEO Adam Stewart and is the first of its kind in Jamaica, differentiating Sandals from the plethora of championship courses available on the island.

Sources

Travelweek. (2008), November 13, p. 30.

Personal communication with Tracy McCann, PR specialist with Sandals.

www.sandals.com.

2. Environmentally-friendly products

International leisure travellers are increasingly motivated to select a destination for the quality of its environmental health and the diversity and integrity of its natural and cultural resources. Studies indicate that environmental considerations are now a significant aspect of travellers' destination-choosing process. Certainly in North America, the growth in special-interest, nature-oriented travel reflects an increasing concern for the environment. A recent study also showed that approximately 80 per cent of American travellers believe it is important that hotels take steps to preserve and protect the environment. According to the study, 70 per cent are willing to pay as much as $150 more for a two-week stay in a hotel that has a 'responsible environmental attitude' and 55 per cent are more likely to book a hotel that purports to be environmentally friendly (*Tourism*, 2002).

In response to demand for greener tourism, hotels, attractions, restaurants and even golf resorts are increasingly adopting green policies in an effort to operate in an environmentally friendly manner. A good example of this is the Water Smart Landscapes Program in Las Vegas (see Chapter 9 for more details), where the Southern Nevada Water Authority has managed to persuade 26 of the 48 eligible Las Vegas courses to participate in a programme that eradicates unnecessary grass, reduces irrigation and returns the environment to a more sustainable level. Some golf clubs like the Mauna Lani Resort on the Kohala Coast of Hawaii's Big Island are selling recycled and biodegradable green golf products like tees, golf shirts and golf visors. They are seeing an increase in the number of golfers who have questions about the environmental standards of the golf course. Pinehurst Resort in North Carolina has also seen a demand for greener golf and offers bamboo golf tees and even a biodegradable golf ball.

3. Nostalgia

Nostalgia has become a big driver in destination choice. The more rapidly people are propelled into an uncertain future, the more they yearn for the imagined security of the past. Not only have tourists become more interested in history, but the scale, richness, and diversity of the history they are interested in has also expanded enormously in the past 30 years (Leadbeater, 2002). Nostalgia tourism provides an alternative to the present by recourse to an imagined past, a version of reality that people carry around in their heads. A consequence of this emergence in nostalgia tourism is the increasing desire to re-visit a specific country or city with a sentimental association instead of discovering somewhere new. A 2007 survey in the UK found that 90 per cent of British travellers use their holidays to re-visit a specific country or city with a sentimental association to their lives and the top reason is a desire to re-live youth. More than a quarter (27.7%) said they go back to a destination where they had a memorable childhood holiday while more than a fifth (21.5%) go to where they lived or studied in their younger years (Davies, 2007).

Fairmont has responded to the demand for the past by introducing a Heritage Golf Experience at its Banff Springs Course in Canada. In 2008, golfers were given the opportunity to play the course the way Stanley Thomson designed it and use equipment from the 1930s. The experience includes a heritage caddie clad in period plus-fours, who helps golfers choose from a selection of hickory-shafted clubs, including a brassie, spoon, jigger, mashie and niblick. Golfers also get three golf balls pressed to replicate those used in the 1930s and some tips on how to swing the mashie. For the Heritage round, the distance from the tees has been reduced from 7083 to 6301 yards to compensate for the vintage technology. This type of golf is called Hickory Golf and has been growing in popularity since the first modern hickory golf championship was held in the USA in 1998.

4. Health-consciousness

A more health-conscious society is often attributed to the influence of the baby boomer. Baby boomers are generally healthier, financially better off, better educated, and more interested in novelty, escape, and authentic experiences than were previous cohorts of older people. Many baby boomers and senior adult groups are consequently opting for more physically challenging and 'adrenalin-driven' activities.

Health and wellness centres are also springing up in many tourism destinations, and many destinations are combining spas with golf tourism. Bulgaria is diversifying away from both ski resorts and the sun-and-sand destinations of the Black Sea Coast to focus on spa and wellness tourism combined with golf. Sandanski, for example, in southern Bulgaria, has seen significant development in recent years, and attracts high-spending tourists from all over the world. The town has been known for some time as the best natural health station in Europe for bronchial asthma, but now two signature golf courses are currently under construction between Bansko and Razlog – some 70km north-east of the town.

Resorts are also expanding their spa facilities in order to satisfy the partners of golf tourists as well as the golfers themselves. The Montgomerie in Dubai, for example, has six treatment rooms in its Angsana Spa, with a range of treatments and therapies based around the use of aromatherapy with natural flowers and spices. At the Fairmont Scottsdale Princess in Arizona, the Willow Stream Spa offers a Golf Performance massage, combining massage, stretching and acupressure, or a hydrating golf facial.

Golf tourists are also looking to eat healthier foods on vacation. In 2008, the Pocono Mountain region of northeast Pennsylvania provided a variety of 'spring cleaning' packages and cooking lessons with the goal of creating and maintaining a healthy psyche, body and soul. Shawnee Inn and Golf Resort joined in this promotion by promoting three new health and wellness-focused on-site amenities: the River Room, offering dishes uniquely native to the area such as venison steak and wild boar chops; The Bistro, a seasonal restaurant with optional al fresco dining; and Spa Shawnee, offering a spa dining menu to complement the massage and hydrotherapy treatments already offered.

5. Customization

Requests for customized and personalized vacations are rising sharply, and both agents and traditional tour operators are changing their businesses to meet that demand. In addition to booking air and hotel reservations, agents and outfitters today are arranging customized wine tastings, visits to artisan workshops, and private after-hours tours of attractions such as the British crown jewels and the Vatican. Even at companies like Butterfield & Robinson and Abercrombie & Kent – both of which have been primarily associated with pre-arranged tours – requests for customized trips are increasing. Kristina Rundquist, spokesperson for the American Society of Travel Agents, says that there are two parallel trends now: people who want personalized service and those who want highly specialized trips: 'Many tourists have precious little time for vacations, so they like to make sure they get exactly what they want, whether it's a boutique hotel or a special kind of restaurant. They need someone who will listen and cater to their needs' (Whitlock, 2001).

Customized golf packages have emerged as a result of this trend, and the case study in Chapter 1 described how Wide World of Golf has responded to trends and altered its focus from larger groups to customizing tailor-made tours. Around 80 per cent of its clients now select custom tours that combine golf with fishing, wine tasting, safari expeditions, photography seminars and cooking lessons. Another example is the Create Your Own Golf Package programme offered by Traverce City in Michigan. Golfers can log on to the destination website and choose from among 19 area courses and 25 lodging properties.

6. Convenience and speed

The increasing desire for convenience and speed is having a great impact on various sectors of the tourism industry. In the restaurant sector, drive-through sales are on the rise; in transportation, self check-in terminals are increasingly popular; and in accommodation, business travellers are seeking convenient rooms for shorter stays. An example of the latter is the new hotel concept introduced recently at Heathrow and Gatwick airports in the UK. Owing much to Japanese 'capsule hotels', Yotel cabins are a cross between a hotel and a first-class airline seat. Each self-contained cabin has a double rotating bed, and facilities include an ensuite bathroom with shower, a flat-screen television and a pull-down desk.

This desire for convenience and speed has also influenced the golf tourism product. For example, more and more golf clubs and resorts are offering high quality club rentals to cater for the occasional golfer. Such golfers, who do not have the time to practise the sport very often during their normal day-to-day lives, may be enticed to play when on holiday or attending a conference. Often, a formal golfing programme is included as a supplemental event before or after a convention, and this programme will usually include the rental of clubs. Such occasional golfers prefer the convenience of using familiar golf clubs, and one company called HRS Golf in San Diego, California, has responded to this demand, and will rent golfers a set of brand new TaylorMade or Callaway golf clubs and have them delivered (and picked-up) at any golf course in San Diego.

7. Corporate and social responsibility

In the last few decades, responsible tourism has emerged as a significant trend in the western world, as wider consumer market trends towards lifestyle marketing and ethical consumption have spread to tourism. Tourism organizations are beginning to realize that promoting their ethical stance can be good business as it potentially enhances a company's profits, management effectiveness, public image and employee relations. In a recent survey, 26 per cent of people aged 33–44 said they increasingly used their purchasing power to reward ethically-, socially-, and environmentally-aware companies (Hickman, 2006).

One example of a golf organization promoting its ethical stance is Troon Golf, the world's largest golf management company. In 2008, the company, headquartered in Scottsdale, Arizona, announced a new Environmental Management Initiative (EMI). 'Troon Golf EMI is the golf industry's first unified plan for environmental stewardship,' said the company's website. The initiative consists of a set of policies and procedures produced by combining three environmental programmes. These include the Troon Golf Environmental Management System (EMS), their long-established Troon Agronomy Standards, and the Audubon Cooperative Sanctuary Program for Golf Courses. Jeff Spangler, senior vice president, science and agronomy, said: 'Responsible environmental management has always been a key component of Troon Golf's operating philosophy and we are eager to continue to set the standard for environmental leadership' (Troon Golf, 2008).

8. Spiritual enlightenment

The desire for spiritual enlightenment on a vacation has led to a boom in religious tourism. Even monks are taking advantage of this growing trend. Monasteries and temples provide the perfect backdrop for peaceful periods of mediation, prayer and reflection for world-weary business men and women. Often set in beautiful scenery, more religious institutions are jumping on the tourism band-wagon and opening their facilities for one– to three–day stays. Southern Koreans for example, have around 36 different Buddhist temples to choose from for their retreats from everyday life. The notion of combining religion and tourism is also gaining momentum in other countries, notably Japan, where the Wakayama region is attracting day trippers from Kyoto and Nara. Visitors can also stay overnight in rooms ranging from simple to luxurious. With views of the Pacific from ancient forest trails, tourists learn about Shinto and Buddhist theory by day. By night, accompanying their vegetarian meals served by the monks, guests can also enjoy sake and beer.

Promotional literature persuading western golfers to visit Asia often comments on the attractiveness of Buddhist temples. Holiday Golf Thailand, for example, has a section on the company website that includes information on getting permission to enter temples and acceptable behaviours when entering a temple. Japanese golf is also often promoted as a spiritual experience, one that goes beyond the game of golf (see Snapshot on the golfing experience in Japan). Interestingly, one of the new religions of Japan, Perfect Liberty Kyodan (*kyodan* means church in Japanese), is one of the most successful. Generally known as PL to its members, it is also called the 'golf religion' because several PL churches feature rooftop driving ranges so members don't have to travel to practise self-expression. The nickname was bestowed by outsiders, but the church accepts it, believing that by stirring curiosity, the name attracts converts to the fold!

9. Service quality

Service quality has been increasingly identified as a key factor in differentiating service products and building a competitive advantage in tourism. The process by which customers evaluate a purchase, thereby determining satisfaction and likelihood of repurchase, is important to all marketers, but especially to services marketers because, unlike their manufacturing counterparts, they have fewer objective measures of quality by which to judge their production. Many researchers believe that an outgrowth of service quality is customer satisfaction. Satisfying customers has always been a key component of the tourism industry, but never before has it been so critical. With increased competition, and with more discerning, experienced consumers, knowing how to win and keep customers is the single-most important business skill that anyone can learn. Customer satisfaction and loyalty are the keys to long-term profitability, and keeping the customer happy is everybody's business. Becoming customer-centred and exceeding customer expectations are requirements for business success.

One of the research studies referred to earlier found that after resort facilities, resort service was the most important predictor of overall satisfaction for golf tourists (Petrick and Backman, 2002b). Experts tend to agree. Commenting on their recent list of top golf courses in North America, Forbes said: 'You cannot have a top-notch golf resort without incredible golf, but most travellers seeking a luxury experience also demand quality accommodations, service, cuisine, activities and amenities. Golf resorts realize that great golf isn't enough' (Olmsted, 2008). As to how you make this list, Ritz Carlton Reynolds Plantation, Georgia, apparently offers the finest 19th-hole meal in American golf. The resort is also home to the nation's only TaylorMade Tour Experience, a super high-tech club fitting and swing evaluation centre. At the Jack Nicklaus-designed Four Seasons Punta Mita, Mexico, golfers meet the head chef at the resort's dock before teeing off in the morning, and choose their fish for dinner from the daily haul. At Sea Pines, South Carolina, the European-style boutique hotel Inn at Harbour Town has a butler service on every floor. Palmilla in Mexico goes one step further with its wing of butler-only suites among the world's finest lodgings, and has the only satellite of Charlie Trotter's famous Chicago eatery. Even the golf carts are air-conditioned.

10. Experiences

According to Pine and Gilmore, today's consumer desires what the industry is calling 'experiences', which occur when a company intentionally uses services as the stage, and goods as props, to engage individual customers in a way that creates a memorable event. More and more travel organizations are responding by explicitly designing and promoting such events (Pine and Gilmore, 1998).

Experiences have always been at the heart of the entertainment business – a fact that Walt Disney and the company he founded have creatively exploited. But today the concept of selling an entertainment experience is taking root in businesses far removed from theatres and amusement parks. At themed restaurants such as the Hard Rock Cafe, Planet Hollywood, and the House of Blues, the food is just a prop for what's known as 'eatertainment'. And stores such as Niketown, Cabella's, and Recreational Equipment Incorporated draw consumers in by offering fun activities, fascinating displays, and promotional events (sometimes labeled 'shoppertainment' or 'entertailing'). But experiences are not exclusively about entertainment; companies stage an experience whenever they engage customers in a personal, memorable way. For example, WestJet and Southwest Airlines go beyond the function of transporting people from point A to point B, and compete on the basis of providing an experience. The companies use the base service (the travel itself) as the stage for a distinctive en route experience – one that attempts to transform air travel into a respite from the traveller's normally frenetic life.

The Legend Golf and Safari Resort in South Africa is a good example of golf tourists seeking experiences rather than just a game of golf. Golfers can not only combine their golf with the wildlife experience, but the golf course itself is unusual. After playing the regular 18 holes, each one designed by one of the world's top golfers, players can take a helicopter ride up to the tee of the Extreme 19th, promoted as the longest and the most dramatic par 3 in the world (see the Spotlight at the beginning of this chapter for more details).

Case study: Golf tourist typologies in Scotland

St Andrews, Scotland, courtesy of VisitScotland

According to VisitScotland, golf tourism is worth approximately $150 million to the Scottish economy, of which $105 million is attributed to UK visitors to Scotland, and $42 million is spent by overseas golfers. For many years, a major element of the tourism strategy in Scotland has been the attempt to create or develop niche tourism markets by capitalizing on Scotland's major assets. As Philip Riddle, Chief Executive of VisitScotland says 'Scotland is the home of golf, and with 520 golf courses, we have something to offer to all types of golfers. We have the best golf courses in the world, and although there is a big demand to play the signature courses such as St Andrews and Turnberry, we encourage people to look beyond the big courses and play our island courses and even our municipal courses as they create a great contrast in experiences.'

A New Strategy for Scottish Golf Tourism was launched in July 2000 aimed at increasing the annual spending on golf tourism by over 4 per cent and securing more internationally prestigious international golf tournaments. One of the aims of the golf strategy was to improve the industry's market intelligence by research- ing golf markets and golf consumers. So in 2006, VisitScotland commissioned a research study to gain a better understanding of the current and potential leisure golfing market to Scotland. One specific objective of the research was to create golfer typologies to optimize marketing and communications activity. Golfers were segmented according to their attitudes and motivations towards golf and golfing short breaks and holidays. The research was conducted by Scott Porter Research, an independent research agency, and involved eight focus groups, 15 face-to-face interviews, and 64 surveys with regular UK and Irish golfers. From the data, eight golfer segments were identified.

Golf buddies

For golf buddies, the social elements of the break are as important as the golf. They tend to take regular breaks in the UK and seek a lively location that offers good facilities apart from the golf, such as restaurants and pubs. They also look for a number of quality courses within close proximity that are suitable for a variety of skill levels. The golf buddies often travel in large groups, and bonding and having fun together are key motivators, although competition on the golf course is an integral part of their holiday. They are typically males, aged between 40 and 70, and are often empty nesters.

Golfing escapees

This segment has a stronger focus on the golfing side of the break and places less emphasis on the socializing. Like the golf buddies, they are usually male, but younger (25–45) and travel in small groups. They are not interested in signature courses because of the expense, but they like a challenge, and tend to look for one or two good courses. For this group, escape is the key motivator and they seek to have valuable time with friends who have a shared interest.

Luxury golfers

This group seeks an exceptional experience, which is golf centred, and likes to take in a number of signature courses. However, they also have a strong require- ment for sophistication and luxury.

They want to stay in high quality accommodation and desire immaculate service both on and off the golf course. Aged between 30 and 50, Luxury golfers tend to travel in large groups, and there are more couples than in the previous two segments. They will take their shorter golf breaks in the UK, but their main holiday is likely to be spent in Portugal, the USA, South Africa and Thailand.

Golfing tourists

This segment seeks a more leisurely break where golf is a key part of a more rounded experience incorporating good accommodation and a range of leisure ac- tivities. They look for accessible, less challenging courses which offer good value.

The key motivation for this mixed gender group is intimate shared time, and they tend to travel with close friends or couples. Aged between 45 and 70, the golfing holiday is more a vehicle for relaxation and a shared leisure experience. Golfing tourists take three or four holidays a year, and are quite likely to travel to France, Portugal and Spain.

Activity golfers

For this segment, a shared outdoor activity is the key motivator, and they look for a destination first, and golf second. They tend to be couples or families, are aged between 45 and 70, and are keen golfers. Activity golfers are keen on outdoor pursuits that are stimulating, energizing and uplifting, and for them, golf is a vehicle for experiencing nature and the countryside. They often seek scenic or quaint accommodation and they are more cost-conscious than other groups. They take two or three breaks a year, normally in Europe.

Golf purists

Golf purists are characterized by highly competitive golfers with low handicaps who are seeking new and exhilarating golf challenges through playing top quality courses. Other requirements are peripheral, and focus on accommodation that provides easy access to a range of such courses and good food. They tend to be small groups, aged 25-40, and they are serious golfers, always competitive and testing their skills. Socializing after golf tends to be low key for the golf purists, although they do want the opportunity to relax. They typically stay in three-star hotels, chosen for ease of access to golf and value for money.

Serendipity golfers

For this group, golf is an enjoyable opportunistic leisure activity on holiday, but tends to fit around other activities. The profile of this group is both male and female and they are often travelling with families. They are aged between 25 and 50, and are of mixed handicap. Golf facilities are not evaluated at the holiday planning stage, and taking the golf out wouldn't detract from the actual break. For this group, golf should be very accessible and even visible. They often rent clubs and look for courses that offer good value.

Golfing opportunists

The final group have a lot in common with the serendipity golfers, but they have stronger intention to play golf on holiday. Although golf is not the strong drive of destination choice, it might be the clincher, and the destination and accommodation selection is likely to be affected by proximity to a golf course. They are keen golfers and are more likely to take their own clubs than rent. They are also similar to golfing tourists, and, like that group, look for accessible, less challenging courses which offer good value for money.

This research has been used by VisitScotland to develop specific messages for the different target markets. 'We find that the North American golfers are often here specifically for the golf, whereas other nationalities, like the Swedes, are here for a number of activities apart from just golf,' said Riddle. 'We are seeing an increasing number of golf courses catering to families or couples for whom golf is not the number one priority when they come to Scotland.' VisitScotland's latest marketing initiative, of which golf played a major part, was Homecoming Scotland 2009, a year-long celebration in honour of the 250th anniversary of the birth of Robbie Burns, Scotland's national poet.

Sources

Interview with Philip Riddle, Chief Executive of VisitScotland, 21 January, 2009

'Attitudes Towards Golf Breaks In Scotland Research: Golfer Typologies', prepared for VisitScotland by Scott Porter Research & Marketing June 2006, accessed 5 January, 2009 at www.visitscotland.org/golfer_typologies-2.pdf.

References

Correia, A. and Pintassilgo, P. (2006) 'The golf players' motivations: the Algarve case', *Tourism and Hospitality Research*, 6 (3), 227-238.

Davies, P. (2007) 'Nostalgia tourism uncovered as new trend', accessed from http://www.travelmole.com, 15 December, 2008.

Hennessey, S.M., MacDonald, R. and MacEachern, M. (2008). 'A framework for understanding golfing visitors to a destination', *Journal of Sport & Tourism*, 13 (1), 5–35.

Hickman, M. (29 May, 2006) 'How ethical shopping is making business go green', *The Independent*, 2.

IBISWorld (2008) *Golf Courses & Country Clubs in the US*, IBISWorld, Los Angeles, p. 9.

KPMG (2008) *Golf Travel Insight in EMA 2008*, KPMG Advisory.

Lang Research. (2007) 'Golfing while on trips of one or more nights': A profile report, Travel Activities & Motivation Survey, 3 October.

Leadbeater, C. (2002) 'Longing for the way we were', *Financial Times Weekend*, 6–7 July, p. IV.

McCarten, J. (2008) 'Lady driven,' *Up!* May, 100.

McGinnis, L.P. and Gentry, J.W. (2006) 'Getting past the red tees: constraints women face in golf and strategies to help them stay', *Journal of Sport Management*, 20 (2), 218-247.

Mintel. (2006) 'Golf tourism', *Travel & Tourism Analyst*, 5: Mintel International Group, London.

National Golf Foundation (2003), *The US Golf Travel Market*, 2003 Edition: NGF, Jupiter, Florida.

National Golf Foundation (2008) *Golf Industry Overview*, 2008 edn, NGF, Jupiter, Florida.

Olmsted, L. (2008) 'North America's top golf resorts' accessed 21 February 2008 from http://www.ForbesTraveller.com.

Petrick, J.F. (2002) 'Experience use history as a segmentation tool to examine golf travellers` satisfaction, perceived value and repurchase intentions', *Journal of Vacation Marketing*, 8 (4), 332–342.

Petrick, J.F. and Backman, S.J. (2002a) 'An examination of the construct of perceived value for the prediction of golf travellers' intentions to revisit', *Journal of Travel Research*, 41, 38–45.

Petrick, J.F. and Backman, S.J. (2002b) 'An examination of the determinants of golf travellers' satisfaction', *Journal of Travel Research*, 40, 252–258.

Pine, B.J. II and Gilmore, J.H. (1998) 'Welcome to the experience economy', *Harvard Business Review*, 76 (4), 97–108.

Tourism (2002) 'Americans going green?' *Tourism*, 6 (8), p. 12.

Troon Golf (2008) 'Troon golf wins inaugural Golf Inc. Green Award', http://www.troongolf.com/company/press_room/story/410.php, **accessed** 22/09/2008.

VisitScotland. (2007) 'Golf Visitor Survey Year End 2007': Sports Marketing Surveys.

Whitlock, S. (2001) 'The world on a platter', *Travel + Leisure*, September, 176–178.

Wilson, J. and Thilmany, D. (2006) 'Golfers in Colorado: the role of golf in recreational and tourism lifestyle and expenditures', *Journal of Travel & Tourism Marketing*, 20 (3/4), 127–144.

3   The Golf Tourism Product

Junior Golf Camp at Celebration, Florida,
courtesy of Celebration

Disney never misses a trick when it comes to marketing and providing products for families. It has even delved into the world of golf with an 18-hole, championship golf course, designed by father and son team, Robert Trent Jones Sr. and Jr. Established at Disney's flagship Florida community in 1996, Celebration Golf Course also features a renowned Golf Academy and a three-hole junior course for ages five to nine. There are five different tee boxes at each hole on the course, facilitating play for all levels of ability.

Run by Celebration Golf Management, the Club has hosted over 3500 tournaments, including the annual Robert Gamez Celebrity Invitational every March, the US Senior Open Qualifier in 2002 and various national and state championships. Rated 4½ Stars in *Golf Digest*'s 'Best Places to Play' since 2004, Celebration provides a comprehensive events package including an uplink GPS system with electronic scoreboard, televised results and sponsor ad programme, souvenirs for every player and even a Scottish bagpiper to welcome and lead out golfers. To counteract the hot weather, two pre-iced coolers are provided for every golf cart and iced wet towels are distributed on hotter days.

With top service one of Disney's tenets, there are bag valets, costumed 'greeters', a full-time professional Golf Event Manager, shuttle services to and from the practice range, and even red carpets leading from the bag drop to registration. Celebration has thought of everything from club cleaning after the event to Caddy Shack-style 'goofy' activities which include putting with broomsticks, teeing off in a chair, playing left-handed or using only three clubs.

The Golf Course and Academy has also achieved national recognition as the site for the finals of the Golf Channel's Junior Drive, Chip and Putt competition aired on American Thanksgiving Day – 26 November, 2008. Patti Covert has been Academy Coordinator for Celebration since 2005. Covert says Celebration is a prototype in many ways, pioneering junior golf as part of its model, environmentally-friendly lifestyle and avoiding urban sprawl in its picket-fence perfection. The TV exposure was a great promotional tool for the golf course: 'It's cool because we had our stage set up and everything worked out really well for the television production and exposure. It definitely helps encourage kids into the sport and to come to Celebration. We have a lot of local kids, too, because of our community,' said Covert.

The golf course is user-friendly for pros, families and novices. Ranked in the 'Top 25 Public Courses' by *Golf World*'s 2009 Readers' Choice Awards, the course has a broad appeal as confirmed by its ratings in the Top 25 Best Family Golf Resorts and in the Top 30 Courses for Women by *Golf For Women* magazine. 'We have tee boxes set half way up the fairways which are used mostly by juniors and women golfers,' explained Covert. 'That way they get to play a regular, beautiful course and enjoy the round as opposed to playing the forward tee box and not scoring well. It's more motivational this way.'

There are golf instruction summer camps for destination visitors (who can stay in the picture-postcard Celebration Hotel nearby) as well as weekend and after-school programmes for local kids. 'These camps attract kids from all over as we are the number one tourist attraction in the world, being Disney,' said Covert. School parties also attend customized courses – one South American group comes regularly from the American Explorer School, in Colombia. Kenny Nairn, a Scottish PGA professional golfer, is head pro at Celebration. 'Golf is a game of integrity, respect, citizenship, friendship and rules. The South American school is using golf – as part of their curriculum – for these aspects plus the enjoyment of the sport,' said Nairn.

For local Florida juniors there are bi-monthly free golf clinics as well as complimentary 30-minute lessons awarded to honours students from Celebration's public schools. The club also uses grants from the USGA to target under-privileged children with three different teaching groups. Lost-and-found golf clubs are also donated to junior golf.

Celebration's General Manager, Gene Garotte has tracked the ratio of out-of-state visitors at 60 per cent during the popular January–April period. Annually, though, destination visitors number 35 to 45 per cent of the course's clientele. The course is promoted in partnership with the nearby Celebration, Mona Lisa and Radisson Hotels. Celebration is also a member of the Orlando Convention and Visitors' Bureau (OCVB), Visit Florida and the Orlando Golf Trail, cooperating on joint marketing programmes with neighbouring courses. 'We work very closely with third party packaging companies. Our guests looking for accommodations, travel and golf are referred to companies such as Golf Pac, Tee Times USA, Captain's Choice and Merit Travel,' said Garotte. Celebration Golf Management also encompasses Legends Golf & Country Club in Clermont, Florida; the International Club, Myrtle Beach, South Carolina; and Crockett Ridge Golf Course in Kingsport, Tennessee.

Sources

www.celebrationgolf.com, www.cgmgolfproperties.com, www.legendsgolforlando.com

Personal interview with Patti Covert, December 2008.

Interviews with Gene Garotte and Kenny Nairn, February 2009

Golf tour operators

A large number of tour operators cater to the golf tourism market, and a few of these are referred to on page 57 in the Spotlight on Celebration Golf Course. As mentioned in Chapter 1, many of these operators are represented by the International Association of Golf Tour Operators (IAGTO). In 2009, IAGTO had more than 330 tour operators as members from 46 different countries. Most golf tourists travelling abroad will purchase a golf package from one of these tour operators, as they are responsible for more than 80 per cent of the international sales of golf packages. The package will usually include pre-payment of green fees and pre-booking of tee-times, as well as transportation and accommodation. Laura Golf Tour, for example, is a small incoming agency for golf tourism in Antalya (the Mediterranean area of Turkey) whose main services are guaranteed tee-time and hotel reservations, transfer services between airport and hotel and hotel and golf course. The company also offers car rental, flight counseling, customer care services, and guiding services. Laura Golf deals with over 7000 golf tourists annually, who mainly arrive from the UK, Germany and Japan.

According to a 2008 golf tour operator survey in Europe and the Middle East, 73 per cent of respondents reported an increase in the number of golf tourists, whilst only 10 per cent noted a decrease in the number of golf tourists (see Figure 3.1). Almost half of the surveyed tour operators indicated that high-end golf holidays were becoming more and more popular and that allocated budgets for golf packages were increasing. However, this data was collected before the recession had really taken hold of most of Europe towards the end of 2008.

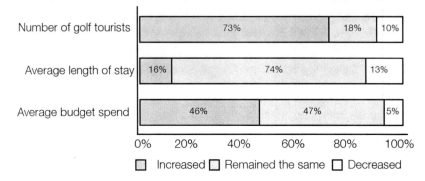

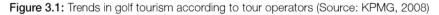

Figure 3.1: Trends in golf tourism according to tour operators (Source: KPMG, 2008)

Golf tour operators tend to sell a variety of golf tourism products. Your Golf Travel.com for example, is a UK-based operator that has a client base of over 100,000 customers. The company breaks its offerings into six different areas: Golf Breaks, primarily catering to leisure golfers who are looking for a short, close-to-home golfing break; Golf Holidays, golfing getaways to Spain, Portugal, France and further afield; Golf Tours, which are golf packages in Europe combining accommodation and a choice of golf courses; Hospitality Packages, the fastest growing area according to the company, offering golfers the chance to watch tournaments such as the US Masters at Augusta National or the World

Matchplay at Wentworth; Corporate Golf, which includes corporate golf days and breaks, corporate golf venues, team building and incentives and charity golf days; and Society Golf, whereby the company will manage a society golf day from the first moment to last, including lunch and dinner menus, and tailor-made competitions and prizes.

Some golf tour operators focus on one particular part of the world. Eagle Golf Tours, for example, specializes in selling golf tours for British golfers to the Carolinas in the USA. Neil Cutler, managing director of the company, says that 90 per cent of his business is to that part of the world, and that 99 per cent of his packages are tailor-made. Many of his customers (about 60 per cent) come back year after year, and they come to him because of his experience in that market. Cutler set up business in 1990 when very few operators were selling golf tours from the UK to America, and has visited over 50 times. 'The British love the climate in South Carolina,' he says, 'and they find the golf terrific value for money.' About 60 per cent of his business is with groups of men and then the other 40 per cent is couples. However, he is seeing an increasing number of women buying his golf packages.

It was mentioned in Chapter 2 that requests for customized and personalized vacations are rising sharply, and golf tour operators are changing their businesses to meet that demand. Robert Lewis, president of TravelGolf.com, a golf publication network, suggests the top three locations in North America for customized golf vacations are Las Vegas, Nevada, Arizona and Myrtle Beach, South Carolina. One interesting package in the USA, sold by the PGA, is the Ultimate Tour Player Experience at TPC Sawgrass, Florida (see the Snapshot on page 60). The package is promoted by the PGA as 'the first time everyday golfers have had the opportunity to experience what it is like to be a PGA Tour player competing in a PGA Tour event as part of the Tour player experience'. The price for this package in 2009 (single occupancy) was $1615.

If imagining life as a professional is not enough, then golfers can always pay to play with a professional. For example, in January 2009, for $999 per person (double occupancy), golfers could join Natalie Gulbis, one of the rising stars on the LPGA tour, for a weekend at the Fairmont Newport Beach in Southern California. The package included two nights' accommodation in an Executive Club room, breakfast, a Friday night welcome reception with Gulbis, a Saturday practice session with Gulbis at Pelican Hill Golf Course, a round at Pelican Hill, a gift bag from her sponsor, Adidas/TaylorMade, and airport transfers. American Express was also giving golfers the opportunity to play with a pro in the EDS Byron Nelson event in May 2009. The Play with a Golf Pro package included airfare and six nights' lodging and the chance to play with a pro in the Wednesday pro-am, the day before the actual tournament. The price was $2500, and that was without the chance of being paired with a Tiger Woods-type pro, as they are usually committed to sponsors, such as Nike, as special guests.

Snapshot: PGA Tour Experiences

The Sawgrass Golf Resort & Spa, a Marriott Resort, Ponte Vedra Beach, Florida, courtesy of Sawgrass Golf Resort & Spa

With some 28,000 members, the Professional Golfers' Association (PGA) of America is the world's largest working sports organization. These members are recognized worldwide as the experts in developing, instructing and managing the game of golf. They also serve millions of people via a network of 41 PGA sections across the USA. Founded in 1916, the PGA has established itself via international spectator events, education and training programmes, outreach initiatives and award-winning promotions, such as the PGA Fall Expo.

One of the spin-offs of the PGA is the PGA Tour which is a tax-exempt membership organization of professional golfers who tour the world taking part in high-profile championships. PGA Tour Experiences is the licensee and fulfilment arm of the PGA Tour. It serves as the tour operation side of the PGA, providing topnotch golf vacations, instructional centres and corporate events and tournaments, all emulating the lifestyle of golf's top professionals. Signature packages include four-day trips to the Hyatt Regency Jacksonville Waterfront with tickets to the Players Championship and behind-the-scenes privileges. The company handles travel and accommodation, VIP tournament tickets and all golf bookings. 'We come up with unique experiences so golf consumers can experience a day-in-the-life of a Tour player,' says Travis Velichko, Director of Business Development for PGA Tour Experiences. 'It's 50 per cent corporate business on incentive and executive trips and 50 per cent your average Joe golfer.'

The flagship facility for the PGA Tour is at TPC Sawgrass, in Ponte Vedra Beach, Florida.TPC (Tournament Players' Clubs) is a network of private and destination golf clubs across the USA which have hosted over 200 professional golf tournaments. The Ultimate Tour Player Experience is a VIP package available at TPC Sawgrass, with guests staying at the Marriott Resort and living and golfing like a pro. So far, clientele has been 90 per cent male typically staying one night with one day golfing.

'In the morning they take a shuttle to the golf course and meet the head pro and a PGA Tour Experience rep. Then there's a guided tour through the clubhouse, giving them the background and history of the organization,' explains Velichko. Visiting the pros' locker room is a highlight: golfers find a golf shirt already hanging in their locker, in their size. The locker is marked with their name, date and the name of one of their favourite players. Following breakfast in the private dining area, they take the Walk of Champions to view past pro golfers and then go to meet their caddies who sport bibs with each golfer's own name. 'They really get a sense and feeling of what it's like playing in a tournament. I speak from experience as I took my Dad who was visiting from Edmonton through it. It was a great experience from the golf to the service and the feeling in the locker room and rubbing shoulders with other players,' says Velichko. Golfers go home with their caddie bib, the framed locker name plate, golf balls, and professional action photos taken at the 16th, 17th and 18th holes.

TPC Sawgrass, set up in 1980, has been the golf instruction flagship for the PGA Tour Academy since 2006. It goes a step further than mere teaching with a programme called Golf for Life launched in spring 2009, incorporating fitness, nutrition, course management and even spa treatments and wine tasting. 'It's a five to seven day course, derived from what top players in the Tour are doing to keep healthy,' explains Velichko. The facility also features one of only two TaylorMade putting labs in existence.

The Tour Academy's On the Road programme travels around the USA in a specially equipped Hummer providing instruction to TPC members. Courses include personalized instruction, advanced training tools and technology, video analysis, take-home DVD or personal online website for guaranteed improvement. Membership in the TPC also entails golfing privileges at other clubs within the network's 23 facilities, including private clubs, daily fee courses and resort venues.

The Tour Academy on the Sea is an instructional programme offered on Norwegian Cruise Line ships. Piloted in early 2009, it comprises a variety of Tour Academy programmes, including private lessons, state-of-the art club-fitting and lessons for junior golfers. Golfers can also play at courses on land during the cruise. Packages include golf fees, club rentals and transportation to and from the golf course back to the ship.

Event management is also within PGA Tour Experiences remit, with a complete package of lodging, transportation, food and beverage, amenities, web design and construction, Internet registration, and tournament management available.

Sources

Personal interview with Travis Velichko, Director of Business Development for PGA Tour Experiences, February 2009.

www.pgatourexperiences.com

www.tpc.com

Golf is being paired with numerous activities, even learning a new language, but a big trend is to match golf with culinary activities. *Travel + Leisure Golf* magazine had an article in 2008 that paired playing golf with beer festivals, and the same magazine ran a print ad for PerryGolf advertising their 'Tee Times You Can Taste' golf packages (*Travel + Leisure*, 2008). The company was combining golf with tapas in Andalusia, wine in New Zealand, cooking classes in Lake Como and Scotch in Scotland. Golf courses and vineyards can be found near each other in locations all over the world, but Greg Norman's design – The Course at Wente Vineyards – is actually located inside a vineyard in California's Livermore Valley, east of San Francisco. Designed for male and female players of all levels, The Course at Wente Vineyards played host to the Wine Country Championship, the fifth stop on the PGA's Nationwide Tour for the past three years.

Another golf course located within a vineyard can be found in Argentina. There, a new oenological project in the city of San Rafael, Mendoza, is tapping into the demand for golf and wine tourism. Algodon Wine Estates Viñas del Golf is situated on 350 hectares of mountains and vineyards which feature a 9-hole golf course that intermingles with nearly 170 acres of vineyards, water reserves and fruit trees. Each hole has been named after its specific surroundings or location within the vineyard. For example, the 3rd hole is set among Malbec vines so is called 'Malbec', whilst the 5th crosses a Bonarda vineyard so is aptly named 'Bonarda'. Argentina has more golf courses than any other South American country, and in 2007 won the IAGTO award for the 'Best Golf Destination in Latin America and the Caribbean'.

Combining golf and wine is also popular in Europe. The La Rioja region of Spain, for example, is attracting a growing number of golf tourists seeking to combine the two activities. Brittany Ferries, Golf in Spain, and Golf and Wine Spain, are just three companies that offer golf and wine packages in La Rioja. These tours are particularly popular when the wine festivals take place in June, August and September. Logroño, the capital of La Rioja, hosted the 2006 Spanish PGA Open. South Africa is also using golf and wine tours to tempt tourists to the Western Cape during the destination's winter months. Cape Town Routes Unlimited (CTRU), for example, has put together several self-drive itineraries for tourists wishing to combine playing on some of the region's 75 golf courses with wine-tasting at the 200 cellars in the Cape Winelands, the largest wine producing region in the Western Cape. For real golf and wine buffs, this might include a visit to the cellars of Engelbrecht Els Vineyards in the Stellenbosch – a partnership between golfer Ernie Els and Jean Engelbrecht, one of the top producers in South Africa.

Another trend in golf tours is the emergence of the golf trail or golf safari. There is an increasing tendency for golf courses in the same area to pool their resources to promote their region as a golfing destination. Golf Mesquite, Nevada, is an example. Prospective golfers can log on to a dedicated website and build a customized golf tourism package from the eight golf courses and numerous hotels listed on the website. Also in Nevada, the Divine Nine is a group of nine year-round Lake Tahoe/Reno area golf courses. The group's 'build your own golf package' option started as low as $50 in 2009 including lodging and tee time. 'It's a great promotion,' said Darryle Fukano, one of the pros at Empire Ranch Golf Course along the Carson River. 'We are competing against each other but also trying to help each other out. Everybody tries to find a niche' (Sonner, 2007). Further north, a separate joint venture called 'Golf the High Sierra' now has 20 courses as partners. Together, the Divine Nine and Golf the High Sierra ventures include courses designed by Robert Trent Jones Sr, George Fazio, Hale Irwin, Peter Jacobsen, Johnny Miller, Jack Nicklaus and Arnold Palmer. Both rely in part on annual promotions to fly sports and travel writers in from around the country to spend time playing the courses, dining at restaurants and chatting with business leaders to get a taste of what the region has to offer.

In Canada, the newly established Thompson–Okanagan Golf Trail features 14 golf resorts. 'The idea of a golf trail is nothing new, but it is around these parts,' notes Miles Proden from the Okanagan Tourism Association. The trail features championship courses linked together so that the longest drive between layouts is just 78 kilometres. The 14 participating golf courses are linked via the Internet on a homepage that features real-time, online tee-time bookings at each course. The website – togolfbc.com – also features weekly green fee specials, course details and scorecards, vacation packages and helpful tourist information.

Golf trails are not just confined to North America. The Snapshot below profiles the Ho Chi Minh Golf Trail in Vietnam, a co-operation between seven golf courses.

Snapshot: The Ho Chi Minh Golf Trail

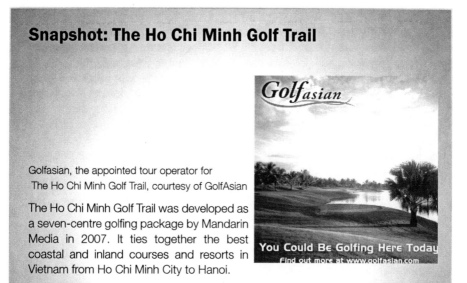

Golfasian, the appointed tour operator for The Ho Chi Minh Golf Trail, courtesy of GolfAsian

The Ho Chi Minh Golf Trail was developed as a seven-centre golfing package by Mandarin Media in 2007. It ties together the best coastal and inland courses and resorts in Vietnam from Ho Chi Minh City to Hanoi.

Golfasian is the appointed tour operator for the Trail. They advertise it online as 'an out-of-the-box exploration of golf, history and culture that reveals tropical Vietnam for what it is – one the most dynamic, affordable, safe destinations on Earth.' Also promised are world-class golf, 'posh' accommodation, French colonial charm and a diverse variety of cities and countryside experiences featuring beaches, national parks and mountains. Holidays are packaged with golf, hotel, transportation, domestic airfares and sightseeing trips, such as visiting the 'Perfume Pagoda' or the silk handicraft village at Van Phuc.

Golf courses include the Chi Linh Star Golf Course near Hanoi, which is developing a new five-star hotel and villa complex. Also in Hanoi area, is the Tam Dao Golf Course, set in Vietnam's largest national park. The Dalat Palace Golf Course, built by Bao Dai, Vietnam's last emperor in the 1930s, tops the list as Vietnam's premier course. Ocean Dunes Golf Course, designed by Nick Faldo, is at Phan Thiet bordering the South China Sea. And also included on the varied itinerary are Dong Nai, King's Island and the Vietnam Golf & Country Club, the most established course in Ho Chi Minh City.

Golfasian's Managing Director, Mark Siegel says the southern part of the Trail, including Saigon, Phan Thiet and Dalat, is the most popular, with one week trips for $1500. The full 15-day package – including Hanoi, Halong Bay, Saigon, Dalat and Phan Thiet – costs around $3000 per person. 'The trail attracts avid golfers who are mostly middle-aged couples looking for a new and exotic golf destination. Most of the travellers are European, but more and more come from North America,' says Siegel.

Specializing in both luxury and value-for-money tours in the three countries, Golfasian offers either single resort or multi-centre trips, with pre-set and tailor-made packages available. Golf is the primary focus, but sightseeing, shopping, fine dining, nightlife and even Thai massage are all thrown in for rounded appeal every second day. Cultural side trips include Vietnam War sites, battlefields, museums and World Heritage sites such as Hoi An.

Set up in 1997, the IAGTO-licensed company now has a customer base of nearly 10,000 golfers – 75 per cent male and 25 per cent female. 'Golfasian is probably the fastest growing golf holiday-related business in Indochina, and that is due to repeat and word-of-mouth customers who keep coming back because of their good experiences and our reputation for service. We have the widest selection of golf holidays in Indochina and think we offer the most value for the money,' says Siegel. And ironically the world economic recession actually helped business for Golfasian whose profits were up 20 per cent in 2008. 'What is happening is that golfers are not cancelling their travels, but looking for more economical destinations,' explains Siegel. 'Indochina fits this bill well, as golf trips cost less here than other top golf destinations, while the quality of golf is as good as it gets anywhere!' Siegel has noted a shift in focus away from the traditional golfing areas of Scotland, the US and Australia, to the newer golfing centres of Thailand, Vietnam and Cambodia.

Due to the success of the Ho Chi Minh Golf Trail, Golfasian went on to launch the Indochina Golf Trail in 2008, this time combining three countries in a golf tour showcasing the premier clubs, top-class resorts and major cultural and historical sites across Thailand, Vietnam and Cambodia.

Sources

Shale, T. (1995) 'Bogged down on the Ho Chi Minh trail', *Euromoney*, June, p. 18.

E-mail communication with Golfasian's Managing Director, Mark Siegel, January 2009.

http://www.hochiminhgolftrail.com, http://www.golfasian.com

http://www.vietnamgolfvacation.com, http://www.thailandgolfzone.com

Golf cruises

Golf cruises are a relatively new and growing sector of golf tourism, and all of the major cruise lines now offer golfers the chance to play golf ashore as part of an organized excursion. Golfers on a cruise can play on almost every continent, and golf cruises are standard in the Caribbean, Mexico, the British Isles, Hawaii, the Bahamas, and Bermuda. New Zealand, Australia, and the South Seas' itineraries also sometimes include a golf package. Silversea Cruises even offers the opportunity to play courses in Africa as part of its Silver Links Golf Cruise programme. Caribbean Cruise Lines Ltd has set up a company called GolfAhoy.com to distribute golf cruises, and the company customizes golf packages on most Princess, Royal Caribbean, Celebrity, Carnival, Seabourn or Silversea worldwide cruise itineraries. GolfAhoy.com has entered into a strategic alliance with Golf Holidays International, a leader in 'land-based' golf holidays packaging.

A new cruise for the company since 2008 is a South African Indian Ocean golf cruise. In the company of a PGA professional, golfers can enjoy a 14-day cruise that takes in golf courses in Mauritius and South Africa. On board, the GolfAhoy PGA professional works with golfers to perfect their technique using the golf simulator and the indoor golf course, supported by state-of-the-art video analysis and simulation technology. The company has also introduced a number of golf and spa cruises in Hawaii and the Caribbean, and this seems to be a trend in the golf cruise market. Elite Golf Cruises also packages a 'Guilt Free Golf & Spa Program' for both the golfer and the non-golfer.

Often, cruise line staff will arrange tee-off times, carts, caddies, and transportation to the golf course. Golfers can also rent all the necessary equipment if they haven't brought their own. Carnival Cruises, for example, has an arrangement with Callaway Golf to use their clubs in their equipment rental packages. Back on the ship, golfers can take advantage of teaching computers, video lessons, and professional advice (often from PGA professionals) to improve their game. Carnival provides lighted and covered 'practice ranges' and holds golf clinics and putting contests throughout the voyage. Golfers who stay on the new Costa Luminosa, part of the Costa Cruises portfolio, can enjoy a golf simulator that boasts 37 virtual courses, as well as an outdoor putting green. Norwegian Cruise Lines have recently introduced the Tour Academy on the Sea, an instructional programme that includes private instruction, club-fitting and lessons for junior golfers. The Tour Academy on the Sea also offers on-the-course golf instruction with an Academy professional at select ports. Packages include golf fees, club rentals and transportation to and from the golf course back to the ship.

Golf cruises are not just restricted to the large cruise companies. For example, Jet Stream Sailing and Golf Charters is a small charter company that designs cruises to Caribbean islands for guests who would like to blend sailing and golf vacations. In 2008, owner Tim Schaaf offered a seven-day golf cruise starting at St Croix with rounds at the Carambola Golf and Country Club and the Buccaneer Golf Course. From there, the cruise moved on to Puerto Rico for golf at El Conquistador. Schaaf is a former PGA professional, so when his captain's duties allow, he will go ashore as a playing partner, or as a teacher (about $300 per round). His catamaran accommodates up to six passengers in three cabins. Gourmet dinners are provided nightly by Schaaf's partner, Marsha McCoskrie, a professionally trained chef. Another smaller cruise company offering golf cruises is American Safari Cruises which sailed the Hawaiian Islands for the first time in 2009 offering golfing enthusiasts the chance to play a number of courses in Hawaii from its small, 36-berth yacht, the *Safari Explorer*.

Even barge cruises sometimes offer golf-themed trips. European Waterways, for example, has 'golf barging' on eight ships – each carrying four to12 passengers - in four countries. Golfers can combine playing golf with cruising the rivers and canals of England, Scotland, Ireland, and France. The cruises are usually a week long and include gourmet cuisine, and four or five rounds of golf. The cruise along the River Thames in England for example, on board the *Magna Carta*, offers golf at Hampton Court Palace Golf Course, Walton Heath Golf Club, Wentworth, Sunningdale Golf Club, and Temple Golf Club.

Golf hotels and resorts

Golf hotels and resorts date back to the early 20th century. The case study at the end of the chapter profiles Fairmont Hotels & Resorts, the Canadian hotel group that has over 20 golfing resort properties around the world.

One of the first golf resorts to be built was the Gleneagles Hotel and Resort in Scotland. The Hotel's Grand Opening Gala was on 7 June 1924 but its history began 14 years prior to that day. In 1910 Donald Matheson, General Manager of the Caledonian Railway Company, was on holiday in Strathearn. His railway line ran through the valley and, as it was the era of 'Grand Hotels' he was so impressed by the surrounding countryside in Scotland that he conjured up the vision of a large country house hotel, built in the style of a palace which would provide leisure in the form of golf to the travelling public. Gleneagles is today one of Scotland's most luxurious five-star resorts and a member of The Leading Hotels of the World. Set in 850 acres of Perthshire countryside, Gleneagles is home to three of the top Scottish Championship Golf Courses. One of them, the PGA Centenary Course is the venue for the 40th Ryder Cup Matches in 2014.

Another large British hotel group targeting the golf tourist is De Vere which has a portfolio of eight golf hotels in England, including Cameron House, a stylish baronial mansion on the shore of Loch Lomond, now one of Scotland's finest luxury hotels. Its golf course, The Carrick on Loch Lomond, opened for play in 2007. Nearby, Loch Lomond Golf Club is well known for hosting the Barclays Scottish Open in July each year. In 2008, De Vere signed a contract with the Calidona Group to manage Roda Golf and Beach Resort, a 140-bedroom hotel, spa, beach club and 18-hole golf course in the Murcia Region of Spain. A new hotel is expected to open in the summer of 2010.

In North America, Pinehurst in North Carolina is probably the largest and best known golf resort. James Tufts purchased Pinehurst for $1/acre in 1895, as a health-centred winter retreat. In 1900, Scottish-born Donald Ross was hired as golf professional for the first 18 holes built in the area. Ross would later redesign Pinehurst No. 1 and design No. 2, No. 3 and No. 4 for the Tufts Family. He has been credited with the design or redesign of over 400 golf courses throughout North America during his career. Many of the world's rich and famous have crossed the thresholds of Pinehurst – the Rockefellers, DuPonts and Morgans to name a few. Oprah Winfrey and others have vacationed at Pinehurst, and Amelia Earhart landed her plane at the resort's airstrip! The Resort's famed No. 2 golf course has been the home of the 1991 and 1992 PGA Tour Championships, 1994 US Senior Open, and 1999 and 2005 US Open Championships. It will be the site of the 2014 US Open.

Pinehurst boasts three world-class hotels. Holly Inn, opened in 1895, was Pinehurst's first inn. It has recently undergone a multi-million dollar renovation of its (now) 85 rooms, including eight suites. Carolina, opened in 1901, has 217 rooms and three suites. The Manor, opened in 1923, offers casual accommodations with its 46 guest rooms and houses a popular Pinehurst restaurant – Mulligan's Sports Bar and Grill. Pinehurst also offers 40 four-bedroom villas, each with a connecting parlour; and 135 one-bedroom condominiums, each with a full kitchen and located adjacent to several golf course fairways or lakeside. Apart from its eight 18-hole championship golf courses, Pinehurst has 24 tennis courts, three croquet courts, a championship lawn bowling course, a 200-acre freshwater lake for sailing, canoeing, paddle boating, kayaking, fishing and swimming, two outdoor swimming pools, a fitness centre and spa, and a number of restaurants and pubs. It also has numerous meeting and banquet facilities spread amongst the hotels.

A significant trend in golf resort development is smaller golf-oriented properties: inns, lodges, and boutique hotels with fewer than 125 rooms – some as few as 15 – and access to championship courses designed by big-name architects. These smaller properties provide environments where the focus is almost entirely on golf, on and off the course. Everything is more personal and intimate than at a high-volume golf resort. Examples are The Lodge at Torrey Pines (La Jolla, California), that has 75 rooms, a gourmet restaurant and access to a golf course that hosts an annual PGA Tour event; The Lodge at Sea Island Golf Club (Sea Island, Georgia), a 40-room lodge that resembles an elegant English manor, and provides access to three championship golf courses; and The Lodge at Bandon Dunes (Bandon, Oregon), a 19-room inn on Oregon's coast, that has a restaurant, a Scottish pub, and offers access to three new golf courses.

Corporate golf

According to a 2006 survey of corporate meeting planners undertaken by trade publication *Successful Meetings*, golf is third in importance to the business portion of the meeting and free time. The survey says golf is more important than providing attendees a beach, a spa, shopping, cultural attractions or other outdoor sports. According to a 2008 Meetings Market Survey conducted by the Professional Conference Managers' Association, 37 per cent of meeting planners indicated that one or more of their meetings involved golf events. The majority of respondents (81%) hosted between one and three of these events each year (PCMA, 2008). Corporate golf has also become the choice for many companies wishing to showcase their business to key clients or reward high-performing employees. Groups make up about 55 per cent of business at Pinehurst Resort in North Carolina, and another popular incentive destination for golfing groups is Mauna Lani Resort in Hawaii, where 20 per cent of business at the resort is business groups and meetings.

Destinations are therefore becoming very proactive in attracting the business golf traveller. Puerto Rico for example, has positioned itself as a golfing destination for the group market and many of the island's top meetings/conference hotels have one or more courses on their property to meet the needs of groups who want to incorporate golf as part of their programme. 'Puerto Rico offers some of the best golf facilities in the Caribbean and North America. In addition to year-round temperatures at about 82 degrees, Puerto Rico is an ideal golfing destination for the group market', said Christine Hinz, a public relations specialist for the Puerto Rico Convention Bureau.

The Puerto Rico Convention Bureau works very closely with the meetings market to promote the golf element as part of an overall meetings experience on the Island. Since 2003, the Bureau has hosted an annual golfing tournament with meeting planners who book group meetings/conferences in Puerto Rico. Co-sponsored with top golf properties (as well as with San Juan properties and nearby top golf facility, Bahia Beach), this has proven to be one of the most successful initiatives for the Bureau in bringing group business to the island. The three-day event is conducted in partnership with Primedia, the parent company of such meeting publications as *Corporate Meetings & Incentives*, *Association Meetings*, *Financial & Insurance Meeting* and *Medical Meetings*.

Hotels themselves are also promoting the convenience of nearby golf courses to impress the planners who book meetings and conventions. Crowne Plaza Hotels and Resorts, for example, used professional golfer, Phil Mickelson in its 2009 television commercials promoting meetings at its 293 hotels. Gina LaBarre, a Crowne Plaza vice president, said upscale business travellers' affinity for golf makes it a natural hook for promoting meeting facilities. 'As marketers, we are thinking of golf more than ever before when targeting meeting planners', she said (Stoller, 2008).

In October 2008, construction began on a new JW Marriott in San Antonio, which plans to attract meetings and conventions with two PGA Tour golf courses. 'Meetings and group business are expected to generate more than half of the revenue when the 1002-room resort opens in 2010', said Mike Kass, director of sales and marketing. Golf course designer Pete Dye and former British Open champion Greg Norman are designing the two adjacent golf courses. They're the newest ones being built by the PGA Tour, which will also manage them.

Tom Pasha, owner of Contact Planning, which books hotels and golf outings for corporations and associations, has seen the effects of the hotels' increased emphasis on golf. 'Hotels, for the longest time, only had an in-house golf pro promoting their golf program,' Pasha said. 'But they now have a lot more sales people selling and marketing golf.' A growing number of meeting planners are adding golf events to their itineraries, said Pasha, whose company books 100,000 rooms and 30,000 rounds of golf a year (Stoller, 2008).

Golf Digest ranks Georgia's Sea Island as the best US resort for business meetings and golf. Sea Island has three courses and 17,000 square feet of meeting space. The magazine ranks California's Pebble Beach Resorts, with its four courses and 19 meeting rooms, as number two. Table 3.1 lists the top 15 resorts for business meetings and golf according to *Golf Digest*.

Table 3.1: The top 15 resorts for business meetings and golf (Source: Adapted from Stoller, 2008)

Resort	Location
Sea Island, The Cloister & The Lodge	Sea Island, Georgia
Pebble Beach Resorts	Pebble Beach, California
Four Seasons Resort Hualalai	The Big Island, Hawaii
The American Club	Kohler, Wisconsin
Four Seasons Resort Lana'i at Manele Bay	Lanai, Hawaii
Four Seasons Resort Maui at Wailea	Maui, Hawaii
Pinehurst Resort	Pinehurst, North Carolina
The Broadmoor	Colorado Springs
The Greenbrier	White Sulphur Springs, West Virginia
CordeValle	San Martin, California
The Ritz-Carlton, Kapalua	Maui, Hawaii
Kiawah Island Golf Resort	Kiawah, South Carolina
The Ritz-Carlton, Naples	Naples, Florida
The Boulders	Scottsdale, Arizona
Grand Wailea Resort	Maui, Hawaii

A number of tour operators cater to the corporate golf market. Your Golf Travel. com, mentioned earlier, profiles hundreds of corporate venues in Britain including what the company promotes as 'the James Bond experience' at the Stoke Park Club in the South of England. As a film location, Stoke Park played host to the game of golf in *Goldfinger* (1964) when James Bond defeated Auric Goldfinger on the 18th green. *Goldfinger* was the first of two James Bond films to be shot at Stoke Park, the second being *Tomorrow Never Dies* (1997). More details on Stoke Park and its association with film can be found in Chapter 7.

Golf schools and instruction

Golfing instruction has been increasingly offered as a central or an add-on feature of golfing packages, and the number of golf schools all over the world is growing. However, the US is still the leader in golf schools, and Table 3.2 profiles the top 25 golf schools according to *Golf Magazine*.

Table 3.2: Top 25 golf schools in America (Source: *Golf Magazine*, 2008)

Golf School	Location	Cost of 3-day programme ($)	Specialization
Wright Balance Golf Academy	Mission Viejo, California	1195	Over 25 hours of total instruction
Kris Moe Golf Schools	Glen Ellen, California	1275	Small learning groups; wine-country
Vision 54	Phoenix, Arizona	2495	Two Top 100 teachers emphasize scoring
Butch Harmon School of Golf	Las Vegas, Nevada	2900 (incl. lodging)	A 2:1 student-teacher ratio
Extraordinary Golf	Carmel, California	1200-1850	Customizes lessons to complement abilities
Aviara Golf Academy	Carlsbad, California	1795	8 hours of lessons a day
McGetrick Golf Academy	Denver, Colorado	975	Intense digital analysis and fittings
Jim Mclean Golf School	Ft. Worth, Texas	2295	New 14,000-sq. ft. performance centre
Chuck Cook Golf Academy	Austin, Texas	1750	Led by teaching legend Chuck Cook
Academy of Golf Dynamics	Austin, Texas	950-1,095	3-hole Nicklaus teaching course
Kapalua Golf Academy	Lahaina, Maui, Hawaii	1295	23-acre practice facility, great views
Jack Nicklaus Golf Academy	St. George, Utah	1250	Low student–teacher ratio
Todd Sones Impact Golf	Vernon Hills, Illinois	495 (1-day programme)	Top 100 Teacher-led school
Crystal Mountain Golf School	Thompsonville, Michigan	739 (incl. lodging)	Lessons and playing in vacation setting
Rick Smith Golf Academy	Gaylord, Michigan	1195	Lesson plan includes on-course filming
Kingsmill Resort Golf Academy	Williamsburg, Virginia	1671 (incl. lodging)	Golf vacation wrapped in a golf school
Pinehurst Golf Academy	Pinehurst, North Carolina	2045 (incl. lodging)	Top 100 Teachers; play Pinehurst No. 2
Dana Rader/Ballantyne Resort	Charlotte, North Carolina	795	Dana Rader hosts a variety of programmes
Classic Swing Golf School	Myrtle Beach, South Carolina	369-469	Flexible lessons; excellent facilities
Phil Ritson-Mel Golf School	Myrtle Beach, South Carolina	495-595	Experienced; priority is giving more yards

David Leadbetter Golf Academy	Champions Gate, Florida	975 (half days)	Crown jewel of the 28 Leadbetter academies
Mike Bender Golf Academy	Lake Mary, Florida	1000-2000	Attention to small groups
Brad Brewer Golf Academy	Orlando, Florida	1304	1-on-1 lessons with a Top 100 Teacher
Arnold Palmer Golf Academy	Orlando, Florida	749	Lessons based on the 'Palmer Method'
Grand Cypress Academy of Golf	Orlando, Florida	1870 (incl. lodging)	Excellent facilities, and technology

One golfing academy with national recognition profiled at the beginning of the chapter is the Celebration Golf Academy. But the largest chain of American golf schools is that of former English golfer John Jacobs. Established over 30 years ago, the John Jacobs' Golf Schools are at 32 resort hotels in 15 states. John Jacobs has an in-house travel department that offers complete golf tourism packages including airfare and accommodation. The company also provides corporate golf programmes at resorts and courses across the country, combining golf instruction and business presentations that address sales training and management, strategy, team building and leadership. These programmes are designed for sales and team building events, employee recognition, tournaments, client entertainment, and golf business seminars. Previous clients include Citibank Foreign Exchange, Canadian Pacific Railway, Ford Motor Credit, TAP Pharmaceuticals, Seagrams Beverages, and The Oilmen. Examples of the corporate programmes offered by John Jacobs (taken from their website) are outlined below.

Corporate golf school examples

(Source: John Jacobs Golf Schools, 2009)

♦ A major national bank hosts a Private 1 Day John Jacobs' Golf School for their top corporate banking clients. The programme begins with a brief breakfast meeting. Four hours of golf instruction follows during which one bank staff member is paired with senior managers from four different client companies followed by lunch. The afternoon is spent putting the lessons learned to work on the golf course. Golf foursomes comprised of a bank management representative and three clients hit the course for an afternoon of improved golf skills and networking.

♦ A regional branch of a major national investment firm hosts Monthly Private 1 hour John Jacobs' Golf Schools Golf Clinics for their top performing sales representatives and their clients. Each clinic focuses on a specific area of the golf game, full swing, short game, etc.

♦ A major independent resort taps John Jacobs' Golf Schools for their corporate group guests to provide educational entertainment during cocktail receptions. Jacobs' instructors utilize a portable swing analysis unit that allows partygoers the opportunity to have their golf swing computer analysed and take home a CD of their swing compared to a PGA professional.

Another one of the largest and oldest golf school operators is VIP Golf Academy which has grown from two sites in Florida over 20 years ago to 18 locations in the United States and the Caribbean today, all picked to include the most desirable areas for golf and golf vacations. VIP specializes in personal 'One to One' golf lessons. Its golf schools are located around the country in golf vacation resort locations where each student receives individual golf lessons from one of VIP's PGA or LPGA teaching professionals. VIP sites include Palm Springs Golf School in California, Phoenix Golf School and Scottsdale Golf School in Arizona, PGA Village Golf School in Florida, Hilton Head Golf School in South Carolina, Las Vegas Golf School in Nevada, Denver Golf School in Colorado, Atlantic City Golf School in New Jersey, Syracuse Golf School in New York, and golf schools in Puerto Rico and the Dominican Republic. Like John Jacobs' Golf Schools, the company's Corporate Golf Division creates customized programmes for business clients or top executives.

The Golf University in the USA is another option for golf tourists. Since 1988 over 4000 students have graduated from its golf schools in Florida, Arizona, Myrtle Beach, and Las Vegas. Their PGA or LPGA professionals work with golfers of all abilities. Prior to arrival golfers are asked to complete a 20 question profile that allows the University to match player with instructor. They recommend their two- and three-day programmes for golfers who are looking to 'tune up' and get ready for the upcoming season. For the golfer looking to 'take their game to the next level', their four-day school is probably the best choice. For beginners or newer golfers, their three-day programme is the recommended choice. They also offer programmes that include hotels located at the golf course.

As mentioned in the Snapshot earlier, the PGA also has its own Tour Academies. These offer golf schools and clinics for all levels of player; private lessons with PGA and LPGA professionals; player development including the World Golf Foundation's new Get Golf Ready programme; club-fitting programmes; and short-game clinics. There are six permanent locations in the USA – including the World Golf Village at Scottsdale – as well as a unique travelling academy and even instruction at sea. Each venue attracts around 1200 golfers per year, flying in from all over the world, typically for a three-day golf school, staying at the resort. The 2008 credit crunch has affected participation in the Academies: 'We're down about 10 per cent in some locations. One item which is hurt in recessions and fluctuates with the DOW is the golf schools because they are a luxury item. People will still go on golf vacations regardless but will drop the golf school when the economy is bad,' explained Travis Velichko, Director of Business Development for PGA Tour Experiences, speaking early in 2009. He considers the PGA Tour brand resilient enough to withstand the economic depression.

Golf attractions

Chapter 1 referred to the World Golf Hall of Fame in Florida, but there are a number of other similar attractions. Another in the USA is the United States Golf Association (USGA) Museum, an educational institution dedicated to fostering an appreciation for the game of golf, its participants, and the Association. It serves as a caretaker and steward for the game's history, supporting the Association's role in ensuring the game's future. The origins of the USGA Museum can be traced to 1935, when George Blossom, a member of the USGA's Executive Committee, first proposed the creation of a collection of historical golf artifacts. One year later, in an effort to formalize the Museum, the USGA Museum and Library Committee was created with the primary function of collecting historically significant artifacts and books. The first significant donation to the Museum – Bob Jones' legendary putter, Calamity Jane II – followed in 1938. For most of its institutional history, significant resources were devoted to the traditional museum functions. However, in recent decades, the USGA Museum has dedicated extensive resources to its educational responsibilities, and has developed a variety of programmes to disseminate information, scholarship, and educational programming to a broad and diverse audience.

Golf museums can also be dedicated to golfers themselves. The Tiger Woods Museum is undoubtedly one for the future (he already has an exhibit devoted to him in the California Museum Hall of Fame), but for now, golf enthusiasts can visit the Jack Nicklaus Museum. Located in the heart of the Ohio State University sports complex in Nicklaus's hometown of Columbus, the Museum is a 24,000 square-foot educational and historical facility. Visitors can take an immersive journey through the golfer's career including trophies, photographs and various mementos from his unparalleled 20 major championships and 100 worldwide professional victories.

Canada is also host to several golf museums. The Canadian Golf Hall of Fame and Museum in Oakville, Ontario, celebrates the game of golf in Canada. A Hall of Fame/Trophy Room contains representations of the Honoured Members. Visitors can also try their luck at putting with a replica 200-year-old putter and a 'featherie' ball. The British Columbia Golf Museum and Hall of Fame is located at the 17th tee of the University Golf Club in Vancouver. The mission of the museum is to research, collect, preserve and display the history of golf and golfers in British Columbia. On display is an extensive collection of clubs (dating back to 1790), bags and golf balls. There is also a library of over 5000 volumes of collectible books, reference books and general interest titles. An important function of the museum is the maintenance of a reference library filled with information on virtually every golf course that has ever existed in British Columbia, along with over 1500 player biographies, and the tournament records from all events dating back more than 25 years.

Outside North America, the British Golf Museum in St Andrews, Scotland, charts the history of golf from its beginnings to modern day. The focus is on British golf, with the museum telling the story of British golf chronologically, exploring the events, personalities and equipment used throughout the ages. The museum has a number of galleries, a kids' section, and a library containing a number of books that look at the history of the game of golf. After officially opening on 19 September 1990, the museum won seven major awards and is currently one of nine museums that have reached the five-star standard in the Scottish Tourist

Board's Visitor Attractions Grading Scheme. The Heritage of Golf Museum is a nearby attraction near the village of Gullane, not far from St Andrews. The one-room museum is viewed by appointment and is run by resident curator, Archie Baird. A consummate amateur golfer, Baird opened his golf museum in 1980, the same year he supposedly retired.

Another well-established museum in Europe is the Golf Museum in Regensburg, Germany. Created by golf historian Peter Insam, the museum is in the heart of the city, close to the famous cathedral of Regensburg. Artefacts include a display case showing club heads made of lead and pewter, which are more than 400 years old; Delft tiles with golf subjects of the 17th and 18th century; and legendary 'Featheryballs', which revolutionized golf at the beginning of the 17th century. There are also 'Morris woods and clubs' made of iron as well as brass putters in weathered leather bags dating from 1780–1930. Visitors can also see a 1922 score card of King George V of England with its 'lousy score' of His Majesty of 117 strokes.

Far away in Australasia, the Australasian Golf Museum, located in Bothwell village, Tasmania, tells the story of how golf has evolved into Australia's most popular participation sport. The museum illustrates why the early settlers in historic Bothwell became Australia's first golfing community, with the nearby Ratho Golf Links recognized as Australia's oldest golf course, and the township having as many as five different golf courses. The evolution of the game is explained through the different eras, as defined by the changing golf ball; from Feathery (1400s to mid-1800s) to Gutta-percha (1850s to 1900) to Haskell (turn of the century to World War II) and the modern balls. Many of Tasmania's champion golfers are featured, from Australia's first-born champions, the Pearce Brothers, to Lucy Arthur, Len Nettlefold, Elvie Whitesides, the Toogoods and the Goggins. Founded in 1996 by former Australian champion golfer, Peter Toogood, the museum is housed in a sandstone heritage building, formerly the State Primary School. It displays items of national and international significance. Prominent Australians who have given their support and donations to the museum include Greg Norman, Peter Thomson, Lindy Goggin, Norman Von Nida, the Toogood and Nettlefold families and Ian Baker-Finch, who donated his 1991 British Open-winning putter and sand iron.

Case Study: Golf at Fairmont Hotels & Resorts

Fairmont has been targeting golfers since it first took over Canadian Pacific properties at the end of the 19th century. In 2009 it had 13 golf resorts, purveying 300,000 rounds of golf annually, as well as five more properties allied to neighbouring, high-end courses. The Fairmont golf foothold extends from North America to the Caribbean, Kenya, South Africa and St Andrews.

As a luxury, high-end specialist, Fairmont promotes golf and spa packages, in order to appeal to golfers as well as their non-golfing partners. Golfing Coordinator, Lindsey Thuell says couples are responding well to packages which provide either a round of golf or a credit to the spa. At Fairmont's Willow Stream Spas

Fairmont Banff Springs in Canada,
courtesy of Fairmont Hotels & Resorts

there are even golf-specific treatments, such as golf stretching and golf facials intended to counteract sun damage. And it's not just women enjoying these treatments. The Fairmont Scottsdale in Arizona attracts just as many men for treatments at its 'man spa', the MVP Room in the Willow Stream Spa. The Fairmont Sonoma Mission Inn and Spa, in California, is capitalizing on the Pilates craze, positioning the ballet-inspired exercise as a mental and physical conditioning blend ideal for golfers.

Around 60% of the Fairmont brand's business is corporate and group travel. But the farsighted company has identified a trend towards family golfing holidays, facilitating this with complimentary (or discounted) junior rounds for every paid adult round. 'It is where the industry is going, golfers want to be with the family more, especially at weekends,' explains Thuell. Looking to attract beginners and, in particular, women, the Fairmont Jasper Park Lodge established a Spring Swing Clinic which is becoming increasingly popular. The Lodge boasts eight Canadian PGA members on its pro staff.

Some Fairmont properties are offering more innovative options for the non-golfer, such as 'Cooking with Chef' packages available at the Algonquin with additional lessons in social etiquette. Activities off the golf course focus on safaris, hiking and African adventures at the Fairmont Mount Kenya Club.

Fairmont's Executive Director, Golf and Retail, Justin Wood says that golf travel has really evolved, making the game a central focus of a much broader active luxury lifestyle for golfers and partners. 'Fairmont is well-positioned to complement their lifestyles because our properties offer such a diverse collection of unique, engaging activities and amenities. By blending in elements such as fitness, spa treatments, and ancillary activities that allow them to be immersed in the environment and culture of the destination – in addition to providing our guests with world-class golf – Fairmont is able to provide a much richer and more valuable golf vacation experience,' he says.

Fairmont is endeavouring to make golfing on business or leisure trips easier for its guests. Members of the Fairmont President's Club (FPC) can reserve complimentary golf clubs to save packing bulky clubs while travelling. The Fairmonts in Scotland and Scottsdale, Arizona, both have dedicated golf concierges to book tee times, organize transportation etc. Wood says that superior service is all about anticipating guests' needs to make the travel experience as comfortable and enjoyable as possible: 'Providing top-of-the-line golf equipment on property or assisting the guest by arranging golf for them at other courses within a certain destination frees the guest to enjoy their time with us without worry or inconvenience. We also make available other benefits to our Fairmont President's Club members – such as Adidas workout shoes and clothing, Aveda travel kits and complimentary use of TaylorMade golf clubs at select hotels. These benefits make it easier for our guests to travel with just a carry-on bag and avoid baggage fees. Plus, it helps us to build relationships with our guests. They rely on us and they appreciate the fact that we are looking after their needs.'

Golfing instruction is being promoted by Fairmont to encourage all levels of golfers. A perk at the Fairmont St Andrews, Scotland, is an exclusive clinic at the St Andrews Links Golf Academy which occasionally provides free tuition for corporate groups. The St. Andrews' Head Pro, John Kerr provides topnotch individual lessons. Guests can also package in club-fitting and instruction programmes. The Fairmont Chateau Whistler, in Canada, offers guests premier instruction at the David Leadbetter Academy, with computer and swing analysis technology.

With a strong emphasis on protecting the environment via the 'Greening our Greens' initiative, Fairmont golfers also get ecological peace of mind when they book their trip. To date, seven Fairmont courses have achieved full certification in the Audubon Cooperative Sanctuary Program, with others enrolled and working towards the designation. 'Golf is a unique sport. The environment in which it is played is intimately entwined in the overall golf experience,' says Wood. 'You simply cannot separate the two. Being good stewards of the land not only makes moral sense, it is imperative for the game itself. By making our golf courses healthy environments for indigenous species of plants and wildlife it makes the golf experience better for our guests. It makes our properties more vital elements of their larger communities, and it allows us to help preserve the beauty that attracted our guests to the destination in the first place.'

Fairmont is owned by Fairmont Raffles Hotel International, a global hotel company with 91 hotels worldwide under the Raffles, Fairmont and Swissôtel brands. Golf is being touted at various Fairmont lounges and restaurants around the world via an ingenious promotion: a new golf-inspired cocktail menu. You can sample Sea Breeze from the Fairmont Southampton Golf Course in Bermuda, for example.

Sources

Personal interview with Fairmont Golf Coordinator, Lindsey Thuell, 2 February 2009.

Interview with Justin Wood, April 2009.

Remington, R. (2008) 'Old tyme golf: Wood-shaft clubs make a comeback', *Calgary Herald*, B3.

Keenan, T. (2008) 'Why spas aren't just for women', *Calgary Herald*, 24 September.

Meetings & Conventions, Jun 2008, Part I, Vol. 43, Issue 7, p 30.

Boettcher, S. (2008) 'Drink this: Shaken or stirred', *Calgary Herald*, Lifestyle, 29 May.

Corcoran, D. (2008). 'Off-Season Island Idyll', *Incentive*, June , pp. 74-76.

Levack, K. (2008) 'Preserving Paradise', *Successful Meetings*, November, p 13.

References

Golf Magazine (2008) 'Top 25 golf schools in America', *Golf Magazine*, November, pp. 73–76.

John Jacobs Golf Schools (2009) Accessed from http://www.jacobsgolf.com/corporate-golf-schools-examples.php, 10 February.

KPMG (2008) *Golf Travel Insight in EMA 2008*, KPMG Advisory Ltd, pp. 6.

Professional Convention Management Association (2008) The 17th Annual Meetings Market Survey, PCMA, Chicago, IL.

Sonner, S. (2007) 'Golf courses in Eastern Sierra team up to promote tourism', *USA Today*, 9 June.

Stoller, G. (2008) 'Hotels play up golf angle for meetings', *USA Today*, accessed from http://www.usatoday.com, 2008.

Travel + Leisure (2008) 'Oktoberfest Golf', *Travel + Leisure*, 65, p. 46.

4 Planning for Golf Tourism

ANZ Ladies Masters Tournament, Royal Pines Resort, Queensland – the Richest Women's Golf Tournament in Australia, courtesy of Queensland Tourism

A golf course is second only to a major body of water in terms of creating added value to residential development, according to Australian property analyst, Michael Matusik. 'In a correctly conceived and researched development, the premium price obtained for fairway frontage and the marketing advantage of a golf course community can greatly exceed the course construction and operating costs,' he says.

The Queensland-based researcher has been studying the golf property development business in northeast Australia since 2000. Matusik has determined that, despite the economic downturn and property market slump in Australia, golf course communities are still being built and golf estate homes still being sold at a premium. He attributes this ability to buck the trend to something more than just the golf. With only 20–25 per cent of golf estate residents actually playing golf, he says 'most buy into a golf estate because the course is often 60 to 70 hectares of permanent and maintained open space, which adds prestige and lifestyle appeal to a residential development.'

His company, Matusik Property Insights, produces a regular newsletter with updated statistics and research results about the Queensland property market in general with a specific focus on golfing developments. Matusik maintains that once the initial lure of the golf has worn off, it is secondary facilities – such as non-golfing, inter-generational activities, lap pools, lounging areas, themed architecture etc. – that sustains demand. With prospective residents comprising up to 75 per cent non-golfers (compared to around 50 per cent in the USA), Matusik says it is critical to plan for non-golfing activities in Australian developments.

The target market for golf course developments is predominantly baby boomers in Australia: 'The traditional golf course buyer household is either an older family with teenage children living at home, with household heads between 45 and 55 years of age, or an empty nester couple aged between 55 and 65 years,' says Matusik. Younger families are also buying into the lifestyle (particularly as telecommunications enable working from home away from urban centres) but often further away from the actual course where property prices are lower.

Profit margins can be high for golf real estate but it is paramount to plan developments carefully, focusing on social and economic conditions, competitive analysis and demand analysis. Some items that planners should consider are whether there are few golf courses in the area or if the existing courses are overcrowded; are land costs relatively low; will the estate contain mid and upper income housing; is the existing market sufficient to absorb premiums required; can capital costs of the course be amortized over several years and over at least hundreds of dwellings; and could the course be sold without detracting from the ongoing marketing of the residential product?

Environmental planning is, of course, key for the sustainability of golf course developments. Australia's Gold Coast saw large overseas investment during the 1980s in reaction to changes in government legislation. Too many golf course developments were subsequently planned, approved and built during this period, some circumventing normal business and environmental planning processes. The result was an over-concentration of golf facilities in environmentally-sensitive areas and an over-supply in relation to demand. By contrast, other areas are learning from this example, addressing these issues in advance of projects. Alexandrina in South Australia, for example, has written into its local council development plan specific controls on water use, vegetation and heritage preservation for golf developments. This has now been recognized as a best-practice model.

Planning for views is also crucial for the marketability of golf course housing. Many courses line allotments down both sides of a fairway with residences placed at a 90-degree angle to the course. 'Providing less angled allotments, changing building setbacks and envelopes, sacrificing some allotments, realigning streets, walking trails and cart paths can direct views toward focal points on the course and elsewhere within the estate. By opening up views to the widest possible audience a developer can maximize the overall base price, premiums and rate of sale,' says Matusik.

He's also convinced that a championship course is not always preferable – the potential clientele must be taken into consideration and most golfers don't boast the necessary handicaps. He recommends numerous tee placements at each hole. Provisions for the non-golfer are vital: 'A golf course provides a great way to integrate pedestrian access throughout the estate. Also, do not rely on the golf course alone, offer other open space and facilities such as pocket parks, BBQs, teenage sports' equipment and play gyms outside the golf course itself,' he advises.

In 2008 he concluded that buyers will pay up to 92 per cent more to live on a golf course. Signature designers, such as Greg Norman, Adam Scott and Karrie Webb, have been partly responsible for the rise in profile of golf course living in Australia. 'Property in branded projects sells faster and for more than in generic golf estates,' Matusik avers. Exclusivity has also helped boost sales – to be a member of the newer courses, golfers must own property in the estate. Premiums can also be affected by water frontage on estates as well as proximity to signature greens.

In a golfing estate the clubhouse can develop into the 'corner pub' of old: a focal point for socializing and also for neighbourhood outreach. Clubs are widening their offerings to fill this need. Settlers' Run, a new Greg Norman-designed golf development near Melbourne, holds a 'This is the Life' festival which features live jazz, wine and food tasting and children's activities – thus appealing to all demographic groups in the estate.

Other developments go a step further in providing a full lifestyle for residents. Shell Cove, on the New South Wales south coast, is part of a $1.5 billion project including a seaside tourist hub with boat harbour, boardwalk and retail/cafe district, residential area and two golf courses. Nicely combining both 'sea and tee', the development also includes schools in order to attract families as well as retirees.

Sources

Centenara, J. and James, B. (August 2008) 'Looking for a Tee-Change', Golf Australia, pp. 93-106.

Matusik, M. (2000) 'Under par', *Matusik Snapshot*, June, No. 81.

Matusik, M. (2003) 'Under par #3', *Matusik Snapshot*, June, No. 203.

Matusik, M. (2005) 'For the record', *Matusik Snapshot*, December, No. 287.

Matusik, M. (2008) 'Sea and tee', *Matusik Snapshot*, February, No. 359.

Warnken, J., Thompson, D., and Zakus, D. W. (2001) 'Golf course development in a major tourist destination: implications for planning and management', *Environmental Management*, **27** (5), pp. 681–696.

Introduction

As the opening Spotlight indicates, planning is critical for the sustainability of golf course developments. In parts of Australia, poor planning resulted in an over-concentration of golf facilities in environmentally-sensitive areas and an over-supply in relation to demand. This chapter focuses on planning issues, outlining the initiatives and solutions most frequently applied in planning for golf tourism development. A section on the planning process is followed by an analysis of golf course types and different layout options. The next section focuses on the four types of courses suitable for golf tourism: 'Trophy' courses; single integrated resorts; golf courses associated with property developments; and networks of courses forming golf regions. There are a number of design considerations in the planning and development of golf courses and these are discussed in turn, followed by a final section on the costs of development and development problems that might arise during the planning process.

The planning process

Tourism planning was originally seen as a simplistic process of encouraging new hotels to open, ensuring transport structures existed, and then instigating a tourism promotion campaign. But in the era of mass tourism development in the 1970s and 1980s, destinations paid the social and environmental consequences of unplanned tourism development. An example was given in the Spotlight where too many golf course developments were planned, approved and built in the 1980s on Australia's Gold Coast, circumventing business and environmental planning processes. Today, planning usually applies a comprehensive and integrated approach, which recognizes that all development sectors and supporting facilities and services are interrelated with one another and with the natural environment and society of the area (Priestley, 2006).

According to Inskeep (1991: p.28) there are eight steps to the planning process:

1 Preparation and organization for the project

2 Determination of development goals and objectives

3 Undertaking of surveys and inventories of the existing situation

4 Analysis and synthesis of the survey information

5 Formulation of the plan, including development policy and the physical plan

6 Recommendations on plan-related project elements

7 Implementation of the plan

8 Continuous monitoring and feedback.

Inskeep (1991) also provides a road map for the planning of resorts specifically. The first step is to conduct a market analysis for the type of resort under consideration. The next stage is the conceptual stage where regional business and community relationships are explored and a resort plan drawn up after consultation with key stakeholders. This is followed by the development phase when various forms of financing are secured in order to complete the project. Larger projects usually require set stages of development during which various forms of financing are secured and different types of revenue generation are pursued to maintain debt repayment and cash flow. This has been the case for the Revelstoke development in Canada discussed in the Case Study at the end of this chapter. When original co-investors Don Simpson and Robert Powaduik pulled out in response to the economic downturn, Northland Properties took the reins. Founded by the Gallarti family, Northland owns the Sandman chain, Moxie's, Denny's and Chop restaurants, the Shark Club in Vancouver and other real estate developments. Northland's counsel, Bernie Malach explained that Gallarti was an expert in rescuing companies from potential bankruptcy with several successful turn-around projects in the past. 'At Revelstoke it will mean doing everything planned but doing it a bit slower,' said Malach.

There are a large number of stakeholders involved in the golf tourism planning process (Priestley, 2006). These include national and regional political authorities who are responsible for macro-scale policies and legislation. At the local and municipal level, the key stakeholders are political organisms, the general public, lobby groups and land owners. Others with a direct interest in golf tourism planning are property developers and building contractors, golf course designers, tourism suppliers (e.g. hoteliers) and tourism operators. On a national and regional scale, there are those in favour of golf development and those who prefer to restrict its growth. For example, in Eastern Europe during the socialist era, golf was associated with capitalism and was consequently banned for more than 40 years. Golf was therefore unable to develop. At the same time in other parts of Europe, such as Spain and Portugal, golf was recognized at national, regional and local levels as a key tourism product. The Costa del Sol, for example, is proud to promote itself as the 'Costa del Golf', stretching beyond the Mediterranean Malaga coast into the Atlantic provinces of Cadiz and Huelva.

Another Spanish-speaking country seeking to emulate the 'Costa del Golf' is Mexico, where authorities see golf resort development as a major niche for the future. This trend towards targeting a high-end, sophisticated tourist is a deviation from years past, when Mexico positioned itself as a bargain destination. More recently it has recognized the importance of seasonally-focused tourism (including golf, honeymoon and youth tourism) in a bid to receive market segments that were overlooked in the past. Golf courses, in particular, were previously seen to take up too much precious land that could be utilized for more important structures such as accommodation wings, restaurants and retail, and swimming pools, etc. Most championship golf courses are located near high-end, coastal resorts, in a popular 'Sea and Tee' combination, but there are also private golf clubs in inner Mexico, particularly in the Greater Mexico City area, which accept visitors. The Snapshot on page 82 profiles golf tourism development in Mexico.

It is important that stakeholders involved in the planning process understand the real strengths and weaknesses of golf tourism (Priestley, 2006). The main weaknesses normally attributed to golf tourism development are land speculation, negative environmental and landscape impacts, and excessive water consumption due to irrigation. On the positive side, the economic benefits of golf development are universally recognized and golf tourism helps to alleviate problems of seasonality and contributes to product diversification. Golf development can reduce pressure on seafront areas, as development can occupy inland terrain, enhancing the value of adjoining real estate which would otherwise be of little value. Similarly, golf contributes to the prestige and image enhancement of destinations and tends to improve their overall quality. It is the responsibility of authorities to establish rules for development in order to mitigate the negative effects. As mentioned above, Alexandrina in South Australia has written into its local council development master plan, specific controls on water use, vegetation and heritage preservation for golf developments.

In recent years, golf architects have realized that preserving the environment is a great selling point, and numerous publications discuss environmentally responsible design, construction, and management of golf courses. Huge areas of golf development are now given over to nature, in the shape of watercourses, nature trails and flora and fauna. An example is the Trump National Golf Club in Los

Angeles, featured in Chapter 5. Trump paid $27 million for the property in 2002 and then invested $261 million in redesigning the course. 'This is the most expensive golf course ever built,' he boasted. Public trails meander through the golf course, providing access to the beach and a public park. Environmentally sensitive areas line many of the holes but don't come into play, and each hole has an ocean view. One page on the club's website is devoted to 'The Environmental Story' and says 'Trump National is dedicated to protecting the environmentally sensitive habitat that plays host to several protected plant species and the endangered Coastal California Gnatcatcher (a small migratory bird).'

At the planning and development stage, sustainable development has become an important consideration. Initiatives such as the Audubon International Signature Programs have been created for resort community projects to assist landowners from the design stages through construction and then in establishing a maintenance programme that focuses on sustainability. To achieve the Audubon Signature Certification, developers must design and implement a Natural Resource Management plan to include wildlife conservation and habitat enhancement, water quality monitoring and management, integrated pest management, water conservation, energy efficiency, and waste management. Audubon International has partnered with the United States Golf Association, and the PGA of America, to create Golf & the Environment, which is dedicated to the game of golf and the protection and enhancement of the natural environment.

Snapshot: Planning for golf in Mexico

Pacifico Golf Course in Mexico, a Jack Nicklaus signature design, courtesy of Four Seasons Hotels Ltd

In Mexico, the $13 billion tourism industry is almost as important to the economy as manufacturing. With over 200 golf courses already and a 365-day golfing calendar, authorities see golf resort development as a major niche for the future. Jacques Rogozinski – head of the government tourism development fund, known as Fonatur – says that the government would rather finance a seaside golf resort project in Baja California than a mega-project like Cancun. 'We are not going to put one more cent into those kinds of (Cancun-style) projects,' he affirmed.

Although golf has not traditionally ranked as a popular sport in Mexico, the General Tourism Development Department of the Ministry of Tourism (SECTUR) identified it as 'a national sport' for Mexico's US and Canadian tourists. Mexico is second only to Hawaii in attracting US tourists and the first choice annually of around 590,000 Canadians who rank among the most prolific golfers per capita in the world.

In a 2009 report 'Golfing trends and behaviour in Mexico', it was deemed that golf could easily be encouraged as a sport, boosting domestic participation by almost double and attracting large numbers of tourist players. 'Golf could be a very important cornerstone for encouraging and developing tourism, as it is a very social and family-oriented sport,' the report concluded. The plan was to change the equation so that no longer would golf be a function of tourist areas, but tourism would develop as a function of golf courses.

With $100 billion earmarked for golf development (Contreras, 2008), sites for future golf resorts in Mexico include Guaymas, which is located on the eastern shore of the Sea of Cortez, Hidalgo, located one hour north of Mexico City, Quintana Roo, on an 81-mile stretch of land south of the Sian Ka'an reserve and north of Belize, and Huatulco. Celebrity endorsement has been integral to Mexico's boost to golf developments. Jack Nicklaus – named by BEST's Golf Guides to Mexico as 'Best Golf Course Architect in Mexico' in 2006 – has had a hand in around 30 developments in Los Cabos, Puerto Vallarta and Cozumel. Further celeb cachet is provided by Tom Fazio at Chileno Bay, two championship courses designed by Phil Mickelson and David Love III at the Diamante Cabo San Lucas golf community, and Pete Dye's Cabo Riviera Marina and Golf Resort opening in 2010.

In 2009, Mexico was flouting the economic downturn by forging ahead with a $500 million investment on the Pacific Coast, including golf courses and marinas. Twice the size of Cancun, the development in Escuinapa is aiming to be one of the foremost destinations in Mexico attracting 3 million tourists annually and a local population estimated to reach 500,000 by 2025. Planning has involved a strong environmental commitment with 155 species of birds and four types of mangroves co-existing in the 5800 acre plot. The project will create 150,000 new jobs.

Mexico's confidence is based on the supposition that Americans are trading in their long-distance vacation plans for destinations closer to home with connectivity and affordability being prime motivators. Airlines – such as Aeromexico and Jet Blue – are also responding to this trend by adding new flights to Mexico, making it easier to reach destinations throughout the country.

Planning for tourism has to include variety and options nowadays. Baby boomers don't all want to be herded; they like to be able to tailor vacations to their own specifics. One of Mexico's newest tourism destinations, the Riviera Nayarit, on the Pacific coast, is adding ecotourism to its combo of beach, golf and spa offerings. Accessible by the Puerto Vallarta International Airport, the area boasts four major golf courses, one designed by Jack Nicklaus at the Four Season Punta Mita. Eco-attractions include zip-lining, canopy tours in the jungle, swimming with dolphins and whale watching. Culture-centric activities are being marketed at the Hilton Los Cabos Beach & Golf Resort to attract gourmands and oenophiles. There are traditional Mexican interactive cookery classes and Mexican wine-tasting classes.

Sources

Contreras, J. (2 June, 2008) 'Putter Up: New Latin Links', *Newsweek*, **151** (22).

Mexico Tourism Board E-Newsletter (Industry) – http://travelagentdeals2.com/mexico/pages_nov08/industry.html.

Travel Courier (2009) 'Riviera Nayarit execs bring growth message', *Travel Courier*, October, p. 14.

'Mexico looks to golf for a tourism boom', http://www.worldgolf.com/travel/mexico/golf-tourism.htm accessed 17 June 2009.

Travel File (2008) 'Martour offers new Mexico program', *Travel File*, September, p. 16.

'Golfing trends and behaviour in mexico', Secretaria De Turismo, Mexico.

www.visitloscabos.travel

Golf course types

Grudnitski (2003) suggests that golf courses can be divided into three general types: private; daily fee or public; and semiprivate or hybrid. The use of a private golf course is restricted to members and their guests, so a private course would not normally attract golf tourists (unless they are spectators at a golf event). A daily fee or public course is open to anyone who pays a green fee, whereas the semiprivate or hybrid course is a common response to the rising popularity of golf and the continually spiralling cost of operating a golf course facility. A semi-private club normally limits green fee play so as to afford its members greater opportunity to enjoy the facility. Research in Las Vegas found that there was an adjustment in price (upwards) of 12.5 per cent, 6 per cent, and 5.7 per cent to the value of houses located in private, semiprivate, and public golf course communities, respectively, over similar houses located in communities that do not have a golf course (Grudnitski, 2003).

Walter (2009) has expanded on these three general types by suggesting eleven categories of golf courses (see Table 4.1).

Table 4.1: Categories of golf courses (Source: Walter, 2009)

Type	Features
Private	Only allow members of their club, organization or community to play on their facilities. If you are not a member, you cannot play unless you are invited to play by someone who is a member.
Public	Can be played by anyone who can afford the green fees. They can be operated by a private organization or a civic organization.
Semi-private	Allow members access at any time but restrict public use to certain days or times. The term is often used to make courses seem more exclusive.
Municipal	A type of public course that is owned and operated by a local government. Anyone who can afford the green fees can play on them.
Daily-fee	Public courses that charge on a daily basis for use of their facilities. Municipal, resort, residential, military, private estate and industrial golf courses may be daily-fee courses.

Resort	Owned and operated by a resort or hotel. They may be public courses, or they may only allow guests to use their facilities.
Residential	Owned and managed by a community. They are usually private or semi-private, reserved for community members only.
Military	Owned and operated by the military for the military. They can be public or private, but their main purpose is to serve military personnel and their families.
Private estate	Owned by an individual or family and are located on their private estate. They are private courses that you can only gain access to by means of a personal invitation from the owner.
Industrial	Owned and operated by a private business. The courses are private and only employees of the company are allowed to use the facilities.
University	Owned and operated by a college or university. They can either be private or public courses.

One relatively new type of golf course not included in this list is the executive golf course. Dubbed the 'mini-me' of golf courses, executive courses are much shorter than full or championship courses, sporting a majority of par 3 holes with a smattering of par 4s and sometimes 5s. The overall par would be in the upper 50s or lower 60s for 18 holes although courses are often 9 holes and, occasionally, 36. Green fees are generally cheaper than full-length courses – an important differential in an economic recession. Sometimes viewed dismissively as second-class citizens in the regulation-ruled world of golf, they can often be a very successful money-spinner in space-crunched, fast-living city centres or tourist destinations. San Diego has a dense concentration of 22 executive and par 3 courses in its metropolis. The Snapshot below gives some examples of this type of golf course.

Snapshot: Executive golf courses

Mystic Ridge Executive Golf Course at Oakville, Canada, courtesy of Mystic Ridge

Old-school golfers have traditionally not taken short courses as seriously as regulation golf which requires a minimum of 6000 yards. But, increasingly, planners are hiring brand-name architects to design executive courses to lend their experience and cachet to help attract multi-standard players. Club quality turf and classic designs are helping convince the old guard of their validity.

Mission Hills, in China (the world's largest golf club with 12 courses) has a par 3, executive course designed by Schmidt-Curley Design Inc. It is an 18-hole course and, according to Brian Curley, it has helped in counteracting antagonism towards shorter courses in the area. 'One of the battles in Asia is that there is a stigma associated with anything less than a par 72 course,' he says. For the past decade Curley has encouraged golf course planners to build courses commensurate with their clientele: 'If a course is too long or too tough, there can be a backlash. Finally, in Asia people are beginning to understand that shorter, easier courses can be a success without having to create a behemoth every time,' he explains.

Mystic Ridge Golf Course at Oakville, near Toronto, Canada, is an executive length, 18-hole course. Designed by Rene Muylaert, one of Canada's leading golf course architects, it opened in 1989. Another regulation-length, par-36, 9-hole course (Angel's View) was subsequently added and these two Oakville courses have been consistently ranked as one of the area's premier public golf facilities. Co-owner Alexandra D'Cunha says her family intended to corner the executive golfing market in the Toronto area from the outset: 'Part of it was that we didn't have the size holding for a bigger course, but on the outskirts of Toronto there is a large population of time-pressed individuals, all juggling commuting, family and work, so we felt strongly that a shorter course would do well.' The four-hour 18-hole course and two-hour 9-holer attract a high percentage of women, drawn also by the healthy, high quality fare in the clubhouse. 'A lot of women don't just want hot dogs and hamburgers. They like to sit with friends in a nice atmosphere and have something healthier to eat. It's about the whole package for women,' says D'Cunha. She also thinks that players don't get so frustrated with shorter driving, less challenging holes and quicker rounds.

As well as seniors and juniors, the public course attracts male golfers, often executives who have limited spare time or who don't belong to a private club. 'Maybe they want to come out with their wife who already likes our course or their children. We also offer men's and ladies' leagues and that works well for us, too, catering for those who don't have friends or spouses who play golf,' says D'Cunha. Weekends are the busiest by far, with weekday mornings and lower-priced twilight slots also popular.

With short courses starting to lose their second-class stigma, golf real estate developments are even embracing the concept. Promontory in Utah, Sunriver in Oregon and Suncadia in Washington are all developing executive courses. The Welk Golf Resort in San Diego is a 36-hole executive golf resort. Lake San Marcos, also referred to as the South Course, is nestled within San Diego's only lake resort community. Open to the public daily, this 2700 yard, par 58 executive course offers four par 4s as well as 14 par 3s. There's also a private, full-length par 71 course for resort members.

Although equipped with instruction programmes, clinics, clubhouses, and all the paraphernalia of a typical golf course, executive courses often circumvent the rigid regulations and etiquette of country clubs. This can attract golfers disillusioned with the strict confines of the game and also encourage fledgling golfers to start. In the US short courses are also utilized for the First Tee program, an outreach project for underprivileged youth.

Sources

Personal interview with Alexandra D'Cunha, 6 March 2009.

Gould, D. (2009) 'In a Different Light', *Golf Business Magazine*, 28 January.

www.oakvillegolf.ca.

http://sg.pagenation.com/sin/Executive%20Golf%20Course_103.8094_1.4014.map

http://www.golfbusinessmagazine.com/pageview.asp?m=2&y=2009&doc=2047.

Golf courses are also named and categorized by the type of vegetation and scenery they are set in. Table 4.2 lists these different types.

Table 4.2: Golf courses categorized by type of vegetation and scenery (Source: Walter, 2009)

Type	Characteristics
Parkland	Characterized by lush, manicured turf, favourable weather and a few accent trees (Douglas). They are the typical type of course found in the US.
Links	Seaside courses that look like the east of Scotland where the game of golf originated (Hamilton). They are grassy open expanses, with rolling hills, deep roughs and no trees.
Heath-land	Inland courses that are characterized by low growing shrubs, gentle slopes and few to no trees. They are made to resemble the inland golf courses of England and Scotland.
Downs	Made to resemble the English downs and are characterized by gentle slopes and grassy plains.
Ocean-side	Border the ocean, but unlike links courses they are well above sea level.
Forest	Surrounded by dense woods.
Mountain	Usually aren't in the mountains, but do have views of mountains.
Prairie	Usually located in the flatlands of the midwest USA. They are flat with few trees and have views of the prairie.
Desert	Usually located in the arid regions of the southwest USA They are heavily irrigated courses that allow you to play in the desert.

Five basic golf course layouts serve as the models for constructing a regulation golf course (Mill, 2008):

♦   **The core golf course.** In a core course, the holes are clustered together either in a continuous sequence with starting and finishing holes at the clubhouse or in returning nines with two starting and finishing holes at the clubhouse. The planned golf course in Revelstoke, Canada, discussed in the case study at the end of the chapter, will roughly follow this design principle. Figure 4.1 on page 90 shows the Master Plan for this course, due to open in 2011.

◆ **Single fairway continuous.** This layout is a single, open loop starting from and returning to the clubhouse. It consumes the greatest amount of land but offers the greatest amount of fairway frontage for development sites.

◆ **Single fairway, returning nines.** This configuration consists of two loops of returning nines, with the clubhouse in the centre. Playing flexibility and the number of rounds that can be played each day are maximized because of the returning nines, as is the real estate frontage.

◆ **Double fairway, continuous.** This layout consists of a continuous single loop of adjacent, parallel fairways. It offers less frontage for development than a single-fairway course, but is well suited for long narrow sites.

◆ **Double fairway, returning nines.** This configuration is characterized by two circuits of nine holes each, which both start and finish at the clubhouse, and both have adjacent parallel fairways.

The preferred option in most real estate developments is the single fairway returning nines configuration. This yields almost the maximum frontage for real estate, but offers greater flexibility and efficiency in operation over the single fairway continuous configuration by providing two starting holes. The downside is that maintenance costs are higher and the quality of play for the golfer may be lessened. Double fairways save on maintenance costs while providing golfers with a better golf experience – at the cost of frontage development. The Revelstoke Master Plan shown on page 90 has six different areas earmarked for real estate development.

Planning courses for golf tourism

Priestley and Ashworth (1995) have suggested that there are four types of courses suitable for golf tourism: famous championship or 'Trophy' courses; single integrated resorts; courses associated with property developments; and networks of courses forming golf regions. These are discussed below, although it is important to recognize that golf tourists do not restrict themselves to these four types. For example, tourism officials in Hawaii have noticed a trend towards visitors wishing to play on public courses – probably due to accessibility and price.

Trophy courses

Once a golf course has held a championship of note (one of the four 'majors' or at least an international tournament) then it often becomes attractive for golf tourists who represent modern day trophy hunters wishing to play golf in the footsteps of their heroes. Carnoustie Golf Course for example, the scene of the 1999 British Open, has seen a large increase in American golfers keen to tame the course that Tiger Woods found so difficult. Wealthy Japanese and American golfers, in particular, are well known for taking international trips to fulfil their ambitions and play on the world's most famous courses (Readman, 2003). St Andrews and other Open venues in Scotland, England and Ireland are particular favourites. In some cases the trophy to be gained may be a collection of courses

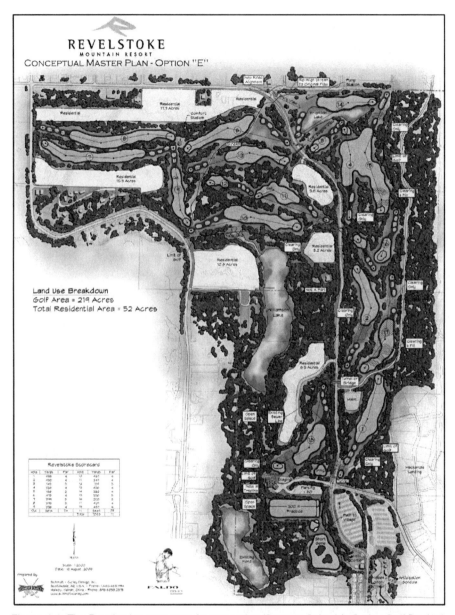

Figure 4.1: The Revelstoke conceptual master plan (Source: Schmidt-Curley Golf Design)

designed by famous designers such as Robert Trent Jones, Dan Maples or, more recently, Jack Nicklaus. Courses holding championship tournaments not only have the effect of ensuring their long-term popularity among golf tourists, but may also serve the purpose of attracting golfers to their regions. In this instance a round of golf on a championship course will form the highlight of a longer tour of the other courses in the area. There can be no doubt that the success of an event can put a destination on the map and raise its status to one of golf trophy in the eyes of the golf tourist. Courses such as Montecastillo (Spain) and

Sun City (South Africa) illustrate this. In an attempt to attract the golf tourist in recent years a whole host of 'championship' courses have sprung up. However, this can sometimes be a mistake as a newly developed course may be too long or difficult to provide a pleasant experience for the average golfer. In the long run this may discourage tourists and local members from playing a course, especially if it fails to attract a well-known event (Readman, 2003).

Single integrated resorts

Priestley and Ashworth (1995, p. 209) define golf resorts as 'self-contained leisure complexes, which include (as minimum requirements) accommodation facilities and one golf course, to which other golf courses and facilities may be added.' These resorts are normally associated with exclusive development and have been called 'islands within islands' (Sulaiman, 1996). Such resorts have been developed in the USA (especially Florida and California), Australia, the Caribbean and other nations and regions wishing to diversify their tourism product. In addition the recent development of golf in Asia has often followed this model with large-scale golf developments being created in Malaysia, Indonesia and Thailand. Examples of these 'megadevelopments' (Cartier, 1998) include the Golden Valley Golf Resort in Air Panas (Malaysia) which was developed as three 18-hole courses on 400 acres of land in 1992 but ended up as 27 holes of golf. This type of destination typically attracts affluent golf visitors who stay on site within the resort rarely venturing out or spending money beyond the walls of these estates, preferring instead to buy inclusive packages of activities from within the confines of the resort. In Japan, memberships of these new resorts in surrounding countries are traded like items in a stock exchange and given as rewards in business incentive schemes.

In North Africa, a number of golf resorts have been developed in tourist areas along the coastline. The courses are often high quality, designed by renowned golf course architects as part of master-planned resorts and golfing communities. Golf tourism is more developed in Morocco because of its proximity to key target markets such as the UK. With Morocco just three hours' flight from London, the British are particularly targeted as customers. Cheaper green fees, high quality food, suitable weather all year, topnotch courses, unspoilt scenery and friendly people are all touted as selling factors in comparison with Portugal and Spain, Britain's most popular golfing destinations. Dependent highly on tourism, there were around 43 courses across North Africa by 2008, mainly concentrated in Morocco. Revenues at most of these courses are generated largely from green fees from tourists (89%) rather than from memberships.

Golf courses associated with property developments

The incorporation of golf courses into real estate development was pioneered in the 1890s at Lake Wales in Florida and at Pinehurst in North Carolina (Boswell and Crompton, 2007). However, the contemporary evolution of golf course real estate development started in the 1950s, with the Hilton Head development in South Carolina. Since then, developers and real estate brokers have included golf facilities as vehicles for adding value to large real estate and resort developments. Such developments can provide benefits to local communities by improving the recreational infrastructure, increasing land values, adding or expanding specific economic activity (e.g. tourism) and job opportunities (Warnken *et al.*, 2001). In the 1980s and 1990s, approximately 35 per cent and 46 per cent, respectively, of new courses were associated with a real estate development (Nicholls and Crompton, 2005).

Boswell and Crompton (2007) studied particular golf course development in the USA whereby the city partnered with commercial firms to develop jointly a golf course community. The city received 44 per cent of the revenues from the sales in the development, and these funds, along with revenues from property taxes, were used to retire the debt charges in creating the golf course and the development's infrastructure. The researchers suggested that the venture was both financially successful and effective in enhancing the image of a declining city. However, there are economic risks associated with golf development. In the financial meltdown of 2008, the golf industry had its victims. Scottsdale-based golf real estate magnate, Lyle Anderson was one. Anderson's directors at Superstition Mountain, Las Campanas and two other properties had to be replaced with creditor-appointed directors. Meanwhile, the Utah golf property group, Promontory agreed to enter Chapter 11. Publicly traded WCI (which developed Old Palm Golf Club in Florida) also went bankrupt, as did the developer of Lake Las Vegas, where turnaround specialists the Atalon Group are now in charge of the project's residential component.

Developers often have no interest in operating a golf course because it is a distraction to their core business of creating subdivisions and selling lots (Nicholls and Crompton, 2005). In the 1990s residential developers automatically designed homes around golf courses believing that the golf would help sell their properties and the course itself would make a healthy profit. However, few clubs make a major contribution to the bottom line, and an increasing number of developers find they are required to continue to accept responsibility for operating and subsidizing courses because no other entity will accept them (Sargent, 2003). Some developments may include a golf membership to entice buyers. The Coronado Golf Resort in Panama for example, that surrounds four Tom Fazio-designed golf courses, is offering new owners free membership to the equestrian, social, golf and beach clubs.

One could assume that a substantial proportion of property buyers in golf developments play golf, but research suggests that only 25–30 per cent of people living in golf communities play golf regularly (Nicholls and Crompton, 2005). Non-playing residents appear to be attracted by the presence and views of the golf course, the natural environment and open space, and the community atmosphere. Other prominent features in the decision to live in golf communities are prestige, status, image and exclusivity. For those not wishing to purchase real estate on a golf course, but who would like to spend a long vacation on a private course, there is an increasing array of membership options. The Concession Golf Club in Florida, for example, has a $60,000 non-equity, fully refundable Golf

Cottage Membership that allows golfers to stay in a cottage for 28 days. Golfers then pay just one month of dues.

Networks of courses forming golf regions

Chapter 3 discussed the emergence of golf trails or golf safaris, whereby golf courses in the same area are pooling their resources to promote their region as a golfing destination. The Snapshot in that chapter profiled the Ho Chi Minh Golf Trail in Vietnam, a co-operation between seven golf courses. These networks are often destinations that develop separately at first, but then cooperate in joint marketing campaigns. This has the effect of persuading the golf tourist to buy a package that may include a combination of accommodation and golf courses in one area all in one go. This results in an extension of the tourist stay and a spreading of the resultant economic benefit throughout the region. A good example of this type of development exists in Alabama where a group of courses all built by the same designer, Robert Trent Jones, are marketed together as the Robert Trent Jones Trail. Elsewhere, the Costa del Sol (Spain) is now marketed as the Costa del Golf and in Myrtle Beach, South Carolina, the South Carolina Tourist Board will tailor packages of the area's many golf courses to the needs of the visitor.

Design considerations and principles

Mill (2008) has suggested there are a number of design considerations in the planning and development of golf courses. These include the size and shape of the property, topography, soil and vegetation characteristics, land costs, water supply, climate, maintenance, and the target market.

Size and shape of the property

Many developers underestimate the amount of land needed for a golf course. While 120 to 130 acres might be sufficient for a regulation 18-hole course on a flat site with few facilities, the same course on more difficult terrain might need upwards of 150 acres. If there are plans for real estate development, the required acreage could be much higher. The Trump National Golf Club in Los Angeles, featured in Chapter 5, is set on 300 acres in order to accommodate the golf course and 75 estate homes. Approximately 215 acres are dedicated to the golf course and 85 reserved for residential development. In the Revelstoke development in Canada (see the case study) the golf course area in the master plan is 219 acres, and the planned residential area is 52 acres. Irregularly shaped pieces of land make for potentially more interesting and safer golf courses compared to square or rectangular sites. Long or narrow sites tend to restrict the options of the developer, and a north–south orientation is usually preferred, to avoid golfers facing the morning or afternoon sun, making play more difficult.

Topography

The topography of the site has the greatest impact on the quality of the golf experience (Mill, 2008), and varied terrain with lakes and ponds, for example, increases the selling price of real estate lots. The Faldo-designed Legacy Course at Roco Ki in the Dominican Republic moves through several different environments with diverse native flora and mangrove trees. Every hole at the Trump National is designed to be pleasing to the eye, and representative of Trump's free-flowing creative style are water features that are scene-stealers, even when up against the backdrop of the Pacific. The ideal site should have both sloping and flat areas, with tees, greens and fairways adapted to the contours of the land. The best holes will drop in elevation from tee to landing area and landing area to green (Phillips, 1986). Because the golfer can easily see the hole, play is faster and more enjoyable. Steep slopes can be graded, but at considerable cost.

A signature hole is also desirable as it can attract potential golf tourists. A floating island green, such as the 14th hole at Coeur d'Alene resort in Northern Idaho, is always an attraction. Golfers take a water taxi ride to the putting surface and receive a certification of achievement for hitting the green with their first tee shot. Pebble Beach golf course in California – host to several prestigious US Opens – has as its signature hole the famous seventh, which is considered by experts to be one of the most challenging and beautiful par 3s in existence.

It plays downhill to a green squeezed onto a tiny spit of land, a green which at its narrowest point is only eight steps wide. But perhaps the most interesting signature hole of recent times is the unique 19th hole at Legend Golf and Safari Resort in South Africa, referred to in Chapter 2. The Extreme 19th is the longest, most dramatic par 3 in the world, set high up on the Hanglip Mountain with the tee reached only by helicopter. Measuring 400 metres, it is played from a vertical height of also 400 metres after a short flight up to the escarpment. The picture right shows Spanish golfer Sergio Garcia at the top of this remarkable golf hole.

Sergio Garcia on Legend Golf and Safari Resort Signature 19th Hole, courtesy of Legend Golf and Safari Resort

Soil and vegetation characteristics

Soil fertility depends to a large extent on the previous use of the land, but several types of land that cannot be used for other development can make excellent golf courses, although construction costs may be high. Examples include wetlands, floodplains, drainage channels and dry streambeds (Phillips, 1986). It is said that a site can never have too much topsoil (Mills, 2008). Topsoil is crucial to the healthy growth of turf grass. In coastal areas, alluvial soil allows for low-cost development. But designing golf courses by the sea brings its own challenges and requires some smart engineering. Before Donald Trump purchased Trump National Golf Club it was called the Ocean Trails Golf Club, and in 1999 – just days before its opening – the heart of the 18th hole toppled into the sea. The neighbouring 9th and 12th holes also fell victims to the natural disaster, and the course opened as a 15-holer and stayed that way for five years. Its original owners spent $20 million and went bankrupt trying to save it (Lewis, 2004). Rebuilding the 18th hole cost Donald Trump $61 million. 'If I'm ever in California for an earthquake,' he said, 'this is where I want to be standing' (Lewis, 2004).

Next to slope, vegetation is the most important influence on the overall character of a golf course. Wooded areas, such as the site for the Revelstoke development, enhance the visual and ecological appeal of a course by separating fairways. At the same time, they provide opportunities for compatible recreational uses such as hiking, mountain-biking, and cross-country skiing in the winter months. Obviously, for heavily-wooded sites the cost of clearing and landscaping will be higher, so this is an important consideration in planning a golf course. Natural hazards can reduce construction costs as fewer artificial hazards need to be constructed. Hazards such as streams, ravines, ponds, and rolling terrain make a course more interesting aesthetically and more challenging from a golfing perspective.

Land costs

The cost of building a top-rated golf course runs between $200,000 and $400,000 per hole (Mill, 2008). This includes the money spent on clearing, grading, drainage, the irrigation system, seeding and grassing as well as the construction of tees, fairways, greens, sand bunkers, and cart paths. However, Brian Curley from Schmidt-Curley Design (see the case study) estimates that turning the side of a mountain or a dead flat desert into a golf course could cost up to $50 million. Donald Trump spent $261 million in redesigning the Trump National Golf Club in Los Angeles, featured in Chapter 5. The average construction cost for a typical 18-hole golf course in Europe and the Middle East in 2005 was $4.54 million (about $250,000 per hole), but costs do vary widely, with Eastern Europe recording an average cost of $1.6 million, whereas in the Middle East the average cost is $7.8 million (KPMG, 2005).

Water supply

According to Schwanke et al. (1977), an average 18-hole golf course needs between 1.5 and 3.5 million gallons of water per week, depending on the type of turf, the irrigation system, and the climate. Courses in Las Vegas for example, require considerably more water than courses in Scotland although many Vegas courses are giving the desert the chance to fight back in an ingenious turf reduction project initiated by Southern Nevada Water Authority (see Chapter 9). Water quality is also a concern – the concentration of soluble salts should be less than 2000 parts per million for grass to grow well (Mill, 2008). Water hazards, streams and rivers can be tapped as sources of water, and more and more courses are using treated wastewater for irrigation purposes. Irrigation systems for golf courses have become increasingly complex since being introduced in the late 1800s. In desert areas like Las Vegas, the system has to cover the entire course, whereas in other parts of the world, a single-row or double-row fairway system is sufficient.

Systems can be either automatic or manual. The former is more expensive to install but less costly to operate than the latter. In many parts of the world – in Indonesia, for example – computerized irrigation systems have allowed golf superintendents to be much more efficient as far as maintenance is concerned (Chen, 2004). An example of a typical single-row system is in place at Grey Wolf Golf Course in Panorama Mountain Village, Canada, featured in Chapter 5. The design is typical of courses built in the last 15 years and is still the practice of choice in this part of the world,' said Chad Thomlinson, Head Professional. 'There are a couple of manual systems still in place in this area but they are inefficient by using too much labour and not being able to control the amount and location of irrigation with great precision.' Describing his irrigation system, he says: 'there are several 6 inch main lines that leave the main pump station and feed the course. Each hole then typically has three secondary lines that feed off the mainline, one for the green area, one for the teeing area and one for the fairway. From this secondary line a 2 inch pipe loops around the area (tee, green or fairway) and feeds individual irrigation heads. There is a wire that travels alongside each 2 inch loop pipe from the satellite to each individual head. The satellites are connected electronically (underground wire) to a master control box in our offices. This allows us to programme which heads come on at what time and for how long. Some newer systems have wireless heads to avoid the cost of putting expensive copper wire underground.' According to Thomlinson, a typical system costs about $1000 per head for all parts and installation so for a full length 18-hole course it will be close to a million dollars.

Climate

Climate has an impact on construction, the length of playable season and on the costs of maintenance. In Scandinavia, for example, weather delays hinder most golf course developments. Courses in moderate climates, like in Palm Springs or the Mediterranean, accommodate more rounds of golf per year while incurring relatively high maintenance costs year-round. Northern courses have lower maintenance costs during the cold season, but have the disadvantage of a shorter golf season. Golf courses in Canada, for example, are often closed for four to five months over the winter.

One of the reasons that Florida has more golf courses than any other US state is because of its warm climate that allows golf play throughout the year. Golf is a primary activity for many of the millions of tourists who visit the state each year from more northern states during the winter months, as well as international visitors from Europe and Latin America. But in recent years, Florida has been victim to the threat of hurricanes. Hurricane Dennis, for example, caused about $1 billion in damage in 2005, including damage to a number of golf courses, which are always in danger from flooding and felled trees. With Hurricane Dennis, it was the anticipation that may have caused the greatest damage to golf tourism. Many Florida and Gulf Coast courses shut down to prepare for the onslaught, losing green fees revenue. In Gulf Shores, tens of thousands of visitors left at the height of the summer tourist season.

Maintenance

Maintenance tends to be the largest single cost item for a golf course. A study of Florida golf courses, for instance, found that the most significant expense was maintenance, representing 29 per cent of total expenditures or $7139 per acre of turf area (Hodges and Haydu, 2004). Maintenance costs will depend on a wide variety of factors, including the course's location, length of season, type, market, size, and purpose. One could spend a near unlimited amount on a regulation course every year. The challenge for the developer is to determine the point of diminishing returns and to structure a maintenance programme that makes appropriate trade-offs and adjustments. If a course is intended to help sell real estate, then the course will likely contain items that are costly to maintain such as extensive water features. The three elaborate on-course water features on the Trump National golf course in Los Angeles cost $5 million. For the waterfall on the 18th hole, 7000 gallons of water are pumped through the system each minute. The starting price for a residence on the course is $5.2 million, so perhaps these costs are justified. Another major factor in maintenance costs is the type of grass selected. In northern latitudes, it is generally accepted that bent grass provides the best playing surface (Mills, 2008). This type of grass is less practical in the south because of summer heat stress.

Target market

According to Schwanke et al. (1977), four important market-related items must be considered in designing a golf course: the relationship between the golf course and real estate; ability levels and diversity of players; overall level of demand for the course; and frequency of play by the same group of users. Some golf courses are designed for one particular market. Around Lake Garda in Italy, golf courses are being designed or re-designed specifically for the US golfer. Palazzo Arzaga, for example, is a five-star hotel, spa and golf resort, whose first 18 is a typical Nicklaus design – challenging, but with wide fairways, large greenside bunkers, five artificial lakes, five tee positions and numerous pin placements. For all his designs, Jack Nicklaus finds out who is going to play the course most often (resort visitors, members, tour pros) and takes care to include golf's largest demographic – the lesser player who may never break 100 but loves the game just the same (Williams, 2006). For the Revelstoke development, featured at the end of this chapter, the emphasis for planning the course is more on aesthetics rather than difficulty, in order to attract less serious golfers. 'We want it to involve a pleasant walk with different degrees of difficulty so the golf can be fun for the whole family,' said Nick Faldo. At the Legend Golf and Safari Resort in South Africa, featured in Chapter 2, each hole features five different tees to allow for both professionals and amateurs. Similarly, the Dragon's Fire Golf Club in

Ontario, Canada, referred to in Chapter 2, has five massive tee decks that allow the course to stretch from about 5200 yards to nearly 7300, in order to attract golfers that want a fun, playable course.

Other golf resorts target every type of golfer by providing a variety of courses. The Lodge & Spa at Cordillera in Colorado, for example, promotes 'a quartet of courses for golfers seeking a variety of challenges'. These include a tough Nicklaus Signature Summit Course, with uneven lies and fast, undulating greens, and a Dave Peltz Design Short Course where every hole is shorter than 130 yards. However, some say that serving diverse markets can be problematic. 'The hardest thing to do these days is to operate a big, full-service club that brings in business,' says Bradley Klein, architect editor for *Golfweek* magazine (Olmsted, 2008). Citing high labour and food costs, he explains that serving diverse crowds is extremely difficult. Consequently, there has been a trend away from the large 'golf-factory' convention-based resort, and toward boutique, luxury micro-resorts. Typically, they have just one or two courses, a small lodge and cottages or other limited but lavish lodging. Examples are the Lodge at Torrey Pines, Auberge at May River Club at Palmetto Bluff, and the Lodge at Sea Pines.

Development problems and costs

A golf course development project takes on average four years, and construction time is about 22 months (KPMG, 2005). During development, a number of difficulties are likely to arise (see Figure 4.2). A KPMG (2005) survey of golf courses in the EMA region (Europe and the Middle East) found that obtaining the necessary permits was the most frequently cited problem, particularly for Eastern European countries. More than a third of owners and operators mentioned dealing with weather delays as a key obstacle, while a quarter encountered environmental opposition. Another quarter mentioned financing as the most problematic issue. One in four new golf course developments had problems with water availability. Other construction issues – earthwork, keeping in line with the original budget and the unprofessionalism of contractors – were viewed as less significant problems.

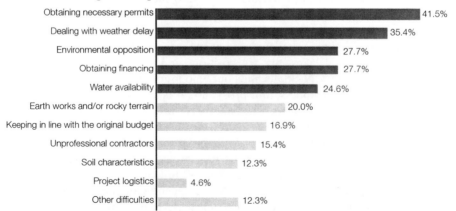

Figure 4.3 illustrates the average breakdown of development costs throughout an entire development project. Actual construction costs typically account for 89 per cent of the total costs (excluding land acquisition, clubhouse, parking space and other on-site facilities). The pre-construction costs include the golf course architect fee. Architects are usually selected through informal channels such as referrals and word of mouth. They are often chosen based on credentials, brand recognition and reputation, but price and quality also play an important role in selection (KPMG, 2005).

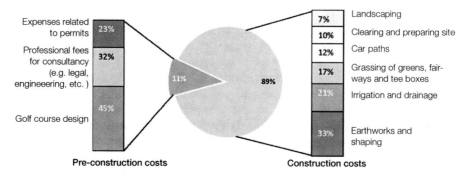

Figure 4.3: Share of development costs in pre-construction and construction phases (Source: KPMG, 2005, p. 20)

Whatever the process used in planning golf developments, it is quite possible that the original plan will require some modification and later stages may be quite different from the original vision. The plans for the Faldo-designed Legacy Course at Roco Ki in the Dominican Republic for example, changed considerably during construction. 'We discovered that one part of the property was swampland so we changed the routing and worked our way toward the headland rather than the beach. We had to raise the fairways two metres and construct a seawall on number 18, which was no small feat,' said Faldo (Faldo, 2008). The 18th at the Ocean Trails Golf Club (now Trump National Golf Club) in Los Angeles suffered a worse fate as was mentioned previously – it toppled into the sea!

Bobby Weed, from Bobby Weed Golf Design in Florida, has ten words that define his philosophy and methodology when designing golf courses: 'This plan is conceptual and subject to change by Designer' (Silverman, 2008: 80). Weed's designs include the Lagoon and Ocean courses at Ponte Vedra Inn & Club, the Golf Course at Glenn Mills, Pennsylvania, The Olde Farm, Virginia, and Slammer and Squire, Florida. 'Everybody thinks this is all thought out in advance,' he says. 'Not for me. This is an art, not a science. We draw with our tractors.'

For golf resorts, sound financial planning is crucial, and there are a number of ways resorts can be financed. One relatively new concept is that of shared ownership. One property company developing resorts in Canada – Stone Creek Properties Inc – is financing two developments in this manner. With two golf courses, one called Silvertip in Canmore and the other Eagle Ranch in Invermere, the company is planning to build hundreds of multi-million dollar homes near the golf courses to be offered on a shared-ownership basis, allowing buyers to pay for just the time they use. As club members, homeowners will pay a one-time fee plus annual dues, choosing from 30-, 45-, or 60-day membership plans ranging from $300,000 to $500,000. 'I truly believe this is the way to finance the future,' said Guy Turcotte, president and CEO of Stone Creek (Hope, 2009). Turcotte says industry research shows people only use their second homes about 17 days a year and to spend millions for that short period of time just doesn't compute. He can see as many as six members sharing the ownership of a home. Among the amenities being offered to members are a concierge service for everything from tee times to dinner reservations, housekeeping and grocery shopping.

Another popular financing scheme for golf developments with real estate is the timeshare concept. Timeshare is a system whereby a guest purchases an accommodation unit for a set period (usually in weekly increments) each year in a resort. The principal characteristic of timeshares is that owners can exchange their properties in order to travel and see other places. This fits well with golf tourists as many golfers do not want to restrict themselves to one golfing destination, and usually timeshares are more affordable than second homes or regular hotel accommodation. For a resort, it is an attractive way to boost cash flow, especially in the development phase, and since a regular flow of timeshare guests can be expected, it will likely increase spending in other areas of the resort business (Murphy, 2008). A number of golf resorts in the USA operate on a timeshare basis. Examples are the Sunterra Resort Royal Dunes in South Carolina, Grand Villas at St Augustine in Florida, and Orange Tree Golf Resort in Arizona. But golfing timeshares are also expanding around the world. The Island Resort and Golf Club in the Bahamas, for example, is popular with golfers from the USA, and Vilar Do Golf Resort in Quinta Do Lago in Portugal attracts golfers from all over the world to play on its four golf courses.

Case Study: Faldo Brands Rockies' Golf Course

Brian Curley and Lee Schmidt have been a golf course design team since their first company, Landmark Golf, was established in California in 1997. Now sporting two offices in Scottsdale and China, their more recent venture, Schmidt-Curley Design was involved in each of the 12 courses at Mission Hills, the world's biggest golf development. Named as number two golf designers (after Robert Trent Sr.) by *Asian Golf Monthly* in 2007, Curley attributes part of their success to their partnerships with PGA Tour pros such as Nick Faldo, Fred Couples, Ernie Els, Annika Sorenstam, Vijay Singh and José Maria Olazabal. In fact on the Mission Hills project, the team worked with 12 of the world's top players.

Most of Schmidt-Curley's work these days is in Asia's growing market: 'The US is so much tied to housing and housing markets come and go. We saw Asia as a new frontier with boundless opportunities on an annual basis,' said Curley. He has found that the economic recession hasn't hit Asia in the same way as the USA and Europe where golf design is not in such demand right now. Another draw in Asia is that developers are cash-rich and do not have to rely on borrowing as local governments often throw in the land as part of the deal.

Author (right) interviewing Sir Nick Faldo at Revelstoke, Canada, photo by Louise Hudson

Despite 90 per cent of their work being outside North America, the twosome began designing and planning a new course in British Columbia, Canada, in conjunction with Nick Faldo. In August 2008, plans for the new course were unveiled to the media with Faldo granting a press conference, mingling with investors, posing for photos driving golf balls off the highest mountain summit, and giving a golf clinic. But the procedure from launch announcements to opening day is very long-term. 'As of right now there's no plan to get started on construction any time soon at Revelstoke – we've got a long ways through with the planning process and plan production and they have to decide when to pull the trigger,' Curley commented in early 2009, adding that no set dates had been missed. A prospective opening date of Spring 2011 was mooted at the press conference.

Faldo has been involved in golf course design on more than 40 different projects over six continents since giving up professional playing. He is also a PGA Tour analyst for CBS and the Golf Channel as well as captaining the 2008 European Ryder Cup Team: 'I'm at the stage where I have to remind myself how good I was,' he joked. He deemed the beautiful site and location for the Revelstoke course a huge 'wow' factor: 'It's an absolutely fantastic project and a great opportunity for Faldo Design. With Brian Curley, I have been on projects all round the world but the mountains you witness here make it a very exciting project.' He was particularly impressed with 'the 19 seconds hang time' when driving off the top of the mountain. Regarding his input into the design, planning and construction, he said 'I'm as involved as anyone in this project. This is my new business and I'm on my eighth project with Brian Curley. It is one of my genuine passions and I love to be involved, giving as much as time will permit. We work well together and see things similarly.' He explained that his challenge at Revelstoke was to find the most beautiful holes rather than the most difficult: 'We want it to involve a pleasant walk with different degrees of difficulty so the golf can be fun for the whole family.' In 2008 he was concentrating on positioning the clubhouse for maximum scenic potential but planned to visit the site at various stages of construction, at the rough shaping and the final shaping, and eventually for the opening ceremony.

Exploiting a celebrity brand for a golfing development can obviously boost overheads but Curley maintains it is well worth the expenditure. 'It may cost extra to get Nick Faldo involved but if the amount is spread over 500 homes then it doesn't add that much. It helps with the absorption rates and his name helps sell 50 houses rather than 12,' he said. Curley was initially impressed with Faldo's commitment to golf course design during their first partnership in China: 'He was getting into the design process and writing little notes every time he played, training himself in the design process. He was much more involved than some of the guys in the business; he just got the boots on and went out walking there.'

Working with golf pros can cause logistical challenges due to hectic international schedules. Curley maintains his role is to make the most of their time: 'We have to work around their schedules to find the optimum times for good input from them.' It's a question of getting the pros involved at key times in the project - during conception and then during the initial stages of construction. 'It's important to have the pros' reactions on what we're starting to build at a time when you can make big adjustments if necessary, such as before the irrigation goes in,' he explained. It's too late for alterations when 18 holes are in and grass down, but it is also important not to waste the celebrity's time too early in the procedure.

Between planning and completion there are often many adjustments made in golf course construction. Schmidt-Curley make regular site visits in order to ensure any changes can be put in place at the right time. 'We're fine and open to adjustment or changes during the process. We don't want to have to put them in when the course is finished,' Curley explained. 'Much of it is really getting the most out of the design and construction process. We don't want to adhere to plan and dig our heels in – we may even find less work is needed than originally intended or we may need to do a bit more cut or fill than expected. Our plans are the guidelines to get the thing going and everyone from contractors to designers must be able to roll with the punches,' he added.

Every project is different – some courses require extensive plans and work to create an entire environment, others utilize the natural topographical attributes of the area, discovering the course as much as creating it. Environmental specialists are used as intermediaries with local government to facilitate planning permission – Curley's team produces documents to help with the approval process.

With his background in real estate, Curley contributes an entire master plan well beyond the golf course for each project. However, the course is intrinsic to the plan in that if a hole has to be altered, it has a domino effect on the entire project. This is why he recommends bringing in golf course architects right from the start: 'We need to be involved in the upfront planning process as early as we can because we know that if a plan goes too far along without golf architect input there can be drastic problems. Say a land planner with zero golf experience did the land plan without a golf architect – which happens all the time because of high fees – then got it approved. If he then brought in a golf architect later, things that have already been approved can't be changed.'

Costs vary from project to project but Curley estimates that turning the side of a mountain or a dead flat desert into a golf course could cost up to $50 million. Key to success, however, is building the right course for the actual demand: 'Golf courses get attention for being photogenic but if you really look at it, a lot of courses with all the accolades are in fact big business losers. They are too expensive to play and to maintain, or get no repeat business. You have to go beyond the design itself and look at the big picture of what you're planning to accomplish.' He cites Las Vegas golf as a case in point, where water and operating costs are so expensive that green fees have to be disproportionately high too.

Schmidt-Curley has added a third office in Kunming, gambling on China as a growth market even though there was a moratorium on building golf courses in 2009. 'There is still good demand for the game and for the golf community lifestyle. In China everyone spends their life living on top of people, so when you have the wherewithal to move to a golf community, it is a huge feather in your cap,' Curley explained. He sees demand coming from the growing middle class: 'As a percentage of the population, the middle class might sound small, but 1.4 billion people is still a big number.'

Sources

Phone interview with Brian Curley, 25 February 2009.

Personal interview with Nick Faldo, August 2008

References

Boswell, W.J., and Crompton, J.L. (2007) 'A city's strategy to fund a golf course by developing homes on proximate property', *Journal of Park and Recreation Administration*, **25** (1), 115–127.

Chen, T. (2004) 'A study of golf courses management: the in-depth interview approach', *Journal of American Academy of Business*, September, 138–143.

Contreras, J. (2008) 'Putter up: new latin links', *Newsweek*, 2 June, **151** (22).

Faldo, N. (2008) 'Behind a Design', *Travel + Leisure Golf*, November/December, p. 70.

Grudnitski, G. (1 April, 2003) 'Golf course communities: the effect of course type on housing prices', *Appraisal Journal*, 145-149.

Hodges, A.W. and Haydu, J.J. (2004) 'Golf, tourism and amenity-based development in Florida', *Journal of American Academy of Business*, 4 (1/2), 481.

Hope, M. (2009) 'Picture perfect', *Calgary Herald*, 28 March, J1-2.

Inskeep, E. (1991) *Tourism Planning: An Integrated and Sustainable Development Approach*, New York: Van Nostrand.

KPMG (2005) From North Cape to Cape Town: KPMG Golf Course Development Cost Survey in the EMA Region.

Lewis, C. (2004) 'Trump goes public in Los Angeles', accessed March 2009 from http://www.golf.com/golf/courses.

Mill, R.C. (2008) *Resorts: Management and Operation*, 2nd edn, Hoboken, NJ: John Wiley & Son.

Murphy, P. (2008) *The Business of Resort Management*, Oxford: Butterworth-Heinemann.

Nicholls, S., and Crompton, J.L. (2005) 'Why do people choose to live in golf course developments?' *Journal of Park and Recreation Administration*, 23 (1), 37-52.

Olmsted, L. (2008) 'North America's top golf resorts', accessed on 15 December 2009 from http://www.forbestraveler.com.

Phillips, P.L. (1986) *Developing with Recreational Amenities: Golf, Tennis, Skiing, Marinas*, Washington, DC: Urban Land Institute.

Priestley, G.K. (2006) 'Planning implications of golf tourism', *Tourism and Hospitality Research*, 6 (3): 170–178.

Priestley, G.K., and Ashworth, G.J. (1995) 'Sports Tourism: the Case of Golf', *Tourism and Spatial Transformations*, Wallingford: CAB International.

Readman, M. (2003) 'Golf tourism', in S. Hudson, ed. *Sport & Adventure Tourism*, Oxford: Haworth, pp. 265–201.

Sargent, P. (June, 2003) 'Tee time', *Leisure Management*, 36–37.

Schwanke, D., *et al.* (1977) *Resort Development Handbook*, Washington, DC: Urban Land Institute.

Silverman, J. (2008) 'Complex affairs', *Travel + Leisure Golf*, November/December, 80.

Sulaiman, M.S. (1996) 'Islands within islands: exclusive tourism and sustainable utilisation of coastal resources in Zanzibar', in Bruguglio L., Butler R., Harrison D., and Filho W.L., *Sustainable Tourism in Islands and Small States Case Studies*, London: Cassell.

Walter, B. (2009) 'Golf Courses', accessed from http://golftrainingaidandteachingtool.com/Golf_Courses_01.shtml 5 March 2009

Warnken, J., Thompson, D. and Zakus, D.W. (2001) 'Golf course development in a major tourist destination: implications for planning and management', *Environmental Management*, Vol. 27, No. 5, pp. 681-696.

Williams, V. (2006) 'Miles to go', *Fairways + Greens*, Winter, 9 (6), 34-41.

5 The Management of Golf Tourism

Clubhouse at Trump National Los Angeles, photograph by author

Located on the Palos Verdes peninsula south of downtown Los Angeles is the Trump National Golf Club. Donald Trump paid $27 million for the property in 2002 and then invested $261 million in redesigning the course. 'This is the most expensive golf course ever built,' he proclaimed. Apart from the wonderful golf course, the club has a 45,000 square foot clubhouse, a pro-shop, two dining options, conference rooms, and a ballroom. A public park sits between the front and back nines providing access to hiking trails. Because it is on the coast, the course is not permitted to go private, so Trump National is the public version of his private clubs elsewhere.

David Conforti is General Manager and Director of Golf at the club. With experience working for Troon Golf and the PGA, Conforti is clearly a highly competent hands-on manager, and speaks openly about the club and its visitors. 'I would say about 30-40 per cent of our visitors are tourists – mainly from other parts of the US, Asia, and Latin America,' he said. 'Corporate golf has been very strong in the past – up to 50 per cent of our business - but 2009 has been slow. Most of our visitors seem to find us through the Internet, but our accolades help.' Trump National has been rated #1 golf course in California by every major western golf publication, ranked #38 in the US by *Golf Magazine*, and recognized as having a 'Top 100 Golf Shop in America' by *Golf World Magazine*.

Trump National also attracts a number of celebrities, which maintains its high profile. Tiger Woods and Phil Mickelson are regular visitors, as is soccer star, David Beckham and American football player, Tom Brady. Actor Mark Wahlberg also plays on a regular basis. 'They just want to come here to escape and they are all such nice people,' said Conforti. The club is featured on television programmes and in commercials quite frequently. 'The PGA America was here last week (April 2009) filming a commercial, and the latest Michael Jordan commercials for Hanes with Charlie Sheen were shot here,' said Conforti. 'H.B.O.'s Entourage was here last year, and the Golf Channel has been here to film a Big Break instalment. We have also had a number of films made here including Step Brothers with Will Ferrell. We will usually charge a site fee for filming, although for the recent Tee it up with Tiger Woods series, filmed over a two week period here for the Golf Channel, we waived the fees as the exposure it gives us is priceless.'

In terms of operations, golf carts are compulsory on the course and the club has chosen electric over gas. 'We are always concerned about the environment here,' Conforti explained. 'But electric carts are also less noisy. I actually think golf carts are the arteries of a golf club operation. Right now we are considering acquiring a new fleet with a new GPS system that we will lease for four years.' The club does all the servicing itself as it has found it too expensive in the past to outsource. 'We have six maintenance staff on site to take care of any problems with the carts,' he added. Cart presentation is also very important to Conforti: 'Our customers notice if the cart is not clean so we spend 15–20 minutes on each cart every night to ensure it is spotless for the next day's golfers.'

It is not just the golf carts where special attention is paid. From the moment guests arrive, the club's mission is to provide a world class experience. 'We take customer service very seriously,' said Conforti. 'Department heads are usually responsible for training but we also bring in an H.R. advisor to provide customer service training.' The club has 280 staff – about 100 full-time and 180 part-time. Aside from management, there are approximately 35 in maintenance, 30 outside, 10 golf professionals, 30 kitchen staff, 12 club house managers, 30 banquet staff and 50 servers or bussers. Managers will meet once a week to discuss weekly events and activities.

According to Conforti, banquets and events are vital to the business. 'We have about 25 large banquets and 100 weddings per year. Saturday weddings are sold out from March to November. Most people find us through the Internet and once we get them here and show them around, 80–90 per cent of them will sign up on the spot.' The club will customize anything from menus to cakes in order to provide a unique experience for guests. The ballroom has seating for 300, and is adorned with a stately, hand-carved fireplace, impressive French doors to the covered balcony, and elaborate crystal chandeliers. The club also hosts a number of events, such as celebrity poker charity events, monthly jazz expression sessions, an annual car show and wine and beer festivals. 'All these events are a great way to keep the community involved,' said Conforti.

The club has two dining options. The Golfer's Lounge is the more casual of the two restaurants, and Cafe Pacific is more upscale, with gold leaf-painted ceilings. Both have an excellent wine list and creative menus. 'We take great pride in our catering and the restaurant here has an excellent reputation. From Monday to Friday most of the diners are locals which I think is really important. We are after all a member of the community. The food is a little more expensive than anywhere else, but it is topnotch food.'

Asked why the club's pro shop has received accolades, Conforti pointed to the range of clothing and equipment as well as attention to detail. 'We are very specific about what we want and we keep a tight control on inventory,' he said. Jennifer Martinez is Merchandise Manager for the shop and is responsible for purchasing. 'All of the vendors come to me, so I don't have to go out buying,' she said. 'We sell a lot of Nike (the Tiger Woods range in particular) and Adidas, and the Tehema brand has done well recently. Many people – even those just coming in for Sunday Brunch – love to take away something with the Trump brand on it – the caps for example, sell very well. We don't get many women coming through so most of our merchandise is for men.' To offload excess inventory, Martinez has a sale every January and also has a permanent sale rack.

To play golf, 2009 green fees were $275 Monday to Thursday and $375 Friday to Sunday. Fees include GPS-equipped golf cart, practice balls, valet parking and locker room services. For those wishing to use the immaculate practice facility, the cost is $23 for unlimited use. Locals have the opportunity to purchase a V.I.P. Card for $700 annually and this gives them 25 per cent off weekday prices and 50 per cent off the weekend green fee. Although it is not a private club, Trump National doesn't like to discount on fees or merchandise to generate sales. 'We think discounting would cheapen the Trump brand and would maybe attract a different demographic', said Conforti.

Asked what his key challenges were, Conforti alluded to having to exceed expectations constantly. 'We have two types of visitors. There are those who are pretty wealthy and expect the best, and there are those who have saved up for a long time for a special event and, again, expect the best. So we are constantly looking to exceed the expectations of both groups. Ensuring people receive value for money is especially important today. Fortunately, we have an amazing staff with very low turnover. In fact, if there is turnover it is induced by us. All of our staff wants to work here – they want the Trump name on their resumes and they love the contact with celebrities. The tips here are excellent, and they can also play cheap golf!'

As for the future, Trump National is partnering up with a new golf resort opening four miles down the road. Terranea Golf Resort, a $450 million resort owned by Lowes, opened in the summer of 2009, and has a 9-hole executive golf course. 'But they will be sending up the serious golfer to us to play here. The partnership should work well – we have a good relationship with them as there are lots of synergies. Having high-end accommodations nearby will certainly help attract more golf tourists,' said Conforti.

Sources

Personal interviews with David Conforti and Jennifer Martinez, 15 April 2009.

FG Staff and Contributors, Reno, NV. 'The West's Best: T is for Trump', accessed from http://www.trumpnationallosangeles.com/files/FGMagazine_The_Wests_Best.pdf.

Diaz, C. (August 2006) 'Living Large', Golf Magazine.

Williams, V. (2008) 'National Pleasure', Fairways + Greens, **11** (5), 15–17.

http://www.trumpnationallosangeles.com/

Introduction

The opening Spotlight highlights some of the key management issues involved in running a successful golf operation. Management issues at golf courses were often neglected in the 1970s and 1980s, because for years, the benefits of a golf course to a real estate project far outweighed its costs (Phillips, 1986). If a golf club ran up large losses it was relatively easy for developers to write the losses off to real estate marketing or other departments. But, as both capital and operating costs have risen, course and club management has taken on additional importance. Developers often now turn their attention to management issues as a means to recover the profitability of a golf course operation. This has led to a wide range of organizational arrangements for management as well as new techniques for operations and maintenance practices designed to control costs and increase rounds played. This chapter discusses such management structures, as well as important operational considerations for golf club managers, such as staffing, pro shops, golf cart fleets, maintenance and course management, customer service, and risk management.

Management structure

One typical organizational structure for a real estate/golf course project is for the developer or owner to retain full operational control, such as at Trump National Los Angeles. The course is structured for accounting purposes as a separate profit centre, and operational responsibility will rest with the club manager, a staff of golf professionals responsible for the pro shop and lessons, and a course superintendent. The advantage for the developer is that they can be assured of ongoing control over operations and it reassures other stakeholders of the project's viability. The disadvantage is that developers may not always have access to skilled managers or golf professionals.

Another popular organizational structure is for the developer to contract with a full-service management company (see the Snapshot on Troon Golf on page 109). This may be suitable for less experienced developers or for those clubs that have been transferred to members or resident ownership. Most of the larger management companies operate nationwide, and even internationally. ClubCorp Inc. for example, operates courses in Australia, China and Mexico as well as the USA; American Golf Corporation has courses in New Zealand and the UK; and Troon Golf has courses in 20 other countries outside the USA including Mexico, the UK, Italy, Japan, Fiji, Australia, Kuwait, South America and the Caribbean. This trend is likely to continue as firms look to increase market share and attempt to achieve economies of scale by minimizing average administration and maintenance costs per golf course.

Some of these management companies specialize in order to differentiate themselves. For example, Florida-based Elite Club Associates specializes in high quality private clubs and upscale residential communities; Honours Golf Company in Alabama concentrates on boutique-style golf course development and management; and Virginia-based Billy Casper Golf has a distinct focus on improving the customer experience, innovative marketing and growing the bottom line. The Walters Group, which owns and operates three golf courses in Las Vegas has specialized in theming its courses. Bali Hai, located right on The Strip offers a taste of the South Pacific, with black volcanic rock, white sands and blue lagoons. Royal Links feature 18 replicas of the most famous golf holes played in the British Open rotation of clubs, including the renowned Hell Bunker at St Andrews. And Desert Pines pays homage to Pinehurst with thousands of transplanted pine trees and bales of straw.

An increasing number of courses which are owned and operated by municipalities are looking to management companies to purchase or run their operations. A recent example comes from Palm Coast Florida, where the City Council hired a management company – Chicago-based Kemper Sports – in 2009 to manage the newly-developed Palm Harbor Golf Club. The city took over the course after developer Centex donated it to the city. 'From day one we knew that it is not just building a golf course but managing the golf course,' said City Manager Jim Landon (London, 2009). 'It is extremely critical for the success of the course not just to maintain it, but to manage it and promote it so people will want to come back. It is important to have a management company, someone who knows the business and will make it operate in the black. We don't have anyone on city staff that has that expertise,' he explained. A study by Gustafson and McLean (1999) examined three cities which privatized their golf services. One hired 11 different contractors to operate the 13 city-owned courses, another hired one contractor to run all five of its golf courses, and the third city created a not-for-profit corporation to operate its five golf courses. All three cities were able to reduce maintenance, capital improvements, and administrative costs by delegating the management of golf courses, totally or in part, to the contracted entity.

Of course, the structure of golf resort ownership varies across countries. In China, for example, approximately 94 per cent of courses are run by the owner, with only 6 per cent operated by an external management company (KPMG, 2008). About half of these facilities are private clubs open exclusively for members, while the other half also allow visitors to play on a green fee basis. Close to two-thirds of the clubs have a pro shop and practice facilities, while about half of them provide additional sport, accommodation and recreation facilities. This reflects the high level of service the majority of Chinese golf courses provide.

Snapshot: Troon Golf takes over the management of ailing golf clubs

Troon Golf is a leading international golf development, marketing and management company. Based at Scottsdale, Arizona, the company also has offices in Hong Kong, Australia, Switzerland and Dubai, serving over 200 golf courses in 27 countries and 32 states. Troon's flagship golf course – Troon North Golf Club – was founded by Dana Garmany in 1990. Since then, the 'Troon Golf Experience' has been disseminated internationally with a sole focus on luxury golf properties and developments. The Troon signature includes pristine course conditions, personalized member service, topnotch food and beverage facilities and high-end retail. Troon runs a private club operating division, called Privé (Private Clubs of Distinction), which includes some of the world's top clubs – for example, The Els Club in Dubai, Bearwood Lakes Golf Club in England, Lion Lake in China's Guangdong Province, as well as clubs in Italy, Portugal, South Africa, Puerto Rico, Korea, Australia and numerous venues throughout the USA.

Troon's aim is to offer its umbrella benefits without compromising a club's character. A series of proprietary operating manuals represents the collective knowledge and expertise of the company and serves as a guide for its field professionals. The manuals include a complex set of metrics designed to measure facility performance across a broad spectrum. The company also monitors ongoing goal achievement, establishes new profitability and cost-savings benchmarks and develops improved operating methods to achieve optimum performance at each golf facility.

However, there is no 'à la carte' programme, according to Tim Greenwell, Senior Vice President, Sales & Marketing, Troon Golf. Instead Troon customizes its solutions for management, development and marketing issues for each client. Fees are usually based on a percentage of sales although they are sometimes fixed at the outset with an incentive based on select performance goals. 'Troon Golf maintains a commitment to maximize an owner's return on investment,' Greenwell explained. 'This provides the gateway to establishing positive relationships with owners. The ability to maximize owner profitability year after year is the means to strengthen and continue these relationships.'

Owner involvement and scrutiny in all phases of its operation is encouraged. Troon Golf's corporate office provides operational oversight and expertise, and offers centralized coordination of accounting, payroll, financial reporting and human resources administration, which ultimately leads to substantial cost savings. Sophisticated training programmes are provided for the club's existing staff and Troon carries out ongoing analysis of operating performance. 'Troon Golf is the world's leading golf course management company with a highly skilled human resources department working to recruit the most qualified associates,' commented Greenwell. 'Corporate human resource teams also provide comprehensive training programmes in conjunction with each individual department to train associates working around the globe.'

Management is headed up by a Vice President of Operations who leads a corporate team to support each property. On the field, a golf course General Manager oversees day-to-day operations. Many existing staff members are kept on although Greenwell said some changes are made occasionally in key facility management positions. Staffing is a top priority with Troon which distributes a monthly newsletter for employees – the *Troon Report* – chronicling happenings at all Troon facilities and including staff promotions, accolades and events around the world. Communication with club members is also paramount and they have their own newsletter, *Troon News*, which covers corporate news, headlines and events.

Whilst basic procedures, principles and philosophies are applied throughout, individual initiatives are also encouraged. In his 2009 website address, Dana Garmany (Troon's Chairman and CEO) said the challenges of the economic downturn meant that innovative budgeting and planning would be vital for clubs, encouraging their input for cost-cutting and efficiency tactics at both corporate and field levels. Typical challenges faced by Troon Golf when taking over management of a club include poor course conditions, poor customer service, high food cost, and low course usage levels. 'Troon Golf uses its expertise in the areas of agronomy, operations, associate training, food and beverage, sales and marketing, and design and development to overcome these challenges,' said Greenwell.

Retail management is a company strength with 11 Troon golf shops ranked in America's Top 100 Shops in 2009. High quality rental golf clubs are provided by Callaway Golf and golf carts are included with each paying customer's round. Most courses have GPS technology for measuring distances to each hole. With *Golf Magazine* Top 100 Instructor, Tim Mahoney as Director of Education, Troon specializes in golf instruction. Mahoney oversees multiple golf academy brands for the company including Troon Golf Academies, ESPN Golf Schools, and Golf Digest Golf Schools.

Troon Golf also assists with golf course design, clubhouse architecture and general destination development. 'In the area of construction, where each delay typically results in lost time and added costs, Troon Golf's team of architectural and design experts scrutinizes every detail of every phase of development, enabling them to recognize opportunities for keeping costs to a minimum and staying within approved budgets,' explained Greenwell. 'From the initial design stage through the final sign-off on each component, Troon Golf's involvement includes extensive budget planning and analysis, implementation of cost controls, and frequent reviews of site, clubhouse, maintenance and other building plans. The end result is a golf facility that, from beginning to end, was designed and constructed bearing in mind the owner's ultimate objective.'

Course makeovers are often a high priority when established clubs seek Troon's involvement and the agronomy team strives for high standards with a focus on sustainability. The Troon Golf Environmental Management Initiative (EMI) won the inaugural Golf Inc. Green Award 2008 in the companies and associations category.

The company's first international venture was at The Westin Turnberry Resort in Ayrshire, Scotland, in 1997. Subsequently, Troon expanded worldwide in both traditional and developing golf areas. In 2007 it allied with the Tourism Development and Investment Company (TDIC) as part of the Abu Dhabi Tourism Authority's plan to develop golf tourism in the region. Troon's management team was appointed to facilitate a $5.5 million plan to upgrade the Abu Dhabi Golf Club. Upscaling the hospitality approach was integral to the new strategy. TDIC also owns the Saadiyat North Beach Golf Resort which is the only Gary Player course in the United Arab Emirates and the only ocean course on the Arabian Gulf. In 2009, the company was planning eco-courses in the wetlands of Saadiyat Island, off the coast of Abu Dhabi, which was being transformed into an international leisure, residential and cultural destination. Troon's first venture in Russia was also slated for a 2009 opening. Agalarov Estates is Moscow's first fully-integrated golf community with 260 exclusive residences planned, 18-hole, 7100-yard championship course, 65,000 square feet clubhouse, townhomes, and other recreational facilities.

There are many advantages intrinsic to using a management company. Troon's philosophy is based on maximum profitability and investment return. Its international purchasing programmes enable clubs to purchase high quality equipment and supplies for the golf course, golf shop and food and beverage areas at wholesale rates and with better terms than those available to individual clubs.

Another advantage is the cross-marketing network spanning its 200 courses and clubs. 'Electronic marketing continues to be a key priority for Troon Golf,' said Greenwell. 'Recognizing the advertising-saturated environment in which we live, our goal has been to allow customers to request information on Troon Golf facilities through all available channels: Tee times (EZLinks), online website registrations, Troon Rewards registrations, and the creative efforts of our staff.' With over 2.5 million records on Troon's customer database, keeping the data current is key to Troon's success. A tenet of Troon's modus operandi is providing a premier customer-loyalty programme. 'Golfers earn one point for every dollar spent, which can be redeemed for rounds of golf (750 points) and Callaway golf equipment,' Greenwell explained. Discount levels from 10 to 20 per cent are based on the number of points accumulated within one calendar year.

Sources

Personal Interview with Brett Brooks, Manager of Marketing Communications for Troon Golf, May 2009.

AME INFO – Middle East business resource – http://www.amerinfo.com.

May, C. (2006) 'New golf tourism developments in Messinia', Buzzle.com, accessed from http://buzzle.com/editorials/8-10-2006-105060.asp

www.troongolf.com.

Revenue and expenses

As mentioned in Chapter 1, golf facility operations make up the largest component in terms of revenue within the golf economy. The revenue that flows through a golf facility comes primarily from green fees, membership fees, range fees, golf cart rentals and associated spending on food and beverages. In the USA in 2005, golf courses, stand-alone ranges, and miniature golf facilities generated $28.1 billion in revenues (SRI, 2005). European golf facilities earn about 30 per cent of the revenue of their US counterparts, broadly in line with the number of courses. This revenue is quite impressive when compared to other popular sports. For example, all spectator sports – including baseball, basketball, football and hockey revenues – brought in a total of $24.4 billion in 2005, and fitness and recreational sports centres had annual revenues of $16.8 billion. However, the golf industry observes a very poor level of profitability. On a year-to-year basis, IBISWorld (2008) believed that golf courses and country clubs experienced a loss between 2000 and 2008. These losses are generally less than 2 per cent of industry revenue, but continued slow economic growth in 2009 and 2010 is expected to lead to further problems within the sector. Towards the end of 2008, a number of golf resort developments fell prey to the credit crunch, with dozens of projects slowing or suspending plans (Blevins, 2008).

Golf courses are largely a fixed cost operation and, with over 85 per cent of courses in the USA operating on a daily fee basis, it means there will be a marginal increase in revenue for every additional round of golf played. Management can therefore have significant implications for profitability. The cost structure of individual players in the industry depends on the type of golf course and facilities being offered, but most revenue from a golf club comes from annual and daily green fees, two to three times as much as from the second most important source – golf cart rentals (Mill, 2008). Golf resorts can be more profitable than individual golf clubs as they have the necessary resources to charge premiums to members and visitors for the use of facilities beyond the actual golf. Figure 5.1 indicates revenue for golf courses in the USA in 2008, showing that golf course membership fees account for 33.9 per cent of industry revenues, with green fees making up 26.2 per cent. Increased golf participation levels for casual and weekend golfers have increased this segment from around 24.3 per cent in 2000.

However, this trend may be softened as an increasing number of golf courses that are owned and operated by municipalities are being sold to private golf course management companies, which tend to charge yearly membership fees. Food and beverage sales are the third largest product segment accounting for 22.4 per cent of industry revenues, with two–thirds of this generated from the sale of food and non-alcoholic beverages and a third from the sale of alcoholic beverages alone. Golf club and other equipment rentals, such as golf carts and trolleys, make up around 7.8 per cent of sales. A smaller, but growing revenue stream is coming from the sponsorship of club signage, such as on scorecards, tee signs and bag tags (James, 2009a).

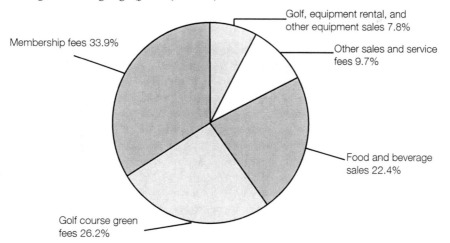

Figure 5.1: Revenue split for golf courses in the US in 2008 (Source: IBISWorld, 2008, p.7).

Payroll is usually the largest expense category for a golf resort or individual club, followed by the cost of merchandise and the cost of food and beverages. Figure 5.2 shows the typical cost structure for golf courses in the USA in 2008. Labour costs make up the largest proportion of expenses at around 36 per cent, showing that the industry is highly labour-intensive, indicative of the high levels of golf course maintenance and development required, and the low concentration of firms participating in the industry. Another major component of a club or resort's expenses is made up of purchases, which includes fertilizers, plants, food, beverages, golf equipment, and other miscellaneous materials. An indication of the high level of capital costs within the industry is the reasonably high percentage of depreciation allowed for (6.9%), and is allocated for vehicles, golf carts and maintenance machinery, office equipment and computer technology.

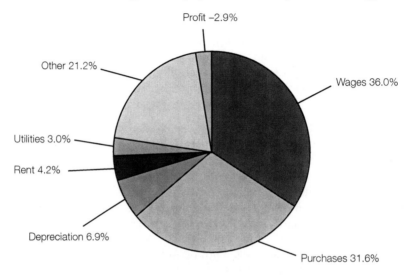

Figure 5.2: Typical cost structure for golf courses in the US in 2008 (Source: IBISWorld, 2008, p. 21).

In order to reduce operational expenditures, there has been a trend towards the outsourcing of course maintenance to third parties. Although this strategy has lowered expenses for some golf courses, it can also result in a loss of control over timing and quality of work being carried out (IBISWorld, 2008). Golf course maintenance companies are often able to lower costs on materials such as fertilizers and turf due to bulk purchases from wholesalers. Insurance costs have also spiralled for golf courses in the last decade (Chen, 2004). Premiums have increased in part due to higher levels of legal action taken by players being hit by golf balls. With all these increased costs, coupled with lower levels of participation in recent years, golf resorts have been forced to look for alternative methods of boosting revenue. This has been achieved through improved food and drink services, a focus on retail sales of golf equipment, promotion of lessons and golfing clinics, and improved practice facilities. An example of a state-of-the-art practice facility can be found at Desert Pines Golf Club in Las Vegas referred to earlier, voted 'Best Driving Range' by *Las Vegas Life*. The Desert Pines Practice Center features an automatic ball delivery system so golfers needn't bend over to tee up each new practice ball. The 58 hitting stations are under cover from the rain and direct sunlight and the centre is climate controlled so it is cooler in the summer and warmer in the winter. The facility is lit for night-time practice and there are two teaching bays with instruction available from PGA instructors.

Banquets can also represent an excellent way of bringing additional revenue to golf clubs, as witnessed in the Spotlight on Trump National in this chapter. According to Mill (2008), an effective marketing plan is crucial for selling banquets, and there are several common sources of banquet business. Golf tournaments and outings represent a logical market segment, and a variety of options can be offered to this market – pre-game breakfasts or lunches, box lunches, and post-game dinners, for example. Other profitable segments for banquets are social events, including weddings and anniversaries, and corporate functions such as group meetings and employee recognition events. An increasing number of golf clubs are targeting females with special events. For example, the Hideaway Golf Club in La Quinta, California attracted 168 women to its 'Wild Flower' three-day member/guest event in February 2008. The festivities included a helicopter dropping rose petals on the practice area, a 'stagette' party, and a final day closest-to-the-pin contest where the winner received a diamond bracelet.

Staffing

As Figure 5.2 indicates, for most typical golf courses or resorts, staffing is a major consideration with payroll expenses accounting for a significant proportion of a club's expenses. The Snapshot on Troon Golf alluded to the fact that staffing is a top priority with the company. Running a golf club or resort can be very labour-intensive, but staff numbers will vary. The opening Spotlight referred to the 280 staff employed by Trump National Los Angeles. The Hyatt Regency golf resort in Coolum, Australia, on the other hand, employs just 50 permanent maintenance and professional staff as well as casual staff for specific events and seasonal activities. Grey Wolf at Panorama in Canada, featured on page 118, employs 80 staff. So numbers will vary depending on geographic location and type of resort. Figure 5.3 shows the average number of full-time staff at golf courses around the world. Chinese courses typically employ more staff than anywhere else (Figure 5.4). According to KPMG (2008) an 18-hole course in China employs on average more than 250 people full-time, while larger courses have 35–40 per cent more staff. Part-time employment is not common, mainly due to the courses' year-round availability and the relatively low cost of labour in China.

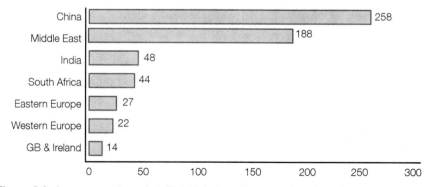

Figure 5.3: Average number of staff at 18-hole golf courses in selected regions (Source: KPMG, 2008 p.16).

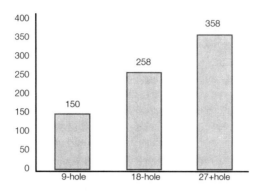

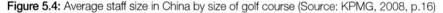

Figure 5.4: Average staff size in China by size of golf course (Source: KPMG, 2008, p.16)

For Trump National Los Angeles, recruiting staff is not too much of a challenge as employees really want to work there. Recruitment is done in-house and the club has a dedicated employment webpage on its website indicating current openings. At Panorama (see Snapshot) there is a small local base of employees but 90 per cent of staff comes from outside western Canada. Around 20 per cent of Panorama's recruiting efforts are focused on Australia and New Zealand where an improved visa programme has facilitated two-year work permits for the under-25s. But they have also noticed a shift towards the 50–65 age group staying in the work force longer.

Other clubs and resorts may choose to use a specialist recruitment company for the golf industry. One such specialist is UK-based Prime Golf & Leisure. Since launching in May 2007, the company has successfully made appointments at a range of golf clubs. Run by Scott Clark, managing director and head consultant, who himself is a former PGA professional and general manager at four different clubs, the company ensures its clients' needs are fully established and understood, before candidates from a large and diverse database of over 1000 people are placed in a post. The company boasts that its 'Perfect Match' Golf Club Recruitment System has a success rate up to 95.2 per cent mainly because of its 7 step 'Top Of The Tree' screening process. Further details of the recruitment process can be found on the company's website, but essentially the seven steps are: The Brief; The Search Process; The First Filter; The Second Filter; The Line Up; Interviews; Final Interviews.

Pro shops

The majority of golf clubs have pro shops, usually located within the clubhouse, where green fees are paid and where golf merchandise is offered for sale. These shops are sometimes run by the professionals at the club (as at Trump National) but they may be managed by a golf management company (as in the case of Troon Golf) or an outside consultancy. Since merchandise sales can account for up to 10 per cent of total revenue for golf clubs, an understanding of retailing is important. A key is to keep overheads low without sacrificing quality and image. A strategic approach to inventory control involves open-to-buy (OTB) which is essentially the difference between how much inventory is needed and how much is actually available. This includes inventory on hand, in transit and any outstanding orders. In order to take advantage of special buys or to add new products, some of the OTB dollars should be held back. This also enables the retailer to react to fast-selling items and quickly restock shelves. There is open-to-buy forecasting software available on the market specifically for golf clubs (Arizona-based, Open to Buy Wizard, for example). Sales of accessories have become increasingly important to net income as the profit margin (often at least 60 per cent) and turnover of accessory inventory is greater than with other pro shop items (Mill, 2008). Some proshops offer merchandise online, such as the PGA which sells apparel, accessories, books and DVDs at its site www.shoppga.com.

As mentioned in Chapter 2, the last decade has seen a new cross-over of golfing designs to fashion and, conversely, the fashion world influencing golf apparel. Fabrics are now technological triumphs with lightweight, heat and sweat wicking properties borrowed from running, tennis and ski wear. Equipment has also evolved, coming a long way from the original wooden clubs and stones characterizing early golf. Nowadays, self-improvement marketing has a strong influence on golfers seeking the latest 'technology'. An increasing number of golf clubs and resorts are responding by offering high quality equipment for sale or for rent to cater for golf tourists. Desert Pines in Las Vegas, for example, will equip golf tourists with the latest Callaway irons, Big Bertha fairway woods, Big Bertha Titanium drivers and Odyssey putters, as well as FootJoy shoes, should they wish to rent equipment. The opening Snapshot mentioned that rental golf clubs at all 11 Troon golf shops are provided by Callaway Golf.

Golf cart fleets

For managers of golf courses, the golf cart fleet is an important operational consideration. In the opening Spotlight, the Director of Golf at Trump National Los Angeles, David Conforti referred to golf carts as 'the arteries of a golf club operation.' In North America, the average fleet size is about 70. This would be higher than at European facilities of the same size, but lower than China where the average cart fleet size is around 90 (KPMG, 2008). In Australia, golf carts are greatly outnumbered by pull carts, as golfers of all ages there prefer to walk the course. Golf courses have to decide whether to lease or to buy their golf carts. While buying may make economic sense in the long-term, leasing is popular because it reduces maintenance problems as servicing is included in many new leases. Leasing also frees up cash for other course projects. The ideal golf cart lease contract is one that allows for a payment schedule in keeping with the cash flow of the resort, that matches a service contract with in-house maintenance capabilities, and that allows payments to be written off as an operational expense (Denigan, 1999). At Trump National Los Angeles the golf cart fleet is leased over a four-year period, but the maintenance is done by the golf club staff.

Inventory control is the key to good fleet operation (Mill, 2008). Rotation of carts on a day-to-day basis can ensure all carts get the same use. One effective management technique is to rotate one-third or one-quarter of the carts out of the lease at a time rather than turning over the entire fleet at the same time. Another important consideration is whether or not to use electric or gas carts. While electric carts are increasingly popular (Victor, 2009) as they are more environmentally-friendly, they do have drawbacks, including the need to have recharging facilities at the club. Two golf courses featured in this chapter, Trump National and Panorama, have chosen to use electric carts as they are both greener and quieter. One recent innovation, perhaps not friendly towards the environment, is the introduction of air-conditioned golf carts, invented to counter the heat in places like Scottsdale, Arizona, where an estimated 12 million rounds of golf are played each year (Resorts, 2008).

Snapshot: Bag boy to Director of Golf in 20 years

Grey Wolf, Panorama, courtesy of Tourism British Columbia

From a part-time job washing clubs as bag boy in 1989, Chad Thomlinson has worked his way up the golf industry ladder. In March 2009 he was appointed as Director of Golf by the Intrawest-owned Greywolf Golf Course at Panorama Mountain Village in British Columbia, Canada.

Thomlinson played golf throughout his teens, competing in his first junior championship at the age of 13. Around that time he started working as a bag boy at B.C.'s Vernon Golf and Country Club, developing his golf prowess until he became a member of the Canadian Professional Golfers' Association in 1995. Three years later, he graduated from Camosun College, in Victoria, B.C., earning a Diploma in Business Administration and Golf Management, which combined his passion for golf with a solid background in management and marketing. In 1999 he took his first full-time golf job as Assistant Professional at B.C.'s Radium Resort where his success led to his nomination in 2000 as Assistant Pro of the Year by the Professional Golfers' Association of British Columbia.

Thomlinson quickly worked his way up, serving as the Associate Professional at the Springs Golf Course in 2001 before taking on the role of Head Professional at Greywolf Golf Course in 2003. He had continued to educate himself while working, earning a Bachelor's Degree in Commerce from the Royal Roads University that year. Six years after joining the Greywolf team, he achieved his ultimate ambition: 'Leading a world class golf operation has been a goal of mine for many years', explained Thomlinson. Forward plans include strengthening Panorama as a premier golf destination in Canada, while promoting it locally with early bird green fees and affordable 'Stay & Play' packages. Greywolf was ranked British Columbia's best golf course by *Golf Digest* in 2003.

With the B.C. golf season running just from May to October, there are many misconceptions about Thomlinson's job. 'The interesting part is that people are fascinated by it because they think it's the dream job,' he said. 'They think it's cool to get to work at a golf course and it must be a lot of fun. People don't really know what we do – they either think we play golf all day or teach or hang out and drink in the club.'

As Director of Golf, Thomlinson's duties revolve around managing the 80-strong team of staff as well as taking on the fiscal responsibilities. 'Essentially it's like running any other business but the biggest challenge is the seasonality,' he explained. 'Sometimes it feels like we're starting from scratch again each season.' The summer months are obviously the busiest golf operational period but off-season Thomlinson's team operates the Nordic Centre at the course, organizing cross country skiing, snowshoeing and rentals for the 13-week winter season. In between seasons, Thomlinson also engages in marketing and trade shows, retail purchasing and planning, preparing for the coming season, recruiting, training, detailing business plans and budgets. 'Once we're open, we're very popular, so there's no opportunity for high level thinking or planning. If we're not ready with that on opening day, then we're in trouble,' he commented.

With year-round employment possibilities in ski and golf – plus great resort-based staff housing – Panorama is in a strong position to attract highly motivated staff. 'We have a small local base but 90 per cent of our applications come from outside western Canada,' said Thomlinson. Around 20 per cent of Panorama's recruiting efforts are focused on Australia and New Zealand where an improved visa programme has facilitated two-year work permits for the under-25s. The remainder are recruited from universities across Canada. The staff typically consists of around 50 males and 30 females with 90 per cent in the 18–28 age group.

With the economic recession, Thomlinson has noticed a dramatic shift away from sheer numbers of applicants towards greater quality. 'It's changed from having 18–25 year olds running the show, when we used to be happy if they showed up 10 minutes late, maybe hungover. Now the market is more competitive and we're seeing the 50–65 age group staying in the work force longer. This amounts to change for the HR world and it's a lot easier to get golf-focused personnel with a strong work ethic.' Increasingly, Thomlinson is able to find a golf-oriented workforce: 'If they love golf and can talk golf it increases the customer service potential.'

Sources

Personal interview with Chad Thomlinson, March 2009.

www.greywolfgolf.com.

Maintenance and course management

As mentioned in Chapter 4, maintenance tends to be the largest single cost item for a golf course, mainly because it is so labour-intensive. These costs will depend on a variety of factors including the course's location, length of season, type, market, size, and purpose. In North America, studies have found that courses in the west are more expensive to maintain than those in other regions. A good deal of this variation can be linked to the amount of natural precipitation and to the length of the season. The type of grass selected and the length of grass are important considerations, but the key to good golf management is taking care of the greens (Chen, 2004). At Stewart Creek in the Canada Rockies (see Snapshot in Chapter 10) the agronomy department works on a high budget because of its location in the mountains and its commitment to environmental stewardship. With snow covering the course into May, there are further challenges in relation to opening on time and having good grass on the fairways and greens.

Construction of new courses in many parts of the world has slowed down, but refurbishment and renovation are the names of the game today (James, 2009b). 'Many clubs want to raise their standards by making the course more attractive and challenging,' said Charlie Greasley, contract manager of John Greasley, a golf course contractor in the UK. The company has seen a growing emphasis by clubs on bunkering. 'The trend is towards strategic and maintenance friendly bunkering. Fairway bunkers, for example, are being repositioned at the correct yardage for the modern game,' he said.

It is beyond the scope of this book to include detailed information on turfgrass management, but for those looking for a guide on this subject, McCarty (2005) has written a comprehensive book that provides in-depth information and tips for growing grass with minimum impacts. Turfgrasses provide soil erosion control, dust stabilization, heat dissipation, noise abatement, air pollution control, wildlife habitat, safety to competitive athletic participants, increased property values, and are an integral component of the landscape. Included in McCarty's book are chapters on best turfgrass for golf courses; golf course design and maintenance considerations for environmentally friendly turf; preventing and managing environmental stresses such as cold, drought and heat stress; irrigation water quantity and quality; and pest management.

Golf course managers in many parts of the world are constantly looking for new ways to fight pests (Chen, 2004). In Indonesia, for example, poisonous snakes are a threat to golfers, and have to be removed. Octogenarian F.X. Sutono made golf course snake clearing his specialty when courses started burgeoning throughout the country over the past two decades (Sudiarno and Nugroho, 2001). Charming the snakes into captivity rather than killing them, the beast tamer was active at around 100 golf courses right into his 80s. He used two matches to 'divine' where snakes were and then pointed out relevant locations to his assistants. His team could clear a 30-hectare course in two days. He brought the captured snakes home to Semarang where some were given to Taman Lele Zoo (where Sutono was Manager and later Chairman) and others were released in appropriate wild habitats. Before the advent of golf in Indonesia, Sutono made his name as a tamer of poisonous insects and animals. He was involved in over one hundred films as an actor, director and officer-in-charge – responsible for shielding crew from bites and stings. He also had a travelling snake dance show with his Nogogini (fire of snake) dance group registered as a pioneer of snake dancing in Indonesia.

Another important consideration for golf course managers is speed of play on the course. A key reason people stop playing golf, or why some never start, is because they don't think they have the time for 18 holes (Mill, 2008). Many courses try to compensate for long rounds by putting more golfers on the course, which is accomplished by decreasing tee-time intervals. Others are introducing GPS technology to speed up play while providing a better experience for golfers (as at Trump National Los Angeles). Golf carts are being equipped with laptop computer screens to give a picture of each hole including yardage and the placement of features such as sand traps. Golfers can use the devices to track yardage and identify potential hazards, the theory being that they will make better shots and speed up play. The position of each cart is known centrally so bottlenecks can be monitored and messages sent to individual carts asking them to speed up play, without having to send out a marshal. GPS is especially useful at resort courses where golfers are not likely to be familiar with the course. There are a number of software programmes also available that will assist in course management. Table 5.1 lists the various packages that are available from one Canadian-based software company called Platinum.

Table 5.1: Platinum golf course software packages as of 1 January 2009 (Source: www.golfcoursesoftware.ca/pricing.html)

Golf Starter Package
Tee Time Reservations
Online Reservations
Member Management
  Price: $18,699.00

Golf Mid Package

Tee Time Reservations	Purchase Orders	Online Reservations
Vendor Management	Tee Time Ballot System	Inventory Control
Member Management	Product Labels	Member Invoicing
Reports Generator	Member Sales Tracking	Member Payments
Point of Sale		

  Price: $24,399.00

Golf Full Package

Tee Time Reservations	Member Management	Online Reservations
Member Payments	Tournaments	Supplier Catalogue
Member Handicaps	Invoicing and Tracking	Tee Time Ballot System
Vendor Management	Lessons Scheduler	Purchase Orders
Greenskeeper Scheduler	Inventory Control	Point of Sale
Staff Management	Point of Sale Cash Out	Payroll
Product Labels	Reports Generator	Activity Scheduler
Comparative Reports	Staff Login/Out	Expenses
Day Planner		

  Price: $36,699.00

Programming

Golf-related programming, such as junior lessons or golf camps, is often the responsibility of the club manager or golf professional. At Trump National Los Angeles, the club offers individual lessons and golf clinics for visitors. The golf professional will take the lessons off the clock and keep the money, whereas the club takes responsibility for running the clinics. As mentioned in Chapter 3, golfing instruction has been increasingly offered as a central or an add-on feature of golfing packages, and the number of golf schools around the world is growing. Disney's Celebration Golf Course, for example, has golf instruction summer camps for destination visitors as well as weekend and after-school programmes for local kids. All-inclusive resorts are also promoting golf instruction. Sandals recently introduced its first Sandals Golf School at Sandals Golf & Country Club, Ochos Rios, Jamaica (See Snapshot in Chapter 2).

Chapter 3 profiled Celebration and discussed a number of other top golfing schools, but there are also many smaller golf schools that have found their niche in this growing market. Summit Golf School, for example, offers learning vacations at its facility located on the ocean in Daytona Beach, Florida. A three-day, three-night package in 2009 was priced at $840 per person and that included hotel room on the ocean, continental breakfast and lunch, instruction, a personalized instruction video, club storage and cleaning, green fees and cart fees for nine holes per day, and free use of the driving range in the evenings. Tim Peightal is the Director of Operations at the Summit Golf School. He started his career at the Disney golf operations and was also the Director of Instruction at the United States Senior Golf Academy for six years. Peightal's goal as a teacher has been to find as many ways as possible to make learning the game of golf fun. 'After all is said and done, it's still just a game,' he said. Peightal feels that every golfer is an individual and that there is no one method that fits everyone.

The most common barriers to taking golf lessons are lesson expense and the time involved (Mill, 2008). To overcome these constraints, golf facilities have begun to introduce a variety of programmes aside from the traditional lesson or clinic. These include video-taping golfers playing or taking lessons, computer instruction and club fitting. Although club fitting is perceived as a valuable tool, a 2005 survey of golfers found that only about half of them have been club fitted (National Golf Foundation, 2005). Of those fitted, 73 per cent said that it was a valuable experience. About the same number of golfers (69%) have used videotaping and found it useful. Although club fitting and videotaping were not perceived as valuable by every golfer, they are both rated more highly than computer instruction.

Programming also includes the hosting of professional tournaments. Developers and top management are often interested in the high visibility of such tournaments, but the exposure can come at quite a price. Donald Trump for example, is not always keen to host big events at his public course in Los Angeles. 'The problem is that we lose play. We're getting $375 a round on weekends, and when you lose that much play over two weeks, which is what it really takes to do an event, it's hard to justify an event. It's a lot easier to do on my private course' (Williams, 2008). Golf events will be covered in more detail in Chapter 8.

Customer service

It was mentioned in Chapter 2 that customer service is having an increasing influence on overall satisfaction for golf tourists (Petrick and Backman, 2002; Olmsted, 2008). Being customer-centered and exceeding customer expectations are therefore important requirements for managers of golf facilities, as witnessed by the importance placed on customer service by Trump National Los Angeles and the Paraparauma Beach Golf Club, both featured in this chapter. As the golf industry becomes more competitive, individual complexes must step things up to maintain customers and challenge rivals (Golf Academy of America, 2009). Baby boomers – who make up a large proportion of golfers – are particularly critical consumers with high expectations but are willing to spend money for excellent service (Coleman et al., 2006).

Providing additional services is one way of exceeding expectations. Many golf courses and resorts have become wireless Internet service providers (ISPs), generating new, recurring revenue streams by offering secure, high-speed Internet access in food and beverage venues, meeting rooms, lounges, hotel rooms, pool areas or community residences. But one frequently overlooked facet of customer satisfaction is the training of a course's employees (Golf Academy of America, 2009). There are a number of customer service training programmes available to golf courses, and some are designed specifically for the golf industry. UK-based Thirdway Consultancy, for example, offers a range of customer service training courses that are tailor-made for the golf industry. Seminar topics include: 'Service Standards in the Food and Beverage Department'; 'Upselling in Retail'; 'Connecting with the Customer'; and 'Together Everyone Achieves More'.

An increasing number of golf resorts are attempting to differentiate on customer service. An example is the Grove Hotel and Resort in Hertfordshire, UK. Home of the World Golf Championships in 2006, the Grove is a pay-and-play facility with a strong service philosophy. Since opening in 2003, the club has introduced many high-end services, with an unstuffy, can-do attitude. All staff members are geared towards the requirements of the guest, and no task is too great or too small. As Spencer Schaub, Director of Golf, says 'The Grove's philosophy is simple: to anticipate your needs even before you realize you want something' (Golf Monthly, 2007). Customer service is also taken seriously at Panorama (see Snapshot). Recruitment focuses on acquiring golf-focused personnel who have a strong work ethic which in turn increases the customer service potential.

As customer expectations have risen over the years, so the need to improve customer service in golf clubs has been acknowledged (O'Sullivan, 2009; Betteridge, 2009). In Scotland, VisitScotland has devised two schemes to improve customer service for golf tourists. The Golfers Welcome and Visiting Golfers Welcome schemes are quality assurance programmes that allow golfers to see at a glance what facilities are available at various clubs and accommodation providers across the country. The Golfers Welcome scheme assesses hotels and accommodation, whilst the Visiting Golfers Welcome scheme assesses Scottish golf clubs. Effectively, both schemes are aimed at raising the bar for the services which target golf tourists. Figure 5.5 is a copy of the Visiting Golfers Welcome scheme criteria.

Visiting Golfers Welcome scheme for golf clubs:

1 A warm welcome should be extended to visiting golfers. A pro-visitor policy or charter should be in place.

2 Signing to tee, and around course should be clear, and in good condition. All facilities should be of a good standard.

3 Catering should be available, or if not available, information on location and opening times of nearest local eating establishments.

4 Visitor changing facilities should be made available to visiting golfers.

5 A lockable area should be provided for safe storage of golf clubs/shoes/equipment etc.

6 Flexibility of payment options including Credit Cards.

7 A commitment to one of the following training courses, Welcome Golfer, No Rough Edges or similar golf related training.

8 Consideration should be given to training members as golfing ambassadors and encouraged to welcome visiting golfers.

9 Value for money golf – different pricing options dependent on capacity.

10 Met Office information (four day forecast) or similar to be provided.

11 Information on location of local accommodation providers should be available, including directions.

12 A range of tourist information should be available, including general information on local area with suggestions for non-golfers.

13 Information should be provided on local sports/golf shops, club shops, coaching, club hire, availability of practice areas, driving ranges.

14 There should be a commitment to training of caddies (where service provided).

Figure 5.5: Visiting Golfers Welcome scheme criteria (Source: VisitScotland, 2009).

Risk management

Risk management has long been associated with resort management, and although financial risk is a regular occurrence, if a golf club or resort takes in guests, there is an extra responsibility of 'duty of care', where management is obliged to protect its guests from harm (Murphy, 2008). A resort could be vulnerable to a number of risks, including food poisoning, accidents, natural disasters and bad weather (Tarlow, 2006). In Canada, there is also the risk of running into a bear – at Stewart Creek in Canmore, Alberta, for example (see Snapshot in Chapter 10).

Risk management is a way to prepare for such risks, and Gee (1996) has identified a four-step process that can assist resorts in the management of risk:

◆ **Risk identification.** This might concern asset risk which involves the major investment in property and facilities that need to be protected; income risk which has a high dependence on external conditions beyond immediate control (such as the credit crunch of 2008–9); legal liability risk, which is increasing as society becomes more litigious. Liability insurance is a major cost factor for all golf clubs and resorts.

◆ **Risk measurement and evaluation.** To control the frequency and magnitude of losses due to risk, it is important to develop recording procedures and to create a repository of past records.

◆ **Risk reduction.** Many common dangers like food, health and safety and fire are regulated and controlled by local by-laws and ordinances. However, such statutes often involve the minimum acceptable precautions, so a resort may choose to follow the Disney example and select higher standards (Murphy, 2008).

◆ **Risk finance determination.** Most resorts can absorb small and infrequent losses brought about by seasonal fluctuations or occasional accidents, but will need to transfer the risk of large business interruptions or liability claims to outside suppliers such as insurance brokers.

Some brokers specialize in the golf industry. UK-based Kerry London Sport and Leisure for example, has an insurance policy specifically tailored to golf clubs. Optional coverage in 2009 included cover for wedding cancellations, designed to reflect the economic situation at the time. The company has a freely accessible risk management database for clients, which offers downloadable documents covering aspects of club operations that may have a bearing on insurance premiums. These include health and safety procedures, public liability, security, buildings maintenance, data backup and financial controls.

Crisis management

Crisis Management is an extension of risk management and is more concerned with taking proactive steps in reducing the dangers of catastrophic business collapse due to crisis or disaster. A crisis for a golf resort is normally the result of external factors impacting negatively on the appeal and marketability of the resort concerned, beyond the direct managerial control of resort authorities. Such factors may be acts of terrorism, national disasters, health issues, crime or international conflict. Since 11 September 2001, there have been more than 3000 major terrorist attacks, most of which have impacted the tourism industry. Although terrorism is not a new phenomenon, what is new is its use to attain political ends as well as the global media attention now given to terrorist incidents. The continuous publication by the media of the horror of terrorist attacks and their subsequent responses and highly publicized results are often enough to sway many international travellers towards reconsidering their vacation plans.

Natural disasters can also have a devastating impact on tourism. In 2005, New Orleans in the USA was hit by Hurricane Katrina which devastated the city. Prior to Katrina, New Orleans received about 10 million visitors a year, but a year after the disaster, hotel bookings were still down by 26 per cent. The hurricane damaged 80 per cent of the city, and killed 1836 people. In response to the threat of hurricanes, hurricane guarantees are now offered by many tour operators and travel agents. In 2005, resorts like Beaches, Sandals, SuperClubs and Club Med were promoting policies that allowed travellers to rebook for another time without penalty if a hurricane ruined their vacation.

Health concerns can also have a negative impact on tourism. The swine flu virus pandemic threat in 2009 had a devastating impact on tourism in Mexico, with the governments of the United States, Canada and Europe advising against non-essential travel to Mexico. With memories of the impact of the 2003 SARS virus still fresh, tourism officials in Mexico were bracing themselves for a slowdown in travel to their country. In 2008 the tourism industry brought in $13 billion to the country, making it the third largest source of foreign currency after remittances and oil revenues. While any reduction hurts, the US is Mexico's key market: 80 per cent of its tourists come from America, according to the government's tourist department.

Responding to crisis

Once a resort or destination has identified and acknowledged it is facing a crisis, it has been suggested that there are three steps to managing the crisis (Beirman, 2003).

♦   Establish a crisis management team. The first step is establishing a crisis management team, and assigning key roles, such as media and public relations, relations with the travel industry in source markets, and destination response coordination with the local tourism industry. In theory, the middle of a crisis is not a good time to formulate a strategy for managing image or reputation, but for many organizations it is precisely when the conversation begins. Businesses and destinations that are serious about their reputation need to manage risk as an ongoing issue and plan for unfortunate events.

♦   Promote the destination during and after the crisis. Promotional campaigns following a crisis are often the only way a destination can persuade visitors to travel. Initiatives can include offering incentives to restore the market, and ensuring that opinion leaders in source markets visit the destination to see that recovery is in place. After the swine (H1N1) flu outbreak in early 2009, the Mexican government approved a $1.3 billion economic stimulus including $15 million for tourism promotion.

♦   Monitoring recovery and analyzing the crisis experience. The final stage in marketing in times of crisis involves monitoring statistical trends and the duration of both the crisis and recovery process. Analysis of source markets, which under- or over-performed during the crisis, assists the destination marketers in determining the allocation of marketing resources to each market. Market research will gauge the effectiveness of marketing campaigns on source markets and segments within those markets.

Case Study: Golf tourism in New Zealand – Paraparauma Beach Golf Club

Paraparauma Beach Golf Club, New Zealand, courtesy of Paraparauma Beach

Paraparauma is on the east coast of New Zealand's North Island, about an hour's drive north of Wellington. It boasts two good courses – Kapati Golf Club and the better-known Paraparauma Beach Golf Club, which has hosted 12 New Zealand Opens. The links course began with nine holes in the 1930s, and was extended with another nine designed by Alistair McKenzie in 1949. Ninety four year-old Ian Uwen – a founding member – considers Paraparauma Beach one of the best links courses in New Zealand. 'I played for Cambridge Firsts in England in 1936. I was a scratch golfer at the time, and played all over the country, so I only managed a 3rd class honours degree,' he said with a twinkle in his eye. Uwen still plays in Men's Day every Wednesday, playing to a handicap of 18 these days. In the local tourist office, officials say they saw a big increase in golf tourists looking to play the course after Tiger Woods came to play in the 2002 New Zealand Open, but the numbers have dropped off in the last few years. 'There was a real buzz around town when Tiger came through,' said one of the members, a detective by day, who was fortunate enough to be appointed as security for Woods during the tournament, watching him play every hole.

The golf demographics at Paraparauma Beach consist of about 60 per cent locals, 30 per cent domestic tourists, and 10 per cent international visitors, according to Course Superintendent and General Manager, Leo Barber. 'Tourists tend to find us through our website, although we know this needs upgrading, and we are working on it at the moment,' he said. The club is using a golf club website specialist to redesign the site – David Bradley Associates – at a cost of around $8000. About 75 per cent of the club's revenue comes from members and 25 per cent from green fees, although Barber would like to see more green-fee paying golfers. 'Golf in New

Zealand is relatively affordable,' he commented. 'And there are more golf courses per capita than anywhere in the world – about 430 courses at the last count.'

Servicing both members and guests is a perpetual challenge for Barber, who arranges visitor times around club events. He also has to schedule course maintenance discreetly, reducing the impact on both club events as well as one-off visitor groups. 'Like any club I guess the biggest challenge for management is the ability to satisfy a large cross-section of people all with differing views and expectations and affiliations and length of time belonging to the club. We also cater for a variety of groups, a mixture of members and guests, golfers and non-golfers. Moving forward we need to implement better systems, a more integrated approach between the departments and foster better relationships with companies and organizations that feed us our clients such as cruise ships, tour operators and accommodation providers,' he said.

With a strong international reputation, tour operator business is important to Paraparauma Beach, which is also patronized increasingly by cruise tourists. Around 60 cruise ships included Wellington in their itineraries in 2008, some of which boasted a Golf Director on board to arrange on-shore games. Barber is working on a database of tour operators, planning future golf packages in various accommodation/meals/transportation combinations. 'We do offer special pricing for tour operators when they come through,' said Barber. Kalos Golf, based out of the USA, is one company the golf club has worked with regularly. 'There is little involvement from our side apart from, of course, delivering the experience once they turn up. We provide imagery for their marketing purposes but they market and provide the guests for us,' he explained.

According to members, Barber has made a tremendous difference to the club since joining in 2006 as Course Superintendent. 'It is fair to say that the club was at a low point with mounting debt, ageing assets, poor course presentation and general member dissatisfaction,' said Barber.

'Often when a club goes through these periods I think one of the mistakes they make is ignoring their core functions and looking for answers beyond where the actual dissatisfaction lies. As an example, the club had been focusing on lengthening the course, adding bunkers and proposing to build new greens when the reality was that the dissatisfaction lay with poor conditioning and questionable maintenance practices. Instead of addressing how to increase revenue from golf it was looking at how to make revenue from other sources such as trees and land sales, etc.'

Barber initiated plans for course conditioning, financial management and delivery of services, starting with a course policy document developed in 2006. Faced with long-term debt and a working capital shortfall, Barber looked to the membership for interest free loans to clear the interest responsibility. 'A reduced playing year - but at full subscription - cleared the working capital position and we then addressed budgeting for surpluses, auditing our expenses and prioritizing and funding asset replacement,' he explained.

Voluntary member participation is intrinsic for Paraparauma's financial health. One of the members has collected the autograph of every winner of the 12 New Zealand

Opens held at Paraparauma Beach and hopes to auction them in a framed picture of the course to raise money for the club. 'This was part of a larger initiative to raise $100,000 that would be put towards the retirement of long-term debt,' Barber explained. 'This initiative fell short of its intended goal but generated a good amount of club spirit with some of the activities that were organized as part of the fund raising efforts such as social nights, wine tasting, tournaments, etc.'

Barber's current task is delivery of services both to members and guests. The greatest challenge is coordinating numerous departments, some of which are contracted out: 'At the end of the day, failure in any one of these departments will impact on the overall satisfaction of the experience. The aim is to deliver the complete golfing experience focused on excellent customer service, superior playing conditions on a world class course, and simple but well presented food and beverage. We are progressing with this but still have some way to go for it to be complete.'

Sources

Personal interview with Leo Barber in November 2008.

http://www.paraparaumubeachgolfclub.co.nz.

References

Beirman, D. (2003) *Restoring Destinations in Crisis: A Strategic Marketing Approach*, Wallingford: CAB International.

Betteridge, M. (March 2009) 'Making an impression', *Golf Club Management*, 37.

Blevins, J. (2008) 'Mountain development slows down', *Denver Post*, accessed from http://www.denverpost.com/business/ci_11172295 23 March 2009.

Chen, T. (2004) 'A study of golf courses management: the in-depth interview approach', *Journal of American Academy of Business*, September, 138–143.

Coleman, L.J., Hladikova, M. and Savelyeva, M. (2006) 'The baby boomer market', *Journal of Targeting, Measurement and Analysis for Marketing*, 14 (3) pp. 191-210.

Denigan, J. (1999) Made to order', Club Management (September/October). *In Improving Golf Cart Fleet Operations* (3rd Edn). Jupiter, Fl: National Golf Foundation, 2001, 21.

Gee, C.Y. (1996) *Resort Development and Management* 2nd edn., East Lansing, Michigan: Educational Institute of the American Hotel and Motel Association.

Golf Academy of America (2009) 'Golf training: increase your course's customer service', http://www.golfacademy.edu/ accessed 2 April 2009.

Golf Monthly (September 2007) 'The Grove: five grand years', *Golf Monthly*, 168–169.

Gustafson, T.F., and McLean, D.D. (1999) 'The operating structure of privatized golf services', *Journal of Park and Recreation Administration*, 17 (4), 39–55.

IBISWorld (2008) *Golf Courses & Country Clubs in the US*, Los Angeles: IBISWorld.

James, T. (2009a) 'Ad timing', *Golf Club Management*, March , 59–60.

James, T. (2009b) 'Modern marvels', *Golf Club Management*, February, 48–50.

London, A. (2009) 'Council picks golf course management', News-Journal Online, accessed from http://www.news-journalonline.com 23 March 2009.

KPMG (2008) *Golf Benchmark Survey in China 2008*, KPMG Advisory Ltd.

McCarty, L.B. (2005) *Best Golf Course Management Practices* 2nd edn., Upper Saddle River, NJ: Pearson Prentice Hall.

Mill, R.C. (2008) *Resorts: Management and Operation* 2nd edn, Hoboken, NJ: John Wiley & Son.

Murphy, P. (2008) *The Business of Resort Management*, Oxford: Elsevier

National Golf Foundation (2005) *Golf Industry Overview 2005*, Jupiter, Florida: NGF.

Olmsted, L. (2008) 'North Americas top golf resorts', accessed from http://www. ForbesTraveller.com 21 February 2008.

O'Sullivan, D. (2009) 'Time for change', *Golf Club Management*, January, 52–53.

Petrick, J.F., and Backman, S.J. (2002) 'An examination of the construct of perceived value for the prediction of golf travellers' intentions to revisit', *Journal of Travel Research*, **41**, 38-45.

Phillips, P.L. (1986) *Developing with Recreational Amenities: Golf, Tennis, Skiing, Marinas*, Washington, DC: Urban Land Institute.

Resorts (2008) 'Next round's on me', *Resorts*, 4 (5), 84-87.

SRI (2005) 'The 2005 golf economy report', from http://www.golf2020.com/reports/GolfEconomyExecSummary.pdf

Sudiarno, T., and Nugroho, C.H. (2001) 'F.X.Sutono, fairway snake catcher from Semarang', *Jakarta Post*, January from: http://www.thejakartapost.com/news/2001/01/07/fx-sutono-fairway-snake-catcher-semarang.html

Tarlow, P.E. (2006) 'Disaster management: exploring ways to mitigate disasters', *Tourism Review International*, 19 (1/2), 17-25.

Victor, C. (January 2009) 'It pays to keep quiet', *Golf Club Management*, 58.

VisitScotland (2009) 'Visiting Golfers Welcome Scheme', accessed 31 March 2009 from http://www.visitscotland.org/golfers_welcome_scheme.pdf.

Williams, V. (2008) 'National Pleasure', *Fairways + Greens*, 11 (5), 15-17.

6 The Marketing of Golf Tourism

Visit Scotland promoting Homecoming Scotland, courtesy Visit Scotland

With Scotland synonymous with golf, the 2009 Homecoming Scotland campaign used its national sport as one of its main marketing levers. The year-long festival celebrated the 250-year anniversary of the birth of Robbie Burns, Scotland's signature poet. The golf component was the 'Drive It Home' campaign, featuring free golf for tourists from participating countries – United States of America, Canada, Sweden, France, Middle East, Germany, Italy, Australia, New Zealand, Hong Kong, Japan, China, Argentina, Brazil, Switzerland, Austria, Norway, Denmark, Finland and The Netherlands. The offer was for free four-ball fixtures at around 100 courses, encouraging groups to book a trip to Scotland via the dedicated website – www.driveithome2009.com. Drive It Home was Scotland's biggest ever golf promotion in its leading overseas golf markets.

With the offer prompting golfers to register online every five minutes of the day during the first phase, the promotion was intended to add around $28 million to the Scottish economy that year, according to VisitScotland. Golfers are estimated to spend about $3500 during an average trip there. In a bid to attract over 8000 golfers to Scotland, a second phase was launched in March 2009 with more courses participating. The initiative was created in collaboration with the Scottish Golf Union, Golf Tourism Scotland and the Scottish Ladies' Golfing Association.

VisitScotland's CEO, Philip Riddle promoted the campaign with a worldwide tour in 2008 to raise awareness among potential overseas tourists as well as the ex-pat community. 'We have a very widespread diaspora,' explained Riddle. 'There are almost as many Scots in Canada, for example, as there are in Scotland. There are very positive associations, too, for millions of people as well as an appreciation of what Scots have done around the world. We want to make 2009 the year for them to come home.' He was hoping to appeal to 'Blood' Scots (of Scottish descent) and 'Heart' Scots (those with a passion for the country and culture). Extending a general invitation to the world 'to anyone with an affinity to Scotland', Riddle toured the USA, Canada, Australia and New Zealand, their main long-haul markets. British golfers – Scotland's biggest target market – were also encouraged. 'There are probably more Scots living in Britain than in Scotland,' averred Riddle.

The Homecoming Scotland campaign consisted of three marketing directions: UK (including corporate and private segments); International; and Business. 'Golf transcends all three of these segments,' he said. 'We're going beyond leisure tourism and talking to business, too.' The Forbes conference, in June 2009, was located at Gleneagles as a quasi business/golf meeting. Internationally, the campaign was targeting the 'mature devotee', particularly from the North American market, who often wants to fit in two rounds per day, but also reaching out to Asian markets such as Korea.

Another major market for VisitScotland is Sweden, with well-heeled tourists spending on an array of associated products during their stay. 'Swedes tend to come not just for golf but to see things, eat, drink and shop,' said Riddle. A second prong of the Homecoming Scotland operation was whisky: 'Of course with golf and whisky, that's a good combination in itself, but we also have the poetry of Burns, our culture, heritage, great minds and innovation on the intellectual side.'

While featuring the country's world famous championship courses, Riddle also wanted to emphasize cheaper golf available in Scotland. 'Scotland is seen as the home of golf with top courses and top golfers which is sometimes off-putting,' he explained. 'We have the best golf courses in the world but we encourage people to look beyond the best ones. There are 550 courses – an immense array and variety. There are island courses, municipal courses and Edinburgh has some of the best value courses with fantastic views for just $25 a round, compared to $400 at St Andrews, for example.' In Scotland, he added, golf is the game for the 'common man'.

Golf combo packages were also promoted. 'In a loose sense, for example in the English market which is our biggest market, the husband will golf and the wife will want to do something else such as painting or visiting historical sites or family activities,' said Riddle. Many Scottish golf courses were also broadening their appeal by attracting beginners. With the scenic backdrop of lush landscapes, quaint villages and local pubs and restaurants, Scotland was also emphasizing golf/fishing combos. 'There is so much compressed into Scotland all within a relatively small area. You could be shopping in Glasgow in the morning, playing a world-class golf course in the afternoon like Loch Lomond, then staying on an island and having dinner in the evening with no-one around,' he added.

The Homecoming Scotland campaign utilized a mix of print and online media advertising placements across travel and lifestyle media (including National Geographic and Scottish-themed magazines). With two main bursts in fall 2008 and spring 2009, the intention was to reach and influence target markets during the key consideration and booking period for 2009 travel. The Homecoming message was sent out monthly via the 'Diaspora' database of 1500 Scots-interest organizations globally, motivating gatekeepers to message their members. It was also dispersed across VisitBritain's global website networks via messaging and online banner advertising. Plans and controversy over the Trump golfing development were also giving Scotland free publicity in 2009. 'It's good for Scotland to have a venture like that. Donald Trump's a publicity magnet so it's good to get all that exposure,' said Riddle.

VisitScotland was responding to the worldwide drop in tourism numbers by creating this concerted campaign. Visitor numbers had recovered after a drop in 2001 but international visitation levelled off in 2008 and was expected to drop further in 2009 due to the economic recession. The project was a $1.6 million investment: 'A lot of money has been put into the campaign by individual businesses as well as government,' said Riddle. VisitScotland incurs an annual expenditure of $140 million for tourism promotion and running 100 visitor information centres spread throughout the country. Two-thirds of that financing comes from the Scottish government, the rest from partnerships with business and local government.

Various high profile events were planned throughout the year and branded 'Homecoming'. These included the Scottish Homecoming Golf Classics in April/May which offered prize-giving banquets 'fit for kings', a 'skirl' of bagpipes, a taste of Scotland's cuisine and traditional entertainment. St Andrews Golf Week was also promoted on the Drive it Home website as well as the July Open at the newly-refitted Turnberry and the Cullen Homecoming Senior 2 Day Open Amateur Tournament in June. The Official Guide to Golf in Scotland 2009 dubbed the country 'The Home of Golf' with an introduction by golf celebrity Sam Torrance, 'Scotland's Ambassador for Golf'. 'Golf is a big part of 'Homecoming Scotland' and rightly so as we gave the game to the world,' said Torrance. The guide included all golf destinations and events for 2009 as well as Homecoming arts, cultural and culinary activities endorsed by actor Sean Connery. Riddle hoped to measure the success of the Homecoming and Drive It Home initiatives by studying participation levels at events and tracking web hits.

Sources:

Personal interview with Philip Riddle, CEO of VisitScotland, 2008.

Walker, T. (2009). 'Drive It Home to expand', *Leisure Management News*, February, accessed from http://www.leisuremanagement.co.uk/newsdetail1.cfm?codeID=1 06353&CFID=5306178.

http://www.homecomingscotland2009.com

Introduction

The Homecoming Scotland campaign highlights the importance of marketing in the golf tourism sector. A $1.6 million investment in promoting golf tourism was intended to add around $28 million to the Scottish economy. Marketing is of vital concern to those involved in golf tourism as it is the principal management influence that can be brought to bear on the size and behaviour of this global market. Even the smallest of clubs are realizing the importance of marketing and have appointed someone to take on this responsibility (Hill, 2009). Marketing has been defined as 'the process of planning and executing the conception, pricing, promotion, and distribution of ideas, goods, and services to create exchanges that satisfy individual (customer) and organizational objectives' (Kotler, 1984: 92). This philosophy defines marketing as a process intended to find, satisfy, and retain customers while the business makes a profit. Central to both these definitions is the role of the customer and the customer's relationship to the product, whether that is a good, a service, or an idea. The golf tourism sector, like other service sectors, involves a combination of tangible and intangible products. For example, a golf resort is a mixture of goods (course, hotel beds, and food) that are linked with a range of services (lessons, clubhouse service, and pro shop services). This package of tangible and intangible products is perceived by the tourist as an experience, and represents the core of the tourism product.

The marketing plan

The term 'marketing plan' is widely used to mean a short-term plan for two years or less. The opening Spotlight described a marketing plan launched by VisitScotland in 2008/09.

A marketing plan serves a number of purposes for any organization involved in golf tourism: it provides a road map for all future marketing activities of the organization; it ensures that marketing activities are aligned with the corporate strategic plan; it forces marketing managers to review and think through all steps in the marketing process objectively; it assists in the budgeting process to match resources with marketing objectives; and it creates a process to monitor actual against expected results.

A systematic marketing planning process consists of eight logical steps, as outlined in Figure 6.1. These stages will be discussed in turn.

1. **Corporate connection**
   – mission & vision statements

2. **Analysis & forecasting**
   – portfolio analysis
   – competitor analysis
   – segmentation

3. **Setting marketing goals & objectives**

4. **Marketing strategy**
   – targeting & positioning

5. **Tactics & action plans**

6. **Resource requirements**

7. **Marketing control**

8. **Communicating the plan**

Figure 6.1: Marketing planning: an 8-step process

1. The corporate connection

Marketing planning should reflect the goals and objectives of the organization as a whole. The mission or vision statement reflects the organization's philosophy, and the goals and objectives as set out in the business plan become the basis of planning for all departments. Marketing's responsibilities in relation to the corporate vision are usually outlined in one or more separate marketing-specific documents. Goals can be defined in terms such as sales growth, increased profitability, and market leadership, whereas objectives are the activities that will accomplish the goals. A vision statement usually answers the question, 'What do we want to be?' while the mission statement will answer the question, 'What business are we in?' Whereas the vision describes where the organization wants to be in some future time, the mission is a broader statement about an organization's business and scope, goods or services, markets served, and overall philosophy.

2. Analysis and forecasting

The next stage of the marketing plan is defining the current situation. It is essential that each component of the business be reviewed in order to ensure that resources can be allocated efficiently. Marketing research is important at this stage, defined as the systematic and objective search for and analysis of information relevant to the identification and solution of any problem in the field of marketing (Green *et al.*, 1988). Unfortunately, in tourism, many smaller organizations feel that 'real' marketing research is a costly and time-consuming luxury only available to large companies that have professional research staff, sophisticated computers, and almost unlimited budgets. This is not true, but research in the golfing sector does tend to be carried out by larger organizations. For example, in 2009, Sport England commissioned IPSOS MORI to conduct research over a four-year period to establish what is important to people in the UK when they take part in golf and how satisfied they are with the quality of their experience. There are some market research companies that specialize in golf research. An example is the Golf Research Group (GRG). Founded in 1989 by Colin Hegarty, GRG has offices in Dallas and London. The National Golf Foundation (NGF) in the USA also undertakes research on behalf of its members. One program, for example, is called the Voice-of-Customer Operating Model (VOCOM) which enables facilities to analyze, track and monitor customer behaviour to develop one-to-one relationships with customers and increase profitability. As part of this program, NGF measures customer loyalty for participating golf facilities, developing a Loyalty Index. Customer Loyalty Awards are given each year to managers of high-performing facilities.

Analysis models

Several models exist for reviewing effectiveness and identifying opportunities, but those proven by time and practical application across a range of industries include portfolio analysis, competitor analysis, segmentation analysis, SWOT (strengths, weaknesses, opportunities, and threats) analysis, and forecasting.

Portfolio analysis first became popular in the 1960s, when many organizations sought to improve their profitability by diversifying their activities so as not to keep all their eggs in one basket. The Boston Consulting Group (BCG) model was one of the most popular approaches to evaluating a very diverse group of goods and services, based on long-term planning and economic forecasts. The model adopts the view that every product of an organization can be plotted on a two-by-two matrix to identify those offering high potential and those that are drains on the organization's resources.

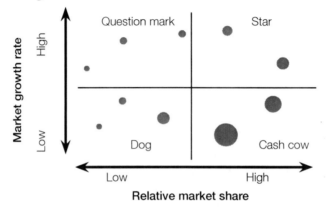

Figure 6.2: The Boston Consulting Group (BCG) model

In Figure 6.2, the horizontal axis represents market share, and the vertical axis represents anticipated market growth. High market share means that a business is a leader in that good or service; low market share indicates that either the marketplace is heavily competitive or a good or service has not had widespread market acceptance. A good or service can then take up one of four theoretical positions on the model. A cash cow is a product that generates cash and turnover, but the long-term prospects are limited. A dog provides neither cash flow nor long-term opportunities and does not hold great promise for improved performance. Stars are products that have a dominant share of a fast-growing market. Although they may not generate a large amount of cash at present, they have potential for high returns in the future. Question marks are fairly speculative products that have high-risk potential. They may be profitable, but because they hold a small market share, they may be vulnerable to competition. Goods or services go through the product life cycle which can affect where they are positioned on the BCG model. A new product may be in the 'question mark' cell; as it becomes successful it moves into the 'star' category, and then moves on to become a 'cash cow' before it starts to decline and becomes a 'dog'.

Information on the number and type of competitors, their relative market shares, the things they do well, and things they do badly will assist in the planning process. Competitor analysis will also highlight market trends and the level of loyalty of consumers. Competitors can be divided into four broad categories: direct competitors offer similar goods and services to the same consumer at a similar price; product category competitors make the same product or class of products; general competitors provide the same service; and budget competitors compete for the same consumer dollars. In addition to the existing competition, there is also the threat of potential competition in the form of new entrants (Porter, 1980: 4).

Segmentation analysis refers to the way in which organizations identify and categorize customers into groups defined by similar characteristics and similar needs or desires. The concept of segmentation is widely adopted in tourism marketing, as few companies in the industry attempt to appeal to an entire market. The principles of segmentation are based on the premise that a market can be readily divided into segments for the commercial purpose of targeting offerings. The core advantage of segmentation is that customers will be more satisfied with the product because it has been designed with their needs in mind. Their social needs are also satisfied because they will be mixing with people like themselves and avoiding incompatible types. If an organization knows exactly which segments it wishes to reach, it can select the media most likely to be read, heard, or seen by those consumers, and so spend less on general mass-market advertising. If it knows the lifestyles and attitudes of that segment and the benefits they are seeking from the product, the advertising message can be made more persuasive. Chapter 7 looks in more detail at the advertising strategies that golf destinations use to attract golf tourists, but the Snapshot on page 141 outlines how Tunisia is targeting British golfers by promoting the destination as excellent value for money relative to Portugal and Spain.

SWOT is an acronym for strengths, weaknesses, opportunities, and threats. A SWOT analysis provides scope for an organization to list all its strengths (those things it does best and its positive product features) and its weaknesses (problems that affect its success). These factors are always internally focused. For hotels and visitor attractions, location may be a major strength, or the strength may lie in the skills of certain staff members. Strength may also lie in historical artefacts or architectural style, or it may reflect having a particularly favourable consumer image. VisitScotland perceives its strengths to lie in the immense array and variety of golf courses, as well as the value for money offered. Weaknesses – ranging from ageing products and declining markets, to surly customer contact staff – must also be identified. Once identified, they may be subject to management action designed to minimize their impact or to remove them where possible. One of the challenges faced by VisitScotland was the lack of consistent service quality for visitors, as mentioned in Chapter 5. Weaknesses and strengths are often matters of perception rather than 'fact' and may be recognized only through consumer research. Opportunities are events that can affect a business, either through its reaction to external forces or through its addressing of its own weaknesses. The Homecoming Scotland campaign was an opportunity for tourism officials to promote golf tourism in the country. Threats are those elements, both internal and external, that could have a serious detrimental effect on a business. In the opening case, VisitScotland was responding to the worldwide drop in tourism numbers in 2008 and 2009.

Because information is never perfect and the future is always unknown, no one right conclusion can ever be drawn from the evidence gathered in the SWOT process. As a result, forecasting becomes an important stage in the planning process to support a SWOT. Forecasting is market research based but future-oriented, and it relies on expectations, vision, judgement, and projections for factors such as sales' volume and revenue trends, consumer profiles, product profiles, price trends, and trends in the external environment. Because the future for tourism and hospitality products is subject to volatile, unpredictable factors and competitors' decisions, the goal of forecasting is not accuracy but careful and continuous assessment of probabilities and options, with a focus on future choices. Forecasting recognizes that most marketing-mix expenditure is invested months ahead of targeted revenue flows. Since marketing planning is focused on future revenue achievement, it is necessarily dependent upon skill, judgement, foresight, and realism in the forecasting process.

3. Setting marketing goals and objectives

Goals are the primary aims of the organization, and objectives the specific aims that managers try to accomplish to achieve organizational goals. Goals can be defined in terms of sales growth, increased profitability, and market leadership. Objectives are the activities that will accomplish the goals. For example, the goal of sales growth for a hotel could become an objective of a 20 per cent increase in accommodation sales and a 30 per cent increase in food and beverage sales. The goal of increased profitability could be translated into objectives of a 15 per cent increase in profits across the board, and a goal of market leadership could be translated into objectives for each city in which a hotel chain operates. The Homecoming Scotland campaign was intended to add around $28 million to the Scottish economy in 2009.

4. Marketing strategy: targeting and positioning

No area of the marketing plan surpasses the selection of target markets in importance. If inappropriate markets are selected, marketing resources will be wasted. Target markets should be selected from a previously developed list of available segments. These include segments currently served by the organization and newly recognized markets. A target market is simply the segment at which the organization aims its marketing message. Implicitly, the non-profitable customers should be given less attention. A target market generally has four characteristics. It should comprise groups of people or businesses that are well-defined, identifiable, and accessible; members should have common characteristics; they should have a networking system so that they can readily refer the organization to one another; and they should have common needs and similar reasons to purchase the product or service. For VisitScotland, there were a number of target markets for their campaign, divided into three major segments; UK, international and business. Attractive markets within these broader segments were also identified, such as the Swedish golf tourism market.

Once the market has been segmented and a target market identified, the next step in the marketing plan is positioning. Positioning is a communications' strategy that is a natural follow-through from market segmentation and target marketing.

Market positioning is ultimately how the consumer perceives the product or service in a given market, and is used to achieve a sustainable competitive advantage over competitors. The Snapshot on page 141 explains how marketers in Morocco and Tunisia are hoping to use golf as part of their repositioning strategy after realizing that the destinations were narrowly perceived as cheap holiday destinations for sunshine and beach activities. Research is often needed to identify the perceived positioning of destinations relative to competitors. A study by Kim *et al.* (2005) found that Australia showed a similarity to Hawaii in perceived image to potential Korean overseas golf tourists; Malaysia, Thailand and the Philippines held similar positions in the minds of Koreans; whereas China did not show any similarity to other destinations.

Three steps are necessary to develop an effective position in the target market segment: product differentiation; prioritizing and selecting the competitive advantage; and communicating and delivering the position. It is important to promote not only one benefit to the target market, but to develop a unique selling proposition (USP), a feature of a product that is so unique that it distinguishes the product from all other products. The goal of a USP is for a company to establish itself as the number one provider of a specific attribute in the mind of the target market. The attribute chosen should be desired and highly valued by target consumers. Attracting visitors is becoming an increasingly important source of income for golf clubs (in addition to memberships) so it is important that a club has a USP that makes it stand apart from other clubs (Hill, 2009). Tourism and hospitality providers try to differentiate their products by using branding, and this is discussed in more detail in Chapter 7.

5. Tactics and action plans

Although no single strategy will be suitable for all organizations, marketing planning provides the opportunity to understand the operating environment and to choose options that will meet the organization's goals and objectives. Planning involves selecting and developing a series of strategies that effectively bring about the required results. Marketing strategies are designed as the vehicle to achieve marketing objectives. In turn, marketing tactics are tools to support strategies. Action programmes comprise a mix of marketing activities that are undertaken to influence and motivate buyers to choose targeted volumes of particular products. A marketing mix programme or marketing campaign expresses exactly what activities will take place in support of each identified product/market subgroup on a week-by-week basis. Further details on communication plans will be given in Chapter 7, but the opening Spotlight described the various tactics used by VisitScotland to bring golfers to Scotland in 2008/09.

6. Resource requirements

The marketing plan needs to address the resources required to support the marketing strategies and meet the objectives. Such resources include personnel, equipment and space, budgets, intra-organizational support, research, consulting, and training. A common error in writing a marketing plan is developing strategies that are probably highly workable but for which there is insufficient support. Of prime importance in analyzing resource requirements is the budget. Setting a budget that provides the marketing department with sufficient resources to deliver its plan is essential. In the opening Spotlight, VisitScotland allocated $1.6 million to promoting golf tourism in 2008/09. However, in most organizations, various departments compete for funds, and it is not always easy to convince management that the marketing budget should have a priority claim in limited funds. Although this is less of an issue in commercially-oriented organizations, it can be a major problem in arts and entertainment organizations and non-profit groups. The idea of spending money on marketing (which is frequently not viewed as a core activity) at the expense of collections, maintenance, acquisitions, or expanding performance programmes is often a very contentious issue.

7. Marketing control

The penultimate step in the planning process is to ensure that objectives will be achieved in the required time, using the funds and resources requested. In order to measure effectiveness, evaluation programmes have to be put in place, and regular monitoring needs to occur. The most important reason for insisting on precision in setting objectives is to make it possible to measure results. Such results for a tourism business might be flow of bookings against planned capacity, enquiry and sales response related to any advertising, customer awareness of advertising messages measured by research surveys, sales response to any price discounts and sales promotions, sales response to any merchandising efforts by travel agents, consumer use of websites and flow of bookings achieved, and customer satisfaction measurements. VisitScotland planned to measure the success of the Homecoming and Drive It Home initiatives by studying participation levels at events and tracking web hits.

8. Communicating the plan

Involving as many staff members as possible in the process of setting objectives and drawing up plans that communicate well is an important aspect of motivating staff at all levels and securing enthusiastic participation in the implementation process. It is especially important for service businesses, in which so many staff members have direct contact with customers on the premises. Marketing plans are also important in communicating with stakeholders outside the company. Approaching banks or other investors – for example, in tourism projects funded by government sources – invariably requires a business plan in which marketing is a primary component. Where money is granted, evidence of results will be required through a formal evaluation process. In terms of presenting the report, many readers, both inside and outside the organization, will be impatient and will want the conclusions immediately. The executive summary is therefore a key section of the report.

Snapshot: Golfing the Sahara

Magazan Beach Resort, Morocco, courtesy of Magazan Beach Resort

Golf in North Africa has been growing since its early origins in the late 19th century when it was first introduced by the British in Egypt. The first private club established there was the Gezira Sporting Club in 1882 for the British Army. This was open to the general public in 1952 and the 18-hole golf course is now a private members' club.

Dependent highly on tourism, around 43 courses had spread across North Africa by 2008, mainly concentrated in Morocco. Three of Morocco's 18 courses are at Royal Dar Es Salaam in Rabat which hosts the annual King Hassan II golf tournament. Egypt now has approximately 14 courses, concentrated in Cairo, Alexandria and several tourism resorts. Tunisia has 10 and Algeria has launched golf with a course at Deli Ibrahim. There – and also in Libya and Sudan – golf is played mainly on sand courses but there were a few grass courses in the pipeline in 2008. The majority of courses are set in touristy areas along the North African coastline. They are often high quality, designed by renowned golf course architects as part of master-planned resorts and golfing communities. Revenues at most of these courses are generated largely from green fees from tourists rather than from memberships.

Andrea Sartori is Head of Golf Advisory Practice in Europe, Middle East and Africa for KPMG Advisory Ltd, a market intelligence company. In his report *Golf Benchmark Survey in North Africa*, he surveyed 20 golf course managers from North Africa to create a picture of golf in the region which has an ideal, year-round climate for golf growth. Sartori noted that golf course development in the late 1990s coincided with the rise of tourism. More recently the number of domestic golfers has started to grow with around 9000 golfers living in the region by 2008 – one in 10,000 inhabitants. Over half of these golfers are in Morocco, with Egypt numbering around 3000 and Tunisia almost 1000. Notably, around 30 per cent of local golfers are women and 11 per cent juniors, according to Sartori's statistics. These high figures are due to the large proportion of players being ex-pats whose wives and children also join clubs. Initiation fees are minimal – averaging around $320.

Annual subscriptions start from $800 with a few courses charging $1300 or more. Many courses still charge members green fees on top of subs but green fees are lower in North Africa than most tourism destinations – around $70–80 for 18 holes (compared to $150 in Dubai, for example). Staffing levels are high in North African clubs, particularly in the golf maintenance departments. Large fleets of carts are also offered – around 40–50 on average. Some activities are outsourced to external suppliers – such as pro shop and food and beverage services.

With Morocco just 3 hours flight from London, the British are particularly targeted as customers. Cheaper green fees, high quality food, year-round weather, topnotch courses, unspoilt scenery and friendly people are all touted as selling factors in comparison with Portugal and Spain, Britain's most popular golfing destinations.

In the 1980s and 1990s, Tunisia had the reputation of a cheap holiday destination particularly favoured by Europeans seeking sunshine and beach activities. However, in 2006 Melody Mehta – a marketing consultant for a London advertising agency – was given the job of repositioning Tunisia in the middle and high end of the tourism market. 'Golf will eventually become an important part of that strategy,' Mehta said. 'It's one of the premium elements in the tourism marketplace.' While working on the company pitch for the advertising account, Mehta coincidentally heard a BBC interview with the Tunisian Minister for Tourism, in which he claimed golf development as a high priority.

Mehta's challenge was to come up with a new branding strategy for Tunisia. 'The overarching issue was that Tunisia didn't conjure up a clear picture in people's minds. Egypt, Australia, Canada, for example, all bring clear images to people. In destination marketing you have to have that, so the first objective was image,' she explained. Her method was to create various 'pillars' around which to develop the marketing and advertising campaign. The primary pillar was Sahara. 'It is a very exotic name and no-one actually owns it or markets their ownership of it,' said Mehta. Her second pillar was Carthage which, although famous throughout history and literature, was hard for people to pinpoint on a map. 'A particular segment of medium to well educated people have heard of it but even they don't know where it is,' said Mehta, who utilized the historical association of Hannibal and the elephants to the area to link Carthage with Tunisia. Her third pillar was luxury and the fourth the Mediterranean Sea. Stressing the country's proximity to tourist hubs in Europe, she emphasized the fact that Tunisia is only 20 minutes further by air from the UK than Cyprus.

The first phase of Mehta's strategy was creating visual pictures in people's minds. 'It takes two to three years for those to start getting through so you put that out via advertising until people really start associating those things with Tunisia,' she explained. Elements such as wine production and tasting could then follow. Golf – which pulls on all the pillars of the campaign – could also be run as a future sub-strategy. The target market was Europe in general with a focus on the UK in particular due to the frequency with which the British travel. 'The average British tourist takes five overseas breaks per year so we're leveraging into that,' she said.

So far the rebranding is helping consolidate Tunisia's upmarket image: 'When I started Tunisia was not on any UK lists of popular or desirable destinations. Six months after the launch Tunisia was number six in the ratings,' said Mehta. She hoped that 'Golfing the Sahara' could become a draw for golf enthusiasts. 'It's the sand trap of a lifetime, after all,' she quipped.

Sources:

Interview with Melody Mehta, marketing consultant for Fox Kalomaski, London, 23 March 2009.

Sartori, A. (2008) *Golf Benchmark Survey in North Africa*, KPMG, accessed from www.golfbenchmark.com.

www.royalgolfdaressalam.com; www.morocco-travel.com

Pricing

As seen in the Snapshot on golf in North Africa, pricing is crucial to successful marketing, but it is often the least understood of the marketing mix elements. The prices that an organization charges for its products must strike a balance between gaining acceptance with the target market and making profit for the organizations. The pricing element of the marketing mix is unique in that it is the only one that directly affects an organization's revenues, and hence its profits. The fields of finance and economics have much to contribute in setting prices, but on their own perhaps do not lead to the best pricing decisions. Other marketing mix decisions will often interact with pricing decisions. Product quality (both real and perceived) needs to be considered in light of price. Knowledge of the 'price–quality trade-off' compels decision-makers to recognize that consumers might accept a higher cost for a better quality of product. It was mentioned in Chapter 5 that Trump National Los Angeles felt that discounting would cheapen the Trump brand and would maybe attract a different target market. Similarly, with regard to brand image – often the consequence of marketing communications decisions – lesser-known brands might command lower prices. This would be the case for Kashmir (see the case study) as it seeks to establish itself as a golfing destination. Finally, pricing decisions must take into account the needs of the distributor. Distributors will sell a product only if they will obtain a certain profit margin.

As with other elements in the marketing mix, pricing should be treated as a tool to achieve corporate and marketing objectives. If the target market has been clearly identified, and a decision has been made about where a product is to be positioned, then pricing will become easier to determine. Trump National is clearly positioning its Los Angeles course as an upscale, luxury golf experience, so prices are set accordingly. Companies choosing to position their products in the mass market and to enter a field with many competitors will need to adopt a very careful pricing policy. Those seeking to appeal to niche markets – such as luxury golf cruises in the Caribbean – may have slightly more price flexibility, since they have fewer competitors and perhaps more points of difference between their products and others in the niche. The Old Course Hotel in St Andrews, Scotland, can afford to charge over $2600 for three nights and a round of golf, because no one else can guarantee a tee time on the Old Course, a sought after experience for serious golfers.

Whatever the strategy of the organization is, clear pricing objectives should be established before price levels are set. The key factors determining pricing decisions are shown in Figure 6.3. They are marketing objectives, costs, other mix variables, channel member expectations, buyer perceptions, competition, and legal and regulatory restrictions.

Figure 6.3: Factors affecting pricing decisions (Source: Dibb *et al.*, 1994).

Generally, companies use pricing as part of their positioning of a product, employing one of three strategic approaches: premium pricing, value-for-money pricing, and undercut pricing (Dickman, 1999). In premium pricing, a decision is made to set prices above market price, to reflect either the image of quality or the unique status of the product. Trump National Los Angeles appears to be following this pricing strategy. In value-for-money pricing, the intention is to charge medium prices and emphasize that the product represents excellent value for money at this price. VisitScotland is following this type of strategy as depicted in the opening Spotlight. Organizations with well-established reputations for service generally do well with such a pricing strategy: Fairmont Hotels & Resorts, for example. The objective in undercut pricing is to undercut the competition by setting lower prices, and the lower price is used as a trigger for immediate purchasing. Entrants into the low-cost airline segment use this tactic. Unit profits are low, but satisfactory overall profits are achieved through high turnover. This strategy is often used by organizations seeking a foot in or rapid expansion into a new market. Indian golf courses have been able to get a foothold in the international golf market by charging low green fees compared to other countries. Courses in India charge on average $13 during the week and $18 at the weekend (KPMG, 2008). Despite the fact that tourists are charged two to four times more than the locals, golf remains an elite sport in India.

Any of these policies can be seen as 'fair-pricing' policies. A fair price can be defined as one that the customer is happy to pay while the company achieves a satisfactory level of profit. Thus a premium-pricing policy is acceptable, provided that the customer receives the benefits appropriate to the price. Only when companies are able to force up prices against the consumers' will, such as in the case of monopolies, can it be said that fair pricing is inoperative.

Basic approaches to pricing

Organizations involved in the marketing of tourism, leisure, and hospitality products use different methods of calculation to set prices. Pricing methods fall into three main categories:

♦ Cost-based pricing – the addition of a certain monetary amount or percentage to the actual or estimated costs of a service to arrive at a final price, drawing heavily on the accounting discipline of costing. To use this method, it is necessary to understand the differences in the nature of costs. At the simplest level, costs can be split into two types. *Fixed costs* do not vary with the amount of the service provided. Hence a golf resort has the fixed cost of the accommodation to bear, whether or not rooms are occupied. *Variable costs* increase as more of a service is provided. For example, the energy and cleaning costs of accommodation will increase as more guests occupy the rooms. These two cost elements can be combined with revenue – which should increase as more of the service is sold – to give a picture of when an operation becomes profitable. Having established the cost of doing business, the simplest approach to pricing is to add next a standard mark-up to the cost of the product, known as cost-plus pricing. For example, Stewart Creek Golf Club in Alberta (see Chapter 10) will mark up most inexpensive wines by 100 per cent, and higher end bottles by about 50 per cent. So a bottle of wine purchased at $20 will be sold for $40, and a bottle that cost the club $100 will be sold for $150.

  The concept of marginal costing, which attempts to identify the cost of one or more unit of a product, is an important one in cost-plus pricing, since it offers the marketing manager a flexible tool for pricing. For example, in the case of a golf course, the additional cost of allowing one more golfer on the course is extremely small. Therefore, once break-even is achieved, it becomes very attractive to price the 'marginal green fee' (any fees over the number that have to be sold to break even) at a price that will attract market demand from those unwilling to pay regular fees. Many golf courses offer reduced twilight green fees to attract such golfers.

♦ Demand-based methods – sometimes called 'buyer-based pricing' (or 'sensitivity pricing'), techniques in this category share the feature of giving major consideration to the consumer. These methods allow for high prices when the demand is high and for lower prices when the demand is low, regardless of the cost of the product. This is a tactic used by The Vale Hotel, Golf and Spa Resort in Glamorgan, Wales. During the autumn, when demand is low, the resort offers half-price green fees for four balls, and two-for-one offers for golfing packages. Such pricing is also common for golf resorts in Arizona where golf tends to be more expensive in the winter due to higher demand and cheaper in the hotter months of the summer. In the UK, golf courses are finding that demand for annual memberships is falling, whereas the number of golfers playing is remaining steady. Some have suggested therefore that golf clubs consider a more flexible form of membership whereby a smaller annual membership is charged together with a small fee for playing (O'Sullivan, 2009). Other courses are looking to increase revenues from non-members. Saunton Golf Club in North Devon, UK, for example, has a 60 to 40 per cent ratio of members to non-members (the norm is 70 to 30 per cent) and attempts to offer a more balanced portfolio of products and services than traditional members' clubs. Although the course is number one priority, the club emphasizes excellent service, fine catering and pleasant, comfortable areas in which to change (Victor, 2009).

◆ **Competition-oriented** – in which an organization fixes the prices of products in relation to competitors' prices; this is often also called going-rate pricing. This method offers the advantage of giving the organization the opportunity to increase sales or market share, but it is a dangerous approach to pricing, as it does not focus on either costs or the consumer. The arguments for this approach are that the industry will have developed prices that are acceptable to the marketplace and there is little to be gained by offering different prices (so-called 'industry wisdom'). The counter-argument is that there may be the opportunity to offer different prices (and therefore possibly to achieve better profits) that the majority of the industry has ignored.

For setting prices, marketers need to have an understanding of yield management. *Yield* is the profit that is made on the sales of goods and services; it is calculated based on the number of customers, how much they spend, and the number of products they buy. Yield management is the practice of developing strategies to maximize opportunities for the sale of an organization's perishable products, such as airline seats, hotel rooms, and tour seats, and therefore improving its long-term viability. More simply, it has been defined as 'lowering the price ... according to expected demand, and relying heavily on computers and modeling techniques' (Lundberg *et al.*, 1995). It was initiated by the airline industry in the 1980s as a way to increase revenue from existing routes and aircraft. Computer technology made it possible for airlines to predict the number of seats that would be sold on a given flight – called the load factor. By analyzing costs, and also determining the price sensitivity of various types of airfares, airlines discovered that by offering seats at a variety of special fares they could boost load and revenues. Yield management is also used by golf facilities. For example, Troon Golf applies yield management in order to make pricing decisions at its courses. Members of the Troon Card loyalty programme, for example, are offered rates from 30–50 per cent off the rack rate at participating courses, depending on seasonality. In 2008, the Troon Card programme delivered 73,891 rounds of golf and $5,172,407 in revenue to participating courses (Troon Golf, 2009).

Pricing strategies for new products or service

When a new product enters the market, it is vital to obtain market share and create the desired image for the product in the consumer's eyes. New products face unique problems. If the product is truly new – something never before available in the marketplace – it will be extremely difficult for consumers to develop a sense of what price is appropriate. If there are no similar products with which to compare it, they may either undervalue the innovation or perhaps overvalue it. Detailed research on price sensitivity, clearly outlining the unique features of the new product and researching the best way to communicate this information to consumers, will be important.

Three strategies commonly used for the introduction of new products are prestige pricing, market skimming, and penetration pricing. Prestige pricing sets prices high to position a product at the upper or luxury end of the market. For example, the Marquis Los Cabos hotel in Baja California created a three-night package in 2007 with a private jet and golf with Jack Nicklaus, and set the price at $7 million. Market skimming calls for setting high prices at the launch stage and progressively lowering them as the product becomes better established and progresses through its life cycle. The policy takes advantage of the fact that most products are in high demand in the early stage of the life cycle, when they are novel or unique or when supplies are limited. If the product anticipates a very short life cycle – as in the case of major events such as the Ryder Cup golf tournament – and organizing and marketing costs must be recovered quickly, market skimming is a sensible policy to pursue. Penetration pricing is the opposite of market skimming, as prices are set at a very low initial level. If an organization is trying to achieve maximum distribution for the product in the initial stages, it will probably price at a lower level to obtain maximum sales and market share.

Other pricing techniques

There are a number of other pricing techniques available to marketers. These include promotional pricing, product bundling, price spread and price points, discriminatory pricing, discounting, and all-inclusive pricing. Promotional pricing is used by companies when they temporarily sell products below their normal list price (or rack rate). Usually this is done for a short period of time, often to introduce new or re-vamped products, or to promote a special event. The assumption is made that consumers will buy other items at normal price levels along with the promotionally-priced items. Promotional pricing is often used in conjunction with product-bundle pricing, when a company groups several of its products together to promote them as a package. An example is the Naples Beach Holiday & Golf Club in Florida which had a special room rate in 2009 in conjunction with its annual 'SummerJazz on the Gulf' concert series. The $183 rate included green fees, two reserved beach chairs, tennis, access to the resort's spa and fitness centre, valet parking, afternoon tea and children's activities.

Organizations in tourism and hospitality try to offer a price spread – a range of products that will suit the budget of all target markets. A holiday park, for example, may offer campsites with tents, standard cabins, en suite cabins, and family units, each different from the other in terms of size, location, types of fittings and furnishings. The range of prices that an organization can set is virtually unlimited. However, research in the restaurant sector has suggested that if the price spread is too wide, consumers will tend to order from among the lower-priced items (Carmin and Norkus, 1990). Price points are the number of 'stops' along the way between the lowest-priced item and the highest-priced item. Price points vary among industry sectors and types of business. In a restaurant, it is possible to create a menu with a wide range of dishes and to allot a different price to each dish. Golf destinations may also create a number of price points. The Spotlight on Scotland indicated that the country had 550 courses with a number of price points, ranging from $25 as the cheapest to $400 at St Andrews.

Organizations often alter prices to suit different customers, products, locations, and times. This discriminatory pricing allows the organization to sell a product or service at two or more prices, despite the fact that the product costs are the same. For example, many restaurants charge higher prices in the evening than they do at lunchtime, even if the food is identical, because of demand differences. Golf courses usually charge more for a weekend green fee than during the week because demand is higher on a Saturday or Sunday. The market must be capable of being segmented if discriminatory pricing is going to be an effective strategy. Segments will have highly distinct sensitivities, and being able to price differently to the various segments is key to success in maximizing profits (Hiemstra, 1998). Care should also be taken to ensure that the strategy is legal and that it does not lead to customer resentment.

From time to time, most businesses will need to consider discounting their standard prices. Many tourism organizations engage in volume discounting – offering special rates to attract customers who agree to major purchases. Golf resorts for example, may offer special prices (or upgrades) to corporate clients to encourage volume business, or they may use loyalty programmes to ensure that travellers use their brand. The discount will often reflect the level of overall demand, discounting during slow periods and low seasons. A discounted price is only a wise move if it increases demand, brings new users, or increases consumption by regular users. Organizations that discount key products but don't lower costs to offset the discount are taking an economic risk unless the discount is only for a very short period or is designed to overcome a very specific problem. There is also the risk that discounting may not lead to increased demand.

Other popular strategies include all-in pricing or all-inclusive pricing. This type of pricing was used originally in holiday camps in the UK where customers were provided access to every entertainment facility in the camp for a single price. The strategy proved highly successful, and Club Med built on this model for its chain of holiday resorts around the world. Club Med now advertises 'total all-inclusive' holidays, so that consumers pay for no extras whatsoever. Today, tourists are very familiar with booking all-inclusive holidays in resorts like those in the Caribbean and Mexico, and some are packaging in free golf. Almond Resort's Smugglers' Cove in St Lucia, for example, included three rounds of golf as part of its 2009 all-inclusive package.

Snapshot: New Mexico Golf Tourism Alliance

Black Mesa Golf Club, New Mexico, courtesy of New Mexico Tourism Department, photographer Dan Monaghan

Golf is very important to the New Mexico's tourism coffers. A poll of tourists in 2003 revealed that 4 per cent of visitors to New Mexico came specifically to golf. The area boasts a more equable, all-year-round golf climate than other southern or desert states and rounds are cheaper, even for top quality courses. Golf brings in more than $500 million per year according to an industry-funded study by New Mexico State University. The 2006 research advocated increasing the amount of rounds played by out-of-state visitors as the best way to boost room-nights and associated lodgers' tax collections for local governments.

The 'Golf on the Santa Fe Trail' was established in 2003, featuring eight high desert New Mexico golf courses in the Rio Grande corridor. Golf on the Santa Fe Trail was named in the top two golf trails in the USA in *Golf Magazine* in 2007. The group spent more than $243,000 marketing its courses and the state in general as a golf destination, targeting Dallas, Tulsa, Midland, Houston, Phoenix and Minnesota markets. In 2004, it booked 560 rounds of golf and 288 room-nights, accounting for $35,000 in revenue. By 2006, it had booked 4200 rounds and 1880 room-nights for a total economic impact of $425,000.

In 2005, both golf industry professionals and the local tourism authority saw the potential for a bigger joint marketing thrust, linking all the state's 70 plus golf amenities. Ski New Mexico was created in 1973 to promote New Mexico as a ski destination.

In a bid to create a golfing counterpart, Governor Bill Richardson sought funding to establish a concerted state-wide golf marketing drive. Although domestic golf was on the increase in the region, it was insufficient to sustain the area's golf operations. After many months of planning facilitated by The Albuquerque Convention & Visitors Bureau and the *Sun Country Golf* free newspaper, New Mexico's golf and hospitality industries joined forces in 2006 to create a non-profit alliance to promote New Mexico as a national golf-tourism destination. Under the auspices of the Sun Country Section PGA, the alliance was comprised of representatives from the golf industry, the lodging industry and convention and visitors bureaus. A board of directors was formed with Warren Lehr, director of golf at Paa-Ko Ridge Golf Club, as first president of the alliance. He was also vice president of the Golf on the Santa Fe Trail website. In 2009, he was succeeded by Dan Koesters, director of golf at New Mexico State University golf course.

The new organization's mandate was to develop marketing and advertising strategies to attract out-of-state golfers, encourage golf stay-and-play packages, cooperate with the New Mexico Tourism Department in joint marketing and develop local golf-tourism partnerships among and between local courses, lodgers and restaurants. Short-term, the alliance would focus on developing a unified Internet presence, publishing a printed state-wide golf guide for the 2007 and 2008 golf seasons, and training New Mexico lodging-industry staff to cater to the needs of golf tourists. Longer-term projects included development of a national marketing strategy and identification of core golf-tourism markets, as well as integration of real-time, web-based tee-time reservations with lodging reservations.

Dana Lehner, Tournament Director of the Sun Country PGA, described the alliance's goal as raising awareness. 'New Mexico is an unknown destination. If you live outside our borders, it's easy to confuse us with Phoenix or Dallas when in reality we are much different, based on our higher elevation, it's cooler, so much better weather for golf, and our price points are around half to a third of Phoenix. But, unfortunately, until now we've not done a very good job of educating people outside our borders about that.' The alliance would be a cooperative effort between golf and lodging facilities to pool their resources along with government aid, he explained. The fledgling alliance applied to New Mexico Tourism for a Cooperative Advertising Grant in 2008 and was awaiting official confirmation of the amount in July 2009. 'We spoke with the governor and presented it to the committee last fall and asked for half a million. We were shooting for the stars but our state is having a hard time with the economy so we have no idea how much we'll get yet,' said Lehner. The New Mexico Tourism Department offers Cooperative Marketing Grant Programs to tourism-related, non-profit organizations to promote events and destinations to visitors from 50 miles away or more. The department will match on a 33 per cent or 50 per cent basis. Originally, the Golf on the Santa Fe Trail group had applied for this kind of government sponsorship but was not eligible as their group wasn't state-wide. Lehner said this was one of the spurs that got the wider alliance started. 'So far we're kind of in our infancy. We've been putting the group together but we've not put it all into an official ad campaign yet. We've created some media collateral pieces, sent information out via golf booths around the country and in the Visitor and Convention Bureau, and created the website. A major ad effort will follow in next year or so.'

Initial outreach efforts of the new alliance were funded by golf courses' and lodgers' financial commitments. Individual commitments to the alliance are variable, with tiered levels of exposure available via the alliance's cooperative marketing and advertising. All golf courses – as well as hospitality businesses and tour packagers – in the state are eligible for representation. Ruidoso, Las Cruces, Northern New Mexico, the Four Corners and the existing Golf on the Santa Fe Trail corridor in central New Mexico were natural focuses for packages via the alliance, which was also open to suggestions throughout the state for similar golf-tourism loops.

New Mexico has both variety and quality within its golf product. Lehr's course, Paa-ko Ridge, scored five out of five stars in *Golf Digest/*Fodor's 'Best Places to Play' in 2007. But New Mexico's key marketing differential is cost. 'New Mexico has 11 courses rated by *Golf Digest* at four stars or higher, but the real beauty of the golf here is the value,' said Ken Adams, co-publisher of the Sun Country Golf newspaper. 'We have courses with greens fees of $40 to $100 that would cost $200 to $350 elsewhere. Combine that quality and value with the terrific climate across this state and you have a first-rate, year-round golf destination,' said Adams, who was serving as volunteer executive director of the new alliance.

Sources

http://www.golflink.com/golf-courses/state.aspx?state=NM

http://assets.bizjournals.com/albuquerque/stories/2007/05/28/focus1.html

www.cybergolf.com/

www.golfonthesantafetrail.com

www.paakoridge.com

http://www.nmenv.state.nm.us/cpb/InfFinCon/documents/CooperativeMarketingGrantProgram.pdf

Distribution

An organization's distribution system is centred on the 'place' aspect of a company's marketing mix. Its purpose is to provide an adequate framework for making a company's product or service available to the consumer. In the tourism industry, distribution systems are often used to move the customer to the product. In the Snapshot above, an alliance was formed in New Mexico in order to distribute the golf tourism product, but the first and most simple form of distribution is a direct distribution channel, a channel through which a company delivers its product to the consumer without the outside assistance of any independent intermediaries. In such a case, the service provider is solely responsible for the delivery of its product. Most bed and breakfasts use a direct distribution channel to market products to potential customers. They perform all of the necessary channel functions on their own, without relying on any assistance from outside intermediaries. The accommodations surrounding the Paraparauma Beach Golf Club (see Chapter 5) follow such a strategy.

The second type of distribution channel used to deliver a product is an indirect channel. In this case, the service provider makes use of independent intermediaries to help facilitate the distribution if its product. Outside intermediaries such as travel agents, tour operators, and other tourism specialists assist the supplying company by helping to attract consumers to the product or destination. Most international golf resorts use both methods of distribution to sell golfing holidays. They will target consumers directly through a website, newsletter, videos and promotional written material, but will also use intermediaries – in the form of selected tour operators around the world – to attract customers. The Case Study at the end of the chapter describes how tourism officials in Kashmir were hosting 'fam' (familiarization) tours for leading travel agents and tour operators both from within the country and abroad, order to encourage golf tourism in the region.

Travel agents offer the tourism customer a variety of services, including everything from transportation plans and tour packages to insurance services and accommodation. They are the most widely used marketing intermediaries in the tourism industry. An agency will earn a commission for each sale, the amount depending on the type of product sold. The travel agency market is very competitive. Barriers to entry are low and as a result there are many new entrants, which is especially true for the rapidly growing segment of online agents. Independent travel agents are under pressure not only from e-agents but also from direct selling by tour operators. They therefore seek to differentiate themselves, and add value to the product in order to justify their role in the value chain and retain market share.

Tour operators are organizations that offer packaged vacation tours to the general public. These packages can include everything from transportation, accommodation and activities to entertainment, meals, and drinks. Tour operators typically focus their marketing efforts on the leisure market, which represents the dominant buying group of travel packages. Tour operators have the ability to bring in large volumes of customers. They receive discounted rates from the various service providers in exchange for providing a large number of guaranteed visitors. Tour operators make their profits by providing low-margin travel packages to a large number of consumers. Typically, organizations that offer travel packages must sell between 75 and 85 per cent of the packages available in order to break even. Tour operators are increasingly selling their packages direct to customers cutting out travel agents by using their own outlets or web pages. A large number of tour operators cater specifically to the golf tourism market, and some of these operators were discussed in Chapter 3.

Convention and meeting planners plan and coordinate their organizations' external meeting events. These planners work for associations, corporations, large non-profit organizations, government agencies, and educational institutions. Some combine the task of convention planning with that of corporate travel management, whereas other organizations split up the tasks. The private sector is also involved in the marketing of conventions and exhibitions. It was mentioned in Chapter 3 that golf can be a very important consideration for convention and meeting planners, and a growing number of meeting planners are adding golf events to their itineraries.

Travel specialists are intermediaries that specialize in performing one or more functions of a company's distribution system. Hotel representatives, for example, specialize in providing contact with a hotel's customers in order to identify their specific accommodation needs. Advertising agencies can also act as specialists, performing the promotional aspect of a company's distribution system. By using travel specialists in its distribution system, a company can designate particular functions to the intermediaries that are best equipped to perform them. Focusing on one specific operation within the distribution channel allows the travel specialist to perform effectively the function at hand in the best possible way.

Some stakeholders in the travel industry, such as airlines, car rental companies, and international hotel chains, have been quick to grasp the potential of marketing and selling their services online. They have recognized an opportunity to bypass intermediaries and to sell their basic products and services directly to the customer. Many hotels have developed web-based booking tools for both leisure and group sales. Increasingly, package holiday tour operators are including direct sales via the Internet in their sales strategy, thus bypassing the travel agent. Since the Internet encourages direct and immediate contact between suppliers and customers, together with a decrease in transaction and commission costs, there is a strong case for the elimination of intermediaries entirely. Chapter 7 has a dedicated section on the use of the Internet for marketing golf tourism.

Distribution mix strategy

Organizations must decide how to make their services available to their selected target market by choosing their distribution mix strategy. This can be a complex decision. The mix must provide them with the maximum amount of exposure to potential travellers as well as ensure that the strategy aligns with the company or destination image. In addition, the strategy should maximize control over sales and reservations and should work within the organization's budget.

An organization can consider three broad distribution strategy choices:

1. **Intensive distribution** – in this case the organization maximizes the exposure of its travel services by distributing through all available outlets or intermediaries. This strategy is most useful for an organization that is trying to obtain high market coverage. An example would be Disney's Celebration Golf Course in Orlando, Florida (see Chapter 3).

2. **Exclusive distribution** – here the organization deliberately restricts the number of channels that it uses to distribute its product or service to its customers. Because only a limited number of intermediaries are given the right to distribute the product, the result is often a strengthening of the company's image and an increase in the status of those who purchase the product. This strategy is an effective method for prestige tourism products like The World, the only residential community at sea. In 2009, The World offered a number of golf voyages, the last one being in Australia between 6-18 December. Prices started at $11,150 per person based on double occupancy.

3. Selective distribution – in this strategy, a compromise between intensive and exclusive distribution, a company uses more than one but less than all of the possible distribution channels. Sandals Resorts Golf School, Jamaica would be an example of a resort using selective distribution (see Chapter 2).

Alliances

A further form of distribution is via an alliance – New Mexico has developed an excellent example of this cooperative project (see previous Snapshot). An alliance is a partnership formed when two or more organizations combine resources through a contractual agreement that allows them to overcome each other's weaknesses by benefiting from each another's strengths. In this form of distribution channel, each organization shares everything from information to resources to strategies, but the key advantage to alliances is increased distribution. Those organizations joined through the alliance will enjoy access to new markets through new and diversified sales locations. Also referred to as clusters (Porter, 1998), alliances involve businesses in one geographical area that work collaboratively to draw customers to their common location, where as individual rivals they then compete to draw these customers into their own specific business.

Increasingly golfing organizations are collaborating in order to create a competitive advantage for the area, as was seen in the New Mexico Golf Tourism Alliance Snapshot. Other alliances have been referred to earlier in the book, such as the Orlando Golf Trail, Divine Nine in Nevada, Thompson- Okanagan Golf Trail, and the Ho Chi Minh Golf Trail in Vietnam. Another example is Golf Cape Breton, a group of five courses that have banded together to promote golfing opportunities in Cape Breton, Canada. The alliance was formed in 1996 when each of the courses realized they could achieve more by working together than through solo efforts. Each of the member courses makes a significant financial contribution to the 'destination society' in order to support marketing and promotional activities. The organization has also received ongoing funding from Enterprise Cape Breton Corporation, a local economic development agency. The group is promoted through a dedicated website – golfcapebreton.com – and through an e-newsletter sent out to golfers who have signed up to receive information about Cape Breton golf.

Golf courses often form alliances with those in the accommodation sector. An example was given in Chapter 5, with Trump National partnering up with a nearby resort in the hope that having high-end accommodations nearby would help attract more golf tourists. Another example is Roco Ki resort in the Dominican Republic, referred to in Chapter 4, which has partnered with a nearby boutique property, Sivory, to offer packages to golf tourists. This was because accommodation at the golf resort was not due to be open until 2010.

Case Study: Kashmir – a golfer's paradise?

The Piramal Healthcare presents
J & K Tourism-Air India Golf Tournament
2009, courtesy of Majeed

With Kashmir notorious for civil unrest and terrorism right up until 2007, it will be no mean task for the Tourism Department of Jammu and Kashmir (J&K) to reposition it as a golfers' paradise. Nevertheless, this is the mandate for the J&K department headed up by permanent secretary, Naeem Akhtar. The price is right, with Kashmir golf less than $20 for 18 holes, $10 for cart rental and $3 for a caddy. However, a visible military presence in the area could deter more conservative golf travellers. Despite the waning of terrorist incidents in the past few years, many European countries and the USA still had travel warnings in place in 2009.

Golf in the area dates back over 100 years, introduced during the British Raj. Golfers are now being targeted by the government as higher spenders than the typical backpackers often attracted to the area. Brochures and websites dub the J&K region a 'golfers' paradise'. The tourism department is promoting the mountainous destination through print and electronic media and encouraging fam tours from leading travel agents, tour operators and travel writers from within the country and abroad. Since Ghulam Nabi Azad, former Chief Minister of Jammu and Kashmir, declared his desire for the region to become an international golfing hub, officials have been marketing its golf courses, ski hills and resorts at tourism conferences in Europe and the Middle East. The Gulmarg ski area was featured on Ride Guide (a North American outdoor adventure television production) in 2009 showing free-skiing and snowboarding stars visiting the rudimentary Himalayan resort.

Although much of the state's hotel and hospitality industry is state-run (by the J&K Tourism Development Corporation), private investment is also being encouraged. Pride Group Holdings, a Dubai-based retail, property and investment company was planning a $500 million investment in Kashmir's tourism in 2008. The company's CEO Musadiq Shah, a native of the area, said that Pride Resorts' main aim was to reinstate Kashmir on the tourist map. 'We cherish our culture and the respect for our roots motivated us to form Pride Resorts, a footprint in the hospitality industry in Kashmir, with the intent to revive Kashmir's tourism' said Shah, in his website address. Pride's flagship retail store is Pride of Kashmir, first established in the UAE in 1980. The Kashmir project was projected to create up to 2500 direct jobs in the region – with more than 10,000 indirect job opportunities – over four different five-star developments in Srinagar, Gulmarg, Pahalgam and Tanmarg. Naeem Akhtar pledged the tourism department's support of the project, whose first phase was scheduled for opening in 2010 in Tanmarg. A high-end project, modelled on the resorts of Aspen, Colorado, it would be a ski destination in winter and a golf resort in spring and summer.

High profile events have also been used to stimulate golf tourism. In 2003 the 1st Ambassador's Cup was held at Srinagar's Royal Springs Golf Club in a bid by the government to attract tourists to the area. Envoys from Spain, Singapore, the Czech Republic, Brunei, Argentina, Thailand, Spain, Morocco and Uruguay attended with their families as well as representatives from Delhi-based industries. The Ambassador's Cup is now called the Piramal Healthcare presents Air India-J&K Tourism Golf Trophy. The picture above is from the 2009 event, once again a great success for the Tourism Department of Jammu and Kashmir, which is doing its best to garner tourists by organizing many tournaments and other events.

The event was promoted by Tiger Sports Marketing (TSM), the company responsible for developing the Indian PGA Tour, the Hero Honda Masters, an Asian Tour event, the Madhavrao Scindia Golf Tournament, the Christel House Open, the American Express series and the Air Sahara Series. TSM has been chosen by the Indian Golf Union as marketing and management partners for the amateur and junior golf tours and overall development of the game in India. The company also engages in golf consultancy, player management, sports media as well as television production with its own dedicated television show – *The Indian Golf Show* on Ten Sports – highlighting all the major golf tournaments it manages.

Director of TSM, Sayeed Sanadi is very enthusiastic about Kashmir golf. 'When the gates of the Royal Springs Golf Course opened in 2000, I personally rejoiced. But it was not until 2003 and that too by sheer chance that I could have a first look after hearing so many wonderful stories about the beauty of the course. It truly is an amazing course, one that you have to see it to believe it. A few years later I also met Robert Trent Jones Junior who designed the course and put in 14 years of hard work in shaping the course,' he said. The course was under renovation in 2009, due to re-open 2010. Sanadi said that Gulmarg and Pahalgam are increasingly popular: 'Gulmarg is attracting the crowds and the nine-hole course at Pahalgam is being converted into an 18-hole course. So golfers can enjoy one whole week in J&K playing at three different courses from next year.'

Sanadi also vouchsafed that the area was safer to visit now and already has attracted considerable traffic of domestic tourists due to golf's new image as the fastest growing sport in the country. He also applauded the efforts of J&K Tourism to put the area on the golf map via corporate and pro golf events. 'J&K Tourism has also tied up with a lot of travel and tour operators and since then have been inviting groups for a golf package. They have had a fair amount of success with the tourist inflow,' he commented.

Weather – and poor road infrastructure – can be treacherous during Kashmir's winter but there is a long golfing season stretching between April and November. Lower temperatures in the mountains mean golf can be played for a longer duration than in the plains. Another advantage for the area is the prevalence of spoken English, especially among the younger generations. It is also one of the government's official languages and is used extensively on signage in the area.

There are many websites promoting golf tours alongside adventure travel and house-boating trips. Kashmirhouseboats.com packages golf with floating accommodation plus tours of the Mughal Gardens at Nishat and Shalimar, visits to Dal Lake, local villages, carpet weaving and handicraft centres.

Sources

Personal interview with Sayeed Sanadi, Director of Tiger Sports Marketing, 15 May 2009

Gentleman, A. (2008) 'Kashmir says come on in, the tee times are safe', *New York Times*, 8 April, accessed from http://www.nytimes.com

Gentleman, A. (2008) 'Beware bunkers in Kashmir's 'golf paradise'', accessed from http://scotlandonsunday.scotsman.com

Anon. (2008) 'Dubai-based Pride Group Holdings to invest $500m in Kashmir', accessed from http://www.ameinfo.com/157353.html

www.pridegh.com

Ahmed, F. (2007) 'Heritage and history sparkle at Kashmir Golf Course', accessed from http://www.twocircles.net/2007jun03/heritage-and-history-sparkle-kashmir-golf-course.html

References

Carey, R. (2009) 'Back for more', *Golf Business Magazine*, accessed 28 January 2009 from http://www.golfbusinessmagazine.com.

Carmin, J. and Norkus, G. (1990) 'Pricing strategies for menus: magic or myth?' *Cornell Hotel and Restaurant Administration Quarterly*, 31 (3), 50.

Crawford-Welch, S. (1991) 'Marketing hospitality in the 21st century', *International Journal of Contemporary Hospitality Management*, 3 (3), 21–27.

Green, P., Tull, D. and Albaum, A. (1988) *Research for Marketing Decisions*, 5th ed., Englewood Cliffs, NJ: Prentice-Hall.

Hiemstra, S. J. (1998) 'Economic pricing strategies for hotels', in T. Baum and R. Mudambi (eds), *Economic and Management Methods for Tourism and Hospitality Research*, New York: Wiley, pp. 215–232.

Hill, B. (2009) 'Seen and heard', *Golf Club Management*, February, 12–13.

Kim S.S., Chun, H. and Petrick, J.F. (2005) 'Positioning analysis of overseas golf tour destinations by Korean golf tourists', *Tourism Management*, **26**, 905–917.

Kotler, P. (1984) *Marketing Management: Analysis, Planning, Implementation and Control*, 8th edn, Upper Saddle River, NJ: Prentice Hall.

KPMG. (2008) *Golf Benchmark Survey 2007: Benchmark Indicators and Performance of Golf Courses in India*, KPMG Advisory Ltd.

Lundberg, D.E., Krishnamoorthy, M. and Stavenga, M.H. (1995) *Tourism Economics*, New York: Wiley, pp. 106.

O'Sullivan, D. (2009) 'Time for change', *Golf Club Management*, January, 52–3.

Porter, M.E. (1980) *Competitive Strategy: Techniques for Analyzing Industry and Competitors*, New York: Free Press.

Porter, M.E. (1998) *On Competition*, Cambridge, MA: Harvard University Press.

Troon Golf. (2009) 2008 Sales & Marketing Summary.

Victor, C. (2009) 'Changing Times at Saunton Golf Club', *Golf Club Management*, January, 56-57.

7 The Marketing of Golf Tourism: Marketing Communications

Kiawah Island's KiawahMoments.com web page

Located just south of Charleston, South Carolina, Kiawah Island Golf Resort is rated as one of the country's top golf resorts by *Golf Magazine* and *Travel + Leisure Golf*. It includes The Sanctuary – an AAA Five Diamond and Mobil Five Star-rated, 255-room hotel and spa – and 600 private villas and luxury homes. The resort has five championship golf courses, including The Ocean Course where the 1991 Ryder Cup, the 2007 Senior PGA and 2012 PGA championships were all hosted.

In June 2008, Kiawah Island Golf Resort and Kiawah Development Partners (KDP) – the island's master developer and real estate company – launched a new interactive website. KiawahMoments.com was created by Dana Communications, the resort's agency of record.

This unique site brought Kiawah Island into the realm of social web media by inviting resort guests, property owners and residents to share their Kiawah Island experiences online. Dana's challenge was to meet diverse marketing goals – from attracting leisure guests to supporting luxury real estate sales – with a campaign that seamlessly promotes one destination. Dana developed KiawahMoments.com to integrate a social marketing forum into the campaign and reach a wide audience of Kiawah's target consumers.

KiawahMoments.com was designed to provide a place to capture and post real-life special moments for others to see and enjoy. Both the resort and the real estate company KDP used a 'Capture Your Kiawah Moment' advertising theme to portray memorable experiences, tell a story and prompt readers to visit KiawahMoments.com for the rest of the story. The engaging, interactive site invites users to upload and share their experiences via videos, photos and blogs. The campaign won a 2008 Magellan Award from *Travel Weekly*, which honours best practices in travel. Capture Your Kiawah Moment was a Gold Award Winner in the Destinations–Advertising/Marketing Campaign category.

Thos Paine is a partner and president of Dana Communications. 'Statistics showing that already about 50 per cent of travellers use online social media in some way to research their plans. Advertisers and marketers are pressed to take advantage of the emerging opportunities this new media presents,' said Paine. 'Social networking, or word-of-mouth advertising, is becoming key to staying on the leading edge of communication between advertisers and consumers, as it allows for a more credible, widespread message. Recognizing the importance of this revolutionary pattern in the hospitality and travel industry, Dana created KiawahMoments.com to provide travellers not only with resources for important resort and real estate information but also with personal touches that enable them to relate to existing customers' experiences'.

The new website also encourages visitors to share Kiawah moments with others by submitting friends' e-mail addresses. As an incentive for spreading this viral word of mouth, participants can enter into a draw for a weekend at Kiawah that includes a two-night stay in a villa or Sanctuary guest room, one round of golf for two, and a one-hour spa treatment for two. The site also operates as a reservations platform, with links to golf vacations and packages, and allows online visitors the opportunity to join the Kiawah email list – thus helping to build customer databases for lead prospecting.

Kiawah Island Golf Resort is also active on Twitter (www.twitter.com/kiawahresort) and has a presence on Facebook. 'We're just on the beginning stages of taking advantage of social media,' said Michael Vegis, Public Relations Director, in May 2009. 'We have about 500 followers on Facebook and only about 100 on Twitter. We've just started putting links to those sites on any e-blasts that go out to try to corral more followers'. On the Facebook site, visitors can keep up to speed with events on the island, download promotional literature, look at restaurant menus, and check out special promotional offers.

Sources

E-mail communication with Michael Vegis, Public Relations Director, Kiawah Island Golf Resort, 28 May 2009

News releases on http://www.danacommunications.com

www.kiawahmoments.com, www.kiawahresort.com.

Introduction

Effective communication with target customers is carried out by a variety of methods, referred to as 'marketing communications', and the Spotlight above highlighted the growing importance of websites for golf destinations. In many people's perception, marketing is promotion, for promotion is the highly visible, public face of marketing. However, promotion is only one element of the marketing mix, its role being to convince potential customers of the benefits of purchasing or using the products and services of a particular organization. Promotions' decisions will be determined by the overall marketing plan, as illustrated in Figure 7.1. Marketing objectives are derived from the strategic tools of targeting and positioning. The marketing mix is then used to achieve these objectives, and promotions are just one part of this marketing mix.

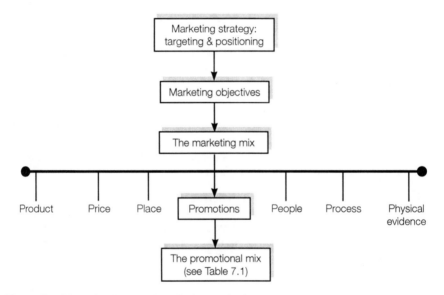

Figure 7.1: The role of promotions in the marketing strategy

The blend of promotional elements outlined in Table 7.1 is known as the promotional mix, and promotional management involves coordinating all the elements, setting objectives and budgets, designing programmes, evaluating performance, and taking corrective action. Promotion can be a short-term activity, but considered at a strategic level it is a mid- and long-term investment aimed at building up a consistent and credible corporate or destination identity. Promotion, when used effectively, builds and creates an identity for the product or the organization. Brochures, websites, advertisements, in-store merchandising, sales promotions, and so on, create the identity of the company in the mind of the consumer, and all aspects of the promotional effort should therefore project the same image to the consumer.

Table 7.1: The promotional mix used in tourism

Promotional tool	Tourism application
Advertising	Television, newspapers, magazines, billboards, Internet, brochures, guidebooks
Sales promotion	Short-term incentives to induce purchase. Aimed at salespeople, distributors such as travel agents, and consumers. Can be joint promotions. Include merchandising and familiarization trips.
Public relations	All non-paid media exposure appearing as editorial coverage. Includes sponsorship of events and causes.
Personal selling	Meetings and workshops for intermediaries; telephone contact and travel agents for consumers
Word of mouth	Promotion by previous consumers to their social and professional contacts. Often perceived by consumers to be the most credible form of promotion.
Direct marketing	Direct mail, telemarketing, and travel exhibitions
Internet marketing	Direct e-mail marketing, Internet advertising, customer service, and selling and market research

Perhaps one of the most important advances in marketing in recent decades has been the rise of integrated marketing communications (IMC): the unification of all marketing communications tools, as well as corporate and brand messages, so they send a consistent, persuasive message to target audiences. This approach recognizes that advertising can no longer be crafted and executed in isolation from other promotional mix elements. As tourism markets and the media have grown more complex and fragmented, consumers find themselves in an ever more confusing marketing environment. Tourism marketers must address this situation by conveying a consistent, unified message in all of their promotional activities. An IMC campaign includes traditional marketing communication tools, such as advertising or sales promotion, but recognizes that other areas of the marketing mix like the Internet are also used in communications. Planning and managing these elements so they work together helps to build a consistent brand or company image.

One final factor to consider in the promotional strategy will be the position of the organization in the distribution channel. For example, does a retailer (i.e. the travel agent) carry out its own promotion for the travel product, or does the producer (i.e. the tour operator or destination) have to promote the product in order to bring the public into the travel agency to buy it? This is known as the choice between push and pull promotional strategies. A push strategy calls for using the sales force and trade promotion to push the product through channels; the producer promotes the product to wholesalers, the wholesalers promote to retailers, and the retailers to consumers. In contrast, a pull strategy calls for spending a large amount on advertising and consumer promotion to build up consumer demand; if successful, consumers will ask their retailers for the product, the retailers will ask the wholesalers, and the wholesalers will ask the producers.

Branding

Before advertising is discussed in any detail, it is important to consider the concept of branding and how it applies to golf tourism marketing. The subject of branding has received increased attention over the last few decades. In an increasingly competitive global marketplace, the need for golf destinations in particular to create a unique identity – to differentiate themselves from competitors – has become more critical than ever. A brand in the modern marketing sense offers the consumer relevant added value, a superior proposition that is distinctive from competitors', and imparts meaning above and beyond the functional aspects.

The process of building a brand should begin with an analysis of the current situation. This stage should consider how contemporary or relevant the brand is to today's consumer and how it compares with key competitors. Once this market investigation is complete, the next stage is to develop the brand identity. Critical to the success of any brand is the extent to which the brand personality interacts with the target market. A brand's personality has both a head and a heart: its 'head' is its logical features, while its 'heart' is its emotional benefits and associations. Brand propositions and communications can be based around either.

The third stage in brand building is to communicate the vision and launch the brand. This may be done through a single announcement or as a part of huge international advertising campaign. This stage involves translating the brand personality and proposition into deliverable messages. A logotype or brand signature and a design style guide, which ensures consistency of message and approach, should also reinforce the brand values. The vision should be expressed in the brand's core values that are consistently reinforced through the product and in all marketing communications. Every execution in all media contributes to maintaining brand presence. The final stage is to evaluate the brand's performance in the marketplace. Continuous monitoring and evaluation of the communications is the key here, in conjunction with open-mindedness and a willingness to embrace change on the part of the brand managers. Any change must be managed with the overall consistency of the brand. The secret is to evolve continually and enrich the original brand personality, building on the initial strengths to increase their appeal and broaden the market.

Chapter 1 opened with a Spotlight that discussed how the Welsh Assembly Government was attempting to challenge the 'giants' of golf tourism. Part of this initiative was the 'Golf as it should be' branding campaign, a phrase used consistently in all marketing materials, and one that was used to reflect the unique nature of the game as it is played in Wales; unhurried, friendly, welcoming and value for money. To encourage participation, Visit Wales created a golf tourism marketing toolkit to help anyone involved in golf tourism to identify new opportunities, attract new markets and increase profit. The toolkit gave practical advice on how to capture the attention – and satisfy the demands – of golfers. One particular print ad, designed to attract women golf tourists, was accompanied by the tagline 'For Ladies who take their golf seriously'. The ad featured a pair of stiletto shoes complete with golf spikes and won a prize at an international ceremony hosted by the International Network of Golf.

Another example of branding comes from Troon Golf, the golf management company featured in Chapter 5. The Troon Golf brand is 'synonymous with luxury golf management, development and marketing' (Troon Golf, 2009). Troon Golf has used the design services of Burisk Communication Design for over 12 years, and in that time the creative execution has evolved with improved layouts and colour sections. In 2009, the corporate ad design reflected colours that included a warm blue/grey with accents of bold eggplant-purple, deep rust and beige. These warm tones were intended to contrast with the cool tones of most golf course images. The creative execution was designed to provide facilities with several options to allow individuality within the Troon Golf brand. However, whatever the type of advertising (corporate or leisure) the objective is the same – to reinforce the Troon Golf brand while driving customers to 1.888. TROON.US and www.troongolf.com. Not only is this achieved through print ads, but it is included on all corporate publications and programmes including *Troon Golf News*, *The Troon Report*, Troon cards, point of purchase displays and website design.

Ad example 1: The Troon gift card, courtesy of Troon Golf

Advertising

In 2009 global advertising spending was expected to reach $453.2 billion despite a fall of about 7 per cent due to the economic recession (*Wall Street Journal*, 2009). Advertising has emerged as a key marketing tool in the tourism and hospitality industries. These industries require potential customers to base buying decisions upon mental images of product offerings, since they are not able to sample alternatives physically. As a result, advertising is a critical variable in the tourism marketing mix, and it covers a wide range of activities and agencies. Its role reflects that of promotion in general, which is to influence the attitudes and behaviour of audiences in three main ways: confirming and reinforcing, creating new patterns of behaviours, or changing attitudes and behaviour. Thus tourism and hospitality companies use images to portray their products in brochures, posters, and media advertising. Destinations do the same, attempting to construct an image of a destination that will force it into the potential tourist's list of options, leading ultimately to a purchase decision. Whatever the tourism or hospitality product, its identity is the public face of how it is marketed, and the importance of advertising in tourism marketing should therefore not be underestimated.

Advertising can be defined as paid, non-personal presentation and promotion of ideas, goods, or services by an identified sponsor, using mass media to persuade or influence an audience. The process of developing an advertising programme includes six important stages. These are illustrated in Figure 7.2 and discussed below.

Objective setting: Communication objectives

Figure 7.2: The process of developing an advertising programme

1. Setting the objectives

In planning and managing advertising, a key factor is the setting of objectives. An advertising objective can be defined as a specific communication task to be accomplished with a specific target audience during a specific period of time. In general terms, advertising has four major tasks: informing, persuading, reminding, and selling. However, advertising in tourism can have many uses. These might include creating awareness; informing about new products; expanding the market to new buyers; announcing a modification to a service; announcing a price change; making a special offer; educating consumers; challenging competition; reversing negative sales trends; and recruiting staff.

2. Setting the budget

Ideally, the advertising budget should be calculated on the basis of the objectives set in the first stage of the process. The media plan must reach sufficient numbers in the target market to produce the size of response that will achieve the sales target. Several methods can be used to set the advertising budget. The objective and task method involves developing the promotion budget by (1) defining specific objectives, (2) determining the tasks that must be performed to achieve these objectives, and (3) estimating the costs of performing these tasks. Using this method requires considerable experience of response rates and media costs, as well as confidence in the accuracy of predictions. Cautious managers prefer to base the advertising budget on what they know from previous experience they can afford to spend. This is often referred to as the affordable method. The percentage of sales method involves setting the promotion budget at a certain percentage of current or forecasted sales or as a percentage of sales price. In tourism and hospitality, the percentage of gross sales generally set aside for marketing is somewhere between 4 and 12 per cent, advertising being allocated about a quarter of this amount. Another way of setting the budget is the competitive parity method, which sets the promotion budget at the level needed to achieve parity or 'equal share-of-voice' with competitors. It may seem unwise to spend significantly less than competitors if you are aiming for a similar share of the same market. In the hotel business the advertising expenditure for the average hotel is 1 per cent of sales, but for limited-service hotels, advertising expenditure is higher, representing 2 per cent of sales.

3. Advertising agency decisions

Since advertising is usually considered the most important tool in the marketing communications mix, companies must decide carefully whether they are going to do the work themselves or hire an outside agency. Only very small businesses, such as guesthouses or local visitor attractions, are likely to undertake their own advertising without professional help. At the very least, advertising agencies can help with the purchase of advertising space at discounted rates. Most advertising agencies enjoy working on tourism and hospitality accounts as they involve intrinsically interesting products, and may welcome the account as a stimulating break from their usual subject matter. There are two main types of advertising agency: the full-service agency and the specialized agency. In advertising, a full-service agency is one that provides the four major staff functions: account management, creative services, media planning and buying, and account planning (which is also known as research). However, tourism and hospitality organizations often use the services of a specialized agency. This type of agency will specialize in certain functions (e.g. writing copy, producing art, media buying), audiences (e.g. minority, youth), or industries (e.g. health care, computers, leisure), or in certain marketing communication areas, such as direct marketing, sales promotion, public relations, events and sports marketing, and packaging and point-of-sale. In the Bermuda print ad example below, Bermuda Department of Tourism used US advertising agency GlobalHue, who specialize in multicultural marketing.

4. Message strategy

The message strategy is the fourth stage in developing an advertising program. Studies have shown that creative advertising messages can be more important than the number of dollars spent on the message. Creative strategy plays an increasingly important role in advertising success. Developing a creative strategy requires three message steps: generation, evaluation and selection, and execution. Providers of tourism and hospitality products face an inherent barrier to effective communication with their customers: the intangibility of the product. Advertisers need to transform an intangible product into a tangible one, using emotion and experience. Although advertisers may create many possible messages, only a few will be used in the campaign, and the second step in developing a creative strategy – evaluation and selection – will determine the final message to be used. In the third step of developing a creative strategy, execution, the creative staff must find a style, tone, words, and format for executing the message.

Here are two examples of print ads using different strategies to target golf tourists. The first is a full page print ad promoting golf in Bermuda that was placed in *Travel + Leisure Golf* in 2008. The print ad was part of an integrated 'Bermuda. Feel The Love' campaign, which also used television and radio. The campaign was designed to position the island as an exceptionally convenient, relaxing and friendly getaway that pampers and caters to every wish with a smile. Advertisers of destinations often try to build a mood or image around the destination, such as beauty, love, or serenity, creating an emotional relationship between the destination and potential visitors. This was the case with this ad. The two heads – a male and a female – sculptured from the landscape of the golf course grab the reader's attention, and this image works with the print copy to gain the readers interest and provoke the desire in them to travel to Bermuda. The website address is included at the bottom of the ad to inspire action.

Ad example 2: A print ad promoting golf that was part of the 'Bermuda. Feel The Love' campaign, courtesy of Bermuda Department of Tourism

In the second full page ad, placed in the same magazine as the Bermuda ad, instead of using just one key visual, two pictures are used. One portrays the golf in San Antonio, but the other uses celebrity endorsement. Bill Rogers resides in San Antonio and is an ambassador for the game there. He won the Texas Open and the British Open in 1981. The strategy here is to play on the heritage and history of the destination and use nostalgia advertising to pique interest. The headline at the top of the ad reads 'Live oaks, deep roots, and perseverance', with a subheading that reads 'Along the river lie legacy and legend.' Nostalgia has become a big driver in destination choice, and researchers expect it to play a much greater role in marketing as the population ages (Muehling and Sprott, 2004).

Ad example 3: San Antonio using nostalgia advertising to pique interest, courtesy of San Antonio Convention & Visitors Bureau

5. Media strategy

The media section in an advertising plan includes media objectives (reach and frequency), media strategies (targeting, continuity, and timing), media selection (the specific vehicles), geographic strategies, schedules, and the media budget. The range of advertising media available to today's advertiser is increasingly bewildering and is becoming ever more fragmented. While these changes offer the prospect of greater targeting, they also make the job of the media planner more difficult. In the Homecoming Scotland campaign featured in Chapter 6, the media plan included using TV, radio, the Internet, newspapers, trade magazines and other promotional vehicles to stimulate people to visit Scotland in 2009. Bandon Dunes in Oregon chose a variation on traditional print advertising in 2009, when they promoted their three golf courses via tear-out post cards in *Golf Digest* magazine. One side of the postcard featured a colour picture of a signature hole from one of the courses, and the flip side had a postcard layout with a few words about each course.

All the different media outlets are referred to as the media mix—created by media planners by selecting the best combination of traditional media vehicles (print, broadcast, etc.); non-traditional media (the Internet, cell phones, unexpected places like the floors of stores); and marketing communication tools such as public relations, direct marketing, and sales promotion to reach the targeted stakeholder audiences. Media planners usually select the media that will expose the product to the largest target audience for the lowest possible cost. Although the Internet is considered to be extremely cost-effective, television is still a good way to reach the mass market. Reaching golfers via the Golf Channel, for example, may still be more cost effective than other media. The channel has 76.8 million subscribers, viewers are the most affluent in cable with a median household income of over $76,000, the median age is 51, and 74 per cent of viewers are male (Golf Channel, 2008). A number of golf destinations have used this media to promote their resorts, including North Carolina, Michigan and Puerto Rico.

6. Campaign evaluation

Managers of advertising programmes should regularly evaluate the communication and sales objectives of advertising. The campaign evaluation stage is often the most difficult in the advertising cycle, largely because while it is relatively easy to establish certain advertising measures (such as consumers' awareness of a brand before and after the campaign), it is much harder to establish shifts in consumer attitudes or brand perception. Despite such uncertainties, the evaluation stage is significant not only because it establishes what a campaign has achieved but also because it will provide guidance as to how future campaigns could be improved and developed. The 'Bermuda. Feel The Love' campaign referred to above generated increased interest and travel from Miami consumers in North America and select markets in the UK and Europe, according to agency Global-Hue (*Target Market News*, 2009).

There are many evaluative research techniques available to marketers to measure advertising effectiveness. Memory tests are often used, and fall into two major groups: recall tests and recognition tests. In a traditional recall test, a commercial is run on television network and the next evening interviewers ask viewers if they remember seeing the commercial. Another method of measuring memory, called a recognition test, involves showing the advertisement to people and asking them whether they remember having seen it before. The persuasion test is another evaluative research technique used to measure effectiveness after execution of a campaign. In this technique, consumers are first asked how likely they are to buy a particular brand. Next, they are exposed to an advertisement for the brand. After exposure, researchers again ask them what they intend to purchase. The researcher analyzes the results to determine whether intention to buy has increased as a result of exposure to the advertisement.

Sales promotions

Whenever a marketer increases the value of its product by offering an extra incentive to purchase the product, it is creating a sales promotion. In most cases, the objective of a sales promotion is to encourage action, although it can also help to build brand identity and awareness. Like advertising, sales promotion is a type of marketing communication. Although advertising is designed to build long-term brand awareness, sales promotions are primarily focused on creating immediate action. Simply put, sales promotions offer an extra incentive for consumers, sales reps, and trade members to act. Although this extra incentive usually takes the form of a price reduction, it may also be additional amounts of the product, cash, prizes and gifts, premiums, special events, and so on. It may also be a fun brand experience. Furthermore, a sales promotion usually has specified limits, such as an expiration date or a limited quantity of the merchandise.

The use of sales promotion is growing rapidly for many reasons: it offers the manager short-term bottom-line results; it is accountable; it is less expensive than advertising; it speaks to the current needs of the consumer to receive more value from products; and it responds to marketplace changes. Sales promotions can also be extremely flexible. They can be used at any stage in a product's life cycle and can be very useful in supporting other promotional activities. In 2008, sales promotion fared better than nearly all other areas of marketing, leading to it accounting for a larger share of marketers' spending (IPA, 2009).

There has also been an increase in joint promotions, where two or more organizations that have similar target markets combine their resources to their mutual advantage. This collaboration can reduce the cost of the incentives offered, and it may be a one-off joint promotion or a long-term campaign such as a trade association campaign using an 'umbrella' brand name. An example of a joint promotion to stimulate golf tourism comes from California where Wente Vineyards golf course in Livermore partnered with chateau-style Lafayette Park Hotel & Spa, in nearby Lafayette, to offer stay-and-play packages. In 2009, these packages started at about $300 a night.

Tactical promotional techniques designed to stimulate customers to buy have three main targets: individual consumers, distribution channels, and the sales force. Some of the main tools used are discussed below, including samples, coupons, gift certificates, point-of-purchase displays (often referred to as merchandising), patronage rewards, contests, sweepstakes, and games.

Sampling involves giving away free samples of a product to encourage sales, or arranging in some way for people to try all or part of a service. As many tourism and hospitality services are intangible, sampling is not always a straightforward process. However, restaurants and bars often give customers free samples of menu items or beverages. Sampling for the travel trade often comes in the form of familiarization trips (commonly referred to as a fam trip). These are discussed later in the chapter.

Coupons are vouchers or certificates that entitle customers or intermediaries to a reduced price on a good or service. CMS Coupon Services reported that 302 billion coupons were distributed in the USA in 2007, a 5.6 per cent increase over the 286 billion coupons distributed in 2006, providing over $386 billion dollars in potential consumer savings. An estimated 142 million consumers used coupons in 2007, with substantial usage across ethnic and demographic lines (CMS, 2007). Companies issue coupons to encourage people to sample new products, to make impulse purchases and to foster brand loyalty. Coupons are used extensively in the tourism and hospitality industries, especially among restaurants, hotels, rental car companies, tourist attractions, and cruise lines. Besides stimulating sales of a mature product, coupons are also effective in promoting early trial of a new product. But many marketing professionals feel that too much promotional use of coupons creates a commodity out of a differentiated product.

Gift certificates are vouchers that are either selectively given away by the sponsor or sold to customers, who in turn give them to others as gifts. Troon Golf, featured in Chapter 5, has two types of gift cards – national or local (facility-only) – that can be sold and/or redeemed for use in the golf shop for green fees and merchandise. All participating facilities are listed on the corporate website. In 2008, $198,000 worth of gift cards were sold, and the total amount of cards redeemed at facilities was $156,560 (Troon Golf, 2009).

Point-of-purchase merchandising is a technique used to promote a product at locations where it is being sold. The value of point-of-purchase merchandising has long been recognized in retailing and is making rapid inroads in restaurants, hotels, car rental companies, and travel agencies. In the food and beverage industry, menus and wine and drink lists are the key tools. In fact, many restaurants now put their menus on the web for customers to view; most wineries now offer free tasting in order to entice customers to purchase; and hotels also use a wide variety of merchandising techniques, including in-room guest directories, room-service menus, elevator and lobby displays, and brochure racks. In order to promote its gift cards, Troon Golf gives all participating facilities a point-of-purchase display which includes sleeves for the cards.

Patronage rewards are cash or other prizes given to customers for their regular use of a company's products or services. Golf courses will often introduce customer loyalty programmes to improve business. Atlantic Golf, for example, with three courses in Maryland, offers a Player's Card to customers which gives 10 points for every dollar spent on green fees, pro shop merchandise or cafe purchases. Goods that are available at each reward level include green fees, equipment and apparel, as well as certificates for local restaurants and even a theme park (Carey, 2009). All members are on a database which is used to leverage the program. For example, to drive business in slow periods, the courses send e-mail offers of double points or 'play three times, the next is free' offers for rounds during particular days or weeks. In 2009, more than 40,000 customers possessed a Player's Card.

Contests are sales promotions in which entrants win prizes based on some required skill that they are asked to demonstrate. Sweepstakes are sales promotions that require entrants to submit their names and addresses. Winners are chosen on the basis of chance, not skill. In 2009 Myrtle Beach Golf Holidays was running a special promotion via its website. Contestants could register for a chance to win a Myrtle Beach Golf Road Trip that included air service to Myrtle Beach, 4 Days/4 Nights with golf, accommodation, limousine service, custom-fitted clubs, half-day lesson and dinner with TV personality Charlie Rymer. Games are similar to sweepstakes, but they involve using game pieces, such as scratch-and-win cards. The use of contests, games, and sweepstakes has been shown to increase advertising readership. These promotional tools can be useful in communicating key benefits and unique selling points, and can be targeted at both consumers and members of the trade.

Snapshot: The Kiwi Challenge Puts New Zealand's North Coast on the International Golf Map

Cape Kidnappers, New Zealand, courtesy of Joann Dost

Legendary Wall Street investor, Julian Robertson devised an innovative marketing strategy which internationally promoted his own golf courses and lodges as well as New Zealand's North Island coastline. He created the Kiwi Challenge – a golf contest between four of the world's best under-30 players – which was sanctioned as part of the PGA Tour's Challenge Events' season. The inaugural 2008 event was televised to around a billion households worldwide and covered by extensive international print and Internet-based media. With a personal fortune of around $850 million, Robertson's ability to put up a $2.6 million prize purse assisted in the celebrity of the event, as did securing sponsorship from SkyGolf.

The golf, lodging and wine millionaire first achieved fame as the 'Wizard of Wall Street', developing his hedge fund firm, Tiger Management, from $8 million in 1980 to $22 billion in 1998. In 2000 he turned his attention to developing an empire in New Zealand, acquiring farmland on the northern coast of the North Island. He employed course architect, David Harman to build his first golf course at Kauri Cliffs in 2000 and in 2004 built a second, nearly 600 km away at Cape Kidnappers, designed by Tom Doak. The two have received many international accolades including ranking 63 and 41, respectively, in the world Golf Magazine polls. Kauri Cliffs was rated 'Best New International Course' in 2001 by Golf Digest. Cape Kidnappers was ranked 'Best in the World' by Britain's Daily Telegraph newspaper.

The Kiwi Challenge linked the two 7119-yard courses in a logistic challenge for the television network, requiring the American producers and crew to film two events over two days 600 km apart. A further publicity coup for Robertson was securing Tiger Wood's caddie, Steve Williams as commentator. It was the New Zealander's first role as a commentator, giving him the ideal opportunity to showcase his country's golf and scenery with aerial footage and panoramic shots. He toured the area by helicopter with a producer, cameraman and sound technician, introducing audiences to some of New Zealand's tourist offerings including 90 Mile Beach, a kiwi bird sanctuary and a rain forest.

The four players were Australia's Adam Scott and America's Anthony Kim, Brandt Snedeker and Hunter Mahan (who took home the $1.5 million first prize cheque). They played 18 holes at each course over two days. NBC Sports televised the 2008 event across the USA and it was subsequently broadcast in India, Latin America, Hong Kong, the Philippines, China, New Zealand, Malaysia, Singapore, Taiwan, Canada and the UK. Extensive print media coverage included everything from Score Golf Magazine to Canada's Globe & Mail and the Dallas News. Reports were aired on YouTube, cybergolf.com, thegolfchannel.com, relaischateaux.com and espanol.video.yahoo.com, among countless other Internet outlets. The limited number of spectator tickets was sold out and proceeds benefited local community charities.

The PGA Tour and Kiwi Challenge signed a three-year deal in 2008 to include the event in the Challenge Events' season, an 11-event annual series. Sponsorship was secured with SkyGolf, LLC, one of the fastest growing companies in golf and maker of SkyCaddie, a PGA-sanctioned Rangefinder. SkyCaddie is the amateur golfer's alternative to a pro's personal caddie – it automatically provides distance information – eliminating the need to search for distance markers – that allows golfers to focus entirely on playing and also helps with club selection.

Robertson has combined his world-class courses with high-end accommodation and spas in lodges which are part of the luxury, Relais & Chateaux network. Green fees are around $400 during high season. Peak season accommodation runs at around $500 per person per night for a suite and $5000 per night for a two-room cottage.

The second annual Kiwi Challenge was set for November 2009 with a 36-hole stroke play event at Cape Kidnappers for a $2 million purse. 'Last year's Kiwi Challenge was a tremendous success and we are thrilled to be hosting it again,' said founder and owner Julian Robertson. 'This year we probably have the best group of players under age 30 to ever to play in a tournament of this type. We are excited to welcome them and the NBC broadcast team to Cape Kidnappers in November.'

Sources

O'Keefe, B. (2008) 'Teeing Off at the Kiwi Pebble Beach', *Fortune*, March, **157**, 6.

Benjamin, M. (2004) 'Julian Robertson', *US News & World Report*, August, **137**, 16.

'Young Guns highlight inaugural Kiwi Challenge', NBCSports.com, 28 July 2008, http://nbcsports.msnbc.com/id/25887539/print/1/displaymode/1098/.

'Inaugural Kiwi Challenge to join TOUR's Challenge Events', PGATour.com, 1 October, 2008, http://pgatour.com/story/print/?http%3A//www.pgatour.com/2008.

'SkyCaddie announces sponsoring The Kiwi Challenge on NBC Sports', worldgolf.com, 14 November 2008, http://www.worldgolf.com/newswire/browse/56295-SkyCaddie-Anno.

'World best golf course in New Zealand', newzealand.com, 9 October 2008, http://www.newzealand.com/travel/media/press-releases/2008/10/recre.

'NBC Sports broadcasts inaugural Kiwi Challenge over the weekend', worldgolf.com, 13 November 2008, http://www.worldgolf.com/newswire/browse/56284-NBC-Sports-broadcasts-inaugural-Kiwi-Challenge-over-weekend.

www.thekiwichallenge.com.

Public relations

Public relations (PR) includes all the activities that a tourism or hospitality organization uses to maintain or improve its relationship with other organizations or individuals. Although public relations has a distinguished tradition, people often mistake it for publicity, which refers to attention received through news media coverage. Public relations is broader in scope than publicity, its goal being for an organization to achieve positive relationships with various audiences (publics) in order to manage effectively the organization's image and reputation. Its publics may be external (customers, news media, the investment community, general public, government bodies) and internal (shareholders, employees).

The three most important roles of public relations and publicity in tourism and hospitality are maintaining a positive public presence, handling negative publicity, and enhancing the effectiveness of other promotional mix elements (Morrison, 2002). In this third role, public relations paves the way for advertising, sales promotions, and personal selling by making customers more receptive to the persuasive messages of these elements. Ultimately, the difference between advertising and public relations is that public relations takes a longer, broader view of the importance of image and reputation as a corporate competitive asset and addresses more target audiences.

A variety of PR techniques are available to tourism and hospitality organizations. Nine of the key techniques are highlighted in Figure 7.3 and discussed below.

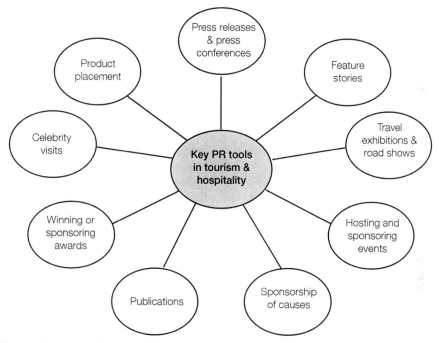

Figure 7.3: selected public relations techniques available to tourism and hospitality organizations

1. Press releases and press conferences

A press release or news release is a short article about an organization or an event that is written in an attempt to attract media attention, which will then hopefully lead to media coverage. It was mentioned above that the Kiwi Challenge received extensive media coverage, and press releases about the event would have been a key contributor to this coverage. Preparing press releases is probably the most popular and widespread public relations activity. To be effective, the release must be as carefully targeted as an advertising media schedule. It should be sent to the right publications and be written in a style that those publications would use. The headline should give a clear idea of the subject. The release should then open with a paragraph that summarizes the main points of the news story by stating who did what, when, why, and where. The style should be that of a news report, and the story must be genuinely interesting to the publication's readers. Ideally, it should tell them something new that is happening and should contain a strong human angle. Other useful contents of a press release include a photograph and quotations, and it is essential to provide a contact name and telephone number in case journalists require further information. Troon Golf distributes an average of six press releases per month, highlighting new management contracts, course openings and course accolades (Troon Golf, 2009).

2. Feature stories

Feature stories or features are articles of human interest that entertain, inform, or educate readers, viewers, or listeners. They are longer and have less immediate news value than news releases. However, such features can be extremely effective, and organizations in the tourism and hospitality sectors often encourage journalists to write stories about their products. Golf resorts should always be seeking to invite golf writers to visit their facility (Hill, 2009). The Dominican Republic, for example, hosted 10 members of the International Golf Travel Writers Association in 2008 to experience the golf offerings of the country firsthand. But it is important that an organization measures the output and outcomes of featured articles. The Ho Chi Minh Golf Trail featured in Chapter 3 has monitored press output since launching in 2007 and says it has been featured in more than 150 media outlets worldwide, including an 11-page article in Outside's GO magazine in 2008. The Trail's dedicated website – http://hochiminhgolftrail.com – publicizes all the media exposure it has received. Some marketers seek to put a monetary value on such media exposure. The Canadian Golf Tourism Alliance for example, valued the 41 media stories on golf in Canada in 2007 at $1.6 million, measured in terms of advertising equivalency.

Familiarization tours or fams were mentioned earlier in the chapter and are a popular method used to expose a product to intermediaries in the channel of distribution. In 2007, Argentina hosted a Golf Super FAM Tour 2007 in an effort to promote the country as a growing golf tourism destination. The seven-day itinerary was arranged by the Tourism Board of Argentina, and included golf at Buenos Aires' most prestigious golf courses, Olivos Golf Club and Pilar Golf Club, both home to past Argentine Open Tournaments. The fam trip also included rounds of golf at Buenos Aires Golf Club (ranked the top course in Argentina by *Golf Digest*) and the Jockey Club, designed by Allister McKenzie. Another example of a golf fam trip took place in Thailand in 2008, when Australian travel agents were invited on a five-day trip to lift the profile of Bangkok and Hua Hin as year-round destinations for Australian golfers. Anin Gujral from the Tourism Authority of Thailand said: 'organizing such trips contributes to the support of Thailand golf tourism on a massive scale. The fams are one of the best ways to communicate with travel decision makers. It gives them first hand golfing experience of each destination' (PR-Inside, 2008).

3. Travel exhibitions and road shows

Many golf organizations exhibit at travel trade shows, exhibitions, or conventions.

Generally, these occasions bring all parts of the golf industry (suppliers, carriers, intermediaries, and destination marketing organizations) together. Exhibiting at a trade show is similar to putting together a small promotional mix. Some exhibitors send out direct mail pieces (advertising) to intermediaries, inviting them to visit their booths. The booth displays (merchandising) portray the available services and may be tied in with recent advertising campaigns. Representatives working the booth hand out brochures and business cards and try to develop sales leads (personal selling). They may also give away free samples or vouchers (sales promotions). When the trade show is over, exhibitors often follow up with personalized mailings (direct mail) or telephone calls (telemarketing).

One popular trade show for those in the golf sector is the International Golf Travel Market (IGTM). It brings together golf tour operators (buyers) with resorts, destinations and country golf representatives (sellers). The event is held annually in early December in different golf destinations, which pay a significant amount to host the event. Previous host destinations include Malaga, the Costa del Sol and Andalucia in Spain, South Africa, the Dominican Republic and Cancun, Mexico. Over 1400 golf tourism professionals from 63 countries attended the event in 2008. Formulated as an intensive business forum, IGTM combines pre-scheduled, one-on-one appointments with social networking opportunities for buyers, exhibitors and press. The four-day event culminates in the coveted IAGTO Awards, the official awards for the golf tourism industry.

4. Hosting and sponsoring events

Event sponsorship is the financial support of an event (e.g. a car race, a theatre performance, or a marathon road race) in return for advertising privileges associated with it. Sponsorships are usually offered by the organizer of the event on a tiered basis, which means that a lead sponsor pays a maximum amount and receives maximum privileges, whereas other sponsors pay less and receive fewer privileges. Investment in sponsorships is mainly divided among three areas: sports, entertainment, and cultural events. Sporting events attract the lion's share of sponsorship revenue. For example, the London 2012 Olympics are expected to attract over £100 million from just the top four to six main sponsors.

Events are occurrences staged to communicate messages to target audiences. Public relations departments arrange press conferences, grand openings, public tours, and other events to create opportunities to communicate with specific audiences. Golf courses and resorts can draw attention to themselves by arranging or sponsoring special events, and this is discussed in detail in Chapter 8. The sponsorship of events is also an effective way of gaining publicity, as it allows the sponsor to invite and host suppliers, journalists, distributors and customers, as well as bring repeated attention to the company's name and products. The Snapshot above is a good example of an event designed to generate publicity. Investor, Julian Robertson devised the Kiwi Challenge in order to promote his own golf courses and lodges in New Zealand.

5. The sponsorship of causes

The sponsorship of causes is part of the wider activity of cause-related marketing, a technique whereby companies contribute to the well-being of society and associate themselves with a positive cause that will reflect well on their corporate image. An example is the Group RCI Christel House Open, an annual event that takes place in different worldwide locations to benefit some of the most impoverished children in the world. The main sponsor, Group RCI, is the world's largest timeshare exchange company. 'We are absolutely delighted to sponsor the Group RCI Christel House Open and are proud to continue the tradition of working with this great organization,' said Geoff Ballotti, president and CEO, in 2009. 'Working with Christel House on this event and others throughout the year allows us to help improve the lives of the children, families and communities that make up the incredible Christel House programmes throughout the world' (*Perspective Magazine*, 2009). The 2009 event took place at 19 courses spanning five continents with 100 per cent of the worldwide proceeds going to programmes and services that directly benefit the more than 3000 children of Christel House. Christel DeHaan, the co-founder of Group RCI, founded Christel House in 1998 with the goal of helping children around the world break the cycle of poverty and become self-sufficient, contributing members of their societies.

Ad example 4: A print ad promotes the 2009 Group RCI Christel House Open, courtesy of Group RCI

6. Publications

Companies rely extensively on communication materials to reach and influence their target markets. Publications such as annual reports, brochures, and company newsletters and magazines can draw attention to a company and its products, and can help build the company's image and convey important news to target markets. The *NorCal Golf Guide*, for example – formerly the *Bay Area Golf Guide* – has been published every year since 1997 and is a comprehensive golf course directory for Northern California. The PGA Professionals' *Guide to Travel* is another example of a publication used as a marketing tool to promote golf, and in particular, the 28,000 PGA professionals. Distributed as a regional destination guide supplement, the guide provides a mechanism for resorts and destinations to reach deep into their markets through a direct mail strategy. In 2009, each supplement consisted of a 32-page, digest-sized, saddle-stitched piece with a print run of 50,000 copies, and was distributed in bundles of 50 copies to 1000 PGA-managed golf facilities. PGA Professionals then made the supplements available in the golf shop, in the locker rooms, and in other areas of the facility. The travel-focused content included advertorial on golf, golf instruction, and non-golf activities.

Audio-visual materials, such as films, videocassettes, and DVDs are coming into increasing use as promotion tools. Many destination marketing organizations use videos to promote their destinations, and some send promotional videos directly to consumers as well as to members of the travel trade. An example of such a promotional DVD is the one produced by Tourism Malaysia called *Malaysia Your Golfing Paradise*. Produced in different languages, the DVD is 11 minutes long, and profiles the top golfing destinations in the country.

7. Winning or sponsoring awards

In many industries, such as the car industry, it has become common practice for companies to promote their achievements. Automotive awards presented in magazines such as *Motor Trends* have long been known to carry clout with potential car buyers. The winning of awards has become increasingly important in tourism and hospitality sectors as well. For individual operators, the winning of an award is a campaign opportunity, a fact recognized by award-winning golf resorts and golf destinations. Most of the awards in the golf industry promote best performance and are often an indication of quality. Winning organizations can therefore use the third-party endorsements in their advertising to build credibility and attract customers. They can therefore provide excellent publicity for winners. An example is the International Association of Golf Tour Operators (IAGTO) Awards, the official annual awards for the golf tourism industry. One winner in 2007 was Vietnam, which won the Undiscovered Golf Destination of the Year. Dr Nguyen Ngoc Chu, general secretary of the Vietnam Golf Association, said 'we used to think of ourselves as the world's best-kept secret, but with the announcement of this award, the secret is out. Vietnam is ready for the big time' (IAGTO, 2007). Another winner that year was Ginn Reunion Resort in Orlando, Florida, which won the North American Golf Resort of the Year Award. Peter Bonnell, V.P. of Sales and Marketing said 'this award is going to brand us. It puts us in an elite status now that we have to protect and maintain.'

8. Celebrity visits

Encouraging celebrities to use tourism and hospitality products can result in considerable media coverage, and can therefore help to promote that particular product. For example, Richard Branson built Virgin Atlantic Airways with the help of a strong public relations campaign that included inviting as many rock stars as possible to fly on his airline. Destinations, too, can benefit from celebrity visits. One popular destination in the Bahamas, Atlantis Resort, generates a considerable amount of publicity by attracting celebrities. Michael Jordan, who favours the Bridge Suite, regularly hosts his own celebrity golf tournaments at the island's onsite golf course. The Spotlight in Chapter 5 referred to Trump National Los Angeles and how the club attracts a number of celebrities, raising the profile of the course. Tiger Woods and Phil Mickelson are regular visitors, as is soccer star, David Beckham and American football player, Tom Brady. Actor Mark Wahlberg also plays on a regular basis. The Mallorcan Tourist Board has also been fortunate to entertain celebrity golfers who endorse their golf tourism product (see the case study in Chapter 8). Michael Douglas and Catherine Zeta Jones for example, have a home perched high up in the hills at Deia, and admit that the quality of golf on the island is a big draw for them. Celebrity visits may be part of an ongoing celebrity endorsement strategy. Canadian golfer, Mike Weir is paid by Taboo Golf Course in Ontario to endorse the course which is marketed as 'Home Course of Mike Weir'. In Hawaii, Honolulu-born PGA golfer Parker McLachlin is used to promote golf on the islands, appearing in a promotional video on the website www.gohawaii.com.

9. Product placement

Product placement is the insertion of brand logos or branded merchandise into movies and television shows, and it is another promotional tactic. Tourism and hospitality companies have been quick to take advantage of this growing trend to generate publicity through the placement of their brands. British Airways was one of the first companies to be endorsed by James Bond in 007 movies, and Virgin Atlantic paid a large amount for a tie-in with the 1999 film, *Austin Powers: The Spy Who Shagged Me*. The movie contained a huge plug for 'Virgin Shaglantic', and star and writer Mike Myers promoted the film in the United States by appearing on posters for Virgin Atlantic with the headline 'There's only one virgin on this poster, baby'. Hotels have also got in on the act. The Plaza Hotel was heavily featured in *Home Alone II: Lost in New York*. In the same movie, the family spent considerable time discussing an Avis car rental.

The value of exposure through television and film has not escaped those in the golf industry. The Snapshot above on the Kiwi Challenge is one example, where the event is a vehicle to showcase two New Zealand golf courses in a favourable light. In Canada in 2008, Prince Edward Island's Department of Tourism announced that the popular Golf Channel series *Big Break* was to be filmed in the province. This was seen as a major marketing coup for the island as PEI's 31 golf courses do not have a high international profile (SCOREGolf.com, 2008). Another example of placement is Trump National Los Angeles, featured frequently on television programmes and in commercials. 'The exposure it gives us is priceless,' said David Conforti, General Manager and Director of Golf at the club. Finally, a club in England – Stoke Park – has quite as history as a film location, and has leveraged this history to its advantage. Stoke Park is featured in the case study at the end of the chapter.

Direct marketing

Direct marketing is a marketing system, fully controlled by the marketer that develops products, promotes them directly to the final consumer through a variety of media options, accepts direct orders from customers, and distributes products directly to the consumer. It is rapidly becoming a vital component of the integrated marketing communications mix. Direct marketing has increased in popularity as businesses have come to place more importance on customer satisfaction and repeat purchase. Direct marketing makes use of databases, which allow precision targeting and personalization, thus helping companies to build continuing and enriching relationships with customers. It was mentioned in Chapter 5, that Troon Golf has a customer database of over 2.5 million names. The data is collected through all possible channels: tee time bookings, online website registrations and Troon Rewards registrations.

There are eight key advantages of direct marketing:

1. **Precision targeting** – direct marketing is aimed at a specific individual. It provides opportunities to target not only general groups of potential buyers but specific buyers individually.

2. **Personalization** – direct marketing provides an opportunity to personalize messages and build stronger links between the company and the consumer. It enables the sender to use names, and thus to target promotions to the individual.

3. **Flexibility** – not only can the contents of each direct marketing message be changed to suit the specific requirements of each participant, but the message can also be delivered to specific geographic locations.

4. **Privacy** – offers made by direct marketing methods are not readily visible to competitors. Direct marketing does not broadcast an organization's competitive strategy as widely as mass communication advertising.

5. **Measurability** – a major advantage of direct marketing is the ability it gives a company to measure the effectiveness of various response fulfilment packages sent out to prospects, in terms of converting enquiries into sales, costs per booking, response by market segments, and so on.

6. **Low cost** – direct marketing has the advantage of generally lower costs per transaction than other forms of communication.

7. **Detailed knowledge** – direct marketing methods allow the gathering of valuable consumer information – not only names and addresses, but also lifestyle information and purchasing behaviour.

8. **Fast or immediate** – because of the format of direct marketing, offers can be made quickly – and can be quickly accepted. This has become more applicable recently with the advent of the Internet.

Direct response advertising is one segment of the direct-marketing industry, and it plays a major role in influencing consumer purchase patterns. It can be defined as advertising through any medium, designed to generate a response by any means that is measurable (e.g. mail, television, telephone, fax, or the Internet). If traditional mass media are used, the message will include a free telephone number, mailing address, or website address where more information can be obtained. The major forms of direct response advertising are direct mail, tele-marketing, the Internet, and direct response television (DRTV).

In 2008, Reynolds Plantation, a golf community in Georgia, used an insert in a number of publications, including *Travel + Leisure Golf*, in order to stimulate a direct response from readers (see insert below). The direct response piece, show-ing attractive visuals of the plantation, incorporated a 'Business Reply Mail' postcard that could be detached from the page. On that card, potential custom-ers were asked to indicate their contact details along with the type of property they were interested in.

Ad example 5: Copy of the Reynolds Plantation insert, courtesy of Reynolds Plantation, Georgia

Figure 7.4 presents some of the communication strategies of the four main forms of direct response advertising, discussed below.

1. Direct mail

Direct mail, in which an offer is sent to a prospective customer by mail, is by far the most common form of direct response advertising. The use of mail is widespread due to its ability to personalize the message (the name can be included in the mailing), its ability to convey lengthy messages (printed sales messages can be sent with reply cards or contracts that can be returned by prospects), and its ability to provide a high degree of geographic coverage economically. There are numerous options available to companies wishing to use direct mail – examples include sales letters, leaflets and flyers, folders, brochures, DVDs, and

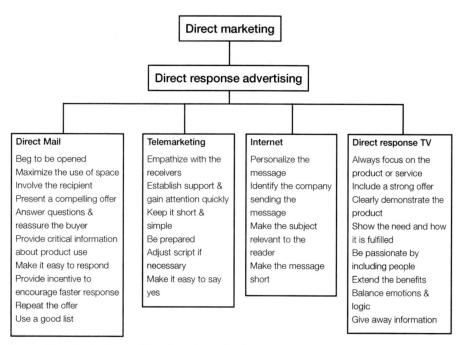

Figure 7.4: Strategic considerations for major forms of direct response advertising

CD-ROMs. The three basic steps involved in direct mail marketing are obtaining a proper prospect list, conceiving and producing the mail piece, and distributing the final version. Lists are secured from internal and external sources. There is no better prospect than a current customer, so a company's internal database must be monitored and updated routinely. The Homecoming Scotland campaign was discussed in Chapter 6, and part of the integrated campaign included a direct mail piece that was sent out to 85,000 prospects in the USA and 26,000 in Canada. The direct mail piece included a letter explaining the Homecoming initiative and a contest to win a free trip back to Scotland. Readers were directed to a website – www.ancestralscotland.com – to enter the competition.

2. Telemarketing

A form of direct marketing that combines aspects of advertising, marketing re-search and personal sales, telemarketing uses the telephone to reach customers or prospective customers. Telemarketing developed massively during the 1990s through the combination of technology-led development of consumer databases, telephone communications, and creation of call centres. The primary advantage of telemarketing is that it can complete a sale for less cost than other techniques such as face-to-face sales calls or mass advertising. However, for this method to be effective, proper training and preparation of telemarketing representatives needs to be as comprehensive as it is for personal selling. Planning the message is as important as the medium itself. A drawback to telemarketing is the fact that consumers react negatively to it.

3. Internet

The role of the Internet in direct response advertising is discussed later in this chapter. Needless to say, direct e-mail marketing, often eliciting a direct e-mail response, is one of the most promising applications in online advertising.

4. Direct response television

Direct response television is one of the fastest growing segments of the direct response industry. Advertisers are attracted to this medium because it allows them to track response rates. Today, savvy advertisers like American Express do very little advertising without a built-in response mechanism that allows them to judge results. There are essentially three forms of direct response television: 60-second (or longer) commercials that typically appear on cable channels, infomercials, and direct–home shopping channels. In all cases, the use of free telephone numbers and credit cards make the purchase more convenient for the viewer. Digital television is likely to have a huge impact on the sale of tourism products and services. In 2009, Canoe Ventures, a group formed by the six largest US cable operators, started rolling out TV ads that allowed consumers to request more information about a product by clicking with their remotes. The group planned to tailor ads by demographic profile of a community, such as age or income, so that those in higher-income areas, for example, would get exotic travel ads.

Personal selling

Personal selling is a personalized form of direct communication in which a seller presents the features and benefits of a product to a buyer for the purpose of making a sale. The high degree of personalization that personal selling involves usually comes at a much greater cost per contact than mass communication techniques. Marketers must decide whether this added expense can be justified, or whether marketing objectives can be achieved by communicating with potential customers in groups. Some tourism organizations favour personal selling far more than others, as for them the potential benefits outweigh the extra costs. In 2008, leading members of the Scottish tourism industry embarked on a sales trip to Russia in a bid to attract high-spending visitors. They hoped Russians' taste for golf, whisky and Robert Burns would draw them to the country as it geared up for Homecoming (see Chapter 6). The delegation – representing 18 businesses such as Gleneagles and Turnberry – met 70 Russian tour operators on the trip, which took in Moscow and St Petersburg. Personal selling may also involve targeting end-users as well as the travel trade. For example, in 2009, in an effort to attract new members, Encanterra, a private golf community outside Phoenix offered a Taste of Trilogy package. For just $149, a couple could enjoy three nights in an onsite home, one round of golf, and two meals at Encanterra's restaurant. The hope was that once visitors had experienced the golf community they would (with some gentle selling) invest in a property.

Objectives of personal selling include achieving sales volume, up-selling and second-chance selling, market share or market penetration, and product-specific objectives. Occupancy, for example, would be a typical measure of sales volume for golf resorts. An emphasis on volume alone, however, leads to price discounting, the attraction of undesirable market segments, cost cutting, and employee dissatisfaction. So exclusive resorts or clubs may restrict prospecting to highly selective segments, believing that price and profits will take care of themselves. Cross-selling occurs when a seller offers a buyer the opportunity to purchase allied products that go beyond the obvious core products. Good opportunities exist for tourism companies, such as hotels and resorts, to upgrade price and profit margins by selling higher-priced products such as suites through up-selling. A related concept is second-chance selling, in which a salesperson may contact a client who has already booked an event such as a three-day meeting. The salesperson may try to sell additional services such as airport limousine pick-up, or try to upgrade rooms or food and beverage services.

The sales process consists of seven steps: prospecting and qualifying, preplanning, presentation and demonstration, negotiation, handling objections and questions, closing the sale, and following up after closing. Prospecting is the process of searching for new accounts. There are two key elements to successful prospecting. The first is to determine positioning strategy, i.e. to whom you should prospect. The second is implementing a process to find and ultimately contact those prospects on a one-to-one basis. A successful sales call, made either by telephone or in the field, requires careful preplanning and preparation.

There are two elements to preplanning a sales call: the pre-approach and the approach. In the pre-approach stage, a salesperson needs to learn as much as possible about the prospect in order to be able to establish a rapport during the sales call and to have the foundation on which to build the sales presentation itself. The approach then follows and involves all the activities that lead to the sales presentation. The salesperson now tells the product 'story' to the buyer, often following the AIDA formula of gaining Attention, holding Interest, arousing Desire, and inspiring Action. According to experts, there are certain words that make listeners take notice. Apparently, the 15 most persuasive sales words are: discover, money, guaranteed, love, proven, safe, own, best, good, easy, health, new, results, save, and free (Brooks, 2002).

Much of selling to the travel trade involves negotiation skills. For meeting planners and hotel groups, for example, the two parties need to reach agreement on the price and other terms of the sale. The hotel salesperson will be seeking to win the order without making deep concessions that will hurt profitability. Although price is the most frequently negotiated issue, other factors may be taken into account, and numerous bargaining tools exist. Sales force members should be taught to negotiate using services or bundled services as the primary negotiating tool rather than price. For the hotel salesperson, negotiations should begin with rack rates, and price concessions should be given only when absolutely essential. Other negotiating tools, such as upgrades, airport pick-up, champagne in rooms, etc., should be employed. In 2007 and 2008, the Prince Edward Island

Convention Partnership offered free golf in order to entice meeting planners into making a booking. If a new meeting was booked with 10 rooms, for a minimum two-night stay, a free round of golf was included for each delegate.

When sales presentations are completed, most prospects ask questions and raise one or more objections. Objections come in all forms, even through body language. Resistance can be psychological (e.g. preference for an established hotel) or logical (e.g., price). There are several effective ways to handle objections. One is to restate the objection and to prove diplomatically that it is not as important as it seems. Another is the 'agree and neutralize' tactic or the 'yes, but' approach. In this approach, sales representatives initially agree that a problem exists, but go on to show that the problem is not relevant or accurate. No matter which approach is used, objection must be met head-to-head. Closing means getting a sales prospect to agree with the objectives of the sales call, which normally implies making a definite purchase or reservation. Knowing when and how to close are the keys to success. As with objections, this again requires careful attention to the prospect's words and body language. Closing techniques include actually asking for the order, offering to help the secretary write up the order, asking whether the buyer wants A or B, asking how the buyer would like to pay, or by indicating what the buyer will lose if the order is not placed immediately.

A salesperson's work is not finished until all the required steps and arrangements are made to deliver the promised services. In some cases, such as the organization of major association conventions or the planning of incentive travel trips, this 'delivery' work is extensive. However, the follow-up is essential if the salesperson wants to ensure customer satisfaction and repeat business. 'Follow up or foul-up' is the slogan of many successful salespeople. It is often advisable to give buyers some kind of reassurance that they have made the right decision. This reduces the buyers' level of cognitive dissonance – a state of mind that many customers experience after making a purchase, in which they are unsure whether they have made a good or bad decision (sometimes referred to as 'buyer's remorse').

Internet marketing

The world is going online in huge numbers. In 2009, 200 million Americans were Internet users representing over two-thirds of the population and, of these, 84 per cent were travellers. In Canada, the Internet stood third – just behind TV and radio – in terms of total weekly time spent by all adults with all media (IAM, 2009). The Internet is the number one medium in terms of per cent share of weekly time spent for both 18–24 and 25–34 year-olds in North America. And while 18–24 year-olds may not be the target market for a whole host of advertisers today, the high levels of Internet usage exhibited by these age groups will become high levels of usage for the 35–54 year-old age group eight years from now. Advertisers whose target market is in that range have only a short time to learn how to use online media channels such as social media to drive results for their brands. The impact of e-marketing can be felt across all sectors of the golf tourism industry, from large resorts to small clubs. The advantage of this business model is that it is based on a sound foundation – consumer demand. Customers are looking to the Internet to research, plan, and book their trips at rates that are increasing every year. Golf courses and resorts are finding that the Internet is becoming an area that guests use to research options when determining where to play golf (Troon Golf, 2009). It is vital therefore for a facility to market itself online and use this forum proactively to communicate and provide online services to its daily-fee guests and private members.

The Internet is also changing the behaviour of consumers when they arrive at a destination, with many now demanding free Internet use. Wireless – or Wi-Fi – provision is becoming quite common in bars, hotels and airports. Internet technology is also being used by travellers as a replacement for printed maps and guidebooks when they arrive at destinations. Consumers are using PDAs to access digital maps or for satellite navigation. Tourists attending golfing events can now use PDAs to gain real-time access to scores. Podcasts are also widely available whereby tourists can download digital guides to attractions to their iPods, rather than having to be led by an audio guide. Podscrolls can also be downloaded onto iPods and these are lists of restaurant reviews stored as photographs. Internet postcards are also commonly available on destination websites where consumers can send an e-mail postcard to friends or family with a choice of pictures that usually promote the destination.

The Internet can be used by those in the golf tourism industry for six key functions: direct e-mail marketing, advertising, information and sales, customer service and relationship marketing, social media marketing, and marketing research.

1. Direct e-mail marketing

One of the most promising applications in online advertising is direct e-mail marketing, in which a user chooses to receive messages from a particular advertiser. This form of advertising is relatively inexpensive, has high response rates and is easy to measure, and is targeted at people who want information about certain goods and services. Unlike banner advertising in its various forms, sending sales messages by e-mail seems quite acceptable to Internet users, since they agree to accept the message. The success of an e-mail campaign – like that of a direct mail campaign – depends on the quality of the list, which can be created in-house or be rented from a list broker. Establishing first contact is the toughest goal of any e-mail marketer. The goal is to have customers make first contact, and then have the marketer follow up. This can be done by giving customers something of real value, such as a special report or newsletter, to encourage them to make contact. It was mentioned above that Troon Golf has a database of 2.5 million contacts, and in 2008 approximately 330 mass e-mails were sent out to these contacts from Troon Golf on behalf of its facilities, equating to nearly 90 million customer impressions (Troon Golf, 2009). As part of the Homecoming Scotland campaign (featured in Chapter 6), VisitScotland sent out monthly e-newsletters to consumers who had registered an interest in Scotland. E-newsletters were sent to 135,000 prospects in the USA, 10,000 in Canada, and 7000 in Australia and New Zealand.

2. Advertising

These days, the Internet is an important part of the media mix, and Internet advertising is seen by some as the convergence of traditional advertising and direct response marketing. Online advertising holds four distinct advantages:

1. **Targetability** – online advertisers can focus on users from specific companies, geographical locations, and nations, as well as categorize them by time of day, computer platform, and browser. They can target using databases, a tool that serves as the backbone of direct marketing. They can even target based on a person's personal preferences and actual behaviour.

2. **Tracking** – marketers can track how users interact with their brands and learn what is of interest to their current and prospective customers. Advertisers can also measure the response to an ad (by noting the number of times an ad is clicked on, the number of purchases or leads an ad generated, etc.) This is difficult to do with traditional television, print, and outdoor advertising.

3. **Deliverability and flexibility** – online, an ad is deliverable 24 hours a day, seven days a week, 365 days of the year. Furthermore, an ad campaign can be launched, updated, or cancelled immediately. This is a big difference from print or television advertising.

4. **Interactivity** – an advertiser's goal is to engage the prospect with a brand or a product. This can be done more effectively online, where consumers can interact with the product, test the product, and, if they choose, buy the product.

Online marketers can advertise via e-mail (as discussed earlier) and by sponsoring discussion lists and e-mail newsletters. But still a common form of advertising on the Internet is the banner ad – an advertisement placed as a narrow band across the top of a web page. In terms of appearance and design, banner ads are often compared to outdoor posters. The content of the ad is minimal. Its purpose is to stir interest, so that the viewer clicks the ad for more information. Once the banner ad is clicked, the viewer sees the advertisement in its entirety, usually via a link to the advertiser's home page. The design characteristics of the banner ad are critical, since the goal is to encourage clicking. The website the ad links to must be interesting, or the surfer will quickly return to the previous page. It was mentioned in Chapter 6 that part of Homecoming Scotland's campaign included the use of banner ads placed on various sites including VisitBritain's global website networks. One of the banner ads used is shown below. Interested golfers could click on the 'Claim Your Free Foursome' button, and enter a name and e-mail address. Golfers would then be given a voucher and sent details on how to validate the voucher for four free rounds of golf.

Ad example 6: Homecoming Scotland banner ad, courtesy of VisitScotland

Advertising money is also increasingly being spent on search-engine advertising, which allows companies to target consumers as they research a holiday. The growth of search engine use for online travel research or booking is staggering, and has been facilitated by the introduction of newer 'travel-specific' search engines such as Kayak, Sidestep, and Yahoo's Farechase. In Britain, seven out of ten people use Google when they trawl the Internet for flights, for instance. The search engine delivers the results and alongside them displays about a dozen 'sponsored links' from companies that have paid to appear on the page. In order to improve rankings of websites on major search engines, marketers employ search engine optimization (SEO). Troon Golf, for example, is continually seeking to enhance the positioning of its clubs. To do this, keywords are researched and applied to the individual pages with an emphasis on club, city and state-specific online searchers. This process is performed prior to the site 'going live' and is monitored by monthly rank reports. The company says that to maintain positioning within the search engines, it is essential that the website content is updated frequently (Troon Golf, 2009).

Marketers are also using the Internet to place ads that may or may not be shown on television at a later date, taking advantage of Internet users' insatiable appetite for online content. In 2007, an ad created by Tourism Australia was downloaded by over 100,000 people in the UK alone before airing on television. BMW expanded the boundaries of advertising formats on the web where its short films featuring BMW automobiles were the attraction, not an advertising distraction. The company launched its first round of films online in the summer of 2001 and the short-film *The Hire*, featuring its Z4 and X5 models, also spawned its own comic book collection. Advertising in online virtual worlds is another opportunity for marketers. An example is Second Life, an online world with a million registered users and a thriving virtual economy. Second Life allows its users to create a new, and improved, digital version of themselves. 'Residents' can buy land, build structures and start businesses. Second Life even has a site for golfers called 'Golf in Second Life'.

3. Information and sales

In the USA, travel sales booked online reached $105 billion in 2008, up 12 per cent from 2007. Travellers used the Internet to help them select lodging (46.5%), learn about destinations (39.7%), find attractions (34.4%), choose an airline (33.2%), and read about local culture, arts, heritage or events (31.8%). The most popular travel services booked online were airline tickets and rental cars (IAB, 2009). In Europe in 2008, for the first time, the proportion of holiday trips booked online exceeded those booked without the help of the Internet. The focus of growth is now firmly on trips actually booked (if not paid for) online, which are rising by about 15 per cent a year. The number of people gathering information about their holiday trips, but not actually making a booking, on the Internet is still rising, but more slowly. About 161 million trips were booked online in Europe in 2008 (ITB, 2009).

The most popular sources of travel information are online travel agencies such as Expedia and Yahoo, search engine sites, travel company sites, and destination sites. The most popular planning activities conducted on the Internet are: searching for maps and driving directions, searching for airfares and looking for places to stay. For golf tourists, there are an increasing number of websites for seeking information on golfing destinations. These include www.travellingforgolf.net, www.golfuniverse.com, and www.learnaboutgolf.com. The latter site includes articles written by 'insiders', and an increasing number of websites have a place for such comments or 'blogs'. Travel blogs give the consumer a credible guide to tourism 'dos' and 'don'ts' without having to worry about advertising exaggerations. Created by travellers, blogs are helping the tourist to become informed before travelling, taking the anxiety out of booking independent trips and also aiding with planning itineraries, booking accommodations and transportation options. Prompted by the success and popularity of blogs, some tourism operations have created their own blogging platforms. Carnival Cruise Lines, one provider of golf cruises, created CarnivalConnections.com in early 2006 to provide a platform for cruise passengers to hook up with former shipmates, plan future sea trips together and share experiences and opinions on cruise destinations and facilities. By mid-2006 this site had attracted 13,000 registered users, of which 2000 had already planned further trips with Carnival's 22 ships. These consumers were predicted to bring in around $1.6 million in revenue which makes the relatively small investment a very high yielding marketing strategy for Carnival.

In recent years, there has been much discussion around the concept of Web 2.0. The phrase Web 2.0 was first coined in 2005 by Tim O'Reilly, a web pioneer, as a way to mark a turning point for web development. It takes into account a fundamentally different point of view, where a website is built around a rich user experience, not a product or service. Customer-centric 2.0 websites require that a company puts itself in the shoes of a website visitor and sees its organization as it appears through the website. According to marketing experts, the success factors for marketing tourism on the web include the following: attracting users, engaging users' interest and participation, retaining users and ensuring that they return, learning about user preferences, and relating back to users to provide customized interactions. Research that has looked at content of web pages suggests that it is crucial that content is accurate, attractive, and easily searchable. Interactivity is also an imperative, as the very behaviour of consumers changes when they log onto the Internet. They not only search for information but also expect interaction and entertainment. A positive experience on the website increases the time spent at the site and therefore increases the dollar amount spent.

Offering virtual tours is one way of providing interactivity, and many destinations offer potential visitors the ability to take virtual tours of an extensive selection of places. Some golf courses are installing virtual tours of the course itself. One such product is the Heli Golf Guide that is based on PGA-style hole-by-hole video. Using low-flying aerial footage combined with ground level footage, professional narration and music, Heli Golf Guide creates videos for each individual course. Heli Golf Guide is a division of Blue Coconut Media Inc. based in Ontario,

Canada, and also makes videos that showcase entire resort properties – a useful tool for selling events, memberships and real estate.

The Snapshot below describes a new interactive golf travel website launched in North Carolina to showcase North Carolina's golf product. A number of golf destinations are following this strategy – providing a one-stop-shop for golf tourists. Another example is Visit Florida, which in 2009 teamed up with the PGA of America and the Florida Sports Foundation to create golf.visitflorida.com. The new website pulls together information from public, private, semi-private, and resort courses across the state. Golfers can search every course in Florida to find exactly what they are looking for, including location, number of holes, par, amenities, course type and rates. The PGA section provides useful instructions and tips from PGA Professionals, tournament coverage and information about players. Visitors to the site can also upload golf pictures and videos of their own, find 'Hot Florida Golf Deals', sign up for Florida golf e-magazines and download the Play FLA Golf e-book.

Snapshot: North Carolina launches interactive golf travel website

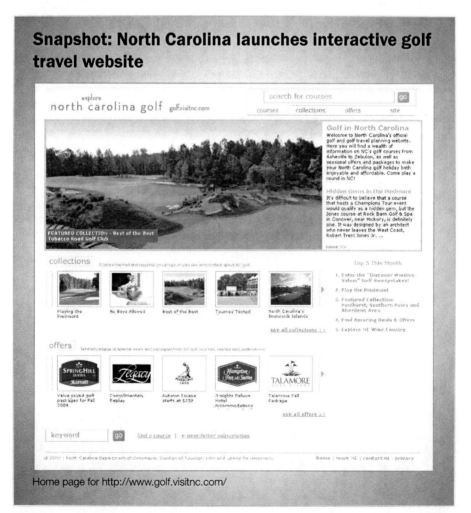

Home page for http://www.golf.visitnc.com/

A new interactive golf travel website was launched in March 2008 by the North Carolina Division of Tourism, Film and Sports Development. The site, www.golf.visitnc.com, is devoted entirely to marketing North Carolina's golf product, providing online cooperative advertising programmes for destinations and amenities throughout the state.

Golf.visitnc.com encompasses all courses that accept outside play (public, resort, semi-private). These are included in the state's database and are accessible from the site at no charge. In May 2009 there were around 430 public course listings as well as golf travel packages and deals reached via multiple primary navigation paths as well as keyword search. Visitors can search 'Mountain', 'Piedmont' and 'Coast' courses by region and rating; resorts and spa and dining listings in proximity to courses; family activities; and 'Girls Golf Getaways'. The site includes a course finder, distinctive golf experiences and tour-planning maps and also highlights courses that host national championships and those ranked by *Golf Digest*. The site links easily to the Division's core consumer website visitnc.com showcasing tourist attractions across the state, including beaches, wine trails, garden tours and historical sites.

In May 2009 performance was measured since inauguration in March 2008 at more than 410,000 user sessions with an average of four pageviews per visit over an average of seven minutes browsing. The site's e-newsletter subscriber base had grown to 17,500 and the regular sweepstakes had attracted over 36,000 entries plus 13,000 leads which the Division shared with participating partners. In the first year, four major sponsors invested around $55,000 to gain added exposure on the site, renewing their sponsorship for 2009.

With North Carolina identified as one of the top golfing locations in the USA, the Division had already dubbed golf travellers among the 'most avid and affluent' tourists. Priority target markets for North Carolina golf are along the USA's eastern seaboard including New York City, Atlanta, Washington DC, Philadelphia and reach into the Midwest and beyond. The website was launched as means to challenge aggressive competitors on state, destination and resort levels such as South Carolina, Alabama, Florida, Georgia, Virginia, Tennessee and Arizona.

The Division's goals in 2009 were to increase golf tourism numbers, increase spending and spark longer stays and/or more frequent visits. To achieve this, it leveraged its golf marketing efforts with partners state-wide, encouraging substantial investment in marketing North Carolina golf travel. The intention was to provide affordable partner opportunities online and in outbound marketing efforts and facilitate direct hand-offs to partner sites for more information and booking options.

The Division wanted to take full advantage of interactive media and transition the online Golf Guide to a self-sustaining online golf travel planning tool to be marketed to avid golf travellers. 'Research indicates the Internet and destination websites specifically are among the top travel planning tools for golfers. Travel Industry Association (TIA) and Golf Digest's 2008 Travel and Destination Study reported 73 per cent of golfers actively use the Internet and destination websites as top sources of information,' said Lynn Minges, Executive Director of the North Carolina Division of

Tourism, Film and Sports Development. 'We are dedicating as many resources as possible to go where the golf travellers are increasingly looking for their information.'

The site marketing embraces SEO/SEM, online media, e-newsletter distribution with further investment made in media relations, selective print and broadcast advertising, consumer golf shows and other promotional efforts. A North Carolina Golf Facebook page – www.facebook.com/northcarolinagolf – was also created to highlight special packages, offers and sweepstakes.

Options for advertisers are three-tiered: formatted offers, display advertising and sponsored collections. The formatted offer option – appealing to accommodations, resorts, schools, courses and packagers – is a 'pay-to-play' section of the site which allows advertisers to choose from different formats which they can adjust once during their 90-day posting. A limited number of display ads – suitable for Convention and Visitors' Bureaus (CVBs), associations, accommodations and packagers – are also available, giving advertisers access to audiences without having to promote a specific offer. The premier level – sponsored collection – enables advertisers, such as associations, destination resorts and CVBs, to buy into an integrated programme, including placement on the home page, enhanced listings for golf courses and packagers, landing page with copy and image gallery, links to their site, the opportunity to feature seasonal offers and sponsored content plus rotation on the home page as a featured destination. Advertisers can also partner with the state on a two-month sweepstakes promotion and are incorporated into the monthly e-newsletter.

Sources

North Carolina Division of Tourism, Film and Sports Development, Golf.VisitNC.com, 8 May 2009 Update.

www.golf.visitnc.com.

Travelweek (2008) 'Dedicated NC golf market website offers planning tool, special deals', *Travelweek*, 22 May, p. 8.

4. Customer service and relationship marketing

The Internet is moving marketers much closer to one-to-one marketing. The web not only offers merchants the ability to communicate instantly with each customer, but it also allows the customer to talk back, and that makes it possible for companies to customize offers and services. The Internet also allows organizations to provide seven-day, 24-hour service response. For example, it is now relatively easy for customers to check on the status of their bookings or their frequent flyer/visitor programmes at any time of the day on the Internet. The main reason consumers have adopted the Internet is that it enables them to shop 24/7 in the comfort of their home. Ease of navigation is then the primary reason for variations in purchase decisions between different online products.

Many consumers, too, are looking to build relationships on the Web. Godin (1999) introduced the concept of permission marketing, in which consumers volunteer to be marketed to on the Internet in return for some kind of reward.

This type of marketing uses the interactivity offered by the web to engage customers in a dialogue and, as a consequence, in a long-term interactive relationship. Permission marketing is based on the premise that the attention of the consumer is a scarce commodity that needs to be managed carefully. Its emphasis is on building relationships with consumers instead of interrupting their lives with mass marketing messages. About two-thirds of hotels are using their online channels to collect information on their customers, and then use that information to drive marketing campaigns (Green and Warner, 2006).

Selective marketing, whereby consumers are shown advertising and promotions related to their browsing interests, is also on the increase. The next stage, according to marketing experts, will come with the spread of digital cell phones with location tracking and automatic short-range communication technology. Electronic coupons, for example, will be delivered to cell phone owners on demand and redeemed by whisking the phone past a cash register, eliminating all the paper.

5. Social media marketing

One major outcome of developing relationships with customers online is the advent of social media marketing. Rather than passively viewing a collection of static pages, today's Internet user is becoming an active participant fuelling a growth in social networking - the creation and sharing of free content made by individual users. It is changing the way people consume media. For example, home video nights have been replaced by YouTube.com, and flipping through photo albums is now done via Flickr.com. The ease of use is the biggest factor driving this trend, both for users and creators. According to the National Golf Foundation (NGF, 2009) social networking is more common with younger golfers, but older golfers are beginning to get on board. A social network community for golfers has been launched by KLM Royal Dutch Airlines. Flying Blue Golf allows golfers to comment on their golf scores and the courses they have played, use KLM frequent flying points to buy golfing equipment, and, of course, book golf trips on KLM. Advertisers are courting social network users because their opinions matter. More than 65 per cent of people said they were more likely to purchase products or services they had learned about by social networking (Galante and King, 2009).

A 2009 study on social media use found that 88 per cent of marketers in North America were using some form of social media to market their businesses (Stelzner, 2009). The study found that Twitter, blogs, Linkedin and Facebook – in that order – were the top four social media tools used by marketers. Respondents reported that the number one benefit of social media marketing was gaining attention for the business, with 81 per cent saying their social media efforts had generated exposure for their business (see Figure 7.5). Though about one in two found social media generated qualified leads, only about one in three said it helped close business, although the percentage was higher (61.6%) among those who had been using social media for longer periods of time. A large percentage (72%) had only just started using social media. According to Forrester Research

Inc., 24 per cent of businesses were planning to cut traditional ad budgets in 2009 to boost social media spending (Galante and King, 2009).

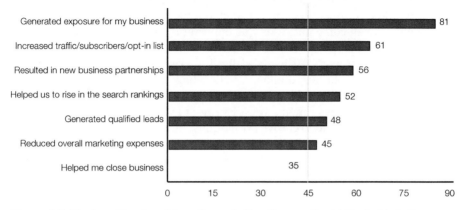

Figure 7.5: The benefits of social media marketing (Source: Social Media Marketing Report, 2009, p. 14)

Founded in 2004, Facebook is the most popular social networking site for consumers, with the number of unique visitors in the USA tripling in 2008, while MySpace, its closest competitor, lost 9 per cent of its users in the same period. Facebook's user base has expanded beyond college students giving advertisers a broader demographic to target (see Figure 7.6). In 2009, Facebook started to use information on users' profile pages to target ads. For example, Facebook helped an Asian airline promote airfares by identifying people who had expressed an interest in Japan in their profile pages. The Snapshot on North Carolina referred to the Golf Facebook page created to highlight special packages, offers and sweepstakes.

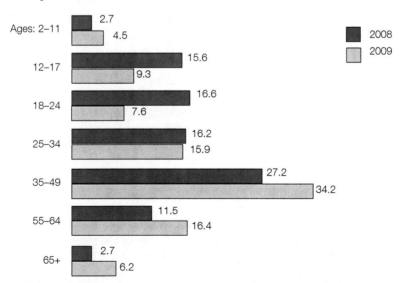

Figure 7.6: US Facebook users: percentage of total by age group (Source: Womack, 2009)

Twitter is a blend of instant messaging and blogging known as 'microblogging' and is intensifying as companies seek new ways to reach consumers. Twitter users in the USA increased 15-fold to 7 million between February 2008 and February 2009. Twitter users post 140-character tweets about whatever is on their minds, giving companies a unique opportunity to pounce on consumers as soon as they express an interest in buying something (Galante and King, 2009). Priceline.com, Southwest Airlines and Jet Blue Airways all post deals on Twitter to entice users who are thinking of travelling. Twitter can also be used to target the trade. Fairmont Hotels and Resorts has a Twitter feed dedicated to travel agents, with news ranging from Fairmont travel secrets and new services to special hotel deals and exclusive promotions. Interactive Friday contests offer up prizes ranging from luxury hotel stays to free gift cards. 'Twitter page is one more way agents can stay abreast of Fairmont news and developments,' said Fairmont's public relations manager Mike Taylor (*Travelweek*, 2009).

LinkedIn is a business-oriented social networking site mainly used for professional networking. As of May 2009, it had more than 40 million registered users, spanning 170 industries. Users maintain a list of contact details of people they know and trust in business, and these people are called 'connections'. This list can then be used in a number of ways such as gaining introductions, finding jobs or seeking business opportunities. A number of golf resorts have signed up to LinkedIn, including Hilton Sandestin Beach Golf Resort & Spa in Florida and Kiawah Island Golf Resort, South Carolina (see opening Spotlight).

6. Marketing research

The Internet has introduced some exciting new ways of conducting surveys. The two main alternatives are using either e-mail or the web to deliver and receive questionnaires. Many hospitality and travel organizations have placed HTML questionnaires on their websites to collect information from people visiting their sites. For example, resort company Intrawest runs regular surveys on its website to collect data from past and prospective customers. Others may poll e-mail subscribers to gather information. The Internet can also be used to get feedback on marketing campaigns. It was mentioned earlier that Travel Michigan was using the Golf Channel to promote golf tourism in the state. This was part of the 'Pure Michigan' tourism campaign, launched in 2007 and continuing into 2009, which included radio and television commercials, as well as print ads and outdoor billboards, all focusing on golf, outdoor activity and lakes. All ads carried the tag line: 'Pure Michigan – Your trip begins at michigan.org'. The website features more than 11,000 attractions, events, hotels, resorts, restaurants and other tourism-related businesses. However, another feature of the website allows visitors to comment on the advertising campaign, providing valuable information to marketers. According to Travel Michigan, for every dollar they spent on out-of-state advertising from 2004 to 2008, new visits motivated by that advertising generated more than $40 of spending (Borgstrom, 2009).

Researchers are still experimenting with online surveys, and there are no conclusive guidelines about the strengths and weaknesses of online research. However, the relative speed and flexibility of online surveys are seen to be two major advantages. Additionally, there is the potential of reaching a large and growing audience of people on the Internet. Internet software is available to take the written survey and convert it into e-mail or web-compatible formats, to e-mail or administer online surveys, and then automatically collect responses, enter them into a database, and calculate descriptive statistics. By using this software on a busy website, it is possible to collect hundreds of responses in a short time period.

Case Study: James Bond adds cachet to England's elite Stoke Park Club

Stoke Park, England, courtesy of Stoke Park

The Stoke Park Golf Club in Buckinghamshire, England, is part of an ancestral estate which dates back to the Domesday Book. The 27-hole championship golf course was added when Nick Lane Jackson bought the estate in 1908 and employed a famous amateur golfer and course architect, Harry Shapland Colt, as designer. Colt's pedigree included Pinevalley, Wentworth, Sunningdale, Muirfield and Royal Portrush. The course hosted the first PGA Matchplay tournament in 1910. A stunning, white Grade I Palladian mansion serves as the clubhouse, surrounded by landscaped parkland and lakes sculpted by Lancelot 'Capability' Brown back in 1750. Built in 1795, the mansion/clubhouse was designed by the architect to King George III, James Wyatt. There are 21 traditional bedrooms within the 50,000 square foot building as well as offices, golf changing rooms, pro shop, dining rooms and reception and conference rooms. The more recent Pavilion, completed in 2002, houses the high-tech 4500 sq. ft. gym, various studios, 13 indoor and outdoor tennis courts, indoor pool, spa (named by *Tatler* magazine as one of the ten best spas in the UK), crèche and playroom. In 2008 28 new contemporary style bedrooms were added to the Pavilion as well as a garden lounge. The adjacent Presidents' room seats ten for private dining. Various dining options include the Michelin-chef's creations, Italian food on the patio, and cream teas with chocolates and champagne.

But Stoke Park's biggest claim to fame came when it played host to the most memorable game of golf in cinema history – James Bond's victorious round against Auric Goldfinger in the 1964 film. Bond, played by Sean Connery, was driving his souped-up Aston Martin, which was auctioned off in a charity event at Stoke Park a few years ago. In the film, Oddjob, Goldfinger's caddie, threatened Bond by throwing his steel-lined bowler like a discus and knocking the head off a plaster statue. The statue is still there because the film's producers created a duplicate for the beheading in the movie. Connery, an avid golfer, hit his own shots in the sequence. On the 17th hole, Goldfinger lost his ball in the rough but Oddjob dropped another down his trouser leg through a hole in his pocket to save his boss a two-stroke penalty. Bond got even on the 18th when he switched Goldfinger's ball. After Goldfinger putted out to win the match, Bond called him for playing the wrong ball because Goldfinger had said at the start they were playing 'strict rules of golf'.

Another Bond film, *Tomorrow Never Dies*, was also partially filmed there in 1997, but the club's first foray into cinematic promotion was in *Dead of the Night* in 1945. Since then scenes for *Bridget Jones' Diary*, *Wimbledon*, *Bride & Prejudice*, *Layer Cake* and *RocknRolla*, among others, have been filmed there. It has also hosted ads, music videos and product launches as well as many TV series (*Midsomer Murders*, *The Professionals* and Discovery Channel shows). *Hello* and *OK* magazines have used the splendid backdrop for their photo shoots. Initially, fees were levied for filming – $250 was charged to the producers of Goldfinger for using the club premises which would be equivalent to around $5000 nowadays.

The club's marketers exploit the links to the film industry by showing clips of the films shot at Stoke Park on their golf course website. There are sections for the various movies and also TV footage as well as a YouTube link for the club. The club also actively encourages film tourists to visit and view the sets used in the films. The majority of articles that review the course include a mention of the James Bond films, and VisitBritain included a stay at Stoke Park in one of its 'James Bond South of England Itineraries', promoted to film tourists in 2009 after the release of *Quantum of Solace*. For Bond fans, Stoke Park at one time themed its exclusive Colt Bar to reflect the film *Goldfinger*. For fans of the movie *Bridget Jones's Diary*, they offered a 'Bridget Jones' Mini Break' in 2009, promoted with the following prose: 'In the summer of 2000, Stoke Park was featured in the award winning film Bridget Jones's Diary. After a hilarious afternoon's rowing, filmed on the glistening lake, the couple (Hugh Grant and Renee Zellweger) retire to our grand Pennsylvania suite. If you need to feel good about yourself and dream of indulging in chocolate dipped strawberries, with a glass of chilled Chardonnay whilst watching movie after movie, than this is the perfect retreat for you.'

Luring film crews and stars to the club in a professional capacity has had side benefits, too, when celebrities decide to join the club. Nicole Kidman and Tom Cruise both became temporary members while filming the Stanley Kubrick psychosexual thriller, *Eyes Wide Shut*. They took golf lessons from club pro, Tim Morrison. Hugh Grant also practised after filming *Bridget Jones' Diary* at the club in 2000 and has been a regular member since then.

Julia Buxton, Public Relations and Communications Manager at Stoke Park, admits that it is difficult to measure the impact filming has on number of visitors.

'However it has enabled the PR and Marketing Department to promote the films at Stoke Park and it is something that the media enjoy writing about. This would in turn increase awareness and sales.' Buxton has also noticed an increase in interest in the club when a new film featuring Stoke Park is released. 'We know when we actively promote the film and its association with us through PR and Marketing that it will have a beneficial effect. We insist on credits and as much additional marketing as we can leverage', she said. Obviously, filming might restrict the movements of members, but Buxton says they make a big effort not to affect the members in any way when they have a film shot there, and in fact members usually get very excited. Stoke Park has a strong relationship with Pinewood Studios, but future plans to encourage filming include building strong relationships with film location managers elsewhere.

Sources

E-mail communication with Julia Buxton, Public Relations and Communications Manager Stoke Park, 9 June 2009.

www.stokeparkclub.com/history.htm.

LaMarre, T. (2009) 'Stoke Park Club: Love lends just the right touch', accessed 6 June 2009 from http://www.golfeurope.com/course-reviews.

http://www.visitbritain.us/campaigns/james-bond/south-of-england-day-1.aspx.

References

Borgstrom, K. (2009) 'Michigan launches first ever national campaign', Travel Michigan News Release, 25 March, http://www.michigan.org, accessed 5 June 2009.

Brooks, B. (2002) 'Prospecting: how to stay in the mind of your prospect and win', *Home Business*, June, 40, 42.

Carey, R. (2009) 'Back for more', *Golf Business Magazine*, accessed 28 January from http://www.golfbusinessmagazine.com.

Carmin, J. and Norkus, G. (1990) 'Pricing strategies for menus: Magic or myth?' *Cornell Hotel and Restaurant Administration Quarterly*, **31** (3), 50.

CMS. (2007) *CMS Trends 2007*, Winston-Salem, NC: CMS.

Crawford-Welch, S. (1991) 'Marketing hospitality in the 21st Century', *International Journal of Contemporary Hospitality Management*, **3** (3), 21–27.

Dickman, S. (1999) *Tourism & Hospitality Marketing*, Oxford: Oxford University Press.

Galante, J. and King, A. (2009) 'Hey, big biz, ur not 2 big 4 #tweets:-)' *Globe and Mail*, 6 April, B12.

Godin, S. (1999) *Permission Marketing*, New York: Simon & Schuster.

Golf Channel (2008) CAB Profile, from http://www.thecab.tv/php/networkprofil es/08profileData/08_pdfs/GOLFCHANNEL.pdf accessed 25 May 2009.

Green, C.E. and Warner, M.M. (2006) 'Hospitality approach to online marketing: Survey of attitudes and approaches', *HSMAI Foundation*, NYU, TIG Global Survey.

Guardian (2006) 'London 2012 organizers expect record sponsorship', *Guardian Sport*, 8 August, 2.

Hiemstra, S. J. (1998) 'Economic pricing strategies for hotels', in T. Baum and R. Mudambi (eds), *Economic and Management Methods for Tourism and Hospitality Research*, New York: Wiley, pp. 215–232.

Hill, B. (2009) 'Seen and heard', *Golf Club Management*, February, 12–13.

IAB (2009) *Canadian Media Usage Trends Study (CMUST)*, The Interactive Advertising Bureau of Canada, Toronto, ON.

IAB (2009) 'September 2008: Online Travel' Industry Stats & Data by eMarketer, from http://www.iab.net/insights_research/530422/ 1675/495034 accessed 26 May 2009.

ITB (2009) *ITB World Travel Trends Report*, Berlin: Messe Berlin.

IAGTO (2007) 'The IAGTO awards', from http://www.IAGTO.com accessed 5 November 2008.

Institute of Practitioners in Advertising (2009) 'The 4Q 2008 Bellwether Report', London: IPA,.

Kim S.S., Chun, H. and Petrick, J.F. (2005) 'Positioning analysis of overseas golf tour destinations by Korean golf tourists', *Tourism Management*, **26**, 905-917.

Kotler, P. (1984) *Marketing Management: Analysis, Planning, Implementation and Control*, 8th edn, Upper Saddle River, NJ: Prentice Hall, 92.

Kotler, P., Bowen, J. and Makens, J. (2003) *Marketing for Hospitality and Tourism*', Upper Saddle River, NJ: Prentice Hall.

Lohr, S. (2006) 'Still holding value,' *Financial Post*, 5 September, FP10.

Lundberg, D.E., Krishnamoorthy, M. and Stavenga, M. H. (1995) *Tourism Economics*, New York: Wiley.

Middleton, V.T.C. and Clarke, J. (2001) *Marketing in Travel and Tourism*, Oxford: Butterworth-Heinemann.

Morrison, A.M. (2002) *Hospitality and Travel Marketing*, 3rd edn, Albany, NY: Delmar Thomson Learning.

Muehling, D.D. and Sprott, D.E. (2004) 'The power of reflection: an empirical examination of nostalgia advertising effects', *Journal of Advertising*, **33** (3), 25–35.

NGF (2009) 'Web 2.0 and the golf industry', National Golf Foundation News Release, accessed 1 April 2009 from http://www.ngf.org.

O'Sullivan, D. (2009) 'Time for change', *Golf Club Management*, January, 52–53.

Perspective Magazine (2009) 'Group RCI returns as title sponsor of the 2009 Christel House Open', 6 May, http://www.theperspectivemagazine.com/ accessed 24 May 2009 from

Pollock, A. (2006) 'Reaching travellers online', *Tourism*, **10** (2), 5.

Porter, M. E. (1980) *Competitive Strategy: Techniques for Analyzing Industry and Competitors*, New York: Free Press.

PR-Inside (2008) 'Thailand golf familiarization trip a success for Australian golf travel agents', from http://www.pr-inside.com accessed 16 December 2008.

SCOREGolf.com (2008) 'Need to know', Short Shots, August/September, SCOREGolf.com, 10.

Stelzner, M.A. (2009) *Social Media Marketing Industry Report: How Marketers are using Social Media to Grow their Businesses*, WhitePaperSource.com.

Sweney, M. (2004) 'VisitLondon plans digital TV channel', *Marketing*, March, 6.

Target Market News (2009) 'GlobalHue is selected as AOR for Bermuda Department of Tourism', from http://www.targetmarketnews.com accessed 12 May 2009.

Travelweek (2009) 'Fairmont on Twitter', *Travelweek*, 19 March, 30.

Troon Golf (2009) *2008 Sales & Marketing Summary*, Troon Golf.

Victor, C. (2009) 'Changing times at Saunton Golf Club', *Golf Club Management*, January, 56–57.

Wall Street Journal (2009) 'Global ad spending seen off 6.9%', *Media & Marketing*, 14 April, B8.

Wells, W., Burnett, B. and Moriarty, S. (2006) *Advertising Principles and Practice*, Englewood Cliffs, NJ: Prentice Hall.

Wilkening, D. (2007) 'Why consumers don't book online travel', accessed 24 April 2007 from http://www.travelmole.com.

Womack, B (2009) 'Facebook bucks economic slump', Calgary Herald, 30 April, E12.

Zeithaml, V.A., Berry, L.L. and Parasuraman, A. (1988) 'Communication and control processes in the delivery of service quality', *Journal of Marketing*, 52, 35–48.

Zeithaml, V.A., Berry, L.L. and Parasuraman, A. (1996) 'The behavioral consequences of service quality', *Journal of Marketing*, 60, 31–46.

8 Golf Events

Spotlight: The draw of Tiger Woods

Tiger Woods after winning the Dubai Desert Classic 2008, courtesy of Tiger Woods Dubai LLC

If anyone doubted the financial and ratings value of Tiger Woods' presence at a tournament, then the slump in viewer numbers and consequent advertising revenue during his forced absence for seven months over 2008/09 proved his unique worth. Ratings fell for TV golf broadcasts and audiences dropped away until his return in February 2009.

Woods had a quicker impact on any sport than any other sporting figure. Following three consecutive US Amateur Golf titles in 1996, he joined the professional PGA Tour. He won his first pro tournament in 1996 just five weeks after joining the tour and won another two weeks later. After being named 1996 PGA Tour Rookie of the Year and *Sports Illustrated*'s Sportsman of the Year, he went on to win four events in 1997 and by 1998 was ranked top golfer on the world golf rankings list.

His dramatic success triggered a surge in TV audience numbers. Audiences increased by nearly 14 per cent for weekend golf telecasts in 1997 and CBS recorded increases of nearly 25 per cent. Sunday ratings for CBS's 1997 Masters Tournament were up 55 per cent from the previous year, broadcasting to an estimated 40 million viewers.

The increase in both viewership and mass appeal of golf was exploited immediately by advertisers and sponsors. Both Nike and Titleist signed Woods to endorsement contracts in 1996, followed by American Express and Rolex. He also took an equity position with The Official All-Star Cafe and signed deals with *Golf Digest*, Sportsline and Warner Books. Nike invested the most in Woods and it paid off when sales of golf clothing and footwear doubled in 1997 to an estimated $120 million. Sales in the first quarter of Woods' connection with the company were up 55 per cent across the company. Researchers have found a direct correlation between Tiger's performance at tournaments and increased profits for Nike.

The 2008 US Open saw record numbers of golf fans – unaware that it would be his last performance of the season due to injury. This was the most watched golf broadcast in cable TV history to date, beating the 2008 Masters. ESPN and NBC shared coverage of the event and ESPN chalked up a 4.2 rating with over 4 million households tuning in. Results were similar online with ESPN.com recording 5.1 million visits (an increase of 256% from 2007) and 36.7 million page views (up 282%). Woods then missed the rest of the 2008 season due to knee surgery and seven months' recuperation.

During his absence, ratings, viewership, advertising and sponsorship all diminished, emphasizing the correlation between golf's popularity and Tiger's presence. In an article for Multichannel News, sports journalist Larry Barrett anticipated Woods' absence having a significant impact on ratings. 'The Golf Channel has histori-cally seen between and 18% and 30% fall-off in events sans Tiger,' he explained. Woods' return in February 2009 at the WGC-Accenture Match Play Championship in Marana, Arizona, was much heralded by TV networks and media in general. Bookmakers were enthusiastic, too, about his return to the sport – betting in-creases by 20% when Woods is playing.

When Woods is playing, golf attracts a wider demographic among TV audiences. He was the youngest Masters' champion ever and the first of African or Asian heritage. In 2001 he became the first golfer ever to hold all four major professional championships at the same time – the Masters, PGA Championship, British and US Opens. By 2008 he was top of the career money list as well as being the leader in career victories among active players on the PGA Tour. In an article for Canada's *National Post*, journalist Bruce Arthur compared him to Michael Jordan whose retirement from the NBA in 1998 resulted in a nose-dive in TV ratings. 'In no other sport does one player, one person, so animate his sport,' said Arthur.

In 2009 two Australian states were battling for Woods' presence at their tourna-ments. The New South Wales government failed to secure his services but he agreed to play in Melbourne for the Australian Masters. Rohan Clarke, writing for *Australian Golf Digest*, said that Woods' fee was believed to be $3 million but would generate around '$19 million in economic benefits to Victoria'. He also expected up to 100,000 spectators to be present, including between 10,000 and 20,000 interstate and overseas tourists.

Sources:

http://web.tigerwoods.com/aboutTiger/bio.

Clarke, R. (2009) 'Australian Golf Digest asks whether golf can become a tourism juggernaut', Australian Golf Digest, from: http://foxsports.com.au/story/0,8659,25576254-23213,00.html accessed on 19 June 2009.

Farrell, K.A., Karels, G.V., Monfort K.W. and McClatchey, C.A. (2000) 'Celeb-rity performance and endorsement value: the case of Tiger Woods', *Managerial Finance*, **26**, (7).

Arthur, B. (2009) 'Sweet relief', *National Post*, 25 February, B8.

Barrett, L. (2008) 'ESPN's perfect game', *Multichannel News*, 23 June, p. 32.

Chapman, J. (2009) 'Tiger's return lifts the gloom', *Golf International Magazine*, April/May p. 164.

Bryan, R. (2009) 'Woods a one-man stimulus package', *Globe and Mail*, 3 March.

Introduction

The opening Spotlight highlights the contribution that golf events – and their high-profile competitors – can make to the overall golf industry economy. As mentioned in Chapter 1, the golf economy is divided into a number of inter-related subsectors. One of those is golf tournaments and the associated endorsements. In 2005 in the USA, the financial contribution of this cluster was over $1.7 billion. In Europe, the Middle East and Africa, golf tournaments and endorsements also generated over $1 billion in 2006 (KPMG, 2008). Much of this income is generated from players and spectators travelling to golf events, so this sector represents an important part of golf tourism. This chapter begins by looking at the different types of golf events around the world, and then focuses on the spectators that attend these events. The hosting of golf events is the subject of the next part of the chapter, looking at issues related to planning, marketing and operational issues. The chapter concludes with a section on the impact of golf events.

Types of golf events

Major tournaments in the USA including the PGA Tour generated approximately $954 million in 2005 (SRI, 2005). In 2006, there were 120 international professional golf tournaments in the Europe, Middle East and Africa region, of which 84 were staged in Europe. In other parts of the world, the Japanese PGA Tour is domestically a hugely popular and rich tour covering over 39 events. Other tours include the Australasian Tour held in countries such as Hong Kong, Malaysia, India, China, the Philippines, Thailand, Australia and New Zealand. The Sunshine Tour meanders through southern Africa during the winter months, November to March. Add to these tours the Ladies Professional Golfers Association (LPGA) Tours of Europe and the USA, the hugely popular Seniors Tour (see the end-of-chapter case study) and a myriad of smaller tours and the result is a continually dynamic world-wide golf tournament. This travelling entourage attracts a large media circus fuelling interest and development of golf in all corners of the globe.

Tournament revenues include fees generated by selling broadcast rights, corporate sponsorship of events, and spectator ticket sales and merchandise purchases. In 1996 when Tiger Woods first turned professional, nine players made over a million dollars on the PGA Tour. In 2008, the same tour boasted 78 millionaires. The total purse in the decade before Tiger's arrival, 1986–96, grew by $37.5 million. In the ten years after 1996, prize money increased by $186.1 million. Men on the PGA Tour play for bigger purses than do the women in the LPGA tournaments, but the men play more rounds of golf over longer golf courses in front of more spectators, and exhibit greater levels of skill than do the women. One research study has found that the professional golf industry appears to reward the absolute level of skill with no gender bias (Shmanske, 2000).

Many of these professional tournaments are preceded by a practice day and a Pro-Am event. For spectators these practice days are the prime time for following players, seeking autographs and for taking pictures. Most major tournaments begin on a Monday and run through to the final round on Sunday. The British Open though has a bonus practice round on the first Sunday making for an eight-day event. In 2008, practice round tickets at Royal Birkdale in Southport, England sold for $45. Pro-Ams will often feature celebrity golfers. For example, spectators at the 2008 AT&T Pebble Beach National Pro-Am could see Bill Murray, Justin Timberlake, Huey Lewis and George Lopez among others.

The economic downturn in 2008/09 undermined the golf event business as it did every other area of the global economy. Many of the 2009 deals were agreed from budgets set in 2008, but in 2010 budgets were lower, and some events fell victim to this credit crunch. The English Open, for example, was postponed for two years after developers at the host Cornish course ran into financial difficulties. An estimated 40,000 spectators had been expected to attend the event, with millions watching it on television. The British Masters, one of the oldest events on the European golf tour, was also dropped from the 2009 European Tour schedule after it was unable to find a new sponsor. The event, which has been staged every year since 1946, was not on the calendar after Quinn Insurance's sponsorship came to an end and no replacement could be found. It had been planned for 17–20 September at The Belfry, where it had been staged the previous three years.

One of the LPGA tournaments, the Corning Classic, also closed in 2009 due to the downturn in the economy and the upturn in tournament costs (Potter, 2009). The tournament had an operating budget of $3.5 million, about 70 per cent of it coming from Corning Inc., a maker of glass and ceramic products. This was just one of five tournaments lost by the LPGA in 2009, most of them in small markets. The men's PGA Tour also lost four title sponsors in 2009 because of the economic downturn. At the end of 2009, the consensus view in the sports business was that elite sports properties would remain popular among sponsors and television – in golfing terms that means the majors, the Ryder Cup and a small handfull of other events around the world – but that the rest of the market was in freefall.

The issue of whether or not sporting professionals can be defined as tourists has been debated in the sport tourism literature (Hinch and Higham, 2001). However, the UNWTO defines tourists as people who 'travel to and stay in places outside their usual environment .... not related to the exercise of an activity remunerated from within the place visited'. For the purposes of this book therefore, professionals are not classified as golf tourists as they are normally remunerated for their endeavours. Those travelling to play in amateur events can be classified as golf tourists as they do not get paid, and aside from the professional tours, there a number of amateur tours that together are a significant component of golf tourism.

One example is the International Pairs competition, endorsed by the International Association of Golf Tour Operators (IAGTO), which is the largest tournament of its kind for club golfers, and attracts players from all over the world. Conceived in the UK in 1998 as a golf tournament to celebrate the millennium, the International Pairs is now firmly established as a major amateur event. Using a betterball stableford format, tens of thousands of golfers take part each year and the tournament is continuing to expand internationally with new countries becoming involved on a regular basis. More than 30 countries have been represented by their national champions since the inaugural World Final in 2004 and the title of International Pairs World Champions has been held by pairs from three different continents. The World Final 2009 was hosted at the famous Carnoustie Golf Links in Scotland. This type of tournament would have a very positive impact on tourism as foreign participants in international events tend to stay longer and spend more money on shopping and other activities (Delpy Neirotti, 2005).

Another unique UK-based amateur event is the Trilby Tour. The brainchild of Savile Row tailor William Hunt – and covered by Sky Sports television – the Trilby Tour provides regular club amateurs with the opportunity to compete in a professionally staged and managed tournament. What makes the event unique is that all competitors are kitted out in the latest fashions from William Hunt's golf range, complete with trilby! The Trilby Tour 2009 comprised four qualifying events. Approximately 400 Amateur Players entered for the qualifiers, with 111 going through to the Amateur final. 100 Professional players also entered for the final. For a one-off entry fee of $375, each competitor received a William Hunt golf outfit, a Callaway tour bag and a boiler-suit for the (compulsory) caddie. Prizes for the amateur winner included lessons with golf coach David Leadbetter, a trip to Orlando Callaway R&D to meet with Roger Cleveland and develop customized clubs, a round of golf with a Callaway star, and a Stewart remote control electric golf trolley.

Some of the larger golf club management companies, referred to in Chapter 5, also manage and promote golf events for amateurs. Troon Golf for example (see Snapshot in Chapter 5) has a number of events designed chiefly to create awareness for the Troon brand. One of these is the Troon Challenge, a series of amateur golf tournaments held annually between May and August at daily-fee Troon-managed golf facilities. Teams of two players participate in one or more regional qualifying events for the chance to advance to the Troon Challenge finals in late August. In 2008, a total of 388 players participated in 13 local qualifying events and 36 players advanced to the finals at the Revere Golf Club in Las Vegas. Revenues generated for Troon's facilities from these events exceeded $57,000 in 2008 (Troon Golf, 2009). The Troon Challenge is promoted via www.troonchallenge.com, Troon Golf's broadcast e-mail system, and point of purchase displays at participating facilities. Troon Golf has also developed the Troon Cup, an inter-club championship for private Troon-managed clubs around the world. In 2008, 17 teams descended upon North Stonington, Connecticut to challenge each other for the right to take home the cup. Another event Troon Golf executes is the annual Troon Card Championship, which is aimed at daily-fee customers. The 2008 event was held at the Quintero Golf and Country Club in Arizona with 120 players participating.

The Executive Women's Golf Association (EWGA), introduced in Chapter 2, also promotes amateur events specifically for women golfers. The EWGA exists to provide opportunities for women to learn, play and enjoy the game of golf for business and for life. The association has over 120 chapters and EWGA activities typically include: an annual 'kick off' event; two to three major tournaments; weekly 'after work' 9-hole league play; business networking and social functions; weekend golf outings; golf rules and etiquette seminars; education programmes; a Chapter Championship (the qualifying event in the EWGA Championship); charity fundraising events; and volunteer installation and recognition events. The EWGA Championship is the largest women's amateur golf tournament in the USA and is designed for players of all skill levels. There are three stages to the championship: one 18-hole qualifying event at the local chapter level; one 18-hole District Semi-Final Championship held at 15 venues across the United States; and the Championship Finals, a two-day, 36-hole event. In 2009 this was held 25–26 September 2009 at the PGA Golf Club in Port St. Lucie, Florida. The Championship, by design, offers two different competitive formats: Stroke Play and Inter-Chapter Team Scramble Competition. Golfers can select the competitive format that best fits their game, personality and skill level.

Many of these events, both elite and non-elite raise considerable amounts of money for charity (see Chapter 9 for more discussion on this). For example, charity events are very popular at Trump National, Los Angeles, featured in Chapter 5. One such event took place in May 2009 when the club hosted the Dodgers Dream Foundation Charity Golf Invitational. There were several ways golfers and sponsors could get involved, but as an example, the entrance price for a foursome was $5500, including golf, on-hole signage, breakfast lunch and dinners, gift bags, photos and participation in tournament contests – and of course the chance to rub shoulders with the rich and famous. The event raised $140,000 and all proceeds went to the Dodgers Foundation that provides educational, athletic and recreational opportunities for the youth of the Greater Los Angeles community. The tournament featured more than 140 golfers paired with a Dodgers player, coach or broadcaster. The event also featured a silent auction with autographed bats, jerseys and balls by Dodgers players. Other items of note included a Vin Scully autographed baseball from the 1988 World Series as well as travel packages to places such as Kapalua, Lake Tahoe and Laguna Niguel. The live auction featured an autographed pin flag from Tiger Woods, a four-night stay at the Terranea Resort in Palos Verdes with a round of golf and an Australian vacation with a five-night stay.

Golf event spectators

Event sport tourism includes both elite and non-elite competitor events (see Figure 8.1). At an elite event, the body of spectators outweighs a small number of elite competitors, whereas at a non-elite competitor event, the number of competitors may be large, but the number of spectators negligible or non-existent. Exceptions to this general rule do exist where non-elite events attract large numbers of family and friends as spectators, and in some instances (such as a marathon) elite and non-elite competitors are accommodated in a single Open event. An example of an elite golf event is the British, the world's oldest golf tournament, which can attract up to 200,000 spectators, depending on the weather, the venue and the closeness of competition in the final stages (Mintel, 2006). By comparison, PGA championships can attract crowds of up to 60,000. Many of the amateur events described above can be classified as non-elite golf events. The Snapshot on page 207 describes how for Abu Dhabi, attracting elite golf events has played a pivotal part in the city's marketing strategy to boost its golf tourism. The inaugural 2006 event attracted 17,500 spectators with TV coverage reaching more than 120 million viewers in 28 countries.

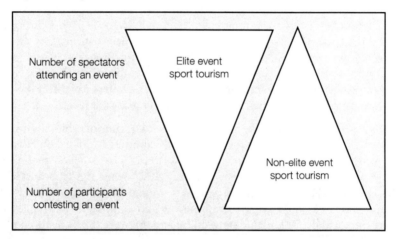

Figure 8.1: Conceptualization of the relative engagement of spectators and participants in elite and non-elite sport contests (Source: Hinch and Higham, 2004, p. 45)

Attending a golf tournament is unique from many other traditional sporting events in that the spectator is watching particular individuals compete rather than teams. Robinson and Carpenter (2003) noted that the action can be viewed by spectators from three different perspectives. They can stay at one hole and watch the whole field play through; they can follow a group for 18 holes; or they can randomly walk the course, watching various golfers at different holes. This is quite different from the usual spectator experience where a fan is confined to a seat in an arena and can see the majority of the action.

There is limited research examining the behaviour and motives of golf spectators (Robinson et al., 2004). McDonald et al. (2002) looked at a number of sports including golf, and found that significant differences did exist between golf spectators and spectators of other sports on the motives of achievement, skill mastery, physical risk, aesthetics, aggression, value development, and self-actualization. Hansen and Gauthier (1994) found that attendees at PGA Tour events enjoyed the scenery more than those on the LPGA or Senior Tour. Spectators at the LPGA events focused more on excitement and drama, shot-making skills and the fitness benefits of walking the course, while Senior Tour attendees were there more for the big names and personalities of the golfers. Robinson et *al.* (2004) also compared the three big Tour events and found a commonality in attendees in that they were all motivated by vicarious achievement – they felt a personal sense of achievement when their favourite player does well, they feel like they have won when their favourite player wins, and they feel proud when their favourite golfer plays well.

One recent study sought to understand the profile of golf tourists attending an international golf event in South Africa by shedding some light on their key trip-related and general golf tourism behaviour patterns (Tassiopoulos and Haydam, 2008). The attendees were mostly between 36 and 50, most likely male, married, with children having left home, and with a professional qualification and possibly self-employed. A large majority (89%) belonged to a golf club. Nearly half of respondents (46%) indicated that they would not have visited the golf tourist destination if the event had not been staged there. The researchers concluded that the golf tourists in South Africa clearly knew what they wanted; they sought to experience quality golf tourism offerings. Although the majority of attendees in this study were male, golf event organizers are noticing an increase in female spectators. At the 2007 British Open in Carnoustie for example, 29% of attendees were female compared to 22% in the 2005 event (Angus Council, 2008).

Snapshot: Abu Dhabi, using elite golf events to boost tourism numbers

Winner Paul Casey teeing off at the 2009 Abu Dhabi Golf Championship, courtesy of Abu Dhabi Tourism Authority

Launched in 2006, the annual Abu Dhabi Golf Championship has played a pivotal part in the city's marketing strategy to boost its golf tourism. Emulating neighbouring Dubai's established golf product, the Abu Dhabi Tourism Authority (ADTA) was targeting affluent golf tourists as part of a campaign to diversify its business and recreational offering. The Championship – a European PGA Tour sanctioned event

– attracts around 120 top golfing professionals vying for the $2 million prize and coveted Falcon Trophy. Held at the topnotch Abu Dhabi Golf Club (built in 2000), the event kicks off the Middle East's 'Desert Swing' trio every January, launching the Tour's yearly events' calendar.

The spotlight was already on the Middle East with the first Tiger Woods' course scheduled to open in 2009 as part of a massive theme park development. Dubbed Dubailand, the course is flanked by 197 palaces, mansions and villas. The Woods' seal of approval helped to open up the Middle East to safety-conscious US travellers. Further reinforcement to international tourists was provided by golfers Colin Montgomerie, Ernie Els, Greg Norman, Sergio Garcia, Pete Dye and Vijay Singh who were also working in the area on course design. In a KPMG 2008 survey the UAE was rated third (to China and Eastern Europe) in the next top golfing hot spots' list.

The ADTA's Chairman, Sheikh Sultan bin Tahnoon Al Nahyan, called the Championship a 'founding pillar' in Abu Dhabi's strategy to utilize high-visibility sports and events to increase the emirate's international tourism profile. The Authority wanted to position Abu Dhabi as a world-class tourism, leisure, business and cultural 'destination of distinction'. Other sports have also been exploited to boost global awareness for the emerging tourism hub. The ADTA secured a Formula One Grand Prix in 2009 and the FIFA Clubs Championship Cup in 2009/10. The Abu Dhabi Adventure Challenge was inaugurated in 2007, attracting teams of four athletes in various endurance trials.

Not content with merely getting the tourists and media there, Abu Dhabi went the extra mile in making its events memorable. Improvements to the luxurious Abu Dhabi Golf Club for the 2009 event included an enhanced spectator village, sponsors' area, hospitality pavilion, perimeter road and complimentary car parking facilities. A new state-of-the-art practice range was added to the national course plus new putting and chipping greens. Pushing the parameters of customer service, the Troon-managed club also provided fun activities for spectators including virtual golf and simulators, free 10-minute lessons with PGA-qualified coaches, plus putting and chipping challenges. There was even a Scalextric track for kids.

The elite club (with green fees starting at $110) features 27 holes designed by Peter Harradine – a former President of the European Institute of Golf Course Architects and the European Society of Golf Course Architects. The par-72, 7510-yard championship course forms an impressive oasis of palms, ornamental trees, shrubs and seven saltwater lakes. The sumptuous clubhouse was built in the shape of a falcon spreading its wings, paying homage to this icon of Arab culture.

The inaugural 2006 event attracted 17,500 spectators with TV coverage reaching more than 120 million viewers in 28 countries. Millions more saw the destination showcased in recorded highlights on news and sports bulletins. With its modern infrastructure and telecommunications, luxurious hotels and restaurants plus inviting weather and crime-free environment, Abu Dhabi was hoping to compete with established destinations in the USA and Europe. It was also contending with fellow newcomers such as Malaysia and China for a place on the international golf leader board. 'While the Abu Dhabi Golf Championship draws spectators from overseas, it's the awareness the event creates among the global golfing community through live television broadcasts and print coverage that is expected to significantly boost golf tourism in Abu Dhabi,' said His Excellency Mubarak Al Muhairi, Director General of ADTA. The ADTA hoped to triple its tourism numbers by 2015 to over 3 million visitors.

Prompted by a comprehensive marketing strategy, the Abu Dhabi Golf Club tracked an increase in rounds from 3305 in 2001 to 8680 by 2005. The strategy included participation in international trade shows such as the World Travel Market; fam trips for key media overseas; ads in leading magazines and promotions with tour operators, airlines and hotels. The club now hosts visitors from Germany, Britain, Scandinavia, Japan, USA, Korea, Malaysia, France, Canada, Belgium and Austria.

Spectator numbers for the third annual Abu Dhabi Golf Championship in 2009 broke previous records with attendance figures upwards of 25,000 for the four-day event. The event, won by Paul Casey, secured a high profile sponsorship line up including Etihad Airways, Aldar, Al Naboodah Construction, and Emirates Palaces as Diamond Sponsors; Etisalat and Standard Chartered Bank as Platinum Sponsors; Nissan, Airbus, Rolls Royce, Rolex and Xerox as Gold Sponsors and Cutter & Buck as official merchandise supplier. The 2009 Spectator Village was a treasure trove of family activities, with competitions and games galore. The UAE's national carrier, Eihad, offered a pair of return tickets to Beijing as part of a putting challenge; Aldar had something for motorsport fans with a full size F1 simulator; and for a relaxing cultural experience, Abu Dhabi Tourism Authority had a Cultural Tent - where guests could sip Arabian tea and watch traditional falconry.

Sources:

Abu Dhabi Tourism Authority. (2006) 'Abu Dhabi poised for larger slice of golf tourism's USD17.5 billion cake', *Travel Daily News*, 10 December, accessed 30 June 2009 from http://www.traveldailynews.com.

Tuchscherer, L. (2009) 'Eden's sister site to be built in Abu Dhabi?' *Leisure Management News*, 19 February, accessed on 30 June 2009 from: http://leisuremanagement.co.uk/.

Al Muhairi, M. (2008) 'Abu Dhabi: set for take off!' *Golf Monthly*, Summer, 8-9.

Hamilton, S. (2009) 'Golf tourism', United Arab Emirates (Dubai & Abu Dhabi).

Pyrih, E. (2009) 'Sand dunes to sand traps: the evolution of golf tourism in the United Arab Emirates'.

Robathan, M. (2009) 'Island of dreams', *Leisure Management*, Vol. 29, 1.

The hosting of golf events

Planning

There are a number of specialist companies that organize golf events, and the case study at the end of the chapter discusses the Son Gual European Senior Tour in Mallorca where German-based Langer Sport Marketing was appointed as the official promoter of the 2009 event. Another well-known company that organizes golf events is International Management Group (IMG). Founder Mark

McCormack was a young lawyer when he agreed to become Arnold Palmer's agent in 1960, and that marked the beginning of IMG. The relationship was based on a handshake and a contract between the two men was never signed, despite it being one of the most valuable and enduring relationships in modern sport. McCormack went on to sign Jack Nicklaus, Gary Player, and Greg Norman among many others. Beginning in 1964 with the World Match Play Championship, IMG has a rich history of creating and producing golf events, including the popular Skins Game and prime-time 'Battle' Series. IMG's capabilities in tournament management include:

♦ Developing creative and profitable tournament concepts;

♦ Securing title and associate sponsorships, site commitments and schedule alternatives;

♦ Cultivating relationships with golf's major tours and governing bodies;

♦ Managing delivery of all marketing, website and event materials, including event tickets, programmes, signage and on-site branding;

♦ Managing day-to-day tournament operations, including vendor relationships, pro-ams, media days and player services;

♦ Integrating new media technology to enhance fan experience (IMG, 2009).

Another golf management company involved in events is UK-based International Sports Management. ISM manages a variety of golf events ranging from professional tournaments on the European Tour through to junior focused grass-roots championships. ISM's Events team offer a range of services including consultancy, staging assistance, as well as a full management service from idea development through to the final finished product, each event being a bespoke product tailored to meet the different business objectives of each client. As the company's website says 'The focus of an ISM managed event is that there is something for everyone – clients looking to use these events as an effective sales and marketing platform, businesses or individuals looking to entertain clients via one of our unique hospitality packages, spectators wanting an unforgettable day out and participants eager to experience a golf event of the highest standard.'

Event management is also within PGA Tour Experiences remit. As discussed in the Snapshot in Chapter 3, PGA Tour Experiences is the licensee and fulfillment arm of the PGA Tour. It serves as the tour operation side of the PGA, providing golf vacations for spectators wishing to see events. Signature packages include four-day trips to the Hyatt Regency Jacksonville Waterfront with tickets to The Players Championship and behind-the-scenes privileges. The company handles travel and accommodations, VIP tournament tickets and all golf bookings. The flagship facility for the PGA Tour is at TPC Sawgrass, in Ponte Vedra Beach, Florida. TPC (Tournament Players' Clubs) is a network of over 20 private and destination golf clubs across the USA which have hosted over 200 professional golf tournaments: 'The golf courses are built to hold modern golf tournaments, which are always presenting new challenges as they grow and the game becomes more popular' says PGA Tour Commissioner Tim Finchen (TPC, 2009).

According to Andrew 'Chubby' Chandler, Managing Director of ISM, to run a major tournament like the British Masters takes about $3 million, most of it for prize money. It was mentioned earlier that the tournament was dropped from the 2009 European Tour schedule after it was unable to find a new sponsor. 'If you can cover the prize money, you can put on a decent tournament,' he said. 'It's a lot of money, particularly when you take into account the fact that the ancillary elements at a golf tournament don't make as much money as you might think. Gate money is never as big as you think it might be' (*Golf International*, 2009, p. 178).

It may also be necessary for a golf club to obtain certain planning permissions to host an event, especially if the event is to take place in a National Park. An example comes from Banff in Canada, where in 2009 the Fairmont Banff Springs Golf Course was competing to host the 2010 TELUS World Skins Games, owned and operated by IMG. Part of those plans involved a review process whereby the Banff National Park Special Events Public Advisory Committee had to review an application from the Fairmont Banff Springs Hotel. A public meeting was held in May 2009 where the proposal to host the tournament was put forward by a hotel representative, followed by question and answer sessions with both the Committee and the general public (Ellis, 2009). Although Parks Canada eventually gave its blessing to the proposed tournament, the organizers decided to host it on Vancouver Island instead.

Even with the assistance of an events management company, a golf club or resort will have the responsibility of ensuring the course itself is in prime condition for the event. The Royal & Ancient (R&A), who are responsible for formulating the rules of golf, has some recommendations for those responsible for setting up a course for events. These are summarized below. The R&A also features short videos on its website showing how the organization presented the Open Championship in July 2008 at Royal Birkdale, UK., which saw 200,000 spectators on site over the week of golf, whilst protecting the wildlife and their habitat.

Recommendations for Course Set-Up for Competitions, Tournaments and Championships (Source: Royal & Ancient)

♦ The golf course will be expected to peak in terms of the standard of playing surface and presentation for major events, be they club, regional, national or international championships. Every course will have a limited number of opportunities to achieve this level of perfection and those responsible for championships must be aware of this and plan accordingly, e.g. do not place the most important event of the year at a time when the course is in relatively poor condition due to climate.

♦ Peaking a course requires ample forethought and preparations need to be planned at least a year in advance of the event. The timing of maintenance procedures such as fertiliser, top dressing, verticutting, as well as frequency of mowing and height of cut, must be considered carefully throughout the course to minimise any negative impact they may have on the playing surface. A period of closure may well be required prior to the event to facilitate the necessary final repairs and presentation.

♦ The authority in charge of the event should be expected to visit the course prior to the start of the championship to make a general assessment of condition and to clarify pin positions in order that specific areas can be protected. These visits must be timed well enough in advance so that any agreed alterations can be implemented without causing any short-term deterioration to the condition of the course.

♦ If your club is hosting a tournament or championship run by one of golf's governing authorities, e.g. a PGA, The R&A or the USGA, then the relevant authority may provide guidance on their requirements for course set-up. Whilst these guidelines may be considered a blueprint for presenting the course in the best possible condition for the standard of play expected, the host should always be consulted to ensure implementation will not have any harmful effects on course condition for an unacceptable length of time post-tournament play. Potential areas of conflict need to be highlighted and resolved before a tournament is accepted.

Source: R&A Course Management Best Practices. Retrieved from https://www.best-courseforgolf.org/

One other important consideration in the planning stage of events is human resource management. Events have unique human resource needs and challenges, especially their usual reliance on volunteers (Getz, 2007). The end-of-chapter case study describes how the Son Gual European Senior Open in Mallorca could not have run without the help of about 50 volunteers, who worked as marshals, caddies, or on parking, and the leader board. Most of them were found through the club's webpage and weekly newsletter as well as a promotional poster placed in golf clubs around the Spanish island.

Hanlon and Stewart (2006) conducted a study of staffing for a major sporting event. They concluded their study by making recommendations for tailored human resource practices, and these are summarized in Figure 8.2. The left-hand side of the model has each of the five main human resource stages, and in the middle are nine special features of major sport event organizations. Tailored event mainstream human resource strategies were identified for each of the five human resource stages and these are listed on the right-hand side of Figure 8.2. The authors recommended that managers be provided with documented guidelines and procedures that reflect the tailored and sport-specific processes required to meet the challenges faced by sport event managers.

Promoting the event

When promoting a golf event, Robinson *et al.* (2004) suggest that the primary focus for marketers should be on the specific golfers who will be playing a particular event. This strategy is employed by the PGA Tour events because of the strong name recognition of a number of its players. The Senior Tour has also relied on this name recognition. The LPGA has also moved in that direction as more of its players have increased their worldwide recognition. As the opening

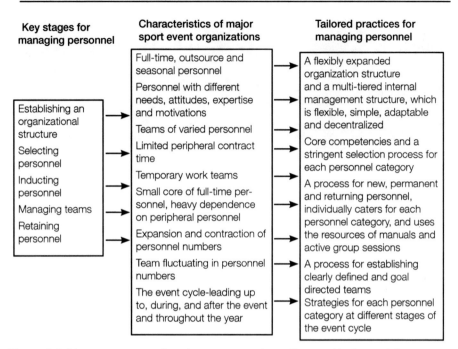

Figure 8.2: Management practices for event organizers (Source: Hanlon and Stewart, 2006, pp. 83).

Spotlight indicated, this plan may backfire if the marketing focus is solely on one player such as Tiger Woods. During his absence in 2008 and 2009, ratings, viewership, advertising and sponsorship all diminished, emphasizing the correlation between golf's popularity and Tiger's presence. As Robinson *et al.* suggest, a better marketing strategy is to identify several well-known players on the tour who should be attending, so as to broaden the scope of the campaign. They also suggest promoting the idea that attending the event as a spectator is also supporting the community. This support Crosset's (1995) study of the LPGA, which indicated the importance of an event to the community. The spectators act as representatives of the community and their presence indicates their support for bringing the event back in the future.

A dedicated website for the tournament is also essential for an elite event, with easily accessible information on ticket sales, maps and directions, corporate hospitality, volunteers, and details about the participating players. Information for media covering the event is also critical. A special media section on the 2009 Crowne Plaza Invitational website included a media guide as well as a one-page fact sheet that could be downloaded by readers. A copy of the fact sheet is shown in Figure 8.3.

Golf events are often branded, one common approach being to use the golf club's or destination's name in conjunction with specification of the type of event, such as the Son Gual, Mallorca European Senior Open featured at the end of this chapter. Another approach is co-branding with a corporate sponsor such as the

Figure 8.3: Fact sheet for the 2009 Crowne Plaza Invitational at Colonial, Fort Worth, Texas

Crowne Plaza Invitational at Colonial, or the TELUS World Skins Games. Celebrities may also use their names as 'hosts', usually to promote a charitable event. An example is the Justin Timberlake Shriners Hospitals for Children Open, held in Las Vegas. Timberlake's involvement with golf is discussed in Chapter 9. Professional golfers too might host an event to promote their own brands. The Ian Poulter Design Invitational is an example. The 4th Invitational took place in July 2009, the day after the conclusion of the British Open. 100 juniors from across the UK competed in the tournament which was televised on Sky.

Securing a title sponsor is critical for most major events, as witnessed by the demise of a number of tournaments in 2009 as mentioned earlier, such as the British Masters, the English Open and the LPGA Corning Classic. Title sponsorship is defined as 'the right to share the official name of a property, event or activity in exchange for payment to the current property, event, or activity owner' (Clark *et al.*, 2009, pp. 170). In general, sponsorship is expected to influence future cash flows as well as build image and awareness with consumers, improve employee morale, and promote goodwill. Prices of sports properties tend to be pushed up because of the extensive media coverage, but according to recent research, golf tournament event sponsorships are priced such that the overall expected NPV of these sponsorships is approximately zero (Clark *et al.*, 2009). In fact, whereas the initial signing of a golf tournament is viewed by investors as a largely insignificant event, investors view renewals of the studied PGA golf tournaments as bad news. The authors of the study suggested that this could have been because the rights fees paid by PGA sponsors rose significantly over the study period.

Certainly, it can be expensive to sponsor a major PGA event. In 2007 the Canadian Open was in disarray. Saddled with a difficult date following the British Open and largely abandoned by former title sponsor Bell Canada, the tournament cost the Royal Canadian Golf Association millions to run. Some speculated it would not survive. However, the Royal Bank of Canada (RBC) stepped in as title sponsor and it is now one of the stronger events on the PGA Tour. The sponsorship is estimated to cost RBC \$3–4.5 million annually until 2012 (Perkins, 2008). RBC is trying to capitalize on golf's popularity with a younger crowd in Canada. For example the 2008 event featured on-site rock concerts.

Another potential income generator for those hosting major golf events is corporate hospitality. Corporate hospitality can be defined as any event for the benefit of an organization entertaining clients or staff, or prospective clients, at the organization's expense (MDB, 2009). The activity can be an effective way of establishing networking opportunities and consolidating customer relationships. According to a recent UK report, sales in corporate hospitality peaked at \$1.5 billion in the UK in 2008, increasing 20 per cent over the previous four years (MDB, 2009). In real terms the report predicts a growth of a further 20 per cent between 2009 and 2013. Despite expected budget cuts, spectator sports are anticipated to retain their majority share of the market, as a result of their reputation as a traditional, popular and nationwide form of corporate entertainment, according to the report. However, the corporate hospitality industry still continues to suffer from a lack of research into the effectiveness of corporate events. Companies find it hard to establish their return on investment in corporate hospitality and more quantitative and qualitative evidence is needed to do this, in order to justify the spending on client entertaining and staff motivation.

In the USA, corporate hospitality at golf events was hard hit by the economic downturn of 2008 and 2009. Corporate hospitality revenue was down at the 2009 US Open, and the US Golf Association (USGA) planned to look at ways of protecting its revenue stream. 'Corporate hospitality has not been immune to the economic slowdown,' said USGA chief business officer Pete Bevacqua. 'The great challenge will be predicting what corporate hospitality will look like in the future. I think coming out of this it will need to be tweaked, it will need to be adjusted. We'll need to show some great flexibility' (Fine, 2009). With spending down during the global economic downturn and companies sensitive over the appearance of frivolous entertaining, only 50 corporate tents were sold at the Open compared to more than 70 when it was last at Bethpage in 2002.

The fee for a 40×40-foot tent can approach a quarter of a million dollars for the USGA, which gets more than 75 per cent of its total revenue from US Open proceeds. 'I think we're at one of those critical junctures where corporate hospitality in all sports and in golf has to take a look at itself and say how will corporations respond to this,' said Bevacqua. Bevacqua said the USGA's projection for corporate revenue at the 2009 Open won by American Lucas Glover was down 20 per cent but he was confident golf remained fertile ground. 'The undeniable fact is that corporate hospitality at golf events is powerful. It works for the corporations. It's a great marketing tool, it's a great way to conduct business,' he said.

Certainly, golf event marketers are becoming quite creative when it comes to corporate hospitality packages. Figure 8.4 shows the variety of packages on offer at the 2009 Crowne Plaza Invitational at Colonial in Texas.

Figure 8.4: Corporate hospitality packages at the 2009 Crowne Plaza Invitational at Colonial (source: www.crowneplazainvitational.com)

River Club at 16 – $49,000
30'x40' air-conditioned venue with private outdoor patio to watch all the action at #16.
Lounge seating with television, linens, lighting and floral decor.
Air-conditioning, access to upscale restroom.
Sponsor board, magazine listing and one full page colour ad in the Tournament Magazine.
100 credentials each day Wednesday – Sunday
Six (6) Clubhouse Medallions; Six (6) Parking credentials (2) Clubhouse and (4) Valet Parking Passes; 10 tickets to Monday's Entertainment Night at Billy Bob's Texas.

Swimming Pool Plaza – $45,000 Hole No. 1
Located in the exclusive Swimming Pool Plaza
20' x 40' tent with outdoor patio seating
Corporate name identification on the pool main entrance.
(100) Credentials per day, Thursday through Sunday; (8) Valet Parking Passes
(10) Tickets to Monday Night's Entertainment Night at Billy Bob's Texas

Colonial Skysuite – $42,000 Hole No. 18.
16'x'24' enclosed luxury private hospitality suite .
Air-conditioned interior with tiered seating for 21 people plus room for 4 standing.
Corporate name identification on the Skysuite entrance.
Sponsor board, magazine listing and one full page colour ad in the Tournament Magazine.
Attractive interior with televisions, floral decor, tables and restroom.
Two (2) playing spots in the Hogan Pro-Am on Monday; One (1) invitation for each Pro-Am participant and guest to Sunday evening's Draw Party.
30 credentials each day Wednesday – Sunday; Six (6) Clubhouse Medallions; Six (6) Valet Parking Passes; 10 tickets to Monday's Entertainment Night at Billy Bob's Texas.

Hawks Nest at 16 – $39,000
30' x 60' air-conditioned venue with shared interior and private outdoor patio.
Fully catered with full beverage service and afternoon snacks.
Sponsor board, magazine listing and one full page colour ad in the Tournament Magazine.
(50) daily credentials to access the Hawks Nest and grounds to include the Lounge

Six (6) Clubhouse Medallions; Six (6) Parking credentials (2) Clubhouse and (4) Valet Parking Passes; 10 tickets to Monday's Entertainment Night at Billy Bob's Texas.
May purchase up to 10 more tickets to entertain a total of 60 per day.

Hogan Skybox at 18 – $29,000
10' x 30' section of a covered private hospitality venue with tiered seating for (20) people.
Fully catered with full beverage service and afternoon snacks.
Sponsor board, magazine listing and one full page colour ad in the Tournament Magazine.
Televisions to keep updated on all the action around the course; fans and WifFi access
(40) dedicated daily credentials to grounds and Hogan Skybox each day, Wednesday-Sunday; (4) Parking Passes, (2) Clubhouse and (2) Valet; (2) Sponsors medallions, good for grounds and clubhouse admission Wednesday-Sunday
(6) Tickets to Monday's Entertainment Night at Billy Bob's Texas

Tennis Lounge – $23,000
Private Hospitality between No. 9 and No. 10 fairways has easy access to golf course, practice putting green, Crowne Plaza Lounge and Fan Fest.
Provides quiet environment to entertain clients, Thursday through Sunday.
Attractive interior with televisions, floral decor, tables and private restrooms.
(50) Credential per day, Thursday through Sunday
(10) Tickets to Monday's Entertainment Night at Billy Bob's Texas

Skybox – $16,000
Locations include: No. 13, 16, and 17 Access Wednesday through Sunday
10' x 20' section of a covered private hospitality venue with tiered seating for (20) people
Rear deck for light food & beverage service plus adjoining entry deck for easy access
Daily Grounds credentials purchased separately in quantities to meet entertaining needs
(4) Valet Parking Passes; (4) Tickets to Monday's Entertainment Night

Log Cabin Village $6000 per day/$20,000 Wed – Sun
Offers opportunity for hospitality before, during and after play in a private park setting.
Space for up to (50) parking places
Nestled on (3) acres across from Colonial Country Club.
Heavily wooded open-air park.
Opportunity to utilize any third-party catering option.
Option to brand hospitality staging space within the park area next to private road

Operational issues

Operations can be thought of as the day-to-day decisions and actions within the event organization, as opposed to strategic and business-level actions (Getz, 2007). Table 8.1 summarizes the unique issues and challenges for events. These include the perishability of event capacity; if tickets or hospitality tents are not sold, the lost revenue cannot be made up later. At the 2009 US Open, with corporate hospitality revenue down, the USGA recouped some revenue loss by selling more tournament tickets to the public. More than 40,000 tickets were sold on each day of the event. However, the event was hampered by heavy rain throughout the week. 'It's a financial monkey wrench and a psychological monkey wrench,' said USGA chief business officer Pete Bevacqua (Fine, 2009). Bevacqua commented on the dreary weather that cut into concession and food sales at Bethpage and added an extra day to the competition. 'You don't want to have an umbrella in one hand and a hamburger in the other. 'It's a downer. It's disappointing but there are only so many things you can control and weather is not one of them.'

Table 8.1: Unique operational issues and challenges for events (based on Getz, 2007, p. 275).

Complex and risky event settings and programmes

Crowd emotions and behaviour

Lack of experience for one-time events

Peak demand periods and simultaneous entry or exit from venues

The perishability of event capacity

The need to be 'green'

The need to be 'green' or environmentally responsible has become an important issue for event organizers. It was mentioned above that Fairmont Banff Springs Golf Course was seeking permission from Parks Canada to host the 2010 TELUS World Skins Games. However, there had to be minimal impact on the environment. The three potential issues were displacement of wildlife during the sensitive spring period, habituation of individual animals to humans and human activities and human–wildlife conflicts. Play would be stopped if a grizzly or black bear was observed feeding on or around the golf course. If necessary, golfers and spectators would be moved away from the bear and the area. Bears would not be removed from the course and Parks Canada would dictate when play resumed (Ellis, 2009).

Snapshot: The experience of Korea hosting an International PGA Tour Golf Event

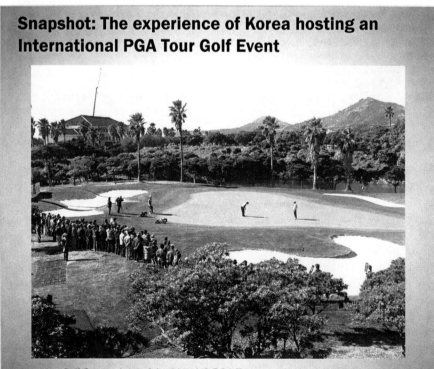

Jungmun Golf Course, host of the 2004 US PGA Tour event in Korea, courtesy of Korea Tourism Organization

Golf has been high profile in Korea since the success of Korean professionals on both the PGA and LPGA circuits. However, 500,000 of the country's 3 million golfers take annual golfing holidays overseas in search of lower green fees and easy tee time bookings. Because of this trend, the Korea Tourism Organization (KTO), in conjunction with other multinational companies, decided to host a US PGA Tour event in Korea, as a solution to help solve the tourism imbalance and to encourage investment in golf tourist destinations. KTO recognized the value of media and commercial advertising that are part of the PGA Tour bandwagon as well as the international spotlight which is focused on each destination on the Tour.

Jeju Island was successful in its bid to host the event to be held in November 2004 at Jungmun Golf Club. The island had acted as base camp for the English soccer team and accompanying media during the FIFA World Cup in 2002. Two main World Cup matches were played there and media focused the spotlight on the island's suitability as an international tourism and sporting events destination.

Over three years of preparations, the KTO and local Jeju Island representatives had to counteract a lack of previous experience in hosting such an event as well as financial problems. There were difficulties faced in aligning the various stakeholders' fiscal systems as well as coordination of research. 30 per cent of the $10 million budget was due to come from sponsors but in 2004, when political upheaval led to impeachment of the country's president and an ensuing election, the sponsors pulled out. The KTO addressed the 30 per cent deficit by reducing the prize purse from $5 million to $3.5 million and cancelled several aspects of the programme. They also invested more KTO funds into the event which prompted criticism from the National Board of Audit for diverting the national budget into the PGA golfing event rather than dispersing it for national tourism promotions.

When the event went ahead, media attention was significant. The value of international TV coverage was gauged at $53 million, domestic TV $5 million and newspaper coverage at $1 million. On top of this there were $7.7 million in free international TV commercial spots and a further $1.5 million in domestic spots. The organizers held eight press conferences and sent out 27 press releases. Online, 132,210 hits were recorded over 40 days surrounding the event. 'The overall assessment concluded that the KTO and Jeju Island has made substantial progress toward the development of a sport tourism market because of its high media coverage, the development of a new trend market, acquiring the necessary professional management skills to organise an international golf event, and because of the positive PR effects' (Lim and Patterson, 2008).

However, one of the main problems with money generated by the event was leakage. Much of the total budget spent by the KTO was paid to the US PGA Tour and the US broadcasting companies. Locals didn't feel that enough profit trickled down directly to their businesses and communities. There was also a low turnout of spectators and key stakeholders were not able to leverage marketing and promotional opportunities offered by the event. It was decided therefore not to make this an annual event.

But even though Korea did not see sufficient immediate benefits to justify them holding a regular event on the Tour, there were positive outcomes. Increased brand recognition helped regenerate Jeju Island's tourism. Being associated with the first US PGA Tour event outside the USA gave the country some credibility in golfing circles and encouraged other sporting events to come to Jeju. In 2006 there were 30 international and 71 national events held there and golf tourism was elevated to third ranking business for the island. With the enhanced experience of handling large golfing events, Korea was able to inaugurate the Korea SBS Tour in 2005.

Sources

Lim, C. C., and Patterson, I. (2008) 'Sport tourism on the islands: the impact of an international mega golf event', *Journal of Sport & Tourism*, 13(2), 115-133.

http://www.jejueco.com.

http://www.visitkorea.or.kr/intro.html.

The impact of golf events

There is an increasing popularity amongst destinations for hosting sporting events in order to generate immediate economic impact, increase future visitation, improve the image of the city or country, or to disperse tourism activities in a wider region (Hudson *et al.*, 2004). The annual Abu Dhabi Golf Championship, for example, has played a pivotal part in the city's marketing strategy to boost its golf tourism (see Snapshot). A smaller community may have other motivations for hosting an event, such as to provide local entertainment and to enhance community pride (Turco, 1998). However, the economic impact is usually the primary motive. It was mentioned earlier that the financial contribution of tournaments and endorsements was $1.7 billion for the USA in 2005. Table 8.2 summarizes the key indicators of this cluster in Europe, the Middle East and Africa for 2006. The contribution was also over $1 billion, supporting approximately 4100 jobs which paid $426 million in wages and contributed $528 million to GDP (KPMG, 2008). Figure 8.5 shows the relative contribution of tournaments and players endorsements to key economic measures of the golf tournaments cluster in the EMA region. In 2007, revenue from the 120 international professional golf tournaments in the EMA region amounted to $329 million. This figure includes the broadcasting rights for the major tours.

Table 8.2: Key indicators of the golf tournaments and endorsements cluster (KPMG, 2008).

2006	Direct	Indirect	Induced	Total
Revenues ($ million)	460	210	375	1045
Contribution to GDP ($ million)	365	57	106	528
Employment*	1,500	1,000	1,600	4,100
Total wage income ($ million)	318	41	67	426

Note: *Employment includes: tournament organizers, broadcasting staff, players involved in endorsements and these players' management.

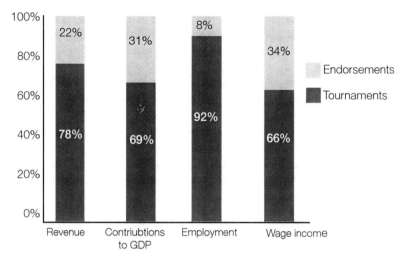

Figure 8.5: the relative contribution of tournaments and players endorsements in the EMA region (Source: KPMG, 2008).

Individually, golf events can have a significant economic impact on a local economy. Table 8.3 gives some examples. A variety of methods have been used to calculate these figures, but normally the impact is determined by visitor spending in hotel rooms, meals, transportation, and shopping. It can be seen that major PGA events can generate vast sums of money. The 2005 Players Championship (TPC) Tournament in Florida, for example, resulted in a $95.8 million dollar benefit for northeast Florida. There were about 72,000 attendees as well as 1267 players, caddies, officials, TV crews, marketing officials and family members. In addition to the $95.8 million in output or gross sales revenues, other economic impacts were $40.7 million in labour income, or net earnings, $6 million in indirect business taxes, and 1398 full- and part-time jobs for northeast Florida (Agrusa and Tanner, 2002).

Table 8.3: The economic impact of various golf events on the local economy

Golf Tournament	Economic impact on the local economy
2000 Buy.Com Louisiana Open Golf Tournament	$69,000
2001 Carolina Golf Association Senior Amateur Championships	$90,749
2004 PGA Championship, Wisconsin	$76 million
2005 PGA Heritage Classic, Hilton Head Island	$84 million
2005 Players Championship (TPC) Tournament, Florida	$95.8 million
2007 British Open, Carnoustie	$22.2 million
2007 Senior PGA Championship, Kiawah Island	$23.3 million
2007 AT&T Champions Classic Golf Tournament	$7 million
2007 Nationwide Tour, Omaha, Nebraska	$8.8 million
2008 NCAA Men's Golf Central Regional Championship, Austin Texas	$1.3 million

Sources: Daniels and Norman. (2003); Agrusa and Tanner (2002); Stevens, Hodges and Mulkey (2007); Nadra (2008); Flowers (2009); Gelan (2003); Angus Council (2008); NorthStar Economics (2004); Decker (2007)

Sometimes these calculations will take into account the economic impact on local charities from the tournament proceedings. A 2004 report estimated that the 140,000 charitable events involving more than 15 million participants raise almost $3 billion every year (NGF, 2004). The majority of outings are conducted by community-based charities and raise roughly $10,000 on average. The PGA Tour of course generates much larger amounts for charitable causes. The Crowne Plaza Invitational, for example, referred to above, raised $6.6 million in total charitable contributions from the tournament, a 50 per cent increase on the year before. PGA Director of Business Development, Travis Velichko says the PGA Tour is the leader among world sports in raising money for charities: 'You could add all the other major sports together and it still wouldn't compare with the charitable contributions we make.'

The media exposure that the event receives can also have a significant long-term impact on the host destination. The PGA Tour, Champions Tour and Nationwide Tour have TV coverage on ABC, CBS, NBC, ESPN, the Golf Channel and USA Network and sell broadcasts to 140 countries worldwide reaching a 240 million audience. Although it is difficult to determine the long-term economic impact of media exposure from a golf event (Gelan, 2003), it is possible to calculate a media value based on advertising equivalency. For example, the British Open in 2007 received 2172 hours of television and media coverage, with Carnoustie area in particular receiving 171 hours of scenic, graphic, and verbal exposure equivalent to $51 million in gross media value. 47 per cent of this was delivered from North America and 23 per cent from the Asia Pacific region, significantly increasing the exposure of Carnoustie country in these areas (Angus Council, 2008). The 2009 Open in Turnberry was also well-received by television viewers around the world, especially given 59 year-old Tom Watson's heroics. Although Turnberry's remote location in south Ayrshire means the R&A lose around $1.5 million in spectator revenue compared to other venues in Scotland (123,000 attended the 2009 event), the organizers know how popular the links is with television viewers.

Because of this potential value of media exposure, destinations will make significant investments in hosting an event. In 2006 for example, the Irish government spent $15 million to stage and market the Ryder Cup golf tournament, in an effort to reverse a five-year decline in North American visitors. Television ads appeared on US channels such as CBS and the Golf Channel. The Ryder Cup was expected to generate about $125 million in business through TV rights, merchandise, tickets, and sponsorship (Cole, 2006). It is not uncommon for destination marketing organizations to be involved in sponsoring such high profile events. The end-of-chapter case study discusses the European Senior Tour event in Mallorca, Spain, where the Mallorcan tourism board, IBATUR, came to the table with the prize money and the sanction fee for the Tour. Also, the Snapshot above describes how the Korea Tourism Organization (KTO) decided to host a US PGA Tour event in Korea, as a solution to help solve the tourism imbalance and to encourage investment in golf tourist destinations.

Malaysia (see Snapshot in Chapter 1) has long followed the strategy of promoting the country's golf industry through the hosting of major golf tournaments. An example is the Malaysian Open, which is sanctioned by the European and Asian Tours and is one of the country's biggest sporting events. The event is telecast worldwide by CNBC and other major sports channels and has an estimated 300 to 500 million viewers (*Malaysian Business*, 2006). The 2009 event was held at the Saujana Golf and Country Club with a prize fund of $2 million. Tourism Malaysia has hosted other international golf tournaments such as the World Cup of Golf and the World Amateur International Tournament Golf Championships (WAITGC), another major golfing event which attracts many foreign golfers.

Emerging golf destinations are also using events to promote golf tourism. The Department of Tourism (DOT) in the Philippines hosts the Philippines-Korea Amateur Golf Tournament in order to promote the country as a suitable golf destination to Korean golfers. Golfers account for a substantial share of Korean arrivals according to DOT officials (*Manila Bulletin*, 2007). The state-run CzechTourism agency, which promotes the Czech Republic as an attractive tourism destination abroad, has also supported a number of golf events in order to showcase the country as a golf tourism destination. CzechTourism was a partner to a series of golf tournaments in 2006 called the Českomoravská golf tour, and one tournament in the series played under the title of the CzechTourism Cup. Chapter 10 has more details on golf tourism development in New Europe.

Sport events have the ability to not only induce travel, but also to promote regional exploration within the host destination (Getz, 1991). Puerto Rico tourism officials were hoping that by hosting a PGA Open – the first Puerto Rico Open was held at the Trump International Golf Club near San Juan in March 2008 – would showcase the security, safety, quality and infrastructure of Puerto Rico's tourism product. The 2008 event was the biggest golfing event in Puerto Rico's history with between 5000 and 8000 spectators showing up each day and an estimated $11-$14 million expected in economic impacts (Cardona, 2009). Hoteliers used the opportunity to attract domestic guests by offering free tickets to the event. In the run up to the Open, Trump International (previously known as Coco Beach Golf & Country Club) represented the island at the 2007 International Golf Travel Market Convention in Mexico. Along with two other major Puerto Rico resorts, the club's representatives attended the premier golf travel convention to showcase its products as well as promote the upcoming tournament. Shortly after the Open, Puerto Rico Tourism leveraged the recent media spotlight by putting a 10-page glossy ad and advertorial in *Travel + Leisure Golf* magazine extolling the virtues of Puerto Rico's golf offerings along with its natural beauty, history, art, culture, cuisine, hiking, sports and shopping opportunities. In 2009 hospitality sales were up 12–14 per cent over the previous year.

Case Study: Golf Son Gual, Mallorca: Host of the European Senior Open in 2009

Billboard publicizing the European Senior Open in Golf Son Gual, Mallorca, 2009, photograph by the author

Watching the planes lining up to land in the distant Palma airport, while sipping beer and eating tapas on the terrace of Son Gual Golf Club, provides visible proof that the Spanish island of Mallorca is the most popular holiday destination in Europe. The attractive combination of geography, climate and culture attracts between 10 and 12 million visitors each year. Traditionally, that popularity has been satiated by package tour operators, but increasingly golf is seen as a hook by which to attract a new clientele. With 23 golf courses on the island by 2009, Mallorca has matured into a perfect short-haul golf destination and a viable alternative to mainland Spain, Portugal and Tunisia – particularly for Germans and British golfers. In 2007, income from the 110,000 golf tourists was 176 million euros, 5.8 per cent more than the previous year.

The island's reputation as a golf tourism destination was given a huge boost in 2009 when Golf Son Gual, a relatively new player on the block, hosted the European Senior Open. German businessmen, Adam and Andreas Pamer, had the original dream behind Son Gual, and three-time German Amateur Champion and course designer, Thomas Himmel, realized it. The 30 million euro course only opened in October 2007, and when the club was chosen as the host, Andreas Pamer, the club's manager said 'It is rare that a golf course succeeds in attracting an event of this stature at such an early stage in its life so it is testament to the efforts of all of our team in providing such wonderful and consistent conditions to play.' Two loops of nine holes fit easily into the 175 acres of land and an extensive earth-moving process has shaped a spectacular and challenging course. One special feature of the course, and one that will bear fruit quite literally, is the incorporation of vineyards around the course, adding to the 800 newly planted olive trees. Fifteen-minute starting intervals ensure there is no waiting around on the tee, and it is customary for golfers to stop half-way round for a few tapas and a drink.

But why did Son Gual choose to host the European Senior Tour? 'When you open a new golf course, you have to think about promoting the product in the right way. Besides lots of press trips and marketing activities the first year we wanted something special, a big tournament with big names but affordable costs. That's why we decided to host a European Senior Tournament,' said Pamer. This is a professional tour for male golfers 50 and over and it is run by the European PGA Tour. The Tour was founded in 1992, and in 2008 had a total prize fund of nearly 8 million euros (quite a way behind the American Champions' Tour in relative prize money). Before the event, Andy Stubbs, European Senior Tour Managing Director said: 'It promises to be an exciting new addition to the European Senior Tour's schedule in 2009. The event is certain to create a great deal of interest in Mallorca and help raise the island's profile as a first-class golfing destination.'

The event was held the week beginning May 6 and began with two days of Pro-Am events, with a capacity for 60 guests each day. Then on 8-10 May, 72 professionals competed for a purse of 300,000 Euros. The event was free for the public with an exhibition area and beer garden open from 10am to 6pm. The first prize of 45,000 euros was won by Mark James after a play-off with former Ryder Cup teammate, Eamonn Darcy. Ian Woosnam of Wales, who won the order of merit in 2008, came in eighth and likened the greens of Son Gual to those of Augusta.

German-based Langer Sport Marketing was appointed as the official promoter of the event. CEO Erwin Langer said: 'It is a great honour to be appointed by the Pamer family to organize this promising new event in one of Europe's prime sun and golf destinations.' Pamer said Langer was contracted because of its long experience in promoting events. 'If we want to see Bernhard Langer playing on our course it is the only way to work with them. But they did an absolute professional and great job. And Mr Erwin Langer was the one who arranged all the big player names to come to Mallorca,' he added.

Operationally, everything ran smoothly, in part because of the help of volunteers. 'You can't run a tournament like this without volunteers' said Pamer. 'We had more volunteers than we needed at the end – about 50 of them, working as marshals, caddies, or on parking, and the leader board. Most of them we found through our webpage and weekly newsletter as well as via a poster we had in every golf club on the island.'

Pamer says it is hard to do a cost/benefit analysis on the event. 'I know the costs exactly because I will have to show them to our main sponsor, the Tourism Board, but it is impossible to measure the benefit.' Altogether the costs of hosting the event were almost one million euros, and at the time of writing, Son Gual was waiting for 330,000 euros from the Mallorcan tourism board, IBATUR, which was used for the prize money and the sanction fee for the Tour. In terms of short-term impacts, Pamer says the number of visitors grew every day till the final on Sunday, when around 2000 spectators came. 'But unfortunately most of them didn't spend a lot on the golf course or in the public area,' he lamented. However, Pamer believes the exposure can only help increase interest in his club in the long-term and therefore attract more golfers. He emphasizes the fact that Son Gual hosted the event in his promotional material. 'I think if you host a European Tour Event, you should also use the right to use their logos and brands for marketing activities,' he explained.

The event generated a fair amount of media exposure, receiving over 50 hours of television coverage in over 20 countries. The only German radio station on the island was a media partner, and was reporting on the event throughout the week before and during the tournament with results and interviews. Patricia Mandado from IBATUR said that they plan to track the success of the event. 'We prefer to make an evaluation after reviewing all the media compilation including the reports related to the tournament made by the press all around the world,' she said.

Despite the hard work involved, Pamer plans to host the event in coming years, especially if he can secure the help of sponsors. The costs he says will not be as high in the future: 'We had to build roads and parking for the public and we had to enlarge the driving range. This won't be necessary in future years. I know how much work it is to organize events like this, if I had known this before I probably wouldn't have done it! But when everything is over and the players write letters of thanks to you, you know why you have done all this work and everybody is looking forward to hosting it again next year.'

Sources

Interviews with Andreas Pamer and Patricia Mandado June 2009.

Simmons, R. (1999) 'Small Island, Big Golf – Golf in Mallorca', *Golf Today Travel*, from http://www.golftoday.co.uk accessed 5 May 2009.

Son Gual Mallorca Senior Open Press Kit.

References

Agrusa, J. and Tanner, J. (2002) 'The economic significance of the 2000 Buy.Com golf tournament on the Lafayette, Louisiana area', *Journal of Sport & Tourism*, 7 (1), 6 – 24.

Angus Council. (2008) 'The Open 2007: economic impact assessment', report by the Director of Infrastructure Services, Angus Council, Report No. 96/08, 22 January.

Cardona, M.M. (2009) 'Puerto Rico golf resorts being upscaled', Associated Press, 8 January, from: http://abcnews.go.com, accessed 17 June 2009.

Clark, J.M., Cornwell, T.B. and Pruitt, S.W. (2009) 'The impact of title event sponsorship announcements on shareholder wealth', *Market Lett*, 20, 169-182.

Cole, C. (2006) 'Ireland has never been greener', *National Post*, 20 September, B8.

Crosset, T. (1995) *Outsiders in the Clubhouse: The World of Women's Professional Golf*, Albany, NY: State University of New York Press.

Daniels, M.J. and Norman, W.C. (2003) 'Estimating the economic impacts of seven regular sport tourism events', *Journal of Sport Tourism*, 8 (4), 214–222.

Decker, C.S. (2007) *An Economic Impact Study Assessing the Impact that the Cox Classic Golf Tournament has on the City of Omaha*, University of Nebraska

Delpy Neirotti, L. (2003) 'An introduction to sport and adventure tourism', In S. Hudson (ed.) *Sport & Adventure Tourism, Oxford*: Haworth, pp. 1–25.

Ellis, C. (2009) 'Parks approves skins golf tournament', *Rocky Mountain Outlook*, 2 July, pp. 1 & 6.

Fine, L. (2009) 'Golf-US Open to tweak corporate hospitality business', Thomson Reuters, from http://uk.reuters.com accessed 2 July, 2009.

Flowers, J. (April 2009) 'The Economic Impact of Golf in South Carolina', for South Carolina Golf Course Owners Association.

Gelan, A. (2003) 'Local economic impacts: the British Open', *Annals of Tourism Research*, 30(2), 406-425.

Getz, D. (1991) *Festivals, Special Events and Tourism*, New York: Van Norstrand Reinhold.

Getz, D. (2007) *Event Studies. Theory, Research and Policy for Planned Events*, Oxford: Butterworth-Heinemann.

Golf International (2009) 'Chubby's Got Talent', *Golf International*, June/July, 174–179.

Hanlon, C. and Stewart, B. (2006) 'Managing personnel in major sport event organizations: what strategies are required?', *Event Management*, 10 (1), 77–88.

Hansen, H. and Gauthier, R. (1994) 'The Professional Golf Product: Spectators' Views', *Sport Marketing Quarterly*, 3 (1), 9–16.

Hinch, T.D. and Higham, J.E.S. (2001) 'Sport tourism: a framework for research', *International Journal of Tourism Research*, 3 (1), 45–58.

Hinch, T.D. and Higham, J.E.S. (2004) *Sport Tourism Development*, Clevedon: Channel View Publications.

Hudson, S., Getz, D., Miller, G.A. and Brown, G. (2004) 'The future role of sporting events: evaluating the impacts on tourism', in K. Weiermair and C. Mathies (eds.) *The Tourism and Leisure Industry – Shaping the Future*, Binghampton, NY:The Haworth Press, pp. 237–251.

IMG. (2009) 'Tournament management', from http://www.imgworld.com/sports/golf/tournament_management.sps, accessed 1 July 2009.

KPMG. (2008) 'The value of golf to Europe, Middle East and Africa', KPMG Advisory Ltd.

McDonald, M.A., Milne, G.R. and Hong, J.B. (2002) 'Motivational factors for evaluating sport spectator and participant markets', *Sport Marketing Quarterly*, 11, 100-113.

Malaysian Business (2006) 'Golf tourism, anyone?' *Malaysian Business*, 1 July, pp. 42.

Manila Bulletin (2007) 'Golf Helps Drive RP Tourism in S. Korea', *Manila Bulletin*, 20 February, from http://www.mb.com, accessed 21 January, 2009.

MDB. (2009) *UK Corporate Hospitality Market Research Report*, February, Market & Business Development, Manchester.

Mintel. (2006) 'Golf tourism', *Travel & Tourism Analyst*, 5, Mintel International Group, London.

Nadra, K. (2008) 'Growth in special events provides economic boon: golf classic, cycling tour generate tourism bucks', San Fernando Business Journal, 31 March.

NGF. (2004) 'The impact of golf on charitable giving in the US', a report by the National Golf Foundation for Golf 20/20.

NorthStar Economics (2004) 'The Economic Contribution of the 2004 PGA Championship on the State of Wisconsin', NorthStar Economics, Madison, Wisconsin.

Perkins, T. (2008) 'RBC shooting at US with golf deal', *Globe and Mail*, 26 July, pp. B6.

Potter, J. (2009) 'LPGA taking final swings at Corning Classic', *USA Today*, 20 May, 2C.

Robinson, M.J. and Carpenter, J.R. (2003) 'The day of the week's impact on selected socio-demographic and consumption patterns of spectators at a LPGA event', *Sport Marketing Quarterly*, 11, 242-247.

Robinson, M.J., Trail, G.T., and Kwon, H. (2004) 'Motives and Points of Attachment of Professional Golf Spectators', *Sport Management Review*, 7, 167-192.

Shmanske, S, (2000) 'Gender, Skill and Earnings in Professional Golf', *Journal of Sport Economics*, 1(4), 385-400.

SRI (2005) 'The 2005 Golf Economy Report,' from http://www.golf2020.com/reports/GolfEconomyExecSummary.pdf

Stevens, T., Hodges, A. and Mulkey, D. (2007) 'Economic impact of the Players Championship golf tournament at Ponte Vedra Beach, Florida, March 2005', EDIS Document FE698, a publication of the Food and Resource Economics Department, Institute of Food and Agricultural Sciences, University of Central Florida.

Tassiopoulos, D. and Haydam, N. (2008) 'Golf tourists in South Africa: a demand-side study of a niche market in sports tourism', *Tourism Management*, 29(5), 870-882.

TPC (2009) 'Tournaments and Events', from http://www.tpc.com/events accessed on 1 July, 2009.

Troon Golf (2009) '2008 Sales & Marketing Summary', Troon Golf.

Turco, D.M. (1998) 'Travelling and turnovers measuring the economic impacts of a street baseball tournament', *Journal of Sport Tourism*, 5(1).

UNWTO (1995) 'UNWTO Technical Manual: Collection of Tourism Expenditure Statistics', World Tourism Organization, 14, http://pub.unwto.org/WebRoot/Store/Shops/Infoshop/Products/1034/1034-1.pdf accessed on 26 June, 2009.

9 The Impacts of Golf Tourism

Aiming for PGA Tour quality, the 303-acre site now features irrigation and drainage systems that re-use and maximize the use of rainwater. There are native grass areas, waste bunkers, lakes and streams that reduce maintenance and more lake areas and re-circulating streams that support wildlife. In place of equipment sheds and a maintenance centre, Timberlake has built a 'Natural Resource Management Centre' which features biodegradable treatment of rinse water.

Timberlake planned to use Mirimichi as the headquarters for his celebrity music career. Although the course is upscale and challenging, he also intends to nurture new golfers there with a nine-hole course called 'Little Mirimichi' and an 18-hole putting course. He wants the club to serve as a social and sporty hub for the local community with special programmes targeting families and children. Costs are relatively affordable – from $59 for weekday rounds and up to $71 for weekends and holidays. It was thanks to considerable family resources that Timberlake was able to open a new course during the economic downturn which had been sparking golf course closures for the previous two years.

The course features artistic stone cart-path bridges, manmade creeks with re-circulating water, Champion Bermuda greens and Patriot Bermuda fairways. Azalea bushes accent the surrounding landscaping with shade-tolerant grass or pine straw under all the trees. Drainage systems in the 80 sand bunkers prevent sand from washing away. Only half the 200-acre course will be mowed as native grasses have been planted in between play areas. Bordered by a forested buffer which prevents any future adjoining development, the new cart paths follow a shady route. The 18 holes have been transformed by Mike MacElhose and Randy Wilson so that the previously flat front nine now features undulating topography and both uphill and downhill shots on the rolling fairways. The workforce comprised around 120 construction and staff workers. In this nature-reserve style atmosphere, Mirimichi staff monitor water flow, count wildlife annually and calculate the club's carbon footprint.

Timberlake has already hosted his own PGA Tour tournament (the Justin Timberlake Shriners' Hospitals for Children Open) and regularly plays with professional golfers. During the 2009 PGA Tour events, the Golf Channel aired a series of short videos called 'Choose your course,' which highlighted the work of superintendents and the environmental benefits of golf courses. The messages were introduced by Timberlake.

Sources:

'Justin Timberlake's eco-golf course', http://blog.sprig.com/blogs/eco_scoop/archive/2008/10/01/justin-timb accessed 1 October 2008.

Kondrat, A. (2008) 'Timberlake to Open United States' First LEED-Certified Golf Course', http://www.takepart.com/2008/10/01/justin-timberlake-to-open-united accessed 1 October.

http://www.timberlake-justin.com/justin-timberlakes-golf-course-gets-award-from-audubon-international/http://mirimichi.com/.

www.commercialappeal.com

Introduction

The unprecedented expansion of tourism has given rise to a number of economic, environmental and social impacts which are concentrated in destination areas (Wall and Mathieson, 2006). Tourism research has tended to emphasize the economic impacts and yet there are increasing concerns about the effects of tourism on host societies and their environments. A number of techniques have been developed to monitor these impacts. Common analytical frameworks include an environmental audit, environmental impact analysis, carrying capacity, and community assessment techniques. It is beyond the scope of this book to cover these techniques in detail, but the tourism manager needs to have knowledge of the most current models. Managers must also have an understanding of the principles of sustainable tourism described as 'tourism which is developed and maintained in an area in such a manner and at such a scale that it remains viable over an indefinite period and does not degrade or alter the environment (human and physical) in which it exists to such a degree that it prohibits the successful development and well-being of other activities and processes' (Butler, 1993, p. 29).

Table 9.1: Positive and negative impacts of golf (Sources: Barcelona Field Studies Centre, 2009; Salgot and Tapias, 2006)

Advantages	Disadvantages
Employment and income benefits, both direct and indirect	Loss of biodiversity
Tax benefits to local, regional and national governments	Eutrophication of river or seawater through use of fertilizers
Attracts new firms to the region	Heavy user of water for irrigation
Health and social benefits. Careers can benefit through 'networking'.	Biocides used to maintain the greenness of the 'greens', control insects, fungicides and weeds, contaminate both the air and water
Attracts the higher-spending social groups	Golf clubs often portray an elitist and exclusive lifestyle
Helps conserve valuable fragments of coastal habitat from encroaching urbanization and agriculture	Leads to an increase in road traffic
Increases local property values	Raises property prices beyond the reach of local young people
Waste can be recycled	Displacement through land occupancy
Quality of tourism increases	Creates elitism
Counteract problems of seasonality	Creates pressures on land

This increasing emphasis on sustainability has important implications for the golf industry, and this chapter focuses on the three pillars of sustainability – the economy, the environment and society. In the past, golf tourism was encouraged for its economic benefits with little consideration for the effects on the environment. But as witnessed in the opening Spotlight, this is beginning to change. For golf tourism to be sustainable, it is vital that its impacts are understood, so that they can be incorporated into planning and management. Table 9.1 lists just some of the positive and negative impacts of golf according to experts, many of which are covered in more detail throughout this chapter.

The economic impacts of golf tourism

As mentioned above, early tourism research focused mainly upon the economic aspects of the industry, with many early impact studies directed at international and national levels. However, there are an increasing number of studies that examine regional and local economic impacts, and this chapter contains a number of such examples (see the Snapshot on the economic impacts of golf tourism in South Carolina). Similarly, there are a growing number of studies that attempt to estimate the impacts of specific events – Chapter 8 referred to several golf event impact studies.

According to Wall and Mathieson (2006) four factors have contributed to both the emphasis on economic impact analysis and the quality of such studies. First, when compared with physical and social impacts, economic impacts are relatively easy to measure. There exist widely accepted methodologies for measuring economic impacts, but in social and environmental sciences these are still in the early stages of development. Second, large amounts of reliable and comparable data have been collected on economic aspects of tourism, often collected routinely by government agencies. Third, research has advanced the application of economic assessment tools in tourism research. Economists have traditionally used input-output (IO) analysis, but other methods such as linear programming, general equilibrium models and cost-benefit analysis have also been employed in recent years. Multiplier analysis is also popular with economists, whereby the money spent by tourists in the area will be re-spent by recipients, augmenting the total. The multiplier is the factor by which tourist spend is increased in this process. For example, research in the Western Cape of South Africa has shown indirect benefits of golf to be positive with a multiplier effect of 1.68 for every rand spent. The final reason for the emphasis on the economics of tourism, especially its benefits, reflects the widespread belief among agency personnel that tourism can yield rapid and considerable returns on investments and be a positive force in remedying economic problems.

The impact of tourism goes far beyond enrichment in purely economic terms, helping to benefit the environment and culture and the fight to reduce poverty. Over the past few decades, the share in international tourism arrivals received by developing countries has steadily risen, from 31 per cent in 1990 to 45 per cent in 2008. Tourism can serve as a foothold for the development of a market economy where small and medium-sized enterprises can expand and flourish. And in poor rural areas, it often constitutes the only alternative to subsistence farming which is in decline. In Rwanda, for example, tourism has become the country's top source of foreign income, overtaking tea and coffee exports in 2007. Rwanda is targeting $75 million in foreign earnings from tourism by 2010. Big emerging markets (BEMs) like Brazil, India, Turkey and Vietnam, also see the potential of tourism as a powerful economic force.

Golf tourism has an important role to play in this economic development. It was mentioned in Chapter 1 that after the Second World War a number of destinations started to develop and diversify their golf tourism products in an effort to lure strong foreign currency, and thus spur economic growth. The attraction of the golf tourist became a key tourism development strategy for many regions around the world. By allowing the building of infrastructure and the import of quality resort builders and operators, countries were able to achieve economic growth by attracting foreign tourists. The case study at the end of the chapter comments on the strategic importance of golf for the Algarve in Portugal since it operates in a counter-cycle to sun-beach tourism. In many other countries, golf tourism has combated problems of seasonality by attracting the higher spending low season tourism (Markwick, 2000).

Golf tourism today attracts millions of holidaymakers worldwide, contributing over 20 billion dollars annually to the global economy. In the USA alone, the domestic and international golf markets together generate a total economic impact of $195 billion, including golf's direct, indirect and induced impacts. Golf provides a direct economic impact of $76 billion in the USA and creates approximately 2 million jobs with wage income of $61 billion (SRI, 2005). In Europe, the Middle East and Africa (EMA), golf generates a direct economic effect of $27.6 billion, golf tourism being responsible for $3.5 billion of this (KPMG, 2008).

As mentioned above, there are an increasing number of government agencies conducting economic impact studies in tourism. SRI International has done a number of such studies for the golf industry in North America. In California, for example, they found that the golf industry pumps $6.9 billion annually into the state's economy, putting it on par with biotechnology ($4.6 billion), wineries ($8.2 billion) and semiconductor manufacturing ($10.0 billion) (SRI International, 2008). When indirect impacts are included – such as the goods and services purchased by golf courses and golf employees from other sectors of the economy – the total direct and indirect impact of the golf industry in California is estimated at $15.1 billion. Golf tournaments in California generated approximately $95.8 million in revenues in 2006, excluding the tournament purses and costs for television broadcasting. Table 9.2 shows the multiplier impacts of golf on California's economy.

In 2006, golf facilities in California represented the largest golf industry segment in terms of revenue, followed by golf real estate, and golf-related tourism. SRI estimated that golf-related tourism spending in California was $1.2 billion in 2006. This figure was calculated by collecting data for two types of figures: the annual number of golf-related trips; and average spending per trip. Table 9.3 shows that nearly 3 million golf tourists spent on average $416 on their trip. This includes spending on accommodation, transportation, food and beverage, entertainment, gifts, etc. Green fees and cart fees are not included as they are already captured in the golf facility operations revenues (Table 9.2).

Table 9.2: Multiplier impacts on California's economy (Source: SRI International, 2008 pp. 25)

Industry	Direct ($ millions)	Indirect/ induced	TOTAL ($ millions)
Golf facility operations	2,846.3	⟶	6,466.8
Golf course capital investments*	325.3	⟶	415.1
Golf-related supplies	951.8	⟶	2,228.1
Tournaments & associations	137.2	⟶	351.7
Real estate**	1,365.2	⟶	2,600.8
Hospitality/tourism	1,245.3	⟶	3,039.8
TOTAL	6,871.1	⟶	15,102.3

Note: Economic impact is calculated on $6,369.2 million of direct golf economy revenues. Portions of two industry segments included in direct economy calculations are excluded from economic impact estimation.

*Golf Course Capital Investments—only new course construction ($163.6 million) is included for this category as other types of facility capital investment are typically financed through facility revenues and therefore, are omitted to avoid double-counting.

**Real Estate—the golf premium associated with golf real estate is considered a transfer of assets rather than new economic activity, so only golf-related residential construction ($1,025.0 million) is included.

Table 9.3: California's golf related travel expenditures in 2006 (Source: SRI International, 2008 pp. 23)

#Golf person trips	2,994,550
Average travel $ per person per trip	416
Total (2006 $ million)	$1,245.3

SRI conducted a similar economic impact study for North Carolina, and found that the average spending per golf trip in 2007 was $58 per day trip and $550 for an overnight trip. Multiplying the total number of golf trips (day and overnight) by average spending per golf trip, SRI found that golf-related tourism spending in North Carolina was approximately $31 million for day trips and $476 million for overnight trips, totalling $507.8 million (see Table 9.4).

Table 9.4: North Carolina's golf-related travel expenditures in 2007 (Source: SRI International, 2009 pp. 25)

# Golf person day trips	534,000
Average travel $ per person per day trip	58.02
# Golf person overnight trips	867,000
Average travel $ per person per overnight trip	550.00
Total ($ million)	507.8

Academics have also looked at the economic impact of golf tourism. Hodges and Haydu (2004), for example, evaluated the economic characteristics and regional impacts of golf courses in Florida in the year 2000. They found that there were residential developments at 54 per cent of Florida's golf courses, with some 756,000 residential units having a total value of $158 billion. Golf industry employment was 73,000 persons. Travel expenses by golf tourists in Florida were estimated at $22.9 billion, of which $5.4 billion were attributed directly to the golf experience. The expenditures had a total impact on the Florida economy of $9.2 billion in personal and business net income and 226,000 jobs. Golf courses had a positive effect on nearby property values in 18 selected counties, with total values for residential properties near to golf courses averaging nearly $20,000 higher than other properties not near a golf course. The research also found that out-of-state visitors to Florida accounted for over 19 million rounds or 32 per cent of golf played. Just north of Florida lies South Carolina, where tourism, and golf tourism in particular, is just as critical to the economy. The Snapshot below focuses on the economic impacts of golf in South Carolina, where golf generates more income than any other single entertainment or recreation activity.

However, not all the economic impacts of golf course development are positive. How many 'golf dollars' stay in the host country is a matter of debate. Anti-golf activist Chyant Pholpoke comments on the Japanese golf tourist. 'When a tourist starts his journey he buys a Nikon camera and then flies with Japan Airlines. Arriving in the Philippines for golf, he takes a Toyota limousine and checks in at a Japanese-owned hotel. He goes up to his room in a Hitachi lift where he takes a drink from a Toshiba fridge, turns on a Sharp air conditioner and a National TV' (Traisawasdichai, 1995). Similar criticisms of leakages have been made in South Africa with suggestions that the money from golf tourism that actually remains in the country is somewhat limited (Enviroadmin, 2005).

In North America, too, there have been criticisms of the economic cost of golf course development. Some complain about the cost to the US taxpayer for the upkeep of courses owned by the military. In 1975 the US Department of Defence spent $14 million a year maintaining the 300 golf courses it owned around the world. Today, the US military claims to own only 172 courses worldwide, but still at a vast cost to the public (Rees, 2008). Similar complaints about military-owned or controlled courses are made in Thailand, Indonesia and Burma.

Snapshot: The economic impact of the golf industry in South Carolina

Fergus Hudson tees off on 18th at the Ocean Course, Kiawah Island, photograph by the author

South Carolina is making significant efforts to understand the golf industry with a variety of research projects and studies into the impacts of this increasingly important industry. Julie Flowers, State Tourism Economist for South Carolina's Department of Parks, Recreation and Tourism has been specializing in tourism – and golf tourism in particular – since 1990. 'Golf generates more income than any other single entertainment or recreation activity in South Carolina,' she said. In fact, since the decline of the textile industry, tourism is the top private industry in the state where it employs over 127,000 people. Figures from 2007 show that the direct and indirect economic benefit of visiting golfers was $2.721 billion in output or sales, creating 33,535 jobs, $834 million in personal incomes and around $276 million in federal, state and local taxes. Green fees and club membership dues accounted for over 39 per cent of state admissions tax collections that year.

With over 350 courses, South Carolina boasts the highest number of golf holes per capita in the USA. Historically, it was also the original home of American golf with the very first course built back in 1786 in Charleston. Nowadays, Myrtle Beach is internationally famous for its 90-plus Grand Strand courses, coastal resorts, and regular internationally-screened championships which help attract both domestic and international golf tourists to the area. The balmy year-round golfing climate is another draw. 'South Carolina's coastal region, with 187 miles of coastline along the Atlantic Ocean, draws about 60 per cent of our visitors with its beaches, championship golf courses, resorts, and history, e.g., Charleston's antebellum period architecture and Revolutionary War and Civil War significance. These amenities are important draws for in-state, out-of-state and international travellers,' said Flowers.

An online survey conducted by Golf Digest Research Resource Center for the Travel Industry Association of America in September 2007 found that more golfers and leisure travellers were choosing South Carolina over Florida. The survey of 4000 avid golfers and affluent travellers revealed that 19 per cent had recently golfed in South Carolina compared to only 15 per cent opting for Florida. South Carolina's top three golf destinations – Myrtle Beach, Hilton Head and Charleston/Kiawah – all made the top 10 on four *Golf Digest* ranking lists generated from the survey results. The survey also recorded useful marketing data, revealing that 73 per cent of golfers use the Internet to plan golf vacations; golfers tend to come in groups of seven and take a seven day trip; they spend around $1000 more than typical affluent travellers and also enjoy dining, shopping and visits to family and friends.

The South Carolina Golf Course Owners' Association co-sponsors the South Carolina Parks, Recreation and Tourism Department's economic impact study as well as co-sponsoring with other golf associations the 'South Carolina Golf Week' which includes a reception for the state's legislature. Flowers' work is also complemented by both university research and industry-driven projects throughout the state. 'Both Clemson University and Coastal Carolina University have golf academic programmes and almost certainly are doing research,' she commented.

A plethora of major annual golf tournaments – including the Heritage Classic held at Harbour Town Golf Links at Sea Pines Resort on Hilton Head Island – bring additional economic benefits to the state. In 2005 the Heritage Classic Foundation commissioned a study by Clemson University to assess the economic impact of the tournament on the island and the region. Visitors to the tournament spent $84 million – $52 million of which benefited area businesses, with 70 per cent of attendees coming from outside the region. In 2007, the Senior PGA Championship held at Kiawah Island had an estimated $23.3 million economic impact on the area, excluding spending by players, officials and the media. Tournaments also contribute substantial amounts to regional charities. And national TV and print media coverage provides another, more intangible benefit for the region's tourism marketing.

Despite the strength of South Carolina's research and marketing, there has been a decline in revenue due to the effects of the international recession. Admissions tax collections from golf revenues were down around 5 per cent between June 2008 and April 2009, according to Flowers. The decrease was more dramatic in the last three months of the period, going from a 10.8 per cent decrease to 16.5 per cent. Golf courses have been responding to the decline in visitor numbers with discount packages and gas card give-aways to offset rising fuel prices. Fewer flights and a reduction in convention and group business have also hit the golf industry in South Carolina, with Myrtle Beach courses experiencing a decrease of around eight per cent in business in fall 2008.

Litchfield Beach and Golf Resort at the southern tip of Myrtle Beach was fighting the recession in 2009 with unbeatable golf deals and stay and play packages. Appealing to families and golfing groups, the sprawling, 600-acre resort offered a broad spectrum of accommodation options including well-appointed self-catering apartments at Seaside Inn, a stone's throw from the 60-mile long Grand Strand beach and a five-minute drive to Litchfield's 10 adjoining golf courses. The resort featured condos, villas and houses on the ocean, overlooking golf courses, or by lakes. Specials during summer 2009 included weekday discounts of 30 per cent; 'Bed and Breakfast Getaways'; 30 per cent reductions on three-night stays at four-bedroom fairway villas; a Freestyle Family Fun package with savings on accommodation and amusement parks; a 'Kids Play Free' golf programme; and the 2009 'Just the Girls' event. Pools, spas, shopping, entertainment and restaurants abound in the Litchfield area, but golf is the main thrust with multiple golfing options over the Waccamaw Golf Trail. In 2009 three rounds of topnotch golf were packaged as low as $103, with a designated golf concierge available in the resort lobby to arrange tee times throughout the internationally-acclaimed Myrtle Beach area. Litchfield's award-winning River Club – designed by Tom Jackson, with Bentgrass greens – was advertising $65 morning golf and $48 for afternoons (including cart), compared to the regular price of $109. In a thrust to fill the famous courses during the hot month of August there were two free rounds of golf offered for bookings before the end of the month.

Sources:

Email interview with Julie Flowers, State Tourism Economist, South Carolina Department of Parks, Recreation and Tourism, 1 July, 2009.

Flowers, J. (2006) 'The Economic Impact of Golf in South Carolina', for South Carolina Golf Course Owners Association.

Flowers, J. (2009) 'The Economic Impact of Golf in South Carolina', for South Carolina Golf Course Owners Association.

Personal visit to Litchfield Beach and Golf Resort July 2009 including interviews with Christa Bodensteiner, River Club.

'SC golf feeling effects of economy', The (Myrtle Beach) Sun News, October 2008, accessed from http://www.scprt.com/files/Research/SCGolfEconomy.pdf.

The environmental impacts of golf tourism

The theory of sustainable tourism emphasizes the critical importance of environmental stewardship. A recent review of tourism journals shows a heavy bias in favour of papers that focus on the environmental issues arising from the industry (Hughes 2005), yet tourism organizations and destinations are generally still inexperienced in handling environmental issues creatively (Hudson, 2008). A substantial fraction of environmental spending relates to the regulatory struggle itself and not to improving the environment, particularly in the tourism sector. But corporate managers in other industry sectors have begun to consider environmental management as a critical component for sustaining competitive advantage, and in the tourism industry it is time for managers to start recognizing environmental improvement as an economic and competitive opportunity, rather than an annoying cost or inevitable threat. Some organizations in the golf industry have responded to this challenge, but before looking at efforts to 'green' the industry, it is important to examine the environmental impacts of golf.

Although most of this section deals with the negative environmental impacts of golf, there are some positive environmental impacts. Golf courses have the potential of improving and embellishing significantly degraded or derelict areas (Markwick, 2000). Many golf courses have been built on floodplain lands that have previously been used for farming, industrial sites that have had a lot of petroleum products put onto the ground and on old mines and quarries (Barton, 2008). Stewart Creek in Alberta, Canada, for example, featured in Chapter 10, was built on top of a disused mine. Golf courses are also green areas which enhance the general landscape, provide space for recreational activities and can also provide a good habitat for local non-hazardous wildlife. These areas often have a positive impact in our environment because they act as giant air-conditioners, they provide massive amounts of oxygen, they clean the air that we breathe from all the pollution that emanates from vehicles, constructions and industry and can also cool down the atmosphere all at the same time. Golf courses can also be treated as water treatment systems due to the fact that the healthy turfgrass they are made of holds pollutants in place which makes them effective disposal sites for waste water (Cuxeva, 2009).

During the 1990s and early 2000s, concern developed over some of the detrimental effects associated with golf course development and operation (Wheeler and Nauright, 2006). The game of golf was originally shaped by the existing landscape and was not a game that shaped the land, but ideas about what golf courses should look like gradually began to change, in part because of television exposure of major events. A phenomenon called 'Augusta National Syndrome' (Keast, 2001 p.37) appeared whereby developers plotted tees and greens in an attempt to emulate the courses that hosted television tournaments. According to Keast (2001) most of the courses built in the last quarter of the 20th century paid little attention to the environmental impacts. However, in the last decade, there have been increasing public concerns about the chemicals used on golf courses and whether they may pose a risk to humans and wildlife; about the water consumption that accompanies the production of 'Augusta-type' courses that so many players desire; and about the effects of course construction on natural vegetation and landscapes.

As a result of these concerns, a number of national and international groups opposed to golf course construction began to appear in the 1990s. Examples include the Asian Tourism Network (ANTENNA) based in Thailand, the Asia-Pacific People's Environmental Network (APPEN) in Malaysia, and the Global Network for Anti-Golf Course Action (GNAGA). These groups joined together on World No-Golf Day in 1993 to launch the Global Anti-Golf Movement. UK-based Tourism Concern is one powerful NGO that has supported World No Golf Day for a number of years, highlighting the environmental and human rights issues connected to golf course development. As they argue on their web-site: 'Maintaining golf courses in prime condition requires massive inputs of fertilisers, pesticides, herbicides and water. An average 18-hole golf course soaks up at least 525,000 gallons of water a day – enough to supply the irrigation needs of 100 Malaysian farmers. Many farming communities lost their land and were evicted either with minimal or no compensation for golf course development. Golf course design has been very much improved as a result of our world-wide campaign' (Tourism Concern, 2009).

Many of these opposition groups have focused their attention on Japan and countries in South-East Asia where weaker government regulations have attracted many developers. The means to halt unsustainable projects is less readily available in underdeveloped countries, resulting in substantial problems for local communities and their surrounding ecosystems. In addition, course maintenance is more difficult and hazardous in tropical regions as they have greater numbers of pests, diseases and weeds to eradicate. In Thailand critics suggest that golf course developers use a variety of dangerous herbicides, including some containing toxic compounds found in Agent Orange (TED, 1996). In 1993, Bruce Bennett produced a documentary entitled 'Green menace: the untold story of golf' which argued the sport was endangering Thailand's environment with pesticides, increasing drought and creating social elitism.

Golf course development in China has also come under fire. Critics have called golf 'green opium' as precious farmlands have been turned into courses causing concern in a country where arable land and water are at a premium. In 2004, the government announced that it would accept no applications for new courses and planned to investigate many of the existing ones because of unauthorized land grabs by local officials eager for economic development (Grange, 2004). When Hu Jintao came to power as China's President in 2002 he focused on a number of issues: the gap between rich and poor; the plight of farmers; and the environment, including water. Golf runs up against all three. It is expensive and elitist, takes scarce supplies of arable land off impoverished farmers, and uses large quantities of both water and environmentally unfriendly pesticides and fertilizers. Golf now has an image problem in China and courses are developing tricks to keep off the radar screen. In Beijing they offer customers the choice of alternative receipts when paying fees: one that records money spent on golf, or the second more popular option, a receipt that says it was spent at a restaurant (McGregor, 2007).

Is it clear from the above arguments that the environmental costs and benefits of golf course development are widely acknowledged in the academic and planning literature. Much of the conflict arising from this type of development results from the fact that different stakeholder interest groups adopt differing positions in relation to these costs and benefits (Markwick, 2000). At one extreme the perceived benefits of developers are economic in nature, in terms of capital growth and potential profits. At the other extreme, for environmentalists and conservationists, loss of habitat and degradation of the environment are seen as the chief costs. Other stakeholders adopt intermediate positions, perceiving a greater or lesser balance between the costs and benefits of development.

When studying golf development interests in Malta, Markwick (2000) found a growing commitment to the implementation of sustainable forms of development. Integrated management of all the environmental characteristics of a golf course is paramount for reducing to a minimum any negative environmental impacts and improving the positive ones (Salgot and Tapias, 2006). In the last two decades, several leading golf nations have implemented environmentally friendly measures aimed at reducing the impact of golf course construction and operation. Most notably, the USA, Europe and Canada have all made progress along those lines (Wheeler and Nauright, 2006). In 1989, the United States Golf Association (USGA) began to sponsor significant amounts of research dealing with environmental issues, with priority given to the effects of fertilizers and pesticides on surface and groundwater resources. Since 1991 the USGA's Environmental Research Program has evaluated the effects of golf courses on people, wildlife and the environment. According to The First Tee (2008) from 1996 to 2006 a US golf course on average implemented five significant environmental improvements including installation of native plantings, creating wildlife habitat areas, implementing erosion control measures and enhancing wetlands.

In 2008, *Golf Magazine* inaugurated 'Green Golf' awards, with 10 properties honoured for 'a serious emphasis on resource conservation and protection.' One of the courses honoured was Mauna Lani Resort on the Kohla Coast of Hawaii's Big Island. Mauna Lani has made environmental stewardship a priority for 25 years, and is a popular incentive destination for groups. Mark Glickman, director of resort marketing at Mauna Lani said that an increasing number of meeting planners have questions about environmental standards on the golf courses. 'Once upon a time the whole green movement was considered more of a fad,' he said, 'but now it is obviously a trend' (Dosh, 2008). In 2009 the resort introduced a Green Golf Package that included free, eco-friendly, golf merchandise. 'Our pro-shop identified some recycled and biodegradable green golf products, like tees, golf shirts, and golf visors that are all green-friendly.'

Another resort that won a Green Golf award in 2008 was Kiawah Island Golf Resort where all five courses plus the grounds at the Sanctuary hotel have recently been certified by Audubon International as Cooperative Sanctuaries (see Spotlight in Chapter 7). The Ocean Course, in particular, has earned acclaim from scientists and environmentalists for its sensitivity to nature. They have praised efforts such as the installation of a unique internal drainage system that recycles irrigation water while protecting adjacent wetlands from run-off, the creation of acres of saltwater and freshwater wetlands, the building of dunes, and the extensive planting of native grasses. Kiawah claims to have been 'green' before 'green' was cool, and any visitor will see that all the resort development has been carefully designed to blend into the island's natural habitat. The commitment to nature preservation has led to many innovative developments including the requirement that all buildings remain behind the secondary dune line to protect critical habitat. There are also no street lights on Kiawah, as the artificial light could attract loggerhead sea Turtles away from the beach, on which they nest for six months of the year. Long before cause-related marketing became popular, the resort was giving guests the opportunity to donate $2 per night during their stay to the Kiawah Island Conservancy, which is dedicated to the preservation of the island. In 2008 alone, this had generated close to $110,000 for the organization.

In Canada, the Royal Canadian Golf Association has a green initiative that seeks to educate member clubs on the advantages of creating balance between quality playing conditions and a healthy natural environment. And in Europe, the European Golf Association ecology unit has created an initiative called 'Committed to Green' that encourages everyone involved in golf to participate in improving the environmental quality of golf courses. Golf clubs can voluntarily participate and receive recognition. It was mentioned in Chapter 8 that the Royal & Ancient (R&A), features short videos on its website, some concerned with sustainability issues. The R&A has also recently introduced a benchmark service whereby golf courses can review their environmental performance over time and compare their performance against similar ones in their own country, and in all countries with similar climates. Clubs can use the benchmarking service to collect data on a number of variables including nutrient and pesticide use, water and energy use and waste management.

The R&A is also proactive in tackling environmental issues when hosting major events. For the 2008 Open Championship at Birkdale, staff were trained and accredited for protected species surveys, and a wildlife booklet was made available to spectators in an effort to keep them informed of the habitat management that had occurred. In the build up to the event, new areas of habitat were created, suitable for colonization favoured by Birkdale's resident species such as the endangered sand lizard and the natterjack toad. In 2009, the R&A worked closely with Scottish Natural Heritage to minimize disturbance to the landscape and its wildlife during the Open at Turnberry. Once again, information was made available to spectators about the management of the links for wildlife and conservation. And it is not just in the UK that golf events are going green. In the 2008 Beyond the Lights Celebrity Golf Classic in Austin, Texas, all carbon emissions from the event were offset. A year before, professional golfer Justin Rose offset the carbon emissions for his entourage's travel for the whole of the 2008 professional tour. The Spotlight at the beginning of this chapter showed how Justin Timberlake is giving celebrity cachet to green golf courses, building an eco-friendly, Platinum LEED certified golf course development in his home state of Tennessee.

Another initiative worth mentioning is the Golf & the Environment Initiative, a collaborative effort between the golf industry, the environmental community, and government organizations. The mission of this voluntary coalition is 'to enhance golf course environmental responsibility and performance through cooperation in environmental stewardship and public education.' The project was initiated by the Center for Resource Management (CRM) as the result of a strategic assessment of the Pebble Beach Resort Company in 1994–95. From the very beginning, the Golf & the Environment Initiative has been guided by a broad-based steering committee that represents the golf industry, the US Environmental Protection Agency, and the environmental community. This group provides direction and balance for all project activities. Some of the initiative's accomplishments include publication of Environmental Principles for the United States; three national stakeholder conferences in Pebble Beach, California, Pinehurst, North Carolina and Orlando, Florida; a *Collaboration Guide* book to encourage and provide guidance for local partnerships and cooperative environmental problem-solving at the community and golf course level; and publication of *Environmental Siting Guide for Golf Course Development* providing golf course developers with practical advice on the golf course site selection process and what 'red flags' they should avoid.

It was mentioned in Chapter 4 that, in recent years, golf architects have realized that preserving the environment is a great selling point, and areas of golf development are now given over to nature, in the shape of watercourses, nature trails and flora and fauna. Many developers, like Donald Trump (see Chapter 5) and Greg Norman, have approached the era of heightened environmental awareness by incorporating environmental issues into their corporate mantra. At the planning and development stage, sustainable development has become an important consideration. Initiatives such as the Audubon International Signature Programs have been created for resort community projects to assist landowners from the design stages through construction and then in establishing a maintenance programme that focuses on sustainability.

To achieve the Audubon Signature Certification, developers must design and implement a Natural Resource Management plan to include wildlife conservation and habitat enhancement, water quality monitoring and management, integrated pest management, water conservation, energy efficiency, and waste management. Audubon International has partnered with the USGA, and the PGA of America, to create Golf & the Environment, a sponsorship initiative which is dedicated to the game of golf and the protection and enhancement of the natural environment. In 2008, more than 2300 courses in the world were in the Audubon programmes – 622 of them from the USA (Barton, 2008). In March 2009, Marriott Golf, a division of Marriott International, announced a new mandate requiring 34 of its managed golf courses in North America and the Caribbean to be Audubon certified by the end of the year.

Environmental challenges facing the golf industry vary, depending on the geography. In Abu Dhabi, for example, (see Chapter 8) water and irrigation are big issues as there is no rainy season. For larger developments that include housing units and hotels the solution is to use grey water – reusing 'clean' waste water to irrigate golf courses. 'The responsibility of the golf community in the world is to be environmentally sensitive and responsible, and all developers that we have been involved with share this responsibility. Fortunately, the development of courses today doesn't need potable water for irrigation purposes and there are many ways to be conservative with the amount of water used, whether by minimizing the grass area or by using effluent water after treating it again,' said Greg Sproule, Managing Director of IMG, which is involved in showcasing Abu Dhabi as a golfing destination.

In North America, a number of courses now use treated effluent water or wastewater instead of drinkable water, irrigating smaller areas of property, irrigating more efficiently with better equipment, raising mowing heights, and using new strains of grass that require dramatically less water (Barton, 2008). The Snapshot below reports on the 'Get Water Smart' programme in Las Vegas and its plan to eradicate unnecessary grass, reduce irrigation and return the environment to a more sustainable approximation of how it should look and perform while still serving modern-day needs. Martha's Vineyard in Massachusetts boasts about being America's only truly organic golf course allowing no pesticides or synthetic chemical treatments. Visitors, in fact, have their golf shoes cleansed before a round to ensure that no weeds are tracked onto the course. The course was winner of the 2008 President's Award for Environmental Stewardship from the Golf Course Superintendents Association of America.

Wheeler and Nauright (2006) argue that the final decision with golf will be left up to the millions of people who play the game. Keast (2001) found that 96 per cent of golfers said they enjoyed seeing and hearing wildlife while playing and that 90 per cent wanted golf courses to increase naturalized areas for wildlife, but that 49 per cent said they still prefer putting areas, tees and greens to be flawlessly green. In a more recent survey of both golfers and non-golfers by Golf Digest (2008), the US adult population was more likely to point a finger at golf for environmental ills than golfers. However, although 91 per cent of golfers felt that golf was already an environmentally friendly sport, nearly as many would accept less-manicured conditions if it meant reducing the use of pesticides and water. Table 9.5 shows some of the results of the survey.

Table 9.5: Golfer perceptions & attitudes concerning golf and the environment (Source: adapted from *Golf Digest*, 2008).

Statement about golf and the environment	Golfers that agree (%)	Non-golfers that agree (%)
Golf is an environmentally friendly/compatible sport	91	66
Pesticides used on golf courses can be a health hazard	40	66
Golf courses should use only enough water to keep the grass alive, not make it lush and green	44	56
Golfers should be willing to play on brown grass during periods of low rainfall	74	69
Government regulation is a necessary approach in addressing environmental issues	68	71

Statement about golf and the environment	Golfers that agree (%)	Non-golfers that agree (%)
Future golf course sites should be restricted to reclaimed land	32	42
New golf courses do not cause as big an environmental threat as the real estate developments that usually accompany them	56	76
If golf courses were more environmentally friendly it would improve golf's image	52	56
Golf should be more environmentally friendly to reduce conflicts with environmental groups	74	63
Willingness to play golf under less-manicured conditions to minimize the use of pesticides on golf courses	64	N/A
Willingness to sacrifice some level of golf-course landscape 'perfection' to save water/prevent groundwater pollution	85	N/A

Snapshot: Selling grass back to the desert: Black Mountain Golf Course in Las Vegas

Black Mountain Golf Course, Las Vegas, courtesy of Louise Hudson

Most Las Vegas golf courses are travesties of nature, verdant oases at variance with the surrounding desert drab. In fact, although the vicarious coolness of incongruous water features, manicured greens and unfolding fairways is most enjoyable, it does inspire guilt in many golfers over the hefty environmental footprint amid such hedonistic excess.

However, many Vegas courses are giving the desert the chance to fight back in an ingenious turf reduction project initiated by Southern Nevada Water Authority

(SNWA). Black Mountain Golf and Country Club received $2 million in rebates from SNWA for xeriscaping its out-of-play areas with drought-resistant foliage.

The Black Mountain course in suburban Henderson conjures up pre-Strip Vegas with none of downtown's glitzy gimmicks. Of course it has some transplanted greenery over the 27 fairways and greens, but it is modestly interspersed among areas of groomed desert scrub. Instead of thirsty forests of relocated monoliths (like showy Shadow Creek where dense foliage prevents players from seeing any one hole from another), there are small pines and low-water desert vegetation. The new square tee boxes are surrounded by gravelly sand rather than rough turf.

The idea behind the 'Get Water Smart' programme is to eradicate unnecessary grass, reduce irrigation and return the environment to a more sustainable approximation of how it should look and perform while still serving modern-day needs. In response to the drastic reduction of the water level in nearby Lake Mead during the worst drought on record in the area, the SNWA has been encouraging both businesses and households to eschew turf since 2005. The authority offers up to $1.50 per square foot in rebates, resulting in reduced water bills thereafter. Black Mountain managed to clock up $2 million in refunds and made money on the deal as restoration work cost only 70 cents per square foot. Some of the surplus was invested in employing a golf architect to landscape the 60 acres of reclaimed desert.

Joan Phillips, director of golf and resident pro, has been with the club for four years, nursing the eco project through initial scepticism from the old-school regulars. 'Some of our senior members date back fifty years with the club and they took some convincing,' she said. In fact, the locals are so set in their ways at Black Mountain that they have roll-over tee times every weekend of the year and will accept no variations. However, the obvious economic savings helped persuade the equity members with lower water bills, less mowing and upkeep, as well as sizeable rebates. 'We do have some new problems to counter though as we now have weed infestation from the old root system which means lots of labour hours as well as more chemicals,' said Phillips.

For the golfer, the change takes a little getting used to visually but it doesn't impair the game as only the rough was removed and replaced by indigenous plants scattered over the sandy gravel. This smooth surface has the added advantage of enabling errant balls to roll or bounce back onto the fairway rather than halting abruptly as they would in deep grass. Although the arid landscaping does nothing to counteract the searing heat, it is welcome balm for the eco-conscience.

Other courses in Vegas are catching on, with Legacy Golf Club and Angel Park (both owned by OB Sports Golf Management) taking significant advantage of the turf reduction project. Legacy – which features the gambling motif with playing card shaped tees on its 10th hole – has xeriscaped 2,056,527 sq ft of its course. Angel Park has converted 3,225,347 sq ft to desert landscape, a sizeable 28 per cent of its 18-hole course. Red Rock Country Club has converted the most, giving 3,769,625 sq ft of grass back to the desert. Prestigious PGA championship course, TPC at Summerlin also took the turf reduction challenge, converting 43,318 sq ft of its out-of-play areas to xeriscape. Even top-dollar club, Cascata – named for the gushing waterfall cascading through its Tuscan-style clubhouse – has replaced 142,924 sq ft of its rough with drought-resistant foliage.

In all, 26 Vegas courses had participated in the Water Smart Landscapes Program by 2008. Summer Ortiz, the conservation programmes coordinator for Southern Nevada Water Authority, said the authority adopted a goal of 250 gallons of water per capita per day by 2010. This meant considerable reductions in both domestic and commercial use with a particular focus on golf courses. 'Although we do not want to see all turf removed from the valley or the golf courses, we do promote the removal of non-functional turf areas,' said Ortiz.

Some of the courses have even gone the extra mile and reduced turf on their driving ranges, too, resulting in extra savings. Ortiz is happy with the 54 per cent success rate of converting 26 out of 48 eligible golf courses to the programme in the first three years, attributing it to developing good relationships with golf course superintendents as well as keeping the industry informed via the SNWA's public information department and website. 'Southern Nevada's consumptive water use declined about 15 billion gallons between 2002 and 2007, despite the fact that there were nearly 400,000 new residents and nearly 40 million annual visitors,' she explained.

Sources:

Personal interview with Joan Phillips at Black Mountain, November 2008.

E-mail correspondence with Summer Ortiz, December 2008.

The social impacts of golf tourism

Social impacts are 'people' impacts, and are concerned with the tourist, the host, and tourist–host interrelationships. In contrast to the economic impact studies, such effects are often portrayed in the literature in a negative light (Wall and Mathieson, 2006). There are a few theoretical frameworks that are applicable to social impact research in tourism. The first was developed by Doxey (1976) who suggested that the existence of reciprocating impacts between outsiders and residents may be converted into varying degrees of resident irritation, depending on the destination. Table 9.6 shows the levels of resident irritation over time.

Table 9.6: Doxey's index of irritation (Source: adapted from Doxey, 1976, p. 26)

Stages of development	Residents attitudes towards tourism
Euphoria	Initial phase of development. Visitors and developers are welcome, but there is little planning or control mechanism.
Apathy	Visitors are taken for granted, contacts between residents and outsiders are more formal (commercial), and planning is concerned mostly with marketing.
Annoyance	Saturation point is approached, residents have misgivings about the tourism industry, and policymakers attempt solutions via increasing infrastructure rather than by limiting growth.
Antagonism	Irritations are openly expressed, and visitors are seen as the cause of all problems. Planning is now remedial and promotion is increased to offset the destination's deteriorating reputation.

Numerous situations provoke irritation or feelings of resentment towards tourists. The most intense feelings appear to develop from three particular conditions (Wall and Mathieson, 2006):

♦ The physical presence of tourists in the destination area, especially if they are in large groups. Congestion is often mentioned as a problem.

♦ The demonstration effect. Residents frequently resent apparent material superiority of visitors and may try to copy their behaviours or spending patterns.

♦ Foreign ownership and employment. The employment of non-locals in managerial and professional occupations provokes resentment.

Some of the points above have been raised in arguments opposing golf developments in developing countries. In South Africa, for example, the Wildlife and Environment Society of South Africa (WESSA) argues that the proliferation of golf estates in the Western Cape is not sustainable. They say that equity and access issues are the most serious weaknesses of golf course development, arguing that golf estates are frequently elitist enclaves, isolated from surrounding communities. 'For society, this cannot be healthy, creating divides between the elite and the surrounding communities, and fostering resentment and tension between the haves and the have-nots. By limiting access to natural resources such as arable land, fuel, water, food and medicinal plants, golf estates further impoverish poor communities, both economically and psychologically' (Enviroadmin, 2005). In 2008 WESSA won a major High Court victory in the Cape Provincial Division when a judge set aside the provincial planning and environmental approvals for the Paradyskloof development in Stellenbosch. The proposed development was to be sited on ecologically sensitive land high on the mountain overlooking Stellenbosch and would have consisted of a golf course, hotel and a 517-unit housing estate.

Another framework for analyzing the interaction of tourists and residents was presented by Wall and Mathieson (2006) based on the work of Bjorklund and Philbrick (1975) who suggested that the attitudes and behaviour of groups or individuals to tourism may be either positive or negative, and active or passive. The resulting combinations to tourism may take one or more forms in the diagram below (see Figure 9.1).

		Active	Passive
Attitude/behaviour	Positive	FAVOURABLE: Aggressive promotion and support of tourist activity	FAVOURABLE: Slight acceptance of and support for tourist activity
	Negative	UNFAVOURABLE: Aggressive opposition to tourist activity	UNFAVOURABLE: Silent acceptance but opposition to tourist activity

Figure 9.1: Host attitudinal/behavioural responses to tourist activity (Source: adapted from Wall and Mathieson, 2006)

Within any community, all four forms may exist at any one time but the number of people in any category need not remain constant. For example, entrepreneurs who are financially involved in tourism are likely to be engaged in aggressive promotion while an often small but highly vocal group could lead aggressive opposition to such tourism development. An example would be Donald Trump's proposed golf resort on the Menie Estate in Aberdeenshire, Scotland. The Trump International Links plan includes two championship golf courses, 950 holiday homes and 36 golf villas. The Scottish government has approved the plans, saying there will be a significant economic and social benefit, including the creation of 6000 jobs, 1400 of which will be permanent. However, members of Sustainable Aberdeenshire – a group made up of environmentalists, local residents and community members – are opposed to the development. They are concerned about a number of things including the impact of the development on protected dunes and wildlife. Construction on the project began in 2008 despite this opposition.

Social impact studies

One interesting social impact study by Gilder (1995) looked at an indigenous rural Hawaiian community's response to the building of a proposed golf course that would save the economic viability of the only hotel in town. A technique called mind mapping was used to determine perceived impacts of the project in Hana, Maui. With mind mapping, an analyst records the conversation and maps out how the situations were described by the respondents. Gilder found that the loss of culture was important to the Hawaiian youth. They do not want this taken away from them with the development of the golf course, and hope that their daily activities and the recreational use of the site can be accommodated. The Hana adults talked more about economic viability of the hotel and jobs, not culture. For them cultural factors must be subordinated to economic factors. As the author commented, adults of any ethnicity in a capitalistic system have to worry about jobs and financial survival. A follow-up study by Wyllie in 1998 found similar differences in opinions amongst residents. He referred to a study funded by actor Kris Kristofferson, who owns a home near Hana, which found that 42 per cent of residents were in favour of the golf course development and 58 per cent were opposed. Wyllie discussed the public dispute between those who felt economically dependent on the development and those who did not. He concluded that the dispute demonstrates that planning tourism in harmony with the local community is no easy matter if the community itself is fractured along lines that divide supporters and opponents of projects into mutually antagonistic camps. In fact, the golf course development did not proceed which was a great disappointment to those who had supported the project.

A study of the golf industry in Alicante, Spain, looked at the opinions of the local population in relation to golf courses in the area (Del Campo Gomis et al., 2006). The authors concluded that communication about the economic benefits of golf courses has to be increased with the local people in order to improve their opinions about golf course development. Locals were more likely than managers and players to think that there were too many golf courses and that the negative social and environmental impacts outweighed the positive economic impacts. Such opposing views can lead to conflict. In 1995, residents of the Mexican town of Tepoztlan halted the construction of a golf complex that was to be built in an ecological reserve above the aquifer supplying the town's water. Environmentalists estimated the golf course alone would need 525,000 gallons of water a day. One man was killed when police opened fire into a crowd of protestors (Rees, 2008).

In Asia, golf tourism is connected to a global panic over rice supplies (Webb, 2008). From Bali to Vietnam, rice paddies are being replaced by golf courses, hotels, villas and industrial parks as Asian economies surge ahead, the standard of living rises and locals opt for higher-paying, less labour-intensive work away from farming. This shift has cut into rice production, a staple food throughout much of the region. A surge in rice prices to historic highs in 2008 sparked fears of political unrest in some parts of Asia and highlighted the dilemma faced by Asian governments about how to balance economic growth with food security in the future. 'The call from Malaysia to Indonesia to China is "return to the land and be a farmer again",' said Song Seng Wun, regional economist at CIMB-GK Research in Singapore. 'The lesson is, food security is important, but people have forgotten that in their rush to industrialize. Longer term, they have to focus on the fact that all these people have to be fed.' In the Philippines, the government, alarmed by its inability to feed a fast-growing population, ordered a halt to the conversion of farmland to other uses. The country is the world's largest importer of rice, and has been hit hard by the surge in rice prices.

Another negative social impact of golf tourism in Asia is the use of female caddies in Thailand and its contribution to the sex tourism trade. Shamelessly promoting their infamous sex tourism industry, Thai entrepreneurs began to require that caddies were women during the 1990s. The women must attend a training school and are paid for their after-game 'services' by the golfers (Wheeler and Nauright, 2006). As Renton (2005 p.3) says 'female caddies who double as prostitutes are one of the special features of the courses of Thailand. In Thailand, each golfer has three or four women caddies – one to carry the clubs, another to tote an umbrella and a third to carry a chair and water' (TED, 1996).

Positive impacts

Despite some of the negative social impacts of golf referred to above, the golf industry does have a very positive charitable and human impact on society. In the US alone, golf generates $3.5 billion for charitable causes each year (Golf 20/20, 2009). The great majority of these funds are generated by thousands of fundraising events across the country designed to benefit local communities and their citizens. National charitable organizations, such as the American Cancer Society, United Way, and Special Olympics, use golf on a regular basis to help raise money for their respective causes. These events are often large and well-attended and typically raise from $25,000 per outing to as much as several hundred thousand dollars (Golf 20/20, 2002). However, the majority of charitable golf outings are conducted by local organizations tied to their respective communities. These include local churches, local law enforcement agencies, and local community causes. These local community outings average about $10,000 per event.

Professional golf tournaments also generate large amounts for charity. An example was given in Chapter 8 where the Crowne Plaza Invitational raised $6.6 million in total charitable contributions from the 2008 tournament. Nearly all of the 100-plus tournaments on the PGA Tour, Nationwide Tour and Champions Tour are structured as non-profit organizations designed to donate 100 per cent of net proceeds to local charities. Collectively they raised more than $135 million for charity in 2008 (Golf 20/20, 2009). The PGA Tour has generated $1.4 billion for charities since 1938. 'The PGA Tour has done a lot for charity over the years, but only because of the passion for giving back shared by our players, tournaments, sponsors, charities, volunteers and fans,' said PGA Tour Commissioner Tim Finchem. 'When we say, "Together, anything's possible", we mean that by rallying behind the common cause of charitable giving, we can create greater awareness and elevate our overall impact, which is so important in these difficult economic times' (pgatpur.com).

One other way that golf has a direct impact on communities is through volunteers. Unlike any other professional sport, the PGA Tour relies upon volunteers to run its events, which is one of the reasons the Tour's charitable model is possible. In order to perpetuate the impact of volunteerism, the Tour has aligned with HandsOn Network, the largest volunteer and civic action network in the USA. The goal of this partnership is to inspire others to serve and connect to volunteer opportunities through HandsOn Network's 250 affiliates and its network of 70,000 non-profit organizations. As part of this partnership, HandsOn will assist select Championship Management events and the TPC Network of Clubs in the development of charitable initiatives and will provide volunteers for community projects and fundraising that fall outside a tournament week. In addition, HandsOn will be able to serve as a volunteer resource in other PGA Tour, Champions Tour and Nationwide Tour event markets on an 'as requested' basis.

A number of researchers have argued that sporting events can have positive impacts on community citizenship. The hosting of sporting events is often a key element that enables communities devastated by economic downturns to regain and enhance their financial foothold in regional, national and global economies. However, criticisms are often raised that local community residents are left out of the process, especially with one-off events. Misener and Mason (2006) suggest that community involvement in the hosting of sporting events – by organizing, watching or participating in an event – can positively impact community citizenship. They argue that so-called 'flexible citizenship' allows those who are seemingly unattached or disconnected from places to develop a sense of place and identity. Proponents of flexible citizenship consider members of a community as more actively involved in the development and shaping of their own civic identity, rather than static recipients of ascribed citizenship status.

Flexible citizenship does not require one to be a community member or a resident of the community to lay claim to the meanings of places and spaces. For example, almost half of the 2002 Manchester Commonwealth Games organizing committee were not residents of Manchester; however, in the final report of the games, all those involved reported a unique sense of identity and attachment to the city (Leather *et al.*, 2003). Golfing events are no different. Volunteers for the Masters in Augusta, for example, come from all over the USA. Hundreds of people from across the States who are lucky enough to land job assignments, for which there are reportedly long waiting lists, take their vacation time to work at the tournament. They keep score, introduce players to the galleries at greens, give signals along fairways and even hold rope lines to keep fans from the field of play. 'People think you're special when they realize you were at the Masters,' said one volunteer, Ron Calahan, who is the general manager for the Savannah office of AIG, an insurance company. 'Working the event makes you feel like you're more a part of what's going on' (Rossiter, 2005).

Many argue that golf leaves a positive mark on communities through the game's foundation of positive values. As one example, the USGA through its 'For the Good of the Game' Grants Initiative supports organizations that use the game and its values as vehicles to improve the quality of life for individuals and for society in general. More than $59 million was dedicated to this initiative between 1999 and 2009. More recently, organizations such as the PGA of America have embraced initiatives designed to support US military personnel and their families, and in particular those who have been injured or perished in the line of duty in Iraq or Afghanistan. For example, the PGA of America and USGA collaborated to create the inaugural Patriot Golf Day in 2007, resulting in more than $1.1 million in donations to military families in need.

According to Golf 20/20 (2009) golf teaches essential life skills to young people – sportsmanship, respect, integrity, honesty and self-control. These positive traits are shared with youngsters through youth development programmes such as The First Tee initiative. The First Tee is a World Golf Foundation youth development initiative dedicated to providing young people of all backgrounds an opportunity to develop, through golf and character education, life-enhancing values such as honesty, integrity and sportsmanship. Through research it was determined that the primary reason more children, and especially economically disadvantaged children, did not play golf was because of the lack of places that welcomed them, places they could physically get to, and places that they could afford. The World Golf Foundation created The First Tee in November 1997 as a way to bring golf to youngsters that otherwise would not be exposed to the game and its positive values.

Case Study: Portugal's golf rich Algarve area strives to achieve environmental sustainability

Portugal's Algarve region was one of the first destinations to recognize the potential for golf tourism to bolster off-season visitation. With an abundance of beautiful beaches fulfilling tourists' needs in the summer, the area actively encouraged high-end golf course developments in the 1980s throughout its 500 square kilometre domain at a time when only lip service was paid to sustainability and environmental responsibility worldwide. The area was voted Established Golf Destination of the Year by IAGTO in 2006.

In 2000 government regulation kicked in with an Environmental Impact Assessment (EIA) Decree-Law limiting golf development to designated tourism areas. Two years later the University of Algarve developed an environmental sustainability blueprint for the region with its Algarve Golf Study. Most courses and developments were built before 2000 and therefore any environmental management plans would be retrospective damage limitation.

With a million rounds played per year, golf tourism is huge for the area's economy. A golf course can generate 150 new beds in a hotel and up to $14 million in revenue, with wealthy golfers spending double the amount of other types of tourists. Over 60 per cent of their spending is outside the actual golf course. The golf industry adds 10,000 jobs to the Algarve region, and has a strategic importance for the Algarve since it operates in a counter-cycle to sun-beach tourism. Around 65 of golf tourists come from England, 8.9 per cent from Ireland, 7.3 per cent from Germany, 5.1 per cent from Holland, 6.1 per cent from Scandinavia, only 1 per cent from Portugal and 6.3 per cent from other countries. The biggest demographic is the 46-61 year-old educated male with 40 per cent staying in hotels, 20 per cent in apartments and another 20 per cent in villas.

A 2002 Algarve Golf Study prepared by the University of Algarve developed a sustainability framework for the golf industry, addressing environmental, economic and social issues. Since many of the Algarve's courses pre-dated the 2000 EIA Decree-Law, they were situated outside planned tourism suitability areas, with a significant number on protected areas and Natura 2000 sites. Only seven of the Algarve's courses had been licensed according to the new law by 2006, according to the study. The researchers found that 17 per cent of courses had certification according to the ISO 14001 standard, 37 per cent had established environmental policies and 30 per cent had environmental programmes in place, with seven of them following the Committed to Green directives.

The 6th hole at San Lorenzo, Algarve, courtesy of San Lorenzo Golf Course

With around 27 million visitors annually, 12,000 registered golfers and over 30 courses in the Algarve, there is an obvious need to balance the impacts of tourism activities, particularly golf, to guarantee long-term sustainability and competitiveness. The major environmental issues for the Algarve are consumption of water for irrigation, consumption of phytopharmaceuticals and fertilizers, energy consumption, waste production, location of courses and implementation of environmental practices by the golf clubs. Around $450 million are generated per year by Algarve's golf tourism, making environmental management affordable particularly for the bigger golf courses and developments. Green Globe-certified Vilamoura, which comprises five golf courses and extensive real estate development, has been leading the way in the region. Antonio Henriques Da Silva, president of the Algarve Golf Association, was a speaker at the 2006 International Conference on Golf and Environment held in Spain. A consultant with Lusotur Golfes (which then owned Vilamoura's five courses), he was also the general director of golf at Vilamoura. His presentation outlined the development's pioneer work in the introduction and certification of the ISO 14001 standard.

Vilamoura, launched in the 1960s, attracted 200,000 golfers in 2006, raking in over $7.6 million in profits. Lusotur first became associated with Green Globe back in 1996. Green Globe's worldwide program was established by the World Travel and Tourism Council to provide guidelines for sustainable development, environmental balance and nature conservation for travel and tourism businesses. Vilamoura was the first tourist and residential development in Southern Europe to achieve Green Globe Destination status and was also given the Green Globe Progress Award. In 1998 Lusotur also achieved ISO 14001 Environmental Certification for its golf course environmental management system – the first company in Portugal to be awarded this certification. Although there are initial costs associated with implementing an eco-friendly golf course management program, there can also be long-term reduced costs for water and energy consumption. Jim Sluiter, Staff Ecologist for Audubon Cooperative Sanctuary Programs, said the Audubon program is recession-proof. 'The program is growing almost daily and continues to grow even with the financial economic impacts of the recession. Environmental stewardship goes hand in hand with savings.' In 2009 Sluiter was looking at Portugal – where there were already three Audubon golf courses in the Lisbon area and one in the Algarve – as a potential 'burgeoning market'.

San Lorenzo Golf Course in Almancil, Algarve, has been a member of Audubon International since August 1998. Golf Director, António Rosa Santos said that San Lorenzo was a natural sanctuary for wildlife and joining Audubon was the best way to ensure its protection. 'We got the 'Environmental Planning' certification for aiming our management towards environmental quality; but we haven't reached the conditions for a total Audubon Certification yet,' he said. He maintained that sustaining high environmental standards for the course is expensive coupled with keeping the course at a superior standard: 'We also keep the golf course lawns at a superior quality, and the turf species are hybrids – far from being indigenously adapted – which depend on artificial support.' Santos said that Algarve courses in general maintain best practices in keeping with Portugal's legal requirements but San Lorenzo has shown the most ecological benefits among its rival courses.

Santos thinks golfers are attracted by environmentally-friendly courses but will not pay more for them. They will, however, pay more for high quality playing conditions. San Lorenzo vaunts its environmental commitment via noticeboards in the clubhouse and a nature trail complete with wildlife viewing structures. So far the government's marketing campaigns have only made minor references to environmental achievements in the region. 'Environmental defence is costly but it preserves the quality of life for the future, and the natural surroundings enhance the satisfaction for the visiting golfers, club members, and public nature lovers,' Santos said.

In 2008 Turismo de Portugal inaugurated its 1st International Conference entitled 'Portugal, A Competitive Golf Destination' with the purpose of addressing golf course management and design and promotion of golf destinations. A session was devoted to key success factors for golf course sustainability with presentations about innovative experiences and good golf course management practices from environmentally-sensitive Portuguese golf courses. There were also sessions from such golfing notables as Severiano Ballesteros. The conference was aimed at businessmen, investors, managers and other players in the golf industry, together with public and private bodies connected to the sector's value chain.

Golf had already been identified as one of the 10 priority products to be developed in Portugal between 2007 and 2015 as part of the National Strategic Plan for Tourism (PENT). The plan recognizes that the golf sector 'will be strengthened by the adoption of principles of sustainability, respect for the environment, active participation by resident populations, ongoing training of human resources, innovation in all business areas, guarantee of quality and safety, compliance with a code of good practices and correct positioning in the purchasing markets.' Conclusions reached by the 2008 Conference included connecting the golf product to landscape heritage factors and to natural resources. 'The golf offer should therefore be tailored to territorial planning instruments, urban and landscape contexts, and environmental management practices, which play a decisive factor in guaranteeing the sustainability of the golf destination,' the report stated. Good environmental practices were recommended during the design, construction and operational stages of golf course development for both financial and ethical reasons.

Sources

E-mail interview with António Rosa Santos, Director of Golf at San Lorenzo Golf Course, Almancil, Loule, Algarve, Portugal, 29 July 2009.

Telephone interview with Jim Sluiter, Staff Ecologist, Audubon Cooperative Sanctuary Programs, 11 July 2009.

Correia, A. and Pintassilgo, P. (2006) 'The golf players' motivations: The Algarve case', *Tourism and Hospitality Research*, **6** (3), pp. 227-238.

Videira, N., Correia A., Alves, I., Ramires, C. *et al.* (2006) 'Environmental and economic tools to support sustainable golf tourism: The Algarve Experience, Portugal', *Tourism and Hospitality Research*, **6** (3), p 204.

http://www.turismodeportugal.pt/eventos/Default_EN.aspx.

http://www.algarve-portal.com/de/sport_leisure/golf/top_golf_travel_awar/.

References

Barcelona Field Studies Centre (2009) 'Impact of golf courses', accessed 27 July 2009 from http://geographyfieldwork.com/golf.htm.

Barton, J. (2008) 'How green is golf?' *Golf Digest Magazine*, accessed 3 June 2009 from http://www.golfdigest.com/magazine/environment.

Bjorklund, E.M. and Philbrick, A.K. (1975) 'Spatial configurations of mental processes', in M. Belanger and D.G. Janelle (eds.) *Building Regions for the Future, Notes et Documents de Recherche No. 6*, Department de Geographie, Université Laval, Laval, Quebec, pp. 57-75.

Butler, R.W. (1974) 'Social implications of tourist development', *Annals of Tourism Research*, 2, 100-111.

Butler, R. (1993) 'Tourism - an evolutionary perspective', in R.W. Butler, J.G. Nelson and G. Wall (eds) *Tourism and Sustainable Development: Monitoring, Planning, Managing*, Department of Geography Publication 37, University of Waterloo, Waterloo, Chapter 2, p. 29.

Cuxeva, I.A. (2009) 'The impact of golf courses in nature', accessed 30 July 2009 from http://ezinearticles.com/?expert=Ivan_A_Cuxeva.

Del Campo Gomis, F.J., Molina Huertas, M.A. and Sales Civera, J.M. (2006) 'Sustainable limits for golf course development in a tourist destination', *World Review of Science, Technology and Sustainable Development*, 3 (3), 197-210.

Dosh, C. (2008) 'Green your golf', Successful Meetings.Com, accessed 28 January 2009 from http://www.mimegasite.com.

Doxey, C.V. (1976) 'When enough's enough: the natives are restless in Old Niagara', *Heritage Canada*, 2 (2), 26-27.

Enviroadmin (2005) 'The Impact of Golf Estates', accessed 6 July 2009 from http://www.environment.co.za.

Gilder, N.M. (1995) 'A social impact assessment approach using the reference group as the standard of impact analysis. The case of Hana: Hawaiians and the proposed golf course', *Environmental Impact Assessment Review*, 15, 179-193.

Golf 20/20 (2002) 'Charitable impact report', 14 November 2002.

Golf 20/20 (2009) 'Economic impact reports', accessed 27 July 2009 from http://www.golf2020.co1m.

Golf Digest (2008) 'Golf and the environment: golfer perceptions and attitudes concerning the game and its relationship with the environment', accessed 15 July 2009 from http://www.golfdigest.com/magazine/environment.

Grange, M. (2004) 'Green opium hooks wealthy duffers', *Globe and Mail Update* October 23, accessed 1 August, 2009 from http://theglobeandmail.com/.

Hodges, A.W. and Haydu, J.J. (2004) 'Golf, tourism and amenity-based development in Florida', *Journal of American Academy of Business*, 4 (1/2), 481_488.

Hudson, S. (2008) *Tourism and Hospitality Marketing: A Global Perspective*, London:Sage.

Hughes, M. (2005) 'An analysis of the sustainable tourism literature', CAUTHE Conference, Alice Springs, Australia, February.

Keast, M. (2001) 'Going for the green', *Canadian Wildlife*, Spring, 37–40.

KPMG. (2008) 'The Value of Golf to Europe, Middle East and Africa', KPMG Advisory Ltd.

Leather, D., White, B., Dobinson, J., Ratt, B., Gallagher, D., Stewart, S. et al (2003) *Post Games Report*, Manchester: Manchester 2002 Ltd.

Markwick, M.C. (2000) 'Golf tourism development, stakeholders, differing discourses and alternative agendas: the case of Malta', *Tourism Management*, **21**, 515–524.

McGregor, R. (2007) 'Green opium' that tees off China. The People's Republic take a dim view of a sport seen as elitist', *Financial Times*, 27 February, 8.

Misener, L. and Mason, D.S. (2006) 'Developing local citizenship through sporting events: balancing community involvement and tourism development', *Current Issues in Tourism*, 9 (4/5), 384–398.

pgatour.com. (2009) 'Finchem, players unveil renewed charity initiative', accessed from http://www.pgatour.com/r/tour_charity/index.html 27 July, 2009.

Renton, A. (2005) 'Learning the Thai sex trade', *Prospect Magazine*, Issue 110.

Rees, E. (2008) 'Taking a swing at golf', *The Ecologist*, **38** (6), 42-45.

Rossiter, E. (2005) 'Volunteers treasure experiences', *Augusta Chronicle*, accessed 28 July 2009 from http://www.augusta.com/.

Salgot, M. and Tapias, J.C. (2006) 'Golf courses: environmental impacts', *Tourism and Hospitality Research*, 6 (3), 218-226.

SRI International. (2005) 'The 2005 golf economy report', accessed from http://www.golf2020.com/reports/GolfEconomyExecSummary.pdf

SRI International. (2008) 'The California golf economy', report commissioned by GOLF 20/20 for the California Alliance of Golf.

SRI International. (2009) 'The North Carolina golf economy', report commissioned by GOLF 20/20 for the North Carolina Alliance of Golf.

TED (1996) 'Asia golf and environment', TED Case Studies Number 249, accessed 30 July 2009 from http://www1.american.edu/TED/asiagolf.htm.

The First Tee (2008) 'Golf's leadership converges on Capitol Hill for First National Golf Day', accessed 24 July 2009 from http://www.thefirsttee.org.

Tourism Concern (2009) 'Golf', accessed 29 July, 2009 from http://www.tourismconcern.org.uk/index.php?page=golf

Wall, G. and Mathieson, A. (2006) *Tourism. Change, Impacts and Opportunities*, Harlow: Pearson Education.

Webb, S. (2008) 'Golf courses, developers nibble at Asia's rice paddies', Reuters, 1 May, accessed 29 July, 2009 from http://in.reuters.com.

Wheeler, K. and Nauright, J. (2006) 'A gobal perspective on the environmental impact of golf', *Sport & Society*, 9 (3), 427–443.

Wyllie, R.W. (1998) 'Hana revisited: development and controversy in a Hawaiian tourism community', *Tourism Management*, **19** (2), 171–178.

10 The Future for Golf Tourism

t

Spotlight: Heli-Golf takes golf vacations to a whole new elevation

An Astar helicopter flies over the 5th green at Fernie Golf & Country Club, British Columbia, courtesy of Ryan McKenzie

Luke Haberman must have one of the golf industry's plum jobs – guiding golf tours via helicopter in Canada's Rocky and Purcell Mountains. Haberman launched the innovative tour company in 2007 in the Kootenay region of British Columbia. Western Canadian Golf Tours specializes in 'Heli-Golf', using helicopters to oversee courses with golf professionals on board to define players' strategy from an aerial perspective before tackling the course.

Haberman studied Golf Management and Operations at Selkirk College in Nelson, BC, and wanted to combine his love for both golf and skiing in his career choices. 'I worked for a heli ski company for a while and did my research with them. I saw the benefit of Heli-Golf in the Kimberley-Fernie area,' he explained. When looking at career opportunities he dismissed the idea of becoming a club golf pro: 'The average CPGA assistant is just scraping by, maybe getting $100 handshakes once in a while but not enough to survive. So I had to find something more lucrative,' he said.

In the early days of golf clubs, pro shops were typically owned and run by the course's golf pro, giving them a secondary source of income. Haberman said initial startups for pro shops are expensive, hence new clubs often want pros to take on the extra financial burden. 'The pros would traditionally get a 15-year contract often, and then it's all gravy after the initial costs,' he explained. 'Now, when pros retire, the clubs are taking over the shops as they want the revenue.'

Backed with the know-how and confidence he garnered from his golf manage-ment course, Haberman started to plan his own golf business in 2006. 'My profes-sors were all ex golf club managers and topnotch people from the industry. It was definitely beneficial because of the contacts I made. If I'd stayed at one specific golf club for those two years then I would have been further up the ladder maybe,' he said. 'But with people to help, experts to call upon, there's a great safety net to try to go it alone.'

Looking for something niche rather than run of the mill, Haberman came up with the idea of running Heli-Golf as well as Heli-Fishing guided tours. A three-handicap himself with the goal of reaching par in 2009, Haberman said that a guide makes all the difference for golfers, saving them three to five strokes. 'Because pros go round with the players they can work on aspects such as their bunker game and solve issues. We are able to use the time to assess the specific coaching needs of each player,' said Haberman. Western Canadian also offers traditional lessons as well as access to practice facilities.

The heli tours are customized to suit both tourists and corporate groups: 'Nothing is cookie cutter, no two tours are the same,' he said. Western Canadian person-nel run players' clubs and equipment by car to the golf club so that everything is ready for the guests when they arrive from their aerial tour of the course. Groups are usually threesomes or sixes with either Haberman or a CPGA professional attending as guide and instructor. 'Before playing, we do a flight over the course to point out signature holes. We then land on the course, hop out and away we go,' said Haberman.

Although clubs were initially worried that helicopters could interrupt other golfers' play, they found that people were fascinated rather than annoyed by the choppers. 'People are infatuated with helicopters so we have no issues with it, they just gather and watch, wide-eyed and excited and wave at us,' he explained.

The Western Canadian Golf Tours' website details various packages, including accommodation, high-end meals, guides, transportation, practice facilities, and home video swing analysis. Haberman has contracts with local speciality res-taurants such as the Old Bauernhaus in Kimberley. The 350-year-old Bavarian building was dismantled and transported to Canada in 1989 and now is renowned for its Alpine cuisine. Packages runs from $2500 for a two-day tour to $8750 for the 'Ultimate Week Heli-Golf Tour' which includes seven days and nights, CPGA lessons, heli flights, guides, and a visit to Ainsworth Hot Springs on Kootenay Lake. 'The three-day tour is the most popular. It's a question of time over money,' said Haberman. Flights can also be provided via Pacific Coastal, Central Mountain Air, Air Canada and Delta.

Haberman is confident enough in the high quality of his product to offer a money-back, satisfaction guarantee. 'It's so unique,' he said. 'Maybe we will get one customer who complains but it's worth offering the guarantee for the revenue generated.'

Guided golf is Western Canadian's number one activity but guided fishing is strong, too. The company runs combos such as a four-day tour including three games of golf and one day's fishing. 'The rivers are phenomenal in this area plus there's Kootenay Lake which boasts a record catch of a 36 lb rainbow trout,' said Haberman. Wildlife viewing is also paramount with the opportunity to see moose and bears during the 25-minute helicopter flight over the Purcell Wilderness Conservatory.

The choppers are contracted from Cranbrook company, High Terrain Helicopters, which leases out A-Stars and Jet Rangers for heli skiing and forestry. Haberman gauges his clientele's attitude to the flying component of the tour: 'If people aren't keen on the whole heli thing, we just fly them regular. But if they are interested in having fun with it, we do more such as running the river at 120 miles per hour – it feels like you are touching the water,' he explained.

He originally looked to Asia for customers but found it 'harder to crack' than anticipated. With an oil boom in Alberta on his doorstep, though, he targeted the domestic market via golf shows in Calgary and Vancouver, venturing also into the USA with shows in Spokane and Portland. 'I get a deal for the golf show stands through Kootenay Rockies Tourism,' he explained. 'So it only costs me $600 for the whole weekend.' He employs a sales and marketing team based from Calgary to tour Canada for PR and promotion and has also established a marketing relationship with Golf Etc, a US golf retail chain which established its first Canadian franchise in nearby Cranbrook. His best marketing coups to date have been getting a two-page feature in the golf section of the *Calgary Sun* newspaper in 2008 and enticing *Fairway Living Magazine*, a US magazine to come for a media visit for a feature article. Also Score Golf Television are featuring the company in Spring 2010 reinforced with an article in Score Golf Magazine, dubbed the 'voice of Canadian Golf', by Haberman.

Now in his third season, he is finding that 80 per cent of his clientele is corporate and 20 per cent leisure. 'Corporate treats, sales schmoozing, wheeler-dealering, it's all giving a good response,' he said. 'But with the oil and gas industry declining right now in Alberta, numbers are down but they will come back.' Unfazed by the economic climate, he extended his territory to the Columbia Valley in 2009 to cover courses at the tourist destinations of Invermere, Radium, Fairmont and Panorama, as well as Castlegar Trail and Rossland. 'The future of golf in this area looks bright as we are starting to see the Americans return and more visits from Eastern Canada,' he explained.

Sources

Personal interview with Luke Haberman in March 2009.

www.westerncanadiangolftours.com.

Introduction

The final section of Chapter 2 focused on ten key trends or demands in consumer behaviour that are influencing golf tourism today. These include the increasing desire for customization, service quality, speed and convenience and a unique experience. This opening Spotlight shows how a Canadian entrepreneur, Luke Haberman, is responding to all these demands by setting up guided golf tours via helicopter in the Canadian Rockies. However even the most savvy of entrepreneurs could not have predicted the severity of the economic recession that the world has witnessed in recent years. This has led many players in the tourism industry to reassess the future and make plans to counter the economic downturn. According to a recent report by Longitudes Group, a combination of a weak economy, a September 11-related travel hangover and fiercer competition for consumers' time and entertainment dollars has crunched margins at many golf resorts, midrange country clubs, small retail stores and daily-fee courses (Rudy, 2008).

Planning for the future is critical for success in any industry, and a key part of planning involves making forecasts. Forecasting is market-research-based but future-oriented, and it relies on expectations, vision, judgement, and projections for factors such as sales' volume and revenue trends, consumer profiles, product profiles, price trends, and trends in the external environment. Because the future for tourism and hospitality products is subject to volatile, unpredictable factors and competitors' decisions, the goal of forecasting is not accuracy but careful and continuous assessment of probabilities and options, with a focus on future choices. In this chapter an attempt is made to make some predictions for the future of the golf industry and golf tourism in particular. Stoddart (2006) argues that considering golf is perhaps the most pervasive of games on a global scale, its social contours have been ignored by academic analysts. He suggests that three themes are likely avenues for investigation: the internationalization of golf and its economy, social access to participation, and environmental issues. This chapter therefore focuses broadly on these three topics.

Internationalization and growth prospects

The recession has a put a hold on many planned expansions, but there is golf course growth in some parts of the world. According to a survey of golf architects, China, Eastern Europe, the United Arab Emirates and India are considered the top locations for significant growth in golf course development for the next ten years (KPMG, 2008). Golf courses are expected to be developed mainly in emerging economies as well as in markets that are especially suited to golf tourism (see Figure 10.1). Low cost flight availability will also influence golf tourism (Garau-Vadell and Borja-Solé, 2008). In North America in 2009, the golf architecture business had contracted to something like 5 percent of what it was just a few years before, when up to 400 new courses were being built annually (Rubenstein, 2009). Architects are therefore trying to expand beyond the United States, although financing is tough to secure and is slowing the pace of development worldwide. Even the course that Tiger Woods designed in Dubai as part of a super-luxurious development was on hold in 2009.

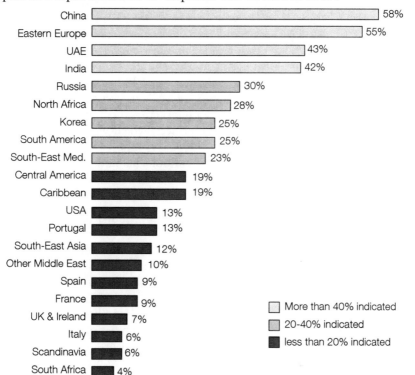

Region	Percentage
China	58%
Eastern Europe	55%
UAE	43%
India	42%
Russia	30%
North Africa	28%
Korea	25%
South America	25%
South-East Med.	23%
Central America	19%
Caribbean	19%
USA	13%
Portugal	13%
South-East Asia	12%
Other Middle East	10%
Spain	9%
France	9%
UK & Ireland	7%
Italy	6%
Scandinavia	6%
South Africa	4%

☐ More than 40% indicated
☐ 20-40% indicated
■ less than 20% indicated

Figure 10.1: Hot spots for golf development (percentage of golf architects who indicated the following countries/regions among their five choices). Source: KPMG (2008)

As Figure 10.1 indicates, golf architects believe that China has the greatest potential for future golf development. If only 1 per cent of China's population plays golf by 2030 – which corresponds to about half of North American participation in the game today – China would have 13 million golfers. This would imply that a supply of 1300 golf courses would be needed in China by then – an increase of 1000 courses in the next 20–25 years. Chapter 1 looked at the development of golf in China in more detail. The number 2 region seen as a hot spot for golf development is Eastern Europe, the focus of the Snapshot below.

Cuba is another country that is setting aside ideological objections and is embracing golf. Investors from Canada and Europe have proposed building gated communities with hotels, villas and condos surrounding 18 and 36-hole golf courses near beach resorts. In 2008, at least 10 golf resort projects were in the pipeline, awaiting approval (Reuters, 2008). At that time, Cuba's capital, Havana, had only one 9-hole course, the former British-owned Rovers Athletic Club, where foreign businessmen and politicians play. The only new golf course since the Cuban revolution was founded in 1998 at Varadero resort after the country opened up to foreign investment and tourism in the wake of the collapse of the Soviet

Union. The 18-hole Varadero Golf Club is on the grounds of Xanadu, a seaside mansion built by US chemical industry millionaire Irenee du Pont.

One unusual golf venture that is sure to divert world attention to Cambodia and Vietnam is a joint venture between the two countries. In 2007, construction began on an 18-hole golf course along the Cambodia-Vietnam border, a project expected to strengthen bilateral ties and economies of the adjoining provinces. The region was heavily bombed by US air forces in the 1960s and 1970s. Under the $100 million project, Malaysian company CVI Resorts Ltd plans to build 9 holes in Vietnam and 9 holes in Cambodia. Along with the Friendship Golf Course there will be a business centre, an international exhibition centre, a casino and a 450-room five-star hotel. The project, which will take five years to build, is expected to create more than 1000 jobs. Cambodia's tourism is increasing rapidly. It has leased five islands in the Gulf of Thailand for $627 million to six local companies and foreign investors to build tourist resorts. In 2008 the country had two golf courses near Phnom Penh and two near Angkor.

Growth in golf development is also expected in the United Arab Emirates (see Snapshot in Chapter 8) and North Africa (see Snapshot in Chapter 6). In India, golf witnessed a 35–40 per cent growth between 2004 and 2008, but mainly for the wealthy elite. Indian real estate developers are keen to sell luxury villas surrounding golf courses in order to cash in on the increased interest in the sport. JP Greens in Greater Noida just outside Delhi is spread over 450 acres with properties on the 18-hole Greg Norman course starting at $1 million and going up to $3 million. As mentioned in Chapter 1, the growing number of international golf events hosted in India and the increasing success of professional Indian golfers on international circuits, will – as in China – lead to more positive exposure for the sport, and a continued growth in golf tourism in the country.

Snapshot: Golf tourism in New Europe

Kempinski Adriatic Golf Course, Istria, Croatia, courtesy of Kempinski Adriatic

New Europe is the contemporary term for former Iron Curtain countries in Eastern Europe. Freed from communist clutches, they are now branching out into tourism and looking at golf for international and domestic revenue. Associated with the excesses and elitism of capitalism, golf was largely banned in the region until perestroika in the late 1980s.

The Czech Republic escaped some of the privations of the other eastern countries, developing golf from the early 1900s. Between 2003 and 2009, the number of courses increased from 40 to 68. CzechTourism sponsored a variety of golf projects in 2006, partnering in golf tournaments, arranging press trips to coincide with the St Andrews & Jacques Leglise Trophies, the Golf Show and the Czech Top 100 Golf Trophy by MasterCard. CzechTourism also hosted Eastgreens, a golf conference held in 2006 in Carlsbad. It partnered with the Czech Golf Federation in a two-year project to promote golf tourism and developed a golf image bank at http://photo.czechtourism.com/index.php?kat=list&kid=000002000. Tourists are encouraged to buy multi-course passes to major courses such as Golf Resort Karlovy Vary (the best known health resort in the Czech Republic), Royal Golf Club Marianske Lazne, and Golf Club Sokolov.

While golf development is still in its infancy in countries such as Slovenia, Romania and Bulgaria, Croatia is looking hot for the future. Istria is at the epicentre of Croatia's golf development with 22 courses anticipated by 2012. The Mediterranean peninsular, which was spared fighting and devastation during the 1990s Balkan War, has already attracted Jack Nicklaus and Robert Trent Jones Jr. Nicklaus's 18-hole signature course at Port Mariccio encompasses a 200 million euro luxury resort and residential community at Barbariga on the western coast of the Istrian Peninsula. The Kempinski Golf Adriatic, the first 18-hole championship golf course in Istria, opened on 1 August 2009 alongside a complex of apartments, villas and a wellness centre, creating 600 new jobs for the area.

In 2006 the World Travel and Tourism Council rated Croatia as the world's fastest growing tourist destination and the government responded by proposing 50 potential golf sites, including some on army land. However, development throughout the country is often impeded by the dangers of clearing mines, complicated red tape and government concerns over environmental impact and unscrupulous practises. Other obstacles include water scarcity, lack of proper waste management planning and local mistrust of newcomers and any development that would affect the lives of small villages near proposed sites. In Istria, locals started a movement against the area's 20 or so proposed golf courses, resulting in the rejection of some plans such as a development at Motovun. Developers are now offering incentives such as schools, hospitals and retirement homes as preparations are being made for public-private partnerships.

Many postwar Balkan countries are turning to golf to boost tourism expenditure. Bosnia and Serbia face similar challenges to Croatia and, furthermore, have no history of foreign tourism. They are both, however, experiencing domestic golf growth. While the Belgrade course opened by Prince Paul Karadjordjevic in 1936 suffered extensive bombing in the 1990s and is now just a restaurant called Golf, membership has quadrupled at a new Belgrade course opened in 2003. Bosnians and Serbians are also starting to cross the borders into Croatia for tee times.

Slovenia also boasts eight courses and golf is becoming a trendy status symbol among burgeoning middle classes.

Nick Faldo has turned his attention to New Europe, embarking on a golf course design project in Moscow. 'I've got one course I'm trying to get going in Moscow but it's slow going there. It's taken four years so far,' he said at a 2008 press conference. Construction was halted there in 2009 due to problems over the location of a gas line beneath the site. Despite such technical difficulties, Russia is starting to see increasing golf development. The Pestovo Golf & Yacht Club is a new residential golf complex just outside Moscow. Designed by UK designers Dave and Paul Thomas, its goal is to become a professional tournament venue with its 6685 metres (7305 yards), par 72, 18-hole championship course. Nicklaus, Gary Player and Ian Woosnam are all active in golf course design in Bulgaria where real estate developments are crucial to commercial viability. Dream Homes Worldwide is focusing on various Black Sea coast projects near golf courses such as Kavarna Hills, Kavarna Gardens and Harmony Hills, near Varna. Woosnam's new 18-hole course at Razlog is helping to make Bansko, Bulgaria's primary ski resort, a year-round destination.

Low domestic demand is a common bugbear for golf courses in Eastern Europe where the average number of rounds per year is only about 10,000 compared with 20,000 in Central Europe and 31,000 in Great Britain and Ireland. Moreover, average initiation fees in the region are comparatively high. 'The relatively high price of golf in Eastern Europe is a key factor, among others, for the low demand,' said Andrea Sartori, head of KPMG's specialist Golf Advisory Services Team. 'Prices are in line with courses in Northern Europe, despite consumers' significantly weaker spending power,' he said. 'However, the great development potential for golf in Eastern Europe is demonstrated by the fact that the golf sector has been growing faster in this region over the past few years than in other European regions. We expect this trend to continue in the forthcoming years.' Participation in the area grew 20-fold between 1990 and 2006 with 135 courses, mainly privately-owned and owner-operated, in operation in Eastern Europe by 2006.

Sources

Press release from Czech Republic 'A Summary of CzechTourism's activities to promote golf in 2006'.

Golf Benchmark Survey in the EMA region 2006, from www.golfbenchmark.com.

'Golf industry set to 'tee up' in Central & Eastern Europe', KPMG, 2003, from http://www.hotel-online.com/News/PR2003_4th/Dec03_EuropeGolf.html.

'KPMG Golf Advisory Practice in EMA: Future of golf in Eastern Europe offers great potential', accessed from http://www.golfbenchmark.com/dbfetch/52616e646f6d 4956b625c469b364021df881aad8c26e9dbc/pr_eastern_europe.pdf.

Harrell, E. and Anastasijevic, D. (2007) 'Croatia's approach shot', Time South Pacific, **40**, p. 58.

'Golf tourism boosts property investment in Turkey', accessed from http://www.estatesturkey.info 19 December 2008.

King, R. (2009) 'Golf tourism is set to become the next ace up Bulgaria's sleeve', Homes Overseas, accessed from http://www.floweradvisor.com.

Golf participation in the future

It was mentioned in Chapter 2 that participation numbers in the USA have been around the 30 million mark for the last decade. Between 2003 and 2007 golf participation actually declined by 7.3 per cent (Rudy, 2008) and forecasts for the next few years show little improvement in participation rates (see Table 10.1). As for places to play, gains in the number of real-estate and resort courses have been offset by disappearing public courses (see Table 10.2). Research shows that course operators are facing problems more complicated than just a reduced flow of customers. Energy costs continue to rise, and fertilizer doubled in price between 2006 and 2008.

Table 10.1: Golfing participation in the US 2004-2014, aged 12 and over playing at least once a year; * = projected (Source: IBISWorld 2008)

Year	Number of participants (million)	Percentage growth
2004	30.2	N/C
2005	29.8	-1.3
2006	30.0	0.7
2007	30.1	0.3
2008	30.0	-0.3
2009 *	29.4	-2.0
2010 *	29.9	1.7
2011 *	30.8	3.0
2012 *	31.0	0.6
2013 *	31.1	0.3
2014 *	31.3	0.6

Table 10.2: Places to play golf 2003-2007 (Source: Longitudes Group as referenced in Rudy, 2008)

Course Type	2003	2007	Percentage change
Real estate	3,141.5	3,411	8.6
Resort	1,312	1,380.5	5.2
Private	4,319	4,452	3.0
Daily fee	8,915	8,693	-2.5
Ranges	1,531	1,375	-10.0

In Europe and the Middle East according to a 2008 golf tour operator survey, 82 per cent of respondents expected a steady growth in the number of golf tourists, (see Figure 10.2). However, this data was collected before the recession had really taken hold of most of Europe towards the end of 2008; and golf tourism in Europe has since then entered a path of growth that is much less intensive than in the past (Garau-Vadell and Borja-Solé, 2008). Respondents ranked Portugal, Spain, Turkey and Dubai among the top golf tourism destinations in the upcoming years (see Figure 10.3). Thailand, Malaysia and Indonesia were also mentioned by several respondents as being emerging golf destinations with potential for future growth.

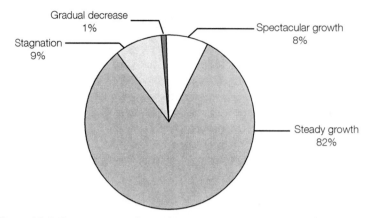

Figure 10.2: Future expectations of tour operators regarding golf tourism growth, Source: KPMG (2008)

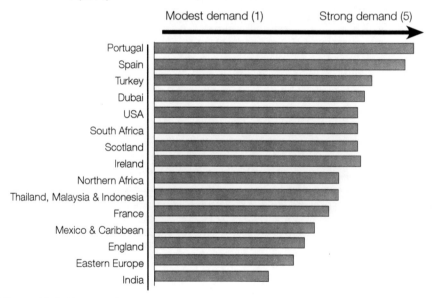

Figure 10.3: Hotspots for golf tourism in the upcoming years, Source: KPMG (2008)

With increased competition among industry participants expected in future years, golf courses and resorts will need to invest additional resources on methods of retaining existing memberships and attracting new members (IBISWorld, 2008). This may involve discounting membership rates, providing reciprocal membership rights in other clubs, and improving club or resort facilities. In 2009, Crown Golf, owner of over 30 golf clubs in the UK, introduced an innovative 'credit crunch membership initiative' in which members can suspend their membership if they lose their job, or transfer it to other golfers if they can no longer afford it. The initiative also allows members of one Crown Golf Club to play up to eight rounds at each of the other clubs owned by the operator.

One consequence of the increased globalization and privatization of golf clubs is the lack of access for local residents. Green (1988), for example, reported on how the Valencia complex in southern California was transformed from a $37 per round facility into a private concern costing $27,000 for individual members and $54,000 for companies. Most locals had to go elsewhere to play their golf. In Hawaii, the state government had to decree a reduced rate of green fees to allow Hawaiian citizens the opportunity to play courses in their own state. In most parts of the world, the game is still geared largely toward the needs of the higher socioeconomic levels, while relatively few municipal courses are being constructed to serve the needs of golf's newcomers.

Some believe that golf has become too expensive and slow and needs to reinvent itself. There may be an increasing market for shorter and more enjoyable courses that can be designed, built and managed more affordably. This may mean dropping course lengths below 7000 yards and perhaps having pars below 70. One such course is being developed in Brampton, Ontario, called Turnberry. The course will have 16 par 3s and two par 4s. Such executive courses were discussed in Chapter 4. Green fees are generally cheaper than full-length courses – an important differential in an economic recession, and many have just 9 holes. An example is a 9-hole course called Mendip Spring in Somerset, which cost just $15 for an adult in 2009.

There have been suggestions that the future of golf course design lies in creating easier courses instead of making each one a 'championship' course (Sargent, 2003). According to a 2005 survey of golfers, a golf course should be 6490 yards long, and the par 3s should be 160 yards, par 4s 375, and par 5s 525 yards. The fairways should have gentle undulation and be of medium width (Frankly Consulting, 2005). It is also recommended that golf courses be part of a mix of activities on offer in a development, not the sole attraction. This is the case at Fairmont Hotels & Resorts featured in Chapter 3. The company packages golf with a number of activities including spas, cooking classes, fitness classes and even safaris, in order to provide a much richer and more valuable golf vacation experience.

Golf clubs may also have to rid themselves of the stuffy private club image with strict codes of dress and decorum. One new club in the Hamptons – The Bridge in Bridgehampton, NY – while no less posh or exclusive, is attempting to make other clubs in the area look out of date. For example, dial up the club and the first thing you hear is James Brown singing 'Take 'em to the bridge!' a lyric from his classic 1970 hit Get Up (I feel Like Being) Sex Machine. The club's founder and principal owner, Robert Rubin, a Wall Street veteran, envisaged a younger, free-spirited membership, a place with a casual vibe and a liberal dress code. The unique clubhouse, which is 80 per cent glass, has a 'green' angle. The roof's overhang shades the granite terrace below, and the blades capture the prevailing winds to cool the building, making the air-conditioning system a seldom-used feature.

Another golf resort seeking to remove the element of elitism in golf is Wintergreen Country Club in Alberta, Canada. Brock Balog was employed in 2009 by

Resorts of the Canadian Rockies to provide recommendations to revitalize the ailing golf club. The beautiful alpine course in a rural village did not have strong connections with the local population and relied heavily on tourism to sustain its short playing season. A ski hill at the same facility had been closed down several years before. Balog – with his background in professional golf and sport marketing – was contracted to observe as Head Professional over a six-month period. He initiated a junior programme to try and involve the local community: 'One of the issues is learning how to get the whole family to the golf course. I'm figuring something out for toddlers so that they can come too, to play and be safe.' He intended to take golf away from expensive elitism towards family values. As one of the architects of the Manitoba golf trail, Balog was also working on partnering with hotels and other golf courses in the area. 'The future for the industry is looking at non-traditional ideas like charging per hole, for example,' he said.

According to many experts, more efforts will be needed in the future to attract juniors, women and minority group golfers (IBISWorld, 2008). The World Golf Foundation's Golf 20/20 initiative is an industry-wide effort to help grow the game, and their First Tee initiative was referred to in Chapter 9. The World Golf Foundation created The First Tee in November 1997 as a way to bring golf to youngsters who otherwise would not be exposed to the game and its positive values. Golf 20/20 has also implemented programmes to bring more adults to the game. One of its most recent programmes – Get Golf Ready – was created based on research that suggested there are a substantial number of men and women who want to play golf but need to be prodded to act. Golf 20/20 asked operators to price at $99 a series of five introductory lessons in a small group environment, as well as instruction in the game's etiquette, rules and values. The theory was that at the end of five lessons, participants would have the tools that could help them transition to playing (and paying) customers. The programme exceeded its 2009 target of 700 participating host facilities. By September that year more than 1000 facilities had expressed an interest in hosting Get Golf Ready sessions, with 805 certified as facilities meeting the criteria for inclusion in the programme.

The PGA of America has also developed Play Golf America, a marketing engine to drive new interest in the game. The initiative includes Play Golf America Days which are free consumer festivals offering golfers of all abilities and all ages a special day of clinics, tune-up lessons with PGA and LPGA professionals, and skill challenges and contests. Another programme that sits under the Play Golf America banner is Take Your Daughter to the Course Week. A total of 1274 courses in North America signed up to be hosts sites for this initiative in 2008.

The sport of golf is also being developed in other parts of the world. In the UK in 2009, Sport England granted England Golf $19.2 million to develop the sport between 2009 and 2013. England Golf, a partnership between the English Golf Union, the English Golf Women's Association and the professional Golfers' Association, intended to put the finding towards supporting the UK's 26 Country Golf Partnerships already in place, and those being formed. The funds will also contribute to increasing and widening the participation from key groups such as women.

In Japan, an increasing number of women are taking up golf, in part because of the emergence of young professional Japanese golfers who receive lots of television coverage. In Japan, the golf-related industry – consisting of equipment, clothing and other accessories – is worth 260 billion yen a year (Japan Today, 2009). The industry grew 5 per cent a year between 2004 and 2009. A spokesperson for Nike Golf Corp, which posts annual sales of 25 billion yen said: 'We've seen sales increase by almost 10 per cent. Women especially in their 30s and 60s are our main customers. While sales of clubs are decreasing, sales of golf wear and related goods are up.' Golf equipment makers are introducing new products targeting women. Bridgestone Corp for example, recently released golf balls featuring pictures of Sanrio Corps 'Hello Kitty'. The women's golf magazine *Regina*, launched in 2006, sells about 60,000 copies a year.

An important concern for the golf industry is adherence or retention. Approximately 3.5 million people in the USA join the game annually, and an equal number quit (Farrally *et al.*, 2003). According to one study, the major reasons why golfers quit are: it takes too much time from the family; too expensive; too long to play 18 holes; they tried but didn't have fun; too difficult; takes too long to learn; and females especially don't want to be embarrassed (see Figure 10.4).

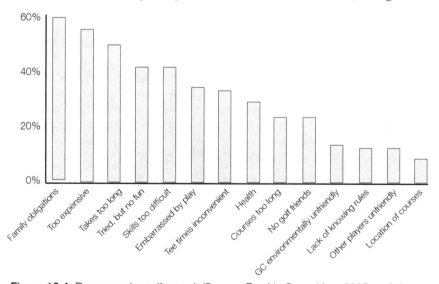

Figure 10.4: Reasons why golfers quit (Source: Frankly Consulting, 2005, p. 21)

Golf 20/20 was initiated to study the issue of retention and stagnation in the game and to develop strategies with a goal of doubling the number of golfers by the year 2020. This will be accomplished by either reducing the outflow of golfers or by engaging the interested bystanders to participate on a consistent basis. Strategies proposed to do this include reducing the intimidation factor, reducing the cost, providing alternative play to reduce the amount of time involved and facilitating the transition from learning to play (Farrally *et al.*, 2003).

A number of the golf resorts featured in this book are looking to the future by attracting juniors into the sport. To ensnare the next generation, Sandals in

Jamaica (see Chapter 2) offers a Junior Golf Camp which runs weekdays for ages 8 to 16, including 20 hours of supervised instruction, competitions and on-course play. At Mission Hills in China, Dongguan Golf Club (Chapter 1) has a golf academy, spearheaded by David Leadbetter, where local kids can take free junior programmes. Celebration Golf Course (Chapter 3) also features a renowned Golf Academy and a three-hole junior course for ages five to nine. Fairmont (see Chapter 3) has also identified a trend towards family golfing holidays, facilitating this with complimentary junior rounds for every paid adult round of golf. The Case Study at the end of this chapter focuses on Englishman, Graham Moore who has been running golf academies for junior golfers since 1990.

Golf and the media

One way of increasing participation is to increase the sport's media exposure. For some, this means changing the game so that it is more entertaining for television viewers. Golf administrators around the world are worried for the future. Aside from a small number of stellar events, the game is finding it harder to punch through media and viewer apathy (Gillis, 2009). Newspaper coverage is declining and television ratings for run-of-the-mill tour events are low. 'We're looking at everything,' says Peter Senior, the former player with, and now in charge of, the Australian Tour. 'We might have to look at 6-hole match plays in a knockout format, that kind of thing' (Gillis, 2009, p. 120). Andrew 'Chubby' Chandler, Managing Director of International Sports Management, also believes that golf needs a fresh angle. 'I don't know whether that's 36-hole tournaments over a weekend rather than 72 holes over four days, or a mixture of medal and stableford or something altogether more radical. The trouble remains that watching modern golf is like watching paint dry and the authorities do zip about tackling the problem,' (*Golf International*, 2009, pp. 177).

One major event with huge media exposure that could have a significant impact on golf participation, and thus golf tourism, is the game's inclusion in the Olympic Games. It seems likely that golf will be included in the 2016 Olympic Games after the International Golf Federation (IGF) submitted a successful bid to the International Olympic Commission's Programme Commission. The IGF proposed a 72-hole individual stroke play with 60 players competing in both men's and women's competition, using world rankings to determine eligibility. Some are opposed to golf's inclusion in the Games, but as PGA golfer, Phil Mickelson said: 'The Olympics brings the game to new markets on a worldwide scale. I think that golf as an Olympic sport is exponentially more important to the game of golf than the majors' (Huggan, 2008, p. 178). Ty Votaw, executive director of the GF Olympic Golf Committee agrees. 'Any sport that is associated with the spectacle of the greatest sporting event on earth will benefit from awareness. If awareness levels are increased and funding is increased as a result, the overall economic viability of golf will be increased. That could benefit tourism, golf course development, equipment sales and employment. All of these things have the potential of increasing the economic impact of golf if it is included in the Olympics,' he said (Alexander, 2008, p. 154).

If golf is allowed into the Olympic Games, it will be the first time since 1904 when 77 golfers from just two nations, the USA and Canada, competed for individual and team titles. Tiger Woods, Arnold Palmer and Annika Sorenstram have helped promote golf's bid to get into the Olympics and Woods has indicated that he would compete if he has not retired by 2016. In a recent interview he said 'I think that golf is a truly global sport, and I think it should have been in the Olympics a while ago. If it does get in I think it would be great for golf and especially for some of the other smaller countries that are now emerging in golf' (Associated Press, 2009).

Snapshot: Juggling needs of people and wildlife at Alberta's Stewart Creek

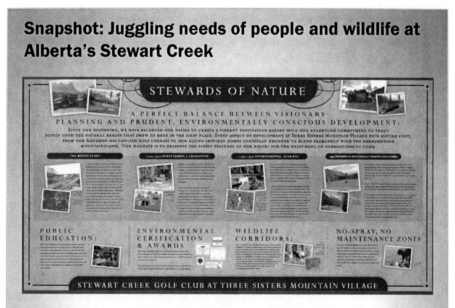

A sign in the club house in Stewart Creek promotes environmental stewardship, courtesy of Stewart Creek Golf & Country Club, Canada

Stewart Creek Golf & Country Club in Alberta's Rocky Mountains near Calgary is a semi-private club affiliated to a high-end property development. The club is working towards becoming fully private when housing and retail development at Three Sisters' Mountain Village is complete. By 2009, Stewart Creek had 330 members and encouraged locals and tourists to round out the numbers. The annual 20,000 rounds were split 50 per cent residents, 35 per cent tourists and 15 per cent corporate. But the unspoiled fairways and greens have also attracted other visitors – the wildlife of the rugged region. Deer, coyotes, elk, moose, wolves and even cougars and various types of bear regularly frequent the course, giving both the service providers and the agronomy department significant challenges managing the people mix as well as golfer/animal interaction.

Stewart Creek's acreage on the outskirts of the town of Canmore is regulated by the Fish and Wildlife division of Alberta's sustainable resource development department. Wildlife corridors form half of Three Sisters' 2000-acre plot and are linked to the 2.8 million acres of protected wilderness of the neighbouring National and Provincial Parks. Around 70 per cent of the golf course is within the wildlife corridor.

Sean Kjemhus has been Director of Agronomy since the club opened in 2000. 'We have to counteract problems like elk footprints and scarring from their antlers in the fall,' said Kjemhus. 'We have deer, bear, wolves, cougars. And we have to maintain a high level of transparency in our maintenance and operations for the public and the government.' The Audubon-certified club has to select environmentally-friendly chemicals and fertilizers which are often very costly. 'We use the latest products which are in the research and development stage to decrease our environmental impact,' said Kjemhus. 'This is unique to a mountain and wildlife area. Golf courses like ours with a higher budget can afford to experiment with these products and we take our leadership role seriously.' Stewart Creek also has to report regularly to the Fish and Wildlife Department regarding water usage and quality.

The high-end course is sculptured into the Rocky Mountain landscape with layered fairways, subtly sloping greens and landing areas defined by pristine forest, mountain streams, lakes and rocky outcrops. It is surrounded by breathtaking vistas of the Cascade and Three Sisters' ranges. Accessed by tree-canopied pathways, each hole has a sense of privacy. To emphasize the unique environment, Stewart Creek utilized indigenous flora and fauna to name many of the holes. It also celebrated the history of mining in the area by restoring the entrances to disused mines and using mining terminology and signage at relevant holes. In 2004 the course received the Environmental Leaders in Golf Award in the International Category by the Golf Course Superintendents Association of America (GCSAA) and *Golf Digest* magazine.

With snow often covering the course into May, there are further challenges in relation to opening on time and having good grass on the fairways and greens. 'The mountains are drastically different from other golf course locations – growing grass in the mountains is like putting ponds in the desert,' commented Kjemhus. The volatile weather also hampers pre-season turf preparation. In April 2009, the agronomy team was resurfacing the 8th green. The 13-day process began with frost removal on 9 April followed by stripping and re-grading the green. The sod - which was imported from the more temperate coastal climate of Abbotsford, British Columbia - had to be artificially heated at the root zone before it was laid.

Under these climatic and environmental limitations, Stewart Creek's agronomy department works on a high budget. With overheads inflated by environmental stewardship and a short, four and a half month season, fees are naturally steep. But Stewart Creek golfers are happy to pay for the chance to play in Stewart Creek's majestic mountain setting, surrounded by pine forest teeming with indigenous flora and fauna. Memberships are $50,000 and corporate memberships run at $75,000 to be divided between three players. Corporate green fees during high season are $195 per person but it's worth it, according to Kjemhus: 'Maintaining such a pristine environment enhances the golfing experience.'

Staffing is crucial to the successful management of any course and Stewart Creek can notch up 100 high season employees. Events' Manager, John Munro said they are chosen for their outgoing personalities: 'With the exception of the kitchen which is a specialty area, we look for friendly, upbeat, smiley people and then teach them the logistics and mechanical parts of the job.' Sourcing staff is the job of the Human Resource Manager who looks for graduates and students at job fairs and universities. The short season brings its own challenges in employee continuity but the local ski hills provide a useful resource for seasonal workers. Every year there are hundreds of winter season employees looking for summer employment to fill the gap. The downturn in the economy has led to a surfeit of resumes at the course, giving managers more choice. 'This year by far the highest percentage of staff ever is returning. Given the economic climate, people are appreciating their jobs more,' said Munro.

Staff training involves an important component of wildlife awareness and safety guidelines. Training sessions with fish and wildlife wardens during orientation familiarize staff with the idiosyncrasies of elk, deer, fox, moose and bear. During the season two permanent golf course ambassadors roam the course, monitoring the emergency response radio system. In case of a potentially dangerous animal sighting, a staff member remains with the animal until wardens arrive and play is stopped temporarily. A 19th hole is in planning so the course would always have a spare in case of shut down.

Stewart Creek's 85-strong cart fleet is electric to reduce noise in the pristine environment. Carts are not compulsory but are advisable as walking in the mountainous area and elevation can be onerous particularly for tourists not acclimatized to the region. The carts are top-of-the-line Calloways, serviced by an in-house mechanic on a two year lease. 'We don't have GPS because our members know the course so well. Also the system is very expensive and it works as the crow flies. Here, with such dramatic changes in elevation, it would not be very effective,' explained Munro.

There are many benefits for members in the sumptuous clubhouse which was completed in 2008. No expense was spared in the rustic wood and ceramic tile decor which attracts a large number of weddings, parties and events during the off-season. 'We sell weddings and parties for non-members Oct 1 to May 1 to the general public. Members get first priority though with the non-members' events second. But it's an important business for us in the off-season as it offsets costs,' said Munro. Members are also on a first name basis with all staff and can sign up to 'play with a pro': 'It's their chance to play with a professional from the club and if they go out with the general manager (who is also a pro), they can air any problems they have,' said Munro. Members have preferential tee times blocked off throughout the season and are kept abreast with golf course news and events via *The Creek News*. As well as club championships and ladies' and men's clubs, Stewart Creek specializes in social events such as wine tasting, barbecues, pig roasts, fashion shows and wine and hors d'oeuvres jazz nights.

Stewart Creek also has a positive effect on the local community, first as a big employer and second in community outreach. 'Usually golf is only introduced to kids in Grade 9 at local schools,' said Munro. 'So we decided to reach out to Grade 8 kids and invite the two area schools to the club. We have a total of 125 kids coming in 25 at a time for an introduction on the range, to hit some balls and learn about golf etiquette.' High school students also frequent the course for weekly instruction and play.

Sources:

Personal Interviews with Sean Kjemhus and John Munro 16 May, 2009.
www.stewartcreekgolf.com.

Environmental issues

It is likely that in the future, more golf resorts will adopt sustainability princi-ples and promote their green efforts. For example, Marriott International has been advertising their 25 golf courses that are Certified Audubon Cooperative Sanctuaries. As mentioned in Chapter 9, Audubon certification requires a high degree of environmental quality with such components as environmental plan-ning, water conservation, wildlife and habitat management, chemical use reduc-tion and safety. The Snapshot above focuses on an Audubon-certified club in the Canadian Rockies that is juggling the needs of people and wildlife.

New integrated golf resorts are also building environmental initiatives into their master plans. The Kalia Eco-Villages development in Costa Rica for example is promoted as being eco-friendly. The villages will be located on Costa Rica's Gold Coast and will comprise over 1000 acres (400 hectares), 432 custom homes and 985 luxurious condominium units. As the company website says: 'Kalia's invitation to participate in this unique lifestyle begins with a master plan that integrates the experience of daily life, a promise to the earth and preservation of resources and an opportunity to engage with local environment and its beauty.' In Kalia Modern Eco-Living resort properties, exterior green features will in-clude solar energy, green roofing systems, site development, cross ventilation, passive cooling water features, water efficiency and grey water recycling.

According to Barton (2008), the game of golf will change because of environ-mental pressures: 'as water becomes scarcer, as organic-management practices increase, as environmentalism and environmental legislation start to bite more than they have, as the economy struggles, and as we come to appreciate the aes-thetics of golf courses in all their many natural, beautiful hues,' he said. He also believes the way it plays will change too, with firmer and faster turf demanding a return to shot-making, creativity, and the bump-and-run. 'It's starting to hap-pen already: the hot courses are not dutiful apostles of Augusta; they are unique, wild and woolly-looking layouts like Bandon Dunes, Sand Hills, Chambers Bay. Americans increasingly love to visit the rugged, natural links of the British Isles, where the game began. That's where we're headed: back to the future.'

Even a decade ago, golf architects were predicting major changes based on en-vironmental grounds. In 2001, Thomas McBroom, one of Canada's leading golf course designers, said that golf courses were changing based in large part on en-vironmental considerations. 'The golf industry has become more understanding of what the environmental issues are and how to design around them,' he added. 'One of the main things you see now is less manicured, irrigated, or groomed space, because we're paying attention to what the environmental issues are – protection of habitat, woodlots, animal homes, and buffer strips by waterways. The focus is trying to keep more acreage in its natural state. That means less chemicals, pesticides, and water, which is good for everyone' (Keast, 2001).

In a recent interview for *Golf Magazine*, Brent Blackwelder, one of America's most prominent environmental advocates, was asked what golf would be like in a perfect world. 'You'd be playing on an organic golf course,' he said. 'The maintenance equipment would be charged by solar power. Recycled water would be used for irrigation, and used efficiently and sparingly. They'd be great variety of wildlife habitats' (Barton, 2008). Golf-course architect, Mike Hurzdon believes that this is not just a dream, as we are going to keep developing better grasses that require less water, pesticide, and fertilizer. 'Seashore paspalum is the biggest miracle in the last 10 or 15 years. You can irrigate it with seawater, and it will do perfectly well in some climates'.

Hurdzan says that if you asked golfers 20 years ago if they would consider playing on a golf course that is not all green, they would probably have said no. But if you asked golfers today, and explained that it is saving millions of gallons of water, they would probably say yes: 'They'd say, "Well, you know it might not be as green as I'd like, but it's good enough, and the game is still fun, and we saved all that water"' (Barton, 2008). Certainly there is a trend towards designing contemporary golf courses that look frayed, timeworn and windblown. One of them is Erin Hills Golf Course in Erin, Wisconsin, a course that the USGA are starting to take an interest in. Previously USGA events were always played on very highly manicured courses. 'Now they're more inclined to go to a Shinnecock or a Newport or an Erin Hills, because they recognize that golf in those kinds of conditions is a better brand of golf. I think that's helping to shift the emphasis,' says Hurzdan (Barton, 2008).

Climate change

Climate change has been identified as an important issue by leading golf organizations around the world. Drawing on the input of over 250 stakeholders – including course managers, union leaders and professional organizations – the Golf Course Advisory Panel at the Royal and Ancient Golf Course at St Andrews identified climate change as one of six issues facing the golf industry over the next 20 years (R&A, 2000). The impacts of climate change can be both positive and negative. Extreme weather conditions, such as flooding or heat waves can reduce golf participation rates (IBIWorld, 2008). On the positive side, a study by Scott and Jones (2007) included a climate change impact assessment in Canada which found that golf participation would increase even under the most conservative climate change scenario. They found the golf industry in some regions of Canada would benefit (in terms of season length and rounds played) from projected changes in the climate more than other regions. Golf courses on the West Coast were projected to benefit the least from a changed climate, as golf is already a year-round activity in many parts of the region. However, golf courses in the Great Lakes region could experience a 10- to 51-day longer average golf season and over 20 per cent increase in rounds as early as the 2020s, and an even more pronounced increase in the 2050s.

Butglobal warming could have a serious impact on golf, and coastal golf courses in particular. Research suggests that of the 1168 coastal courses in the USA less than two metres above sea level, 645 would in part or in total be submerged if sea levels were to rise in the next century (Stachura, 2008). Courses like those at Kiawah Island in South Carolina, the TPC Sawgrass Stadium Course in Florida, and Newport Country Club in Rhode Island, all could be severely affected by a sea-level rise of two metres. Though the conservative projection from the Intergovernmental Panel on Climate Change predicts about a half-metre rise in sea level before the turn of the century, this is a generalization. Others have suggested more alarming projections. A National Science Foundation-funded study in 2006 predicted that if warming continues at its current pace, a six-metre rise in sea level by 2100 is possible. That kind of impact would submerge much of the golf course property in coastal Florida, New Jersey, Maryland, Virginia and the Carolinas. Other scientists believe the warming of the Earth means an increase in the intensity of the kinds of storms that can damage shorelines. In 2007, the Links Course at Wild Dunes in Isle of Palms, South Carolina, fell victim to high tides, higher winds and tropical storms and lost more than half of its 18th hole. The former 501-yard par 5 is now a 190-yard par 3.

Case Study: Junior Golf: The key to the future of the golf industry

Graham Moore with his golf students, courtesy of Graham Moore

Junior participation is intrinsic to the healthy future of any sport industry. Graham Moore has been running golf academies for junior golfers since he noticed a lack of junior facilities in the UK back in 1990. Regarding the future of golf, Moore said 'I think without juniors in any sport, you don't have an industry, you'll have a dying industry.'

Based out of England, he spends five months each year in the USA, touring golf championships with his top juniors. He set up the Graham Moore Golf Tour Ltd, his international junior golf tour division in 2004. A former European Tour player during his teens, he became a fully qualified golf pro by the age of 19. After several years working in the travel industry, he set up Graham Moore International Golf Schools and Junior Academies. 'Everything just piggy-backed from there,' he said. 'I now have junior development programmes, junior academies, plus I work with professionals, too.'

In 2001 he formed the world's first junior only golf club, operating out of Cheshire, UK. Membership varies between 45 and 110 kids, around 80 per cent boys, with an average age of 10. 'It's unique because it's a roaming golf club, fully affiliated to every union as well as the Royal & Ancient in the UK. We use two local public courses and have 75 events throughout the year in addition to the junior tour,' he said. In 2002 Moore received the Vale Royal Sports' Award for his work with golf development and in 2005 he became a fellow of the PGA in recognition of his achievements within the golf industry.

His tour division attracts five to 21-year-old competitors with events held in Britain and Europe. 'It's been sanctioned by all the hierarchy in golf, the English Golf Union (EGU), the English Women's Golf Association (EWGA), the Scottish Golf Union (SGU) and also backed by the Royal & Ancient Golf Club at St Andrews. They give accreditation and handicap adjustments for the older kids,' said Moore. Crans Montana, Switzerland – the home of the Omega European Masters – hosted Moore's European Championship event in 2009. In 2010 the Graham Moore Junior World Championships were scheduled for Providence Golf Club in Florida. Moore's UK events attract between 35 and 65 players, mainly from the UK but also from Germany, Spain and France. Moore expected up to 150 junior players from all over the world for the Crans Montana event. 'And the 2010 World Championships should get a minimum of 150 competitors and maybe as high as 400 for year one of this event,' he added.

Moore's marketing is mainly done online. 'Golf Empire in the UK does e-blasts for me. Also I'm on the US Junior Golf Scoreboard which promotes me on the front of their website as well as all of my tournaments that are two days or more,' he said. He also has links with instructors.com, a US site. His own website gets 25,000 hits per week as well as numerous indirect hits through his affiliations with other companies. 'Word of mouth is also one of our best marketing tools,' he added.

Moore was impressed by the existing framework for junior golf in the USA when he first brought players over from the UK to play in tournaments. 'I created all my junior golf programmes because there was nothing like it available in England and Europe,' he said. 'Bringing my kids over to play in the US world championships was a big eye-opener because they were suddenly playing on major courses having qualified on par 3 courses in England. It was initially very frightening for the kids.'

Moore believes in introducing children to golf at a very young age: 'I'm unique in the UK because no-one does anything like I do. I instruct two-year-olds and up and I start by using golf equipment I developed with the Golf Foundation years ago: a big sponge ball and plastic golf club, linked in to Key Stage 1 and 2 learning.' Every year he selects promising juniors – usually in the 14-16 age group – to attend tournaments, mini tours and programmes from his base in Florida.

Nurturing his juniors up to college age and scratch standard, he then introduces them to three colleges in the USA (Colorado State, University of Colorado at

Boulder and the University of New Mexico in Albuquerque) where he handpicks their coaches to link in with his teaching principles. 'I get the kids ready for the facility and train them for a four-year course stateside to advance them beyond what I can do in the UK where I am limited by the weather and by access.' Many of his junior golfers go on to become PGA professionals.

He says juniors are not necessarily attracted to golf just because their parents play it. 'There's a wide spectrum but two things make it a lot more likely for kids to take it up. Firstly, I give people life skills and people skills because the kids have to spend a lot of time with me and my team of coaches (who I've also trained up since they themselves were kids). It's a good start in life even if they don't want to become a pro golfer. Secondly, I get kids whose parents play golf and have aspiring ideas for their kids. I'm recognized as one of the leading coaches around the world.'

Academy programmes are flexible, usually incorporating around 21 lesson dates over an 11-month period for £235 (around $500). The juniors also compete in five golf competitions, six skills tests, and get club caps and shirts included in the price. Lessons are then scheduled perhaps two at a time with a practice period over three weeks. 'I'm not a believer in too many consecutive lessons. Kids can only take so much information in at one time. They then go on to the next level at the next lesson after they've had a chance to put their new skills into practice,' said Moore. He has developed junior programmes, Levels 1 through 18, with colour-coded merit cards. He now calls these motivational levels the Graham Moore Junior Academy Order of Merit. The kids work towards the various levels in groups of six with Moore or one of his assistants.

Moore also runs private lessons with different pricing for amateurs, pros, beginners, etc. and works with around 600 adult clients. 'My main remit, however, is with junior golf,' he said. He has regulars from Australia and Malaysia who he sees just once a year: 'They've been coming to me for the past ten years, both to England and to Florida, for intensive training. I also have some European lads who come over to England for a weekend four or five times a year.'

Entry fees to events in the junior tours are relatively affordable – anything from around $40 up to $150 for a whole-day event, depending on the location. Moore uses prestigious courses such as four-time Ryder Cup venue, The Belfry, as well as the National Golf Centre at Woodhall Spa (the home of the EGU) and St Andrews. The Crans Montana European Championship costs around $400 per competitor in fees for the full week's events.

Moore has been disappointed with the approach to junior golf in the UK. He compares it unfavourably with Australia where he worked for eight winter seasons using the initiatives from the Victoria Institute of Sport. 'I think we have to learn from these other nations who have got great depth in their sports of all kinds,' he said. He was also impressed with both American and Canadian junior golf which is infused, he said, with the winning spirit. 'UK kids are taught to compete, every other country is taught to win – that's a massive difference,' he commented. Moore has seen growth in junior golf in China and Thailand. He attended the Mission Hills Asian Championships in 2007 and made contacts with several Chinese juniors interested in training and competing in Europe.

For his international fixtures, Moore hooks up parents of juniors with airlines, tourism boards and operators. For US tournaments, he uses GOLFPAC, which packages hotels, car hire, and golf course arrangements – everything except flights. He has a portal on his website promoting GOLFPAC as the preferred operator for the GM 2010 World Championships. 'Bookings can be made directly through my website. It makes life a lot easier now we're going more international. With WorldPay you can pay with a credit card. It creates more business for me with less of a time factor.'

No stranger to celebrity endorsement, Moore has secured sponsorship from his friend, Miguel Angel Jimenez. Jimenez, a Spanish pro golfer now a regular on the Ryder Cup team, has been a friend of Moore's for 30 years. He endorses and is currently sponsoring the GM National Junior Tour, with the inaugural Miguel Angel Jimenez Trophy in August 2009. Villa vacations in Spain will also be put up for first prizes.

Following on his success with juniors, Moore has focused on another neglected segment of the golf market. In March 2009 he inaugurated his Ladies-Only Professional Golf Tour.

Sources:

Personal interview with Graham Moore FPGA March 2009

www.gmintgolfschools.co.uk

References

Alexander, M. (2008) 'A question of sport', *Golf International Magazine*, 84, 154.

Barton, J. (2008) 'How green is golf?' *Golf Digest Magazine*, accessed 3 June 2009 from http://www.golfdigest.com/magazine/environment.

Associated Press. (2009) 'Tiger says he would tee off in Olympics', *Calgary Herald*, 12 August, C5.

Farrally, M.R., Cochran, A.J., Crews, D.J., Hurdzan, M.J., Price, R.J., Snow, J.T. and Thomas, P.R. (2003) 'Golf science research at the beginning of the twenty-first century', *Journal of Sport Sciences*, 21, 753–765.

Frankly Consulting (2005) 'Growing the game survey report', Frankly Consulting LLC.

Garau-Vadell, J.B. and de Borja-Solé, L (2008) 'Golf in mass tourism destinations facing seasonality: a longitudinal study', *Tourism Review*, 63(2), 16–24.

Gillis, R. (August/September, 2009) 'Is golf on verge of a twenty20 moment?' *Golf International*, 120.

Golf International (2009) 'Chubby's Got Talent', *Golf International*, June/July, 174–179.

Green, R. (1988) 'Japanese Investors Move on U.S. Golf Properties', *Golf Digest*, p.44.

Huggan, J. (2008) 'Let's include ourselves out', *Golf International Magazine*, **84**, 178.

IBISWorld (2008) 'Golf courses and country clubs in the US', IBISWorld, Los Angeles.

Keast, M. (2001) 'Going for the green', *Canadian Wildlife*, Spring, 37-40.

KPMG. (2008) 'Golf benchmark survey 2008 – rounds and revenues in EMA', KPMG Advisory Ltd.

R&A (2000) 'On course for change: tackling the challenges facing golf in the first decade of the new millennium', Royal and Ancient Golf Club of St Andrews, Conference Report: R&A, St Andrews.

Reuters (2008) 'Golf embraced to boost tourism', 1 June, Caribbean Update.

Rubenstein, L. (2009) 'New course construction another recession victim', *Globe and Mail*, 5 August, R9.

Rudy, M. (2008) 'How healthy is our game?' *Golf Digest*, July, accessed 1 July 2009 from http://www.golfdigest.com/magazine/2008/07/golfindustry.

Sargent, P. (2003) 'Tee time', *Leisure Management*, June, 36–37.

Scott, D. and Jones, B. (2007) 'A regional comparison of the implications of climate change for the golf industry in Canada', *Canadian Geographer*, **51**(2), 219–232.

Stachura, M. (2008) 'Global warming: our coast is under attack', *Golf Digest*, accessed 3 June 2009 from http://www.golfdigest.com/magazine/environment.

Stoddart, B. (2006) 'Wide world of golf: a research note on the interdependence of sport, culture and economy', *Sport in Society*, **9**(5), 836–850.

Index

Lightning Source UK Ltd.
Milton Keynes UK
16 February 2010

150148UK00001B/9/P